The Formation of Intellectual Capital and Its Ability to Transform Higher Education Institutions and the Knowledge Society

Edgar Oliver Cardoso Espinosa
Instituto Politécnico Nacional, Mexico

A volume in the Advances in Higher Education and Professional Development (AHEPD) Book Series

IGI Global
DISSEMINATOR OF KNOWLEDGE

Published in the United States of America by
IGI Global
Information Science Reference (an imprint of IGI Global)
701 E. Chocolate Avenue
Hershey PA, USA 17033
Tel: 717-533-8845
Fax: 717-533-8661
E-mail: cust@igi-global.com
Web site: http://www.igi-global.com

Library of Congress Cataloging-in-Publication Data

Names: Cardoso Espinosa, Edgar Oliver, 1973- editor.
Title: The formation of intellectual capital and its ability to transform higher education institutions and the knowledge society / Edgar Oliver Cardoso Espinosa, editor.
Description: Hershey PA : Information Science Reference, 2020. | Includes bibliographical references.
Identifiers: LCCN 2018054452| ISBN 9781522584612 (hardcover) | ISBN 9781522584629 (ebook) | ISBN 9781522585091 (softcover)
Subjects: LCSH: Education, Higher--Aims and objectives. | Knowledge workers--Education (Higher) | Information society.
Classification: LCC LB2322.2 .F65 2020 | DDC 378.01--dc23 LC record available at https://lccn.loc.gov/2018054452

This book is published in the IGI Global book series Advances in Higher Education and Professional Development (AHEPD) (ISSN: 2327-6983; eISSN: 2327-6991)

British Cataloguing in Publication Data
A Cataloguing in Publication record for this book is available from the British Library.

Advances in Higher Education and Professional Development (AHEPD) Book Series

ISSN:2327-6983
EISSN:2327-6991

Editor-in-Chief: Jared Keengwe, University of North Dakota, USA

MISSION

As world economies continue to shift and change in response to global financial situations, job markets have begun to demand a more highly-skilled workforce. In many industries a college degree is the minimum requirement and further educational development is expected to advance. With these current trends in mind, the **Advances in Higher Education & Professional Development (AHEPD) Book Series** provides an outlet for researchers and academics to publish their research in these areas and to distribute these works to practitioners and other researchers.

AHEPD encompasses all research dealing with higher education pedagogy, development, and curriculum design, as well as all areas of professional development, regardless of focus.

COVERAGE

- Adult Education
- Assessment in Higher Education
- Career Training
- Coaching and Mentoring
- Continuing Professional Development
- Governance in Higher Education
- Higher Education Policy
- Pedagogy of Teaching Higher Education
- Vocational Education

IGI Global is currently accepting manuscripts for publication within this series. To submit a proposal for a volume in this series, please contact our Acquisition Editors at Acquisitions@igi-global.com or visit: http://www.igi-global.com/publish/.

The Advances in Higher Education and Professional Development (AHEPD) Book Series (ISSN 2327-6983) is published by IGI Global, 701 E. Chocolate Avenue, Hershey, PA 17033-1240, USA, www.igi-global.com. This series is composed of titles available for purchase individually; each title is edited to be contextually exclusive from any other title within the series. For pricing and ordering information please visit http://www.igi-global.com/book-series/advances-higher-education-professional-development/73681. Postmaster: Send all address changes to above address.

Titles in this Series

For a list of additional titles in this series, please visit:
https://www.igi-global.com/book-series/advances-higher-education-professional-development/73681

Preparing the Higher Education Space for Gen Z
Heidi Lee Schnackenberg (State University of New York at Plattsburgh, USA) and Christine Johnson (University of Western Kentucky, USA)
Information Science Reference • ©2019 • 253pp • H/C (ISBN: 9781522577638) • US $175.00

Competency-Based and Social-Situational Approaches for Facilitating Learning in ...
Gabriele I.E. Strohschen (DePaul University, USA) and Kim Lewis (DePaul University, USA)
Information Science Reference • ©2019 • 317pp • H/C (ISBN: 9781522584889) • US $185.00

Autoethnography and Heuristic Inquiry for Doctoral-Level Researchers Emerging ...
Robin Throne (Northcentral University, USA)
Information Science Reference • ©2019 • 163pp • H/C (ISBN: 9781522593652) • US $135.00

Global Perspectives on Fostering Problem-Based Learning in Chinese Universities
Zhiliang Zhu (Northeastern University, China) and Chunfang Zhou (Aalborg University, Denmark)
Information Science Reference • ©2019 • 350pp • H/C (ISBN: 9781522599616) • US $195.00

Prevention and Detection of Academic Misconduct in Higher Education
Donna M. Velliaris (Independent Researcher, Singapore)
Information Science Reference • ©2019 • 324pp • H/C (ISBN: 9781522575313) • US $185.00

Educational Technology and Resources for Synchronous Learning in Higher Education
Jiyoon Yoon (The University of Texas at Arlington, USA) and Peggy Semingson (The University of Texas at Arlington, USA)
Information Science Reference • ©2019 • 356pp • H/C (ISBN: 9781522575672) • US $185.00

Handbook of Research on Critical Thinking and Teacher Education Pedagogy
Sandra P.A. Robinson (The University of the West Indies – Cave Hill Campus, Barbados) and Verna Knight (The University of the West Indies – Cave Hill Campus, Barbados)
Information Science Reference • ©2019 • 446pp • H/C (ISBN: 9781522578291) • US $265.00

For an entire list of titles in this series, please visit:
https://www.igi-global.com/book-series/advances-higher-education-professional-development/73681

IGI Global
DISSEMINATOR OF KNOWLEDGE

701 East Chocolate Avenue, Hershey, PA 17033, USA
Tel: 717-533-8845 x100 • Fax: 717-533-8661
E-Mail: cust@igi-global.com • www.igi-global.com

Editorial Advisory Board

Table of Contents

Detailed Table of Contents

This chapter will focus on the characterization of human, relational, and structural capital, as well as the importance of establishing them as strategic objectives in higher education in Mexico, with the aim of designing academic proposals oriented to optimize and manage intellectual capital. Given that the new economic order demands from academic organizations more efficient ways of producing and transferring education, the context of higher education is pointed out with reference to the capitals in question and the importance of their relationship in such a way that through this it is possible to determine strategic objectives that maximize academic performance and improve teaching-learning models, as well as terminal efficiency in higher education schools in Mexico.

This chapter explores the complex and dynamic environment in which institutions of higher learning (HEIs) have to operate and the imperative for them to transform themselves into learning organizations. This chapter is underpinned by the concept of learning organizations as its theoretical exposition to gauge the capacity of

This chapter is framed within the broader context of the transformative agenda of higher education sector in post-apartheid South Africa. The #FeesMustFall campaign started late October 2015 and the entire 2016 and has grown to become one of the biggest movements ever witnessed in the history of South African student politics. Similarly to the struggle waged by 1976 youth against the dominance of Afrikaans as the medium of instruction, FMF challenges the current government and universities to provide free, quality, and decolonized higher education. The slow pace of transformation, inaccessibility institutions due to fee increment, and Eurocentric curriculum, among others prompted the students to demand accessible financial inclusion and education relevant to their needs and reality. The chapter makes use of qualitative approach with both secondary and primary data extracted from books, accredited articles, and empirical data from selected participants.

The FeesMustFall campaign since October 2015 has grown to be one of the biggest movements ever witnessed in the history of South African student politics. Similarly to the struggle waged by 1976 youth against the dominance of Afrikaans as the medium of instruction, FMF challenges the current government and universities to provide free, quality, and decolonized higher education. Considering the slow pace of economic growth, the realization of free and quality education might be an impossible dream. Thus, dropping the fees seems to be a financial relieve to the poor students, but not the panacea to challenges faced by institutions of higher learning. FMF movement challenges both the government and ANC leadership to walk the talk by implementing policies and resolutions taken to transform higher education from declining. The question is, What are the costs and benefit of free education as advocated through FeesMustFall campaign? Can South Africa afford sustainable free education without compromising other areas of need?

relevance of other knowledge systems. This framework can break superior-inferior, developed-underdeveloped binaries while keeping in mind the core mandate of education, especially in producing skills and a competent and knowledge-based society capable of dealing with both local and international challenges. The academic socialization on IKS would rather require an integrated approach to research which is also interdisciplinary in nature and aimed at interfacing other knowledge systems. This chapter is based on IKS case studies drawn from South African universities. Data obtained from interviews with experts and practitioners in the IKS sector will be engaged to enrich the debates in this chapter.

The objective of the chapter is to provide a proposal of indicators of intellectual capital in higher education for the organizations that comprise it. The importance of valuing intellectual capital in educational organizations is to measure their contributions to society, which complement the financial landscape and allow comparison between similar institutions, in order to compare their performance. Therefore, the conclusion of carrying out this process in higher education is 1) providing adequate information on the value of HEIs to society, 2) assessing and directing the response capacity of the organization towards the needs of the productive and services sector (interest groups), 3) orienting the development of the components of intellectual capital towards a knowledge management that allows to solve in an efficient way the problems of the society, and 4) optimizing the human talent of the institution for the achievement of the organizational objectives.

Preface

Education houses a complex network of paths that lead to a challenge: knowledge. In this path with obstacles, several actors appear that, from different scenarios, give shape to higher education throughout the world; national and international agencies in charge of formulating policies which contribute to improving its quality working in the complicated but satisfactory mission of training for professional performance (González, Tamayo, & Vargas, 2019).

In the same way, the knowledge economy sustains that knowledge is the force of economic development in developed countries, recognizing it as a strategic factor that is a fundamental part of productive processes, along with capital, materials and workforce, which is why its creation, diffusion and use will allow the integral development of the population.

The main characteristics of the knowledge economy are: 1) It is an intangible global phenomenon; 2) It necessarily uses information and communication technologies (ICT) as a means for its different processes and, 3) It supports a considerable and growing flow of intellectual resources, which is why the vision of knowledge as an intangible asset is concrete because it is found above those of a financial and material nature, for which it intervenes in the design of products and processes in organizations (Guzmán & Adriano, 2013).

Based on the above, knowledge is an intangible property of all human beings and is directly related to the ability of people to reason and learn. As mentioned by Nonaka and Takeuchi (1995), knowledge is a flow of information that constitutes a competitive advantage for an organization that manages it effectively and efficiently.

Similarly, the new world order has imposed challenges of all kinds on countries: market volatility, greater uncertainty, intense competitiveness, obsolescence of knowledge, demographic and social change, turn in economic power, sustainable approach, scarcity of resources and technological advance. According to the Organization for Economic Cooperation and Development (OECD, 2011), this new scenario demands professionals capable of adapting to change, of generating creative solutions, and of taking on new challenges.

In this way, the knowledge society appears as a combination of four interdependent elements: the production of knowledge through research, its transmission through education, its dissemination through ICT and its exploitation through innovation. To achieve this, higher education participates in these processes, carrying out the training of professionals and researchers, which is why it is the main strategic resource that allows regional and national development in the countries (European Commission, 2003). For this reason, higher education institutions (HEIs) are the main component of the formation of intellectual capital since they are the key element of the knowledge society, so it is necessary that they continue to be the main source of the necessary skills of the individual (Vera, 2016; Cinque, 2016).

As indicated by Delors (1996), to achieve an adequate adaptation to global changes, the labor market requires highly qualified professionals in the combination of three complementary aspects: cognitive ("knowing"), procedural ("know-how") and the attitudinal ("know how to be"). Faced with this situation, the education system has been forced to react, carrying out a structural reform that allows to approximate the academic offer to the demands of today's society, thus increasing the employability of its graduates, so to achieve this, the paradigm of competency-based training emerged (Martínez & Echeverría, 2009); term that encompasses the set of knowledge, skills and values, ethics and attitudes that determine the ability of a person to respond adequately to the demands of a particular job (Biemans, Nieuwenbuis, Poell, Mulder, & Wesselink, 2004).

Therefore, education has been recognized as the basis of development, as an element of innovation and as a strategic advantage for countries. Nowadays, the globalized world demands with greater force that the superior level is oriented to the training of highly qualified personnel in diverse areas (research, teaching, leadership and management) in order to satisfy in a consistent and effective way the economic needs, political and cultural aspects of society and the labor sector. So, in order to develop a country in the 21st century, competent people who understand their socio-cultural and technological environment are required, so that they integrate both creativity and innovation into their jobs to solve the real complex problems that arise (UNESCO, 2005; Marginson, 2013).

Thus, higher education has acquired, as a main function, the production and transfer of knowledge in order to promote the transformation of society and consolidate scientific and technological progress to carry out the positioning of countries and regions in the geopolitical context. (Mercado, Gil, & Cernas, 2016).

Hence, the interest in managing intellectual capital in HEIs around the world has been aroused because it has been established as an emerging issue for academics, governors and investors (Bezhani, 2010), which has been investigated in industrialized nations due to the fact that it is recognized as the driver of organizational growth in a knowledge-based economy (Lev & Zambon, 2003). However, studies in emerging economies and, specifically, in universities are still insufficient (Tseng & James Goo, 2005).

In this sense, intellectual capital (IC) is the combination of intangible resources and valuable capabilities that allow the organization to transform financial, material and human assets into a system capable of creating value for all the agents linked to it (Edvinsson & Malone, 1998; Sánchez, Elena, & Castrillo, 2009; Cano, Sánchez, González, & Pérez, 2014). A more visionary definition was formulated by Drucker (1993), which highlighted the importance of the arrival of a new society in which knowledge assets dominate and compete for the distribution of IC as a way to achieve a better positioning of the companies in the market. Therefore, its relevance is to allow knowledge to become a profit in the future of the organization and is manifested through inventions, technologies, software, designs and processes (Sullivan, 2001; OECD, 2012; Mercado, Gil, & Cernas, 2016).

Accordingly, the IC has become the intangible that generates value in companies and has an impact on the quality of HEIs, which has led to the need to establish processes that ensure proper management and measurement, aimed at increasing their production, protection and distribution impacting society, government and economy. Thus, the IC has been established as the strategic element to promote national and regional development, which generates innovation in organizations (Edvinsson & Sullivan, 1996; Arrieta, Gaviria, & Consuegra, 2017).

Based on the above, it is necessary to carry out systemically the measurement, management and use of IC in higher education, given that its main asset lies in the creation, development and dissemination of knowledge (Araujo, 2000). That is, what HEIs produce is knowledge, either through scientific research, the dissemination of culture or teaching. In addition, among its most valuable resources are its researchers, teachers, managers and students, along with its organizational processes and networks (UNESCO, 1998; Leitner, Bornemann, & Schneider, 2002; Warden, 2004; Marginson & Marjijk, 2007; Laurenti, 2008).

Also, it is becoming more evident the need to know, manage, store and disseminate knowledge as a means to cultivate the IC of organizations and countries, especially to the extent that the conviction that, the productivity of knowledge and knowledge workers are the decisive factor in the world economy is generalized (Drucker, 1997).

Besides, the massification of information and communication technologies has caused that the generation of knowledge has a very high obsolescence, which is why human capital should be seen as a renewable resource, which is required to update and revitalize permanently with continuous learning, which will provide flexibility and response capacity in an environment in which the only permanent change is, as mentioned by the OECD (1998): "investment in human capital is at the center of country strategies to promote economic prosperity, full employment and social cohesion. Individuals, organizations and nations increasingly recognize that high levels of knowledge, skills and competencies are essential to ensure a successful future" (p. 17).

For this reason, it is necessary to conceive that the management of the IC is linked to the educational management of the organization that considers it as a systemic structure that generates, as a result, a development of effective learning, teaching, research and cultural diffusion environments with respect to the quality system with the purpose of promoting the development of knowledge and its productivity (Johnson, 2010; Rodríguez & Gairín, 2015; Romero, 2018).

So, it is fundamental to consider educational management as an interdependent process of: 1) a multidisciplinary knowledge of pedagogical, managerial and social knowledge; 2) classroom practices, management, inspection, evaluation and governance; 3) value judgments integrated into technical decisions; 4) useful principles for action; multiple actors in multiple spaces of action; 5) different personal, group and social temporalities overlapping and/or articulated (UNESCO, 2013).

As a result, to achieve this, educational management is required to design improvement plans to overcome the areas of improvement obtained through the results of periodic evaluations, in combination with performance evaluations of managers, teachers and institutional self-evaluation processes; thus establishing the basis for the formulation and implementation of improvement plans in which actions are defined for institutional strengthening, which will generate as a consequence that each institution achieves its objectives and goals through organized processes and appropriate management (Farias, 2010; Fontalvo, 2011; Romero, 2018).

Due to the above, educational management will allow the development of the IC of an organization to finally achieve the objective of any educational institution that is to provide a quality service (Romero, 2018); in addition, to position the HEIs in their key role in the economic growth and global competitiveness of the countries (Mercado, Gil, & Cernas, 2016).

In this way, the process of developing the work entitled: "The formation of intellectual capital and its ability to transform higher education institutions in the knowledge society" is a publication derived from various scientific researches which main objective is to provide a state of the art with a systemic vision on the formation of intellectual capital in higher education and its impact on the knowledge society, where topics of great importance for the educational field are highlighted, so this book is aimed at educators, educational technologists, students, researchers, professionals, managers, leaders, administrators and any other person who has an interest in this international issue.

It should be noted that the process carried out for the preparation of the present comprised the following phases by the editor: 1) Submission of book proposal describing the coverage and importance of the topic for its evaluation by the Advisory Board of the Editorial IGI Global; 2) Selection of the evaluation committee; 3)

Invitation at the international level of chapter proposals; 4) Conducting double blind review and judgment for each proposal by at least two evaluators; 5) Sending to the authors the reviews of each evaluator for compliance; 6) Compilation and organization of the chapters that met the evaluation and format criteria and 7) Preparation of the final work.

Finally, it is important to note that the evaluation of each chapter that integrates this work meets the following criteria:

- Originality and meaning of the contribution in congruence with the theme of the book.
- International relevance of the chapter topic and its contributions.
- Coverage of existing prior literature.
- Appropriate use of the methodology used with the respective foundation.
- Establishment of conclusions and previous studies derived from a research process.
- Fulfillment of the formal structure for a chapter.

ORGANIZATION OF THE BOOK

The book is organized into 12 chapters. Here is a brief description of each of the chapters:

Chapter 1 focuses on the characterization of human, relational and structural capital, as well as the importance of establishing them as strategic objectives in higher education in Mexico, with the purpose of designing academic proposals aimed at optimizing and managing intellectual capital.

Chapter 2 explores the complex and dynamic environment in which HEIs must operate and the imperative to transform them into learning organizations through the production of knowledge made by research and management and the dissemination of results.

Chapter 3 focuses on the impact of the processes of economic globalization and acceleration of technological change, which have led to changes in economic and social life worldwide, highlighting the use of ICT, artificial intelligence systems, scanning, connectivity, nanotechnology and biotechnology, among others, and have transformed the national productive structures and human capital that require disruptive technologies nowadays.

Chapter 4 proposes an ecological model of the university including its implications for a transformative change in society in general. The main contribution is that the university within this model becomes an entity, which is constantly committed to itself and its adjacent environment to remain relevant and be part of the solutions to the challenges of society. In this chapter, case studies of South African universities were used as a research technique, including selected interviews with key stakeholders in the higher education sector.

Chapter 5 focuses on identifying HEIs as the strategic element of the knowledge society in Mexico for entrepreneurship through an analysis of the programs taught in the two public universities of the country.

Chapter 6 identifies the potential benefits and opportunities for higher education institutions (HEIs) to promote human-centered intellectual research through the institutionalization of partnerships between the university and the community. The chapter argues that the success of these partnerships depends not only on respect and mutual understanding, but also on the collective vision of all partners to forge the strategy and action plan.

Chapter 7 is framed within the context of the transformative agenda of the higher education sector in post-apartheid South Africa. The FeesMustFall campaign (FMF) began at the end of October 2015 and all of 2016 became one of the largest movements in the history of the South which purpose is to provide free, quality and decolonized higher education. The chapter makes use of the qualitative approach with secondary and primary data extracted from books, accredited articles and also empirical data of selected participants.

Chapter 8 focuses on an analysis of the FeesMustFall campaign (FMF) as a policy that offers a free and quality education in HEIs, determining the costs and benefits from its implementation.

Chapter 9 presents a case study in Mexico focused on analyzing the impact of Project-Based Learning (PBL) to determine the formation of skills such as creative thinking, motivation and meaningful learning supported by the use of ICT for research, analysis, experimentation, simulation and socialization.

Chapter 10 focuses on the importance of generating competitive advantage in the tourism industry based on the definition of intellectual capital and its relationship with the training of professional skills in this strategic area for a country in order to promote productivity and the profitability of organizations.

Chapter 11 establishes that the Incorporating Indigenous Knowledge (IKS) is a proposal that can be used as a reference framework for African research, taking into account the formation of skills in a competent and knowledge-based society capable of facing local and international challenges. Academic socialization at IKS considers an integrated approach to research, which is also interdisciplinary in nature and aims to interact with other knowledge systems.

Chapter 12 is aimed at presenting the development of a proposal of indicators of intellectual capital in higher education in order to measure its contribution to society, meeting the needs of interest groups to optimize the human talent of the institution and thus the achievement of organizational objectives.

FINAL THOUGHTS

In this sense, the relevance of this work is to provide a set of studies on the existence of intellectual capital to measure and manage it in order to develop it and increase it in the context of higher education as the key axis for the economic development of a country, as well as improve the quality of life of its inhabitants.

This book provides insights concerning the use of intellectual capital in Higher Education. This is a cutting-edge and important topic that deserves a reflection, and this book constitutes an excellent opportunity to do it, increasing the understanding of using intellectual capital, providing relevant academic work, empirical research findings, and an overview of this relevant field of study. It is a timely research publication that features the latest scholarly trends, issues, and implications of the use of intellectual capital in higher education, including extensive coverage of pertinent topics.

REFERENCES

Araujo, A. (2000). *Gestión del conocimiento, Universidad y Empresa.* Paper presented at the University Conference on knowledge management in companies and organizations. Centre for University Knowledge Management. Bilbao.

Arrieta, N., Gaviria, G., & Consuegra, J. (2017). Papel del capital intelectual en la calidad de las Instituciones de Educación Superior en Colombia. *Education and Educators*, *20*(3), 419–433. doi:10.5294/edu.2017.20.3.5

Bezhani, I. (2010). Intellectual capital reporting at UK universities. *Journal of Intellectual Capital*, *11*(2), 179–207. doi:10.1108/14691931011039679

Biemans, H., Nieuwenbuis, L., Poell, R., Mulder, M., & Wesselink, R. (2004). Competence based VET in the Netherland. Background and piftalls. *Journal of Vocational Education and Training*, *56*(2), 523–538. doi:10.1080/13636820400200268

Cano, M., Sánchez, G., González, M., & Pérez, J. (2014). El rol del capital intelectual en la innovación de las empresas. *European Scientific Journal*, *10*(28), 348–366. Retrieved from http://eujournal.org/index.php/esj/ article/viewFile/4405/4202

Cinque, M. (2016). Lost in translation. Soft skills development in European countries. *Tuning Journal for Higher Education*, *3*(2), 389–427. doi:10.18543/tjhe-3(2)-2016pp389-427

Delors, J. (Ed.). (1996). *La educación encierra un tesoro.* Madrid: Ediciones UNESCO.

Drucker, P. (1993). La gerencia en la sociedad futura. Bogotá: Norma.

Drucker, P. (1997). The Future that Has Already Happened. *Harvard Business Review*, *7*(49), 64–75.

Edvinsson, L., & Sullivan, P. (1996). Developing a model for managing intelectual capital. *European Management Journal*, *14*(4), 356–364. doi:10.1016/0263-2373(96)00022-9

Edvinsson, L., & Malone, M. (1998). *El capital intelectual, cómo identificar y calcular el valor inexplorado de los recursos intangibles de su empresa*. Bogotá: Grupo Editorial Norma.

European Comission. (2003). *The role of the Universities in the Europe of Knowledge*. Brussels: COM. Retrieved from http://www.ecm.ub.edu/ceuropea/ComUniversidadesES1.pdf

Farias, G. (2010). Espacios de aprendizaje en educación superior: de la profesionalización a la innovación para la transformación social. *Opening*, *2*(2). Retrieved from http://www.udgvirtual.udg.mx/apertura/num13/Articulos/tema2.php

Fontalvo, T., Quejada, R., & Puello, J. (2011). La gestión del conocimiento y los procesos de mejoramiento. *Dimensión empresarial, 9*(1), 80-87.

González, F., Tamayo, A., & Vargas, E. (2019). Aportaciones para un estado de la cuestión sobre pertinencia en la formación profesional turística. *Iberoamerican Journal of Higher Education*, *10*(27), 195–215. doi:10.22201/iisue.20072872e.2019.27

Guzmán, R., & Adriano, A. (2013). Conocimiento, economía, desarrollo y sociedad: trazos desde la complejidad. *In-keys of Thought*, *7*(14), 123-143. Retrieved from http://www.scielo.org.mx/scielo.php?script=sci_arttext&pid=S1870-879X2013000200006&lng=es&tlng=es

Johnson, S. (2010). *TED: ¿De dónde vienen las buenas ideas?* [Vídeo] Retrieved from http://www. ted.com/talks/steven_johnson_where_good_ideas_come_from

Laurenti, T. (2008). Modelling Exogenous Variables in Human Capital Formation throught a Heteroscedastic Stochastic Frontier. *International Atlantic Economic Society*, *14*, 76–89.

Leitner, K., Bornemann, M., & Schneider, U. (2002). *Development and Implementation of an Intellectual Capital Report for a Research Technology Organisation*. Paper presented at the World Congress on Intellectual Capital Readings. 10.1016/B978-0-7506-7475-1.50018-X

Lev, B., & Zambon, S. (2003). Intangibles and intellectual capital: An introduction to a special issue. *European Accounting Review*, *12*(4), 597–603. doi:10.1080/0963818032000162849

Marginson, S. (2013). La Educación Superior como autoformación: El caso de estudiantes transfronterizos. *High School Journal*, *43*(169), 7–24. Retrieved from http://www.scielo.org.mx/pdf/resu/v43n169/v43n169a2.pdf

Marginson, S., & Marjijk, W. (2007). *Globalization and Higher Education*. Paris: Organisation for Economic Co-operation and Development.

Sullivan, P. (2001). *Value-Driven Intellectual Capital – How To Convert Intangible Corporate Assets into Market Value*. New York: Wiley.

Martínez, P., & Echeverría, B. (2009). Formación basada en competencias. *Educational Research Journal*, *27*(1), 125–147. doi:10.6018/rie.27.1.94331

Mercado, P., Gil, P., & Cernas, D. (2016). Validez inicial de una escala de medición del capital intelectual en universidades. *Universitas Psychologica*, *15*(2), 109–120. doi:10.11144/Javeriana.upsy15-2.viem

Nonaka, I., & Takeuchi, H. (1995). *The knowledge-creating company: How Japanese Companies Create the Dynamics of Innovation*. New York: Oxford University Press.

Organization for Economic Cooperation and Development (OECD). (2012). Better Skills, Better Jobs, Better Lives: A Strategic Approach to Skills Policies. Paris: OECD. doi:10.1787/9789264177338-en

Organization for Economic Cooperation and Development (OECD). (2011). *Skills for innovation and Research*. Retrieved from https://biobs.jrc.ec.europa.eu/sites/ default/ files/generated/files/policy/OECD%202011%20Skills%20for%20Innovation%20 and%20Research.pdf

Organization for Economic Cooperation and Development (OECD). (1998). Human Capital Investment. An International Comparison. Paris: OECD.

Rodríguez, D., & Gairín, J. (2015). Innovación, aprendizaje organizativo y gestión del conocimiento en las instituciones educativas. *Education*, *24*(46), 73–90.

Romero, G. (2018). Calidad educativa: Engranaje entre la gestión del conocimiento, la gestión educativa, la innovación y los ambientes de aprendizaje. *Journal of Studies and Experiences in Education*, *17*(35), 91–103. Retrieved from http://www.rexe.cl/ ojournal/index.php/rexe/article/view/597/472

Sánchez, P., Elena, S., & Castrillo, R. (2009). Intellectual capital dynamics in universities: A reporting model. *Journal of Intellectual Capital*, *10*(2), 307–324. doi:10.1108/14691930910952687

Tseng, C., & James Goo, Y. (2005). Intellectual capital and corporate value in an emerging economy: Empirical study of Taiwanese manufacturers. *R & D Management*, *35*(2), 187–201. doi:10.1111/j.1467-9310.2005.00382.x

United Nations Educational, Scientific and Cultural Organization (UNESCO). (2013). *Gestión Educativa Estratégica*. Buenos Aires: Instituto Superior de Planeamiento de la Educación - Ministerio de Educación de la Nación. Retrieved from http://www.buenosaires.iipe.unesco.org/sites/default/iles/modulo02_0.pdf

United Nations Educational, Scientific and Cultural Organization (UNESCO). (2005). Educación para todos: el imperativo de la calidad. Informe de Seguimiento de Educación para Todos en el Mundo. Paris, France: UNESCO.

United Nations Educational, Scientific and Cultural Organization (UNESCO). (1998). *La educación superior en el Siglo XXI: visión y acción*. Retrieved from http://www.unesco.org/education/educprog/wche/declaration_spa.htm

Vera, F. (2016). Infusión de habilidades blandas en el currículo de la educación superior: Clave para el desarrollo de capital humano avanzado. *Akademéia Journal*, *7*(1), 53–73.

Warden, C. (2004). *Valuation and Evaluation of Intangibles in Universities & Research Centres*. Academic Press.

Acknowledgment

The editor would like to acknowledge the help of all the people involved in this project and, more specifically, to the authors and reviewers that took part in the review process. Without their support, this book would not have become a reality.

First, the editor would like to thank each one of the authors for their contributions. Our sincere gratitude goes to the chapters authors who contributed their time and expertise to this book.

Second, the editor wishes to acknowledge the valuable contributions of the reviewers regarding the improvement of quality, coherence, and content presentation of chapters. Most of the authors also served as referees; we highly appreciate their double task.

Third, the editor thanks the Instituto Politécnico Nacional for promoting scientific and technological research. Specifically, the topic of this book came from the SIP project number 20181014.

Edgar Oliver Cardoso Espinosa
Instituto Politécnico Nacional, Mexico

Chapter 1
Human, Relational, and Structural Capital as Strategic Objectives in Higher Education

Jésica Alhelí Cortés Ruiz
Instituto Politécnico Nacional, Mexico

Edgar Oliver Cardoso Espinosa
https://orcid.org/0000-0001-7588-9439
Instituto Politécnico Nacional, Mexico

Rosa María Rivas García
Instituto Politécnico Nacional, Mexico

ABSTRACT

This chapter will focus on the characterization of human, relational, and structural capital, as well as the importance of establishing them as strategic objectives in higher education in Mexico, with the aim of designing academic proposals oriented to optimize and manage intellectual capital. Given that the new economic order demands from academic organizations more efficient ways of producing and transferring education, the context of higher education is pointed out with reference to the capitals in question and the importance of their relationship in such a way that through this it is possible to determine strategic objectives that maximize academic performance and improve teaching-learning models, as well as terminal efficiency in higher education schools in Mexico.

DOI: 10.4018/978-1-5225-8461-2.ch001

INTRODUCTION

This chapter will focus on the characterization of human, relational and structural capital, as well as the importance of establishing them as strategic objectives in higher education in Mexico, with the aim of designing academic proposals oriented to optimize and manage intellectual capital.

Given that the new economic order demands from academic organizations more efficient ways of producing and transferring education, the context of higher education is pointed out with reference to the capitals in question and the importance of their relationship, in such a way that through this, it is possible to determine strategic objectives that maximize academic performance, and improve teaching - learning models, as well as terminal efficiency in higher education schools in our country.

In such a way, the new concepts and models in organizations are taken as a reference parameter due to the success they bring to different structures. Such is the case of intellectual capital that, despite not being a new conception, was not used a few years ago either. And, what has happened in the course of the last two decades is an explosion in certain key technical areas, including information and communication technologies, which have provided new tools with which a global economy has been built. Many of these tools provide intangible benefits that did not exist before, and that have now provided competitive advantages that constitute an asset in institutions (Viedma, 2000).

BACKGROUND

Ulrich (1998) conceptualized intellectual capital as a multiplicative function of competence and commitment. Congruent with the arguments of Ulrich (1998), and Quinn et al. (1996), an examination of the characteristics and features of intellectual capital reveals that it represents a particular case as far as its different components are complementary. This brings about a new dimension in human capital analysis. Without constituting a revolution, this methodology can be used for capital items revealing a high degree of complementarity.

Several studies indicate that unique or scarce resources impact firm performance (Barney, 1991; Castrogiovanni, 1991; Grant, 1991; Mahoney, 1995; Nahapiet & Ghoshal, 1998; Pfeffer & Salancik, 1978; Tsai & Ghoshal, 1998). For instance, Barney (1991) suggests that organizations have a competitive advantage when their assets, capabilities or processes possess specific attributes. That is, when assets, capabilities or processes are rare, valuable, difficult to imitate, and have few substitutes, they represent a critical source for competitive advantage.

However, the bottom line of value creation processes is organizations' combined capacity to employ their, more or less unique, resources, their intangible and tangible assets. The development of the notion of intellectual capital within a human capital framework seems to be a fruitful theoretical refinement to this discussion.

INTELLECTUAL CAPITAL, ITS DIMENSIONS AND RELATIONSHIP WITH HIGHER EDUCATION

Intellectual capital is a topic on which the interest of companies has grown rapidly in recent years, especially in those which benefits derive mainly from innovation and knowledge-intensive services (Edvinsson & Sullivan, 1996). This concept has been used in academic literature for many years; however, it is not until recent times that a small group of companies, including Skandia, Dow Chemicals and the Canadian Imperial Bank, generalize it to refer to all intangible assets.

As mentioned by Viedma (2000), intangible assets, although they cannot be touched, are properly identified and classified in a simple manner as shown below:

1. **Assets of Individual Competence:** They refer to education, experience, "Know How", knowledge, skills, values and attitudes of the people who work in the company (which in this case is our educational sphere). The organization hires the use of these assets with their workers and when they leave home they take with them these assets that are called human capital.
2. **Assets of Internal Structure:** They deal with the formal and informal organizational structure, the working methods and procedures, the software, the databases, the research and development, the direction and management systems, and the culture of the organism. These assets are owned by the organization and some of them can be legally protected (patents, intellectual property, etc.).
3. **Assets of External Structure:** They address the billboard of clients that receives the name of goodwill; the relations with suppliers, banks and shareholders; the cooperation agreements and strategic, technological, and production alliances; the trademarks and the image of the organism. These assets are also owned by the company and in the same way, some of them can be legally protected (brands, commercial, etc.).

Thus, intellectual capital refers to a set of intangible assets related to the knowledge, skills, abilities, talent and creative processes of individuals within an organization, the resources available and the productive relationships that are established inside and outside the institution.

According to the "Intelect" model (Euroforum, 1998), intellectual capital is composed of three key elements: human, structural and relational capital, as shown schematically in Figure 1, observing a synergistic composition that allows obtaining an overview of the intangible assets that the organization possesses, so generating the necessary information for the design of objectives with a strategic sense.

With this denomination, the University Institute Euroforum Escorial (1998), and the consulting company KPMG (1999), have established a model of intellectual capital that is the sum of 3 blocks: Human capital + structural capital + relational capital. Each one of them establishes a temporal scope referring to the present and the future, determining the intangibles that it considers and proposing for each one of them, the most suitable indicators to be able to measure them, as can be seen in Table 1.

In addition, the "Intelect Club" has been created, formed by companies as well as institutions and universities that want to serve as a forum for meeting business experiences and academic knowledge in order to progress in the common goal of measuring and managing intangible assets and knowledge flows. In this sense, for example, the BBVA group, HSBC, Caja Madrid, Indra, and Unión Fenosa, start from this model for their measurement of intellectual capital.

Figure 1. Scheme of intellectual capital
Source: Own elaboration based on Euroforum Escorial (1998)

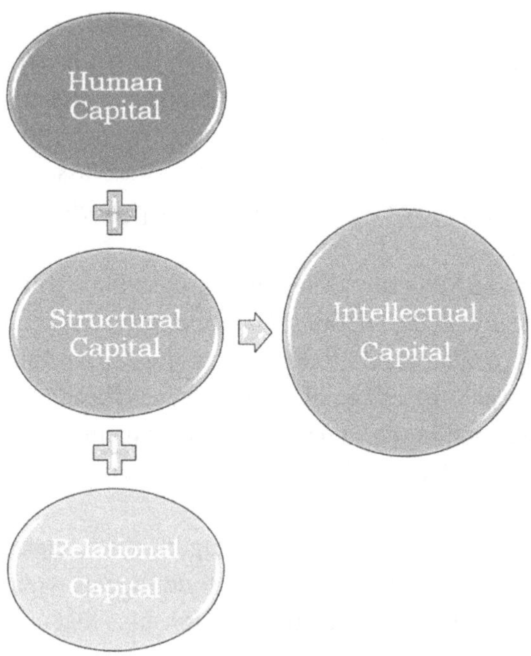

Table 1. Indicators to measure intellectual capital. Intelect model

Human Capital	
	Intangible Assets
Present	• Staff satisfaction • Staff typology • Competences of people • Leadership • Stability: risk of loss
Future	• Improvement of competencies • Innovation capacity of people and equipment
Structural Capital	
	Intangible Assets
Present	• Organizational culture • Business philosophy • Strategic reflection processes • Structure of the organization • Process technology • Product technology • Support processes • Strategic reflection processes • Processes of knowledge acquisition • Mechanisms of transmission and communication • Information technology
Future	• Innovation processes
Relational Capital	
	Intangible Assets
Present	• Relevant customer base • Loyalty of clients • Intensity of the relationship with customers • Customer satisfaction • Support processes and customer service • Closeness to the market • Brand(s) notoriety • Reputation / Company name • Strategic alliances • Interrelation with suppliers • Interrelation with other agents
Future	• Improvement capacity • Recreation of the customer base

Source: Own elaboration based on Euroforum Escorial (1998).

This model conceptually is very similar to the one proposed by Skandia, where three types of capital are highlighted: human, structural and relational, to constitute the intellectual capital, remembering indicators that take into account the present and future in its measurement.

HUMAN CAPITAL

Suarez (1997) defines human capital as the potential economic value of the greater productive capacity of an individual, or of the whole of the active society of a country, which is the result of greater knowledge acquired in school, university or experience.

Due to the fact that the rapid technological advances in telecommunications and information technology are transforming the nature of knowledge, skills and talent of individuals, companies operating in the current globalized world require a different type of worker, with skills, attitudes and intellectual agility that allow a critical and systemic thinking within a technological environment (Bontis, 2002). All this means that one of the dimensions that, in a more repeated way, is considered in intellectual capital models is that related to human capital.

In this sense, it has been defined as a generator of value and a potential source of innovation for the company, that is, it is where the ideas of the organization start (Viedma, 2001), resulting, therefore, a source of innovation and strategic renewal (Bontis, 1998). In other words, it is the thinking capital of the individual, or what is the same, that capital that resides in the members of the organization and that allows to generate value for the company. On the other hand, three components can be distinguished within the dimension dedicated to human capital: (a) competences, in the form of knowledge, skills, talent and know-how; (b) the attitude, which translates into behavior, motivation, action and ethics of the people; and (c) intellectual agility, which generates value for the organization insofar as new knowledge or discoveries are applied to transform ideas into products and services (Roos et al., 2001).

On the other hand, Bontis, Crossan, and Hulland (2002), Bueno (2000), Camisón, Palacios, and Devece (2000), Euroforum (1998), Ordóñez (2002, 2003) and Petrash (1996, 2001) conceive the human capital in a very similar way to the previously exposed, considering that it is integrated by the stock of both tacit and explicit knowledge held by the members of the organization.

Therefore, part of this human capital is the accumulated value of the investments that companies have made in the training of employees (Skandia, 1996). In this same line, Sveiby (2000) in his monitor of intangible assets establishes a dimension that he calls the *workers' competences* and that is defined as the capacity that the members of the organization have to act in different situations and create both material and immaterial assets.

In addition, while it is true that the real owner of this type of capital is not the company, but the workers themselves (Euroforum, 1998; Sveiby, 1998, 2000), it is part of the value of the organization and, consequently, it must be considered as capital for the company and be included in its balance sheet, especially if it is intensive in knowledge and, thus, depends primarily on its personnel.

Hence, human capital is also defined as the knowledge that the company loses when its employees abandon it and, therefore, it presents difficulties to be retained in it. For this reason, organizations must try to retain the most valuable employees (Roos et al., 2001), that is to say, they must adequately compensate those workers who are the bearers of intellectual capital (Sveiby, 2000). However, Malhotra (2000) considers that this circumstance is not totally true, since if it were, it would imply that workers, when they are in their working hours, never think of anything other than the company and that when they go home, they do not take any work problems. Also, this author provides, as another argument for his claim, the fact that there is the possibility of tele-work, which, as its name suggests, allows the company's staff to work outside of it.

On the other hand, Brooking (1997b) presents this dimension with the name of assets centered on the individual and includes, among others, assets such as collective expertise, creative capacity, ability to solve problems and leadership. Along the same lines, Edvinsson and Malone (1999), Nevado and López (2002a), and Sullivan (1999), consider that this perspective is composed of all the individual skills, knowledge, abilities and experience of employees and managers. In a similar way, Pérez (2000) and Fernández, Montes, and Vázquez (1998) define human capital as the individual knowledge and skills of the members of the organization that allow to increase their productivity and their contribution to the generation of value of the company.

It is necessary to take into account the nuance that on human capital Sveiby (1998, 2000) makes. He argues that all workers of the company should not be included within this block, but those who are considered experts, which means, those who are specialists and represent the elite of the personnel. Consequently, the rest of the workforce, that is, those who are dedicated to maintaining and developing both the internal and external structure, must be placed in a different category of intellectual capital (Bontis, 2001).

Thusly, if what is mentioned is analyzed carefully, it is appreciated how the information of the human capital is defined to be applied to institutions of higher education, adapting each of its characteristics to the components and requirements that said institutions demand.

Then, each definition applied to the educational sphere is described in Table 2.

Table 2. Representation of human capital in higher education

Human Capital
• Creation of the academy • Initial diagnostic • Analysis of opportunities. • Workshops for conceptualization • Creation of institutional research lines • Awareness workshops • Workshops for the preparation of preliminary projects • Graduates • Workshops for the training of academic bodies. • Analysis of the requirements of the programs • Incentive programs

Source: Own elaboration based on Romo, Villalobos, and Guadalupe (2012)

RELATIONAL CAPITAL

The relational capital is drawn on the consideration that companies are not isolated systems, but, on the contrary, are related to the outside. Thus, relationships of this type, that add value to the company, are those that should be considered relational capital.

Therefore, this type of capital includes the value generated by the company's relationships, not only with customers, suppliers and shareholders, but with all its stakeholders, both internal and external (Bontis, 1996, Ordóñez, 2003, Stewart, 1998; Roos et al., 2001). That is, it is the knowledge that is included in the relationships of the organization (Bontis, 1998). Seen from another perspective, relational capital is the perception of value that customers have when they do business with their suppliers of goods or services (Petrash, 1996, 2001). In this way, some indicators that show the development of this capital within the organization are, for example, the repeat rate of the clients, the market share or the number of alliances established with other organizations. Otherwise, Sveiby (1989, 2000, and 2001) refers to this dimension as an *external component* and includes relations with customers and suppliers. In this same line, Kaplan and Norton (1997) denominate in this model *"perspective of the client"* to this capital (Network of human resources, 2002) and in it, they analyze how value is created for the client, how his demand is satisfied and why does he pay for it?

As a result, what they intend is to identify and measure explicitly, in order to better manage the proposals for added value that will be obtained with the segments of clients and selected markets (Kaplan & Norton, 1997). Nonetheless, although these authors explicitly limit this external or relational perspective to clients in their model (Bontis et al., 1999), this can be extended to suppliers and, in general, to all the relationships that the company has with its environment (Olve et al., 2000).

In a similar way, Edvinsson (1997) and Edvinsson and Malone (1999), consider that this dimension is integrated, mainly, by the value generated by the relations of the company with its clients. Differently, Brooking (1997b) calls this dimension "*market assets*" and defines it as those resources that give the company a competitive advantage by virtue of the potential that derives from intangible assets that are related to the market. Finally, Camison et al. (2000) call it *social capital* and define it as the set of knowledge assets which accumulation process derives from relationships with customers.

Once the different dimensions of intellectual capital have been presented, it should be emphasized that these dimensions are not watertight compartments in which each dimension is isolated from the rest. Thus, although there are interactions between the different blocks mentioned above, this is a little studied feature in the literature on intellectual capital (Ordóñez, 2001).

However, different authors, including Bontis (1998), Bontis, Chua, and Richardson (2000), Camiso Zornosa et al. (2000), Euroforum (1998), Niven (2003) and Kaplan and Norton (1997), certify the existence of the mentioned connections.

On the other hand, statements such as Edvisson's (1997), who considers that for the management of intellectual capital, the various components of it should be used jointly and not individually, or those made by Edvinsson and Malone (1999) and Sveiby (1998, 2000), who consider that human capital is fundamental for the development of other types of capital, are also signs of the existence of these relationships. As a result of all this, any strategy that aims to develop the intellectual capital of the organization must take into account the existing relationships between the different forms of intellectual capital to perform in this way, the actions that make the total intellectual capital the largest and most convenient for the company (Ordóñez, 2001).

Additionally, the academic field is represented in Table 3 through the aforementioned.

Table 3. Activities for the construction of relational capital in higher education

Relational Capital
• Participation strategy in workshops and internal and external calls. • Strategy for the dissemination of products generated from research projects of academic bodies. • Presentation of research results as speakers at congresses. • Dissemination of the results of the research generated in the institution through the establishment of internal dissemination programs (journals and forums). • Encounters of academic bodies and the productive sector. • Generation of collaboration networks between academic bodies.

Source: Own elaboration based on Romo, Villalobos, and Guadalupe (2012)

STRUCTURAL CAPITAL

Another dimension that integrates intellectual capital is what has been known as structural capital. This type of capital has been described as that knowledge that the company has been able to internalize and that remains in the organization, be it in its structure, in its processes or in its culture, even when employees leave it and, for this reason, it is owned by the company (Edvinsson, 1997). Consequently, it is possible to include in this dimension all the non-human intangibles of the organization, that is, they can be considered within the structural capital from the culture or internal processes to the information systems or databases (Bontis et al., 2000).

For Edvinsson and Malone (1999) and Roos et al. (2001) structural capital can be broken down into three other dimensions that help shape the non-thinking part of intellectual capital and that stays in the organization when the worker does not stay in it. These dimensions are the organization, renewal and development capital. However, it should be clarified that, in certain models, some of these divisions form a specific dimension and are not included in the structural capital.

Starting with the organizational capital, it is the one that includes the value generated by the internal structure of the company and the way in which the operations and processes that take place within it are developed. So, it is understood that internal processes, organizational forms, information flows or the company's own culture are part of this capital.

On the other hand, renewal and development capital refers to any aspect of the company that can generate future value through an improvement, which can be reflected in the intellectual or financial capital. For that reason, the percentage of business from new products, training courses, renewal expenses or new registered patents are indicators of this (Edvinsson & Malone, 1999; Roos et al., 2001).

Diversely, Sveiby (2000) refers to this perspective as an internal component and includes patents, ideas, operating structures, administrative and information organization, etc., elements that are the property of the company and therefore, they comply with the aforementioned property of remaining in it when the employee leaves and that, in turn, have one of their characteristics that can be created within the company or acquired abroad. In this sense, the culture and the organizational environment are also considered internal components.

Similarly, in the definition of structural capital within the Intelect model (Euroforum, 1998), it is mentioned that it includes systematized knowledge, explicit and internalized by the organization, including, thence, the information and management systems, patents or available technology. Consecutively, the authors of this model also highlight the fact that, contrary to what happens with human capital, this type of capital is owned by the company.

Differently, Kaplan and Norton (1997) include this perspective in two of its dimensions, in the internal process (Human Resources Network, 2002) and in part of the perspective of training and growth, since, as mentioned above, this perspective also contemplates aspects related to human capital. The first one identifies those critical processes in which the company must be excellent. In this analysis, by its nature, it is interesting to include the resources and capabilities that the company needs to improve. Thus, some indicators related to this perspective may be the manufacturing time, the number of defective products, the kilograms of waste generated or the number of customer complaints.

In this way, indicators are tried to establish in order to determine if the company can ensure its capacity for long-term renewal and, therefore, its survival. Also, Brooking (1997b) places this type of assets in two dimensions, specifically that of intellectual property assets and that of infrastructure assets. Hence, the former derives from the legal protection that the organization exercises over those assets that have a special value for it, among which are the *know-how*, the manufacturing secrets, the *copyright*, the patents, the rights of designs, among others. Regarding the latter, they refer to those assets that provide order, security, correctness and quality to the organization and the context in which the employees work, as is the case, for example, of the technologies, methodologies and the processes that make the operation of the organization possible, the corporate culture, the methods for the calculation of risks or the information databases.

Finally, the education sector is expressed in table 4 through the concepts cited.

Table 4. Activities to establish structural capital in higher education

Structural Capital
• Support materials for participation in calls and for the preparation of preliminary projects. • Diagrams of procedures for integration of technological project files. • Support material for the standardization of guidelines for early research direction for the degree. • Support materials for the sensitization workshops for researchers, for the formation of research groups of G.C. and academic bodies. • Design and implementation of multimedia materials for the integration of G.C researchers' files. • Design and implementation of web pages. • Development of digital library. • ICTs and LKTs.

Source: Own elaboration based on Romo, Villalobos, and Guadalupe (2012)

MODELS THAT INCLUDE HUMAN, RELATIONAL AND STRUCTURAL CAPITAL TO BE TAKEN AS AN EXAMPLE IN HIGHER EDUCATION

- **Skandia Navigator Model:** Intellectual Capital System. It was presented by Edvinsson and Malone in 1998. Their book arose initially in 1994, as an annex to the company's annual report, where it was shown the contribution of the Intellectual Capital developed within it and clearly identifies the difference between the Financial Capital and the Intellectual Capital of the company; its main objective was to generate a tool to direct the decision-making process.
- **Model of the Balanced Business Scorecard (C.M.I.):** It was developed in 1992, by Kaplan and Norton (2000), and it has been one of the pioneering works in the field of Intellectual Capital; it includes in its analysis the management indicators that had been excluded by inserting only those related to the financial cut, making this compendium a tool for decision making. The C.M.I model presents four perspectives stipulated as follows: a) *The financial perspective*: referred to financial indicators, cash flows, analysis of customer and product profitability, risk management, b) *The customer perspective*: identifies the values related to customers, c) *The perspective of internal processes*: satisfaction of internal and external customers, through innovations, operations, and after-sales service processes, d) *The learning perspective*: refers to innovation, growth, motivation and the ability to learn and grow based on the management of employees.
- **Model of Intellectual Assets Monitor (Sveiby, 1997):** It is presented by Karl-Erick Sveiby (2008); here the intangible assets are taken as a central point. In this order of ideas, Bontis (2000) expresses what was designed by Sveiby as: a) *Human Capital*. It has as a relevant factor the skills of people, based on the ability to act in different situations; there, experience and education are included, b) *Structural Capital* in turn, is subdivided into: internal structure, allusive to the elements created by the company, but which are property of the organization, such as: patents, processes, models, information systems, organizational culture and, external structure, focused on relations with customers and suppliers; sections such as: reputation of the organization, the image of the company and trademarks, are taken into account in the latter.
- **Technology Broker Model (1996):** Annie Brooking (1996) is its proponent; it starts off the same concept of the Skandia model, but includes the assets, both intellectual capital, and tangible assets. In the case of the Broker model, presented by Ascanio (1996), the description of qualitative indicators is reached through the development of a methodology to audit the information related to Intellectual Capital. According to the previous model, intangible assets are

classified into four categories: a) *Market Assets*: brands, customer loyalty, licenses, franchises, b) *Intellectual Property Assets*: patents, copyrights, design rights, secrets of manufacturing, c) *Human Assets*: academic levels, technical knowledge, skills and competencies associated with work and d) *Infrastructure Assets*: technologies, methods and processes that allow the organization to function. The model ends with the referencing and sampling of the audit of Intellectual Capital and the benefits of its measurement within which is confirmed the ability of the organization to achieve its goals, the planning of the research, as well as its development (González et al., 1996).

- **Model of Canadian Imperial Bank:** Prepared by Hubert Saint-Honge in 1996. It is responsible for the measurement of Intellectual Capital of the Imperial Bank of Canada. Its task is to illustrate the relationship between Intellectual Capital and its measurement and organizational learning. It is composed of three elements: a) *Human Capital*, b) *Structural Capital* and c) *Customer Capital*. Additionally, Financial Capital is also found. For McCann (1996), the importance of the model lies in taking the structural concept of Skandia and adding it to the customer capital. The composition of the model is presented as follows: the Knowledge Capital is composed of a holistic system of three elements: a) *Human Capital*: knowledge, skills that employees must have and competences, b) *Structural Capital*: instrumental capabilities to meet the needs of the market and c) *Customer Capital*: they are related to the service, market and loyalty schemes.
- **Model University of West Notario (Bontis, 1996):** It is presented by Pomeda et al. (2002) and developed by Bontis (1996) who make an analysis regarding the cause-effect relationships between the basic elements considered by them as Intellectual Capital (Human Capital, Structural Capital and Relational Capital) and their effect on business results. The success of the model is fundamentally due to the importance of Human Capital in achieving the goals and performance indicators desired and required by the company; likewise, its importance can be reaffirmed within an organizational culture centered on intelligence that leads to structuring knowledge organizations, thanks to the development of that culture.
- **Nova Model (1999):** Created by the company Nova Care and developed by the community Knowledge Management Club of the Valencian Community (Camisón, Palacios and Devece); it is an application model for any type of company; it allows, not only to measure, but also to do process management; it is inclined towards the growth of companies, for which it is divided into four elements: a) *Human Capital*, b) *Organization Capital*, c) *Social Capital* and d) *Innovation and Learning Capital*. By going a little deeper into the above, authors like Osorio (2003) affirm that the essence of the model lies basically

in the direction by competences; likewise, in what refers to the indicators, Pomeda et al. (2002), place them within the range of process dynamics.

- **Dow Chemical Model (Dow, 1998):** As expressed by Sánchez (2000), it arose due to the insufficiency of a scheme that would allow the management of intangible assets to be valued. The methodology, established there, is based on the process of measuring and managing invisible assets and the impact they have on financial activity. This acquires relevance because Dow Chemical, according to Osorio (2003), is a company that managed to develop a method for the codification and management of patent portfolios. The model is structured in three axes: a) *Human capital*, related to the skills to generate customer solutions, b) *Organizational capital*, referred to the organization's capacities to codify and use knowledge and, c) *Customer Capital*, based on the attention and customer service (customer understanding, loyalty generation and franchise management) all these resources, according to the authors, generate the value of the company. It is important to note that the indicators vary according to the type of organizational structure and that said intellectual asset management model consists of six basic steps such as: Business Strategy, Competitor Assessment, Classification of Own Benefits, Valuation, Investment and Portfolio Management.
- **Strategic Management by Competition Model:** The intangible capital. Bueno (1998). Another scheme is the so-called strategic management of the company, Osorio (2003). Professor Bueno, cited by Sánchez (2000), manifests a marked interest in stating that "the center of the model is the Intellectual Capital using the tool of strategic management through competences". The model is based on three essential elements: a) those of *technological origin*, b) those of *organizational origin* and c) those of a *social nature*. The main generic competences are present in this model, namely: a) the attitudinal, b) the aptitude, and c) the evaluative; all referred or related to the members of the organization, through fundamentals of the business of the company and the estimation of what the company is capable of doing. Around this model, authors like Sznirer and Caracho, cited by Osorio (2003) reinforce the company's role, in the sense of focusing all their efforts to acquire and develop that knowledge, skills and attitudes needed to generate business results based on Intellectual Capital.
- **Model of the Five Phases of Nonaka and Takeuchi:** It corresponds to the classic model of Nonaka and Takeuchi (1995); it distinguishes two types of knowledge: tacit and explicit; the first, is the one that physically, is not palpable and that in terms of Intellectual Capital, resembles Human Capital, because it is internal and belongs to each person in particular. The second one refers fundamentally to the representation, by means of physically storable and

transmissible symbols that, for the development of the models of C.I would come to constitute in Structural or Organizational Capital and for others, in Structural or Customers Capital. The model is expressed respectively, by means of the two spirals of epistemological and ontological content; thus, an interaction between tacit and explicit knowledge is developed and it has a dynamic and continuous nature. In such a way, processes appear, and they go from socialization, exteriorization, and combination, to interiorization. After the analysis of the forms and spirals of creation of knowledge, the integral model of the five phases of creation of organizational knowledge is reached, being explained as follows:

- **To Share Tacit Knowledge:** It refers fundamentally to socialization.
- **To Create Concepts:** Tacit knowledge becomes explicit, it is similar to exteriorization.
- **To Justify the Concepts:** The organization determines whether it is really worth developing a new concept, building an archetype, a prototype, an operational mechanism or an abstract model for the case of innovation.
- **To Expand Knowledge:** The diffusion of the knowledge created between the personnel of the divisions and even, with external groups. The knowledge-creating organization, previously exposed under this model, must be an open system of knowledge exchange with the environment.

SOLUTIONS AND RECOMMENDATIONS

Derived from the diverse conceptions and bibliography that describe the Intellectual Capital, which make mention of Human Capital, Relational Capital and Structural Capital, focusing on the business sector, it is observed that the different models have a lot of applicability in different companies, and can really be adapted to the sphere of higher education. For the true development of Intellectual Capital at the institutional level, it is necessary to have elements that promote and participate in circles of research communities, typical of the different sciences of knowledge that commit Human, Relational and Structural Capital as the axis of academic development that becomes a form of valuation of the so-called invisible or intangible assets, which focus on the generations of new knowledge in higher education institutions of the 21st century.

FUTURE RESEARCH DIRECTIONS

OECD (1999) defines intellectual capital as "the economic value of two categories of intangible assets of a company", that is, organizational and human capital. Organizational capital refers, for example, to proprietary software systems, distribution networks, and supply chains (Petty & Guthrie, 2000). Employing human capital theory, we here concentrate on and define the part of intellectual capital that is based on human resources. Human capital theory is well founded both theoretically and empirically, and can be generalized and adapted to constitute a solid platform for the analysis of intellectual capital.

CONCLUSION

The relevance was to determine the status and importance of human, relational and structural capital in companies, to take them as benchmarks in the academic field and design strategic objectives in an internationally recognized higher institution to be used as an example and application in other educational organizations.

It is important to point out that in the information era, the capital that acquires greater importance in strategic analyzes is certainly that which surrounds intangible assets such as human capital. Due to this gradual importance, a total displacement of tangible and physical assets towards intangible and abstract assets is deployed in organizations; these, as well as information technology and innovation incentives, can play a major role in the creation of value. Currently, institutions are concerned with identifying adequate indicators to measure their intangible assets such as human capital (talents and skills of their employees), internal structural capital (administrative systems) and external capital (support and interest of their clients, and the suitability and speed of its suppliers). This type of capital is supported by tacit knowledge, talent management and essential and complementary skills. Competence, or "know how to be", was incorporated into the business vocabulary with the aim of centralizing efforts in the development of efficiency with regard to the training of its employees.

Knowledge-based assets have to be evaluated with extreme caution because their impact on the destination of any business is enormous. It is not enough to have competent people, it is necessary to efficiently use aggregate competences with the intention of strengthening business strategies in order to maintain a long-term competitive advantage.

The knowledge, gross intellectual material, is transformed into intellectual capital from the moment it adds value to products or services; in other words, from the process of socialization of knowledge, and that capital is, in some cases, more valuable than economic capital itself. The socialization of knowledge is based on a complex process of influences, cultural environments, positive and negative conditions, among others, and in the midst of that complexity the individual in his social interaction constructs his own knowledge and shares it with other members of society.

As for the concept of knowledge management, this arose in the 90s, as a proposal to add value to information and facilitate interactive flow throughout the organization. Certainly, the concepts of "intellectual capital and knowledge management" will suffer alterations and will undergo internal strategies of reformulation in the organizational environment. Knowledge management develops systems and processes that are intended to acquire and share intellectual assets; this inevitably reports the full use of knowledge, directing it as a competitive strategic differential of success. This tool shows that the successful companies are not a set of products or services, but knowledge bases with different variants related to the formation of their sets. In as much, the intellectual capital is the key of the competitive advantage of the company with its customers-objective because it creates essential, exclusive competences, and produces better results.

With the approach of knowledge management, the organization, its bases, strategies, structure and culture begin to be seen in a different way, in a competitive environment, where the globalization of the economy, improvements in transport and communications offer to its consumers a range of unprecedented options. The pressures on prices leave no room for inefficiency. The cycle of development of new products is getting shorter and the application of evaluative resources of matrix type more ephemeral. Organizations need quality, added value, service, innovation, flexibility, agility and speed in an increasingly critical way. In a world where the traditional factors of production "nature, capital and work" were exhausted or are in danger of extinction, companies invest vigorously in intellectual capital to increase their competitive advantage, creativity and innovation through ideas that provide knowledge. Much more than what contributes to the total value of the company, knowledge is the basis of its internal structure of an increasingly demanding market, so they have to invest in human resources.

Drucker (2002) says that the means of production, the traditional basis of capitalism, are now in the heads and hands of workers. Evidently, the relativity of the markets and the socio-political development of the companies involved must be considered in this affirmation. Organizational maturity and solidified market referential are required so that the management of the intellectual capital and the assets of the organization can be integrated into a process of planning and development.

ACKNOWLEDGMENT

This research was supported by the Instituto Politécnico Nacional, México (SIP number 20181014).

REFERENCES

APA. (2018). *Publication Manual of the American Psychological Association* (6th ed.). Washington, DC: Author.

Ascanio, A. (1996). *Skandia Navigator model.* Edvinsson.

Bontis, N. (1996). There is a price on your head: managing intellectual capital strategically. Business Quaterly, 41-47.

Bontis, N. (1998). Intellectual capital: An exploratory study that develops measures and models. *Management Decision, 36*(2), 63–76. doi:10.1108/00251749810204142

Bontis, N. (1999). Managing organizational knowledge by diagnosing intellectual capital: framing and advancing the state of the field. *International Journal of the Technology Management, 18*(5-8), 433-462.

Bontis, N. (2001). Assessing knowledge assets: A review of the models used to measure intelectual capital. *International Journal of Management Reviews, 3*(1), 41–60. doi:10.1111/1468-2370.00053

Bontis, N. (2002). *National intellectual capital index: Intellectual capital development in the Arab Region.* Ontario: Institute for Intellectual Capital Research.

Bontis, N., & Chua, W. (2000). Intellectual capital and business performance in Malaysian industries. *Journal of Intellectual Capital, 1*(1), 85–100. doi:10.1108/14691930010324188

Bontis, N., Crossan, M., & Hulland, J. (2002). Managing an organizational learning system by aligning stocks and flows. *Journal of Management Studies, 39*(4), 437–469. doi:10.1111/1467-6486.t01-1-00299

Bontis, N., Dragonetti, N., Jacobsen, K., & Roos, G. (1999). The knowledge toolbox: A review of tools available to measure and manage intangible resources. *European Management Journal, 17*(4), 391–402. doi:10.1016/S0263-2373(99)00019-5

Bradley, K. (1997a). Intellectual capital and the new wealth of nations. *Business Strategy Review, 8*(1), 53–62. doi:10.1111/1467-8616.00007

Bradley, K. (1997b). Intellectual capital and the new wealth of nations II. *Business Strategy Review*, *8*(4), 33–44. doi:10.1111/1467-8616.00046

Brooking, A. (1997b). Intellectual capital. Paidós Empresa.

Brooking, A. (1997a). The management of intellectual capital. *Long Range Planning*, *30*(3), 364–365. doi:10.1016/S0024-6301(97)80911-9

Camisón, C., Palacios, D., & Devece, C. (2000). *A model for the measurement of intellectual capital in the company: the Nova model.* Academic Press.

Daley, J. (2001). The intangible economy and Australia. *Australian Journal of Management*, *26*, 3-19.

Dierickx, I., & Cool, K. (1989). Asset stock accumulation and sustainability of competitive advantage. *Management Science*, *35*(12), 1504–1511. doi:10.1287/mnsc.35.12.1504

Drucker, P. (1993). *Post Capitalist Society*. HarperCollins.

Edvinsson, L. (1997). Developing intellectual capital at Skandia. *Long Range Planning*, *30*(3), 366–373. doi:10.1016/S0024-6301(97)90248-X

Edvinsson, L., & Malone, M. (1999). Intellectual capital, management 2000. Barcelona: Academic Press.

Edvinsson, L., & Stenfelt, C. (1999). Intellectual capital of nations – for future wealth creation. *Journal of Human Resource Costing and Accounting*, *4*(1), 21–33. doi:10.1108/eb029051

Edvinsson, L., & Sullivan, P. (1996). Developing a model for managing intellectual capital. *European Management Journal*, *14*(4), 356–364. doi:10.1016/0263-2373(96)00022-9

Euroforum. (1998). *Measurement of Intellectual Capital. Intelect Model*. Euroforum.

Fernández, E., Montes, J., & Vázquez, C. (1997). The theory of competitive advantage based on resources: synthesis and conceptual structure. *European Journal of Management and Business Administration*, *6*(3), 11-32.

Gibbert, M., Leibold, M., & Voelpe, S. (2001). Rejuvenating corporate intellectual capital by coopting customer competence. *Journal of Intellectual Capital*, *2*(2), 109–126. doi:10.1108/14691930110385900

Harvey, M. G., & Lusch, R. F. (1999). Balancing the intellectual capital books: Intangible liabilities. *European Management Journal*, *17*(1), 85–92. doi:10.1016/S0263-2373(98)00065-6

Huws, U. (1995). *Social Europe follow-up to the white paper*. EC Publication.

Johnston, P. Y Nolan, J. (2000). eWork 2000. *Status report on new ways to work in the information society*. Comisión Europea, Dirección General de la Sociedad de la Información.

Kaplan, R. S. Y., & Norton, D. P. (1992). The balanced scorecard - measures that drive performance. *Harvard Business Review*, 71–79. PMID:10119714

Kaplan, R. S. Y., & Norton, D. P. (1993). Putting the balance scorecard to work. *Harvard Business Review*, 135–147.

Kpmg Peat Marwick. (1999). The incorporation of intellectual capital as a key element of a company's market value. In *Seminar on knowledge management ´99*. Recoletos.

Lev, B. (2001). *Intangibles. Management, measurement and reporting*. Washington, DC: Brookings Institution.

Maisel, L. (1992). Performance measurement. The balanced scorecard approach. *Journal of Cost Management*, *6*(2), 47–52.

Malhotra, Y. (2000). Knowledge assets in the global economy: Assessment of national intellectual capital. *Journal of Global Information Management*, *8*(3), 5–15. doi:10.4018/jgim.2000070101

Nevado, D., & López, V. (2002a). *Intellectual capital: evaluation and measurement*. Madrid: Prentice Hall.

Nevado, D., & López, V. (2002b). A model and accounting report for the measurement of capital intellectual development and applications. Journal of Accounting and Taxation, 229, 161-206.

Niven, P. (2003). The scorecard step by step. Management 2000, Barcelona, Spain.

Nonaka, I., & Takeuchi, H. (1995). *The Knowledge-Creating Company*. Oxford, UK: Oxford University Press.

Olve, N., Roy, J., & Wetter, M. (2000). Implementing and managing the scorecard (Performance drivers). Management 2000, Barcelona, Spain.

Ordóñez, P. (1999). *Strategic importance of the measurement of intellectual capital in organizations*. Magazine Injet.com.

Ordóñez, P. (2001). *Intellectual capital, human resource management system and knowledge management: influence on organizational outcomes* (Doctoral thesis). Oviedo University.

Ordóñez, P. (2002). Evidence of intellectual capital measurement from Asia, Europe and the Middle East. *Journal of Intellectual Capital*, *3*(3), 287–302. doi:10.1108/14691930210435624

Ordóñez, P. (2003). Intellectual capital reporting in Spain: A comparative review. *Journal of Intellectual Capital*, *4*(1), 61–81. doi:10.1108/14691930310455397

Pasher, E. (1999). The Intellectual Capital of the State of Israel: A look to the Future – The Hidden Values of the Desert. Ed. Pasher&Co, Herzlia Pituach.

Pérez, G. (2000). Intellectual capital and knowledge innovation. *X National Congress of ACEDE: Economic integration, competitiveness and institutional environment of the company.*

Petrash, G. (1996). Dow's Journey to a knowledge value management culture. *European Management Journal*, *14*(4), 365–373. doi:10.1016/0263-2373(96)00023-0

Petrash, G. (2001). The intellectual assets management. In Monetize intellectual capital. Techniques to optimize the value of the Organization. Barcelona: Paidós Company.

Petty, R., & Guthrie, J. (2000). Intellectual capital literature review. Measurement, reporting and management. *Journal of Intellectual Capital*, *1*(2), 155–176. doi:10.1108/14691930010348731

Red De Recursos Humanos. (2002). *Some clarification of concepts of fashion*. Author.

Robinson, G., & Kleiner, B. (1996). How to measure an organization's intellectual capital. *Managerial Auditing Journal*, *11*(8), 36–39. doi:10.1108/02686909610131675

Rodov, I., & Leliaert, P. (2002). FiMIAM: Financial method of intangible assets measurement. *Journal of Intellectual Capital*, *3*(3), 323–336. doi:10.1108/14691930210435642

Romo, A., Villalobos, M., & Guadalupe, L. (2012). Gestión del Conocimiento: Estrategia para la Formación de Investigadores. *Sinéctica*, 38.

Roos, G., Bainbridge, A., & Jacobsen, K. (2001). Intellectual capital as a strategic tool. *Strategy and Leadership*, *29*(4), 21–26. doi:10.1108/10878570110400116

Roos, G., & Roos, J. (1997). Measuring your company's intellectual performance. *Long Range Planning*, *30*(3), 413–426. doi:10.1016/S0024-6301(97)90260-0

Roos, J., Roos, G., Dragonetti, N., & Edvinsson, L. (2001). Intellectual capital. The intangible value of the company. Paidós Company.

Sánchez, P., Chaminade, C., & Olea, M. (2000). Management of intangibles. An attempt to build a theory. *Journal of Intellectual Capital*, *1*(4), 312–327. doi:10.1108/14691930010359225

Skandia. (1996). *Supplement to the Annual Report, Customer Value*. Stockholm: Author.

Stewart, T. (1991). Brainpower: how intellectual capital becoming America's most valuable asset. Fortune, 2, 44-60.

Stewart, T. (1998). *The new wealth of organizations: intellectual capital*. Barcelona: Granica.

Sullivan, P. (1999). Profiting from intellectual capital. *Journal of Knowledge Management*, *3*(2), 132–142. doi:10.1108/13673279910275585

Sullivan, P. (2001a). Introduction to the management of intellectual capital. In P. H. Sullivan (Ed.), *Monetize intellectual capital. Techniques to optimize the value of the Organization. Paidós Company.*

Sullivan, P. (2001b). Definitions and basic concepts. In P. H. Sullivan (Ed.), *Monetize intellectual capital. Techniques to optimize the value of the Organization. Paidós company.*

Sveiby, K. (1989). *The invisible balance sheet*. Stockholm: Affersvaerlden/Ledarskap.

Sveiby, K. (1998). *Measuring intangibles and intellectual capital - An emerging first standard*. Documento obtenido en Internet: http://www.sveiby.com/articles/EmergingStandard.html

Sveiby, K. (2000). The new wealth of the companies. Management 2000, Barcelona, Spain.

Sveiby, K. (2001b). *The intangible Assets Monitor*. Academic Press.

Unión Fenosa. (1999). *Annual report 1999*. Madrid: Unión FENOSA.

Viedma, J. (2001). ICBS – Intellectual Capital Benchmarking System. *Journal of Intellectual Capital*, *2*(2), 148–165. doi:10.1108/14691930110385937

Walker, G., & MacDonald, J. R. (2001). Designing and implementing an HR scorecard. *Human Resource Management*, *40*(4), 365–377. doi:10.1002/hrm.1025

Wiig, K. (1997). Integrating intellectual capital and knowledge management. *Long Range Planning*, *30*(3), 399–405. doi:10.1016/S0024-6301(97)90256-9

ADDITIONAL READING

Abdolmohammadi, M. J. (2005). Intellectual capital disclosure and market capitalization. *Journal of Intellectual Capital*, *6*(3), 397–416. doi:10.1108/14691930510611139

Bukh, P. N. D., Larsen, H. T., & Mouritsen, J. (2001). Constructing intellectual capital statements. *Scandinavian Journal of Management*, *17*(1), 87–108. doi:10.1016/S0956-5221(00)00034-8

Curado, C., Henriques, L., & Bontis, N. (2011). Intellectual capital disclosure payback. *Management Decision*, *49*(Issue: 7), 1080–1098. doi:10.1108/00251741111151154

Klein, D. A. And Prusak, L. (1994), *Characterizing Intellectual Capital, Multi-Client Program Working Paper*, Ernst & Young, March.

Nerdrum, L., & Erikson, T. (2001). Intellectual capital: A human capital perspective. *Journal of Intellectual Capital*, *2*(Issue: 2), 127–135. doi:10.1108/14691930110385919

Nonaka, I. AND Takeuchi, H. (1995), The Knowledge Creating Company, Oxford University Press, New York City, NY.

O'donnell, D. (2004). Theory and method on intellectual capital creation: Addressing communicative action through relative methodics. *Journal of Intellectual Capital*, *5*(Issue: 2), 294–311. doi:10.1108/14691930410533713

Organization For Economic Co-Operation And Development. (1996). *Measuring What People Know, Human Capital Accounting for the Knowledge Economy*. Paris: OECD.

Williams, R. L. And Bukowitz, W.R. (1997), "Knowledge managers guide information seekers", HRM Magazine, January, pp. 77-81.

KEY TERMS AND DEFINITIONS

Assets: Set of all goods and rights with value, which are owned by a company, institution, or individual.

Capital: Set of assets and economic goods destined to produce greater wealth.

Goods: Everything material or immaterial.

Holistic: Conception of each reality as a whole other than the sum of its component parts.

Intangibles: That should not or cannot be touched.

Management: To deal with the administration, organization, and operations of a company, economic activity, or organization.

Methodology: A set of methods that are followed in a scientific investigation or in a doctrinal exposition.

Strategy: Adjustable process or set of rules that ensure an optimal decision at all times.

Synergy: Action of two or more causes which effect is greater than the sum of the individual effects.

System: Structured set of related units that contribute to a specific object.

Chapter 2
Grounding Institutions of Higher Learning as Learning Organizations for Developing Intellectual-Knowledge Society

Ndwakhulu Stephen Tshishonga
University of KwaZulu-Natal, South Africa

ABSTRACT

This chapter explores the complex and dynamic environment in which institutions of higher learning (HEIs) have to operate and the imperative for them to transform themselves into learning organizations. This chapter is underpinned by the concept of learning organizations as its theoretical exposition to gauge the capacity of universities to learn and transform themselves. The chapter argues that institutions of higher learning are strategically poisoned to transform themselves as learning organizations. Thus, learning organization-based HEIs could be advanced by transmitting knowledge through teaching and learning, knowledge production through research and managing, and disseminating knowledge through community engagement or service learning. These responsibilities form part of the integral and core business of the HEIs, especially of the universities.

INTRODUCTION

Institutions of higher learning in the developed and developing world operate in a complex, volatile and challenging environment. The demand for these institutions to execute their core business more often exceed the capacity and the financial support

DOI: 10.4018/978-1-5225-8461-2.ch002

they receive from government and public sectors. Higher education sector in the information age and knowledge society is to transcend from what Barnett (2011, p. 31) calls 'knowledge-for-itself' or 'knowledge-in-itself' to 'knowledge-in-world' or 'knowledge-for-the-world'. The era for institutions of higher learning to exist for the privileged few is fading away and considering that higher education institutions are public entities funded from the public purse, there is demand for them to be active role-players in transforming society. Essentially, 'knowledge-in-world' or 'knowledge-for-the-world' (Barnett, 2011) challenges the idea of perceived higher education as an ivory tower, nothing to do with the world miseries, the world over is subjected to endure. In most nations especially those in the third world, the education sector is expected to come up with innovative solutions to socio-economic and political challenges. Since most of the problems are economical in nature, education is viewed as the foundation to the ailing economy (van Rhyn, McMillan, & Ndlebe, 2016).

The proponents of learning organisation theory such as Hudson (1999), Marquardr (2011) and Senge (1990, 2006), view learning organisation as an organisation capable of facilitating the learning of its workforce and harnessing the knowledge capability and experiences for the benefit of all its stakeholders. Organisational learning or learning society is 'a never-ending journey' (Watkins & Golembiewski, 1995, p. 99), 'a vision' (Senge et al., 1994, p. 5); 'a continuous aspiration' (Garratt, 2001, p. x) and scholars such as Marsick and Watkins (1999, p. 219) perceive it as not the real destination. These elements underlie the importance of life-long learning among people and within institutions. Considering the emergence of information age and knowledge society, the chapter interrogate the complex and dynamic environment in which institutions of higher learning (HEIs) have to operate and the imperative for them to transform themselves into learning organisations. The chapter argues that institutions of higher learning are strategically positioned to transform themselves as learning organisations (Bui & Baruch, 2011). Thus, learning organisation-based HEIs could be entrenched through rigorous interface of reaching, research and responsible community engagement. The infusion of the university core function not only helps the institution to forge and brand its identity, but also grounds its relevance in society. Through teaching- research-engagement activities, universities assume the role of using research to identify solutions directed at addressing community challenges (Bender, 2008). It is through the advancement of scholarship that transferring knowledge through teaching and learning, knowledge production through research and managing and disseminating knowledge through community engagement or service learning. These responsibilities form part of the integral and core business of the HEIs especially of the universities.

INSTITUTIONS OF HIGHER LEARNING AS LEARNING ORGANISATION

This chapter is grounded on the notion of learning organisation. The proponents of learning organisation theory such as Hudson (1995), Marquardr (2011) and Senge (1990, 2006), view learning organisation as an organisation capable of facilitating the learning of its workforce and harnessing the knowledge capability and experience for the benefit of all its stakeholders. In order for organisations to attain and sustain comparative advantage, Marquardt (2011, p. 67) advises organisations to learn better and faster from their successes and failures alike. The adoption of learning organisation has been justified on the benefits derived from gaining organisational effectiveness and excelling in the future (Pittinger, 2002; Senge, 1990). From this perspective, learning organisation is a key component in organisations intending to unlock the potential of the people either as individuals or as teams. The idea of learning was developed particularly in the 1960s and 1970s with contributions from Argyis and Schon (1978). It was in the 1980s that the authors developed a link between learning training and company or organisation performance. In the 1980s and early 1990s, Jones and Hendry (1992) also saw a clear link between training, development and human resource management on the one hand, and company performance and competitiveness on the other hand. The authors identified team work and effective communication as key components of an effective learning company.

Learning organisation has some common characteristics such as 1) a learning culture, 2) free exchange and flow of information, 3) commitment to learning and personal development, 4) valuing people, 5) climate of openness and trust (Nakpodia, 2009). Similarly, these features are fundamental to universities as custodians of learning and knowledge production. Firstly, a learning culture entails an organizational climate through which the learning of both staff and students are constantly nurtured. Within the context of a university, teaching and learning culture is instilled through formal lectures, academic debates in seminars and academic excursions. At the centre of university as a learning organisation is innovation where students and academics are challenges to be creative and innovative in coming up with alternative theories and solutions to societal socio-economic and political problems. Through the development of a learning culture, universities are able to understand their environment and human resources available to respond to challenges imposed by both immediate and wider environment (Nakpodia, 2009). Second to a learning culture, is free exchange and flow of information whereby structures, processes and systems are institutionalised to develop academic and administrative expertise. Universities are informational and knowledge producers which run workshops, seminars and symposiums including conferences for the purposes of information exchange and networking. Attending conferences for personal and academic development are part of the key performance areas (KPAs) especially those conferences, which publish presented papers and proceedings as the outcome. Through publication in niche or knowledge expertise areas, academics are rewarded especially by research-based universities and through National Research Foundation (NRF) rating. The third character of a learning organisation in an organisation such as the university is commitment to learning and personal development.

Commitment to learning and personal development is a fundamental principle of any university which makes this institutions to have a competitive advantage. Highly rated and performing universities are those designed to attract well-rounded scholars, academics and researchers of great integrity especially in research production. There is huge investment in higher education not only to attract solid academics, but also to develop and nurture a new crop of young academics eager to integrate all core business of a university for African scholarship. Through the South African Department of Higher Training and Training, there is a drive for recruiting developmental lecturers who are hired and nurtured into academia and given space to complete their PhDs (SANPAD, 2007). This requires the top-management recommitting itself through developing policies that value both individual and collective learning. Commitment to learning and personal development goes along with valuing people as the fourth character by supporting creative ideas and capabilities aimed at developing human intellectual capital in all its facets. Valuing people, be they academics, support staff or students requires an collegial environment whereby free debate of ideas is not subjected to mediocre rather than on intellectual scholarship. The fifth character of a learning organisation is rooted on experiential learning. Universities through their networks and partnership with other higher education institutions, civil society and other private institutions are exposed to an environment for social and dialogical learning. According to Nakpodia (2009), learning from experience implies that learning from mistakes is often more powerful than learning from success. Failure is tolerated, provided lessons are learnt.

Senge (1990) identified five dimensions of organisation that are capable to learn, and continually enhance their capacity to realise their highest aspirations. In one of the dimensions the author opines that people excel and learn voluntarily if there is a genuine shared vision. Having a shared vision is fundamental in growing a learning organisation, yet Senge (1990, 2006) argues without clear goals, values and missions, organisations are unlikely to succeed. Successful organisations thus bind people around a shared picture of the future they wish to create. Senge asserts that team learning for example involves thinking together to allow the group to discover insights not attainable individually. Senge (1990, p. 42) argues that the learning organisation focuses on generative learning, as well as on adaptive learning.

Adaptive learning reacts to events and brings about adaptations retrospectively; generative learning is creative and moves into the future by keeping in touch with the systemic structure of the organisation. These features are the foundation for an organisation which is inspired to expand its horizon by not only responding to the expeditions of its constituencies, but also capable of leverage itself as a comparative entity. Nevis et al. (1995) identified three key qualities of learning organisations that ground learning organisations such 1) pursuing an enhanced knowledge base whereby learning orientated organisations are aware of their strengths for competition, 2) have the capacity of continuous improvement and 3) are able to continuously challenge existing ways of doing things. Within a learning organisation, individual and team learning are equally valued and encouraged hence Senge (2006) argues that organisations learn only through individuals, although individual learning by itself does not guarantee organisational learning. However, the author went further to assert that without individual learning there is no organisational learning take place (Senge, 2006: 129). In essence, learning organisation is about organisational acquisition of knowledge and the capacity to process such acquired knowledge into productive use. In this regard, Nonaka (1991) argues that knowledge is not created until the deep-rooted insights of one individual are successfully internalised and applied by others. As such Nonaka is of the belief that knowledge creation transcends just processing objective information. According to Senge (2006), both individual and organisational learning is enhanced by personal mastery, mental models, shared vision, team learning and systematic thinking. Despite these outlined building blocks towards building a learning organisation, proponents of a learning organisation phenomenon such as De Geus (1997), Garvin (1994), Jackson and Slocum (1999), Marquardt (1999), Watkin and Maarsick (1993)

Despite the prospects and opportunities learning organisation possess in transforming organisation across sectoral divide, the model is without fault. At first glance of evaluating, Shaw (2004, p. 117) is sceptical about how the notion of learning organisation fits comfortably in the management and organisational equation. On one hand evaluation is about outcomes, effectiveness, bottom lines and evidence based practice - accountability. On the other hand, learning organisations are about systems, interaction, process, feedback and improvement (Shaw, 2004, p. 117). The author adds that although there are tensions, proponents of learning organisations argue that lessons learned must be evidentially based, albeit in a variety of ways and not unfalsifiable insights. In practice if not in rhetoric, most evaluation is about incremental change and improvement.

INSTITUTIONS OF HIGHER LEARNING AND KNOWLEDGE SOCIETY

In a knowledge society (Castell, 2001), education plays a decisive and fundamental role, in not only educating the nation, but also broadening opportunities for economic growth and development. World over, the demand for accessible and quality education remains a challenge for both developed and developing nations. Thus, institutions of higher learning, universities in particular, have to transform themselves beyond their comfortable traditional chores of teaching and learning, research and community engagement as their core business (Ramphele, 2008). Primordially, universities have emerged as elite institutions and as custodians of knowledge production and dissemination (Rothblatt, 2006). However, in the modern era, such institutions are challenged to embrace and play a developmental role as one of the critical stakeholders in addressing challenges faced by the modern world. Assumed developmental role saw nations particularly, the developed ones investing huge sums of financial resources in institutions of higher learning with the targeted outcomes of having skilled and competent workforce (Margison & Considine, 2011). The developed nations compared to their developing counterparts have managed to benefit from the globalized economy by taking advantage of their highly competitive higher education systems. In contrast, with competing priories, the developing world including African nations saw the dwindling budgets for higher education and the emergence of private universities (Teferra, 2013). In the context of African universities, issues of transformation, access, quality and curriculum revamping are of utmost importance.

Within this transformative agenda for African universities; is the imperative for Africanizing or endogenising these institutions to serve the intellectual and developmental needs of the African people (Crossman, 2004). In this context, Mamdani (1997 in Makgoba & Chetty, 2010, p. 3) challenges the African universities as institutions of knowledge production to address the African condition and the African identity as a central problem and further recognize the African condition as historically. Mostly affected are the South African higher education institutions, which for decades had operated under the apartheid system with Bantu Education, being the instrument to offer and promote mediocre and inferior education among black population. Verwoed was of the opinion that Blacks should appreciate as ‘hewers of wood and drawers of water’ (in Sehume, 2018, p. 15). This type of education system favoured white South Africans at the expense of their black counterparts, with no doubt the post-apartheid era and the inherence of Bantu Education continue to aggressively entrench exclusion and marginalization. Despite the progress made in developing policies and educational outcomes, the World Bank Group (2018, p. 12) highlighted that the legacy of poor education is the major source of poverty and inequality. This is against the bedrock that education is viewed as the pathway towards securing jobs with high wages. The legacy of Bantu education and its adverse effects continue to undermine the potential of black students whom the majority of them attended mediocre and poor managed schools (Jeffery, 2010). Considering the discriminatory system of Apartheid, imperatives for equity, redress and development of higher education are among some of the priorities post-1994 era (Balintulo, 2004).

INSTITUTIONS OF HIGHER LEARNING AS KNOWLEDGE PRODUCERS

Higher education institutions are the epicentre of knowledge production and its dissemination as such they also have abundance of expectations from stakeholders to be meet. These institutions are created with vision and mission centred on knowledge creation or co-generation and transfer (Rowntree & Fox, 2017). By embarking on research projects either through post-graduate students' research or academic exchange programmes, institutions of higher learning including conventional universities, universities of technology, community colleges and TVET. At the core of generating knowledge, is for higher education institutions to engage their stakeholders equally to create conducive environment for debates and academic scholarship. Equally important is for institutions to develop tools, processes, procedures and structures for stakeholder engagement inclusive of students (primary stakeholders), staff (both academic and administrators) and general society stakeholder. Higher education institutions are reflective of the views, ideologies and struggles of the general society, hence their deliberate engagement with individual and collective stakeholders is of great importance. Thus, institutions of higher learning aspired to excel academically. According to Mazibuko, Chetty, and Mneney (2010, p. 83) this should champion themselves as research-led and outstanding centres in teaching and learning, and community engagement. The integration of all stakeholders is paramount for both institutional transformation and for co-knowledge production and higher education institutions including universities become the sites of knowledge, research outreach and contestation (Cebekhulu, 2013, p. 241). Collaboration in knowledge production especially in interdisciplinary research has seen huge investment from financial institutions and government both in the South and North with monetary rewards for project leaders and researchers. Positively, these knowledge-research endeavours exposed inexperienced staff and post-graduate students under the supervision of senior academics to high quality research methodologies. The quest for all universities to become research-intensive institutions brought with it 'managerialism' as the new governance framework to run higher education institutions. The interface of managerial approach to government and corporate university subject education and knowledge for 'commodification and marketization' (Ndlovu-Gatsheni, 2016, p. 37) and further reduced according to Stewart (2007, p. 141) to 'polytechnic/technikon and industry mode of know-how'. With encroaching culture of managerialism, universities started to operate like corporations with decision-making powers centralised at Senate and management, grounded on decentralisation of administrative duties under appointed school and faculty managers (Chetty & Merrett, 2014, p. 22).

With the internationalisation of higher education, knowledge generating institutions such as universities are entering into collaborative arrangements, among themselves, other knowledge producers and governments. Mosoetsa (2018, p. 36) concurs with the above statement by stating that there is more research collaboration happening between south Africa and the global north, however, she highlighted that there is no adequate collaboration is taking place between South Africa and the rest of the African continent. These partnerships took different shapes and forms yet all have a common mission to pull their human capital and financial resources to undertake research geared towards finding solutions for global challenges such diseases and epidemics, political dilemmas, poverty, unemployment and inequalities (PUI) (Terreblanche, 2012), and climate change including natural disasters such as drought and floods. Due to pressure to provide evidence-based solutions to afore-mentioned challenges, higher education entities embarked on research with the primary intention of generating information for problem-solving strategies and mechanism. Operating within the collaborative problem-solving framework, Ayres and Silvies (2011) argue that it provides a useful framework to address complex community issues and challenges. The power of higher education institutions is based on the quality of knowledge and how the knowledge generated is utilised to influence policy-makers and further empower society. Within the institutions of higher learning, the dominance of Western knowledge systems have been challenged and university community especially the students expressed unhappiness. The relevance of such knowledge is questioned through critical lens that say it does not only perpetuate the colonial education, but is also a weapon for psychological oppression. Critics on the dominance of Western knowledge and its hegemony such as Higgs (2003), Msila (1998), Thiongo (2005) argue for the renaissance of indigenous knowledge systems and their integration into the mainstream academia. Arising from this awakening, higher education institutions began to host forums and seminars deliberating on African scholarship.

Higher education has abundance of knowledge on research methodologies, which both staff and students are required to master in order to produce valid, reliable and quality knowledge. With the emergence of alternative research methods such as action learning approaches, organisations including universities have embarked on engaging communities as part of empowering communities and organisations through information, theories and practices sharing. Academics and researchers interested in forging social and transformative change in society, invest an enormous time, energy and resources with the primary purpose of engaging primary stakeholders as holders of knowledge. Knowledge-based on action research includes its variants such as Participatory Rural Appraisal (PRA) (Chambers, 1994; Chambers, 2003; Cornwall, 2003), Participatory Learning and Action (PLA) (Rifkin & Pridmore, 2001) and community-based research (Minkler & Wallenstein, 2003). These scholars embraced conceptualised knowledge generation through collaborative community-based research and engagement. Through the application of popular participation (Anello, 2003), higher education sector is able to effectively use research techniques to extract valuable information ready to be used by communities for their own development. Purposive knowledge production through the use of participatory methods does not only acknowledge the wealth of communities have, but also graduate people and their communities as reputable knowledge producers and users. Higher education sector is therefore challenged to view itself as a producer of knowledge within the ever-changing environment. Such environment requires these institutions to go about teaching, researching and providing services to the broader society for socio-economic and political transformation. Being relevant justifies massive public investment for higher education institutions either by their respective government or donor-agencies (Yakubu, 2017, p. 4). Considering the knowledge gap between knowledge producers (universities) and knowledge consumers (communities) (Stoecker, 2016, p. 100), knowledge created through participatory action research result in co-creation of knowledge created by university researchers for knowledge generation. Knowledge generated through collaborative work provides opportunities for stakeholders to play an active role in directing research (Skovdal & Cornish, 2015). The authors further state that such research method recognises communities as having a wealth of knowledge and skills that can be utilised in the research process.

POTENTIAL OF IHI IN BECOMING LEARNING ORGANISATION

Senge (1990) identified five dimensions of organisation of learning organisation which continually enhance their capacity to realise their highest aspirations. In one of the dimensions the authors state that people excel and learn voluntarily if there is a genuine shared vision. Having a shared vision is fundamental in growing a learning organisation, yet Senge (1990, 2006) argues without clear goals, values and missions, organisations are unlikely to succeed. Successful organisations thus bind people around a shared picture of the future they wish to create. Senge states that team learning involves thinking together to allow the group to discover insights not attainable individually. Senge (1990, p. 42) argues that the learning organisation focuses on generative learning, as well as on adaptive learning. Adaptive learning reacts to events and brings about adaptations retrospectively; generative learning is creative and moves into the future by keeping in touch with the systemic structure of the organisation. These features are the foundation for HEIs to inspire and expand their horizon by not only responding to the expeditions of its constituencies, but also leveraging themselves to be comparative entities. Nevis et al (1995) identified three key qualities of learning organisations that ground learning organisations such as 1) pursuing an enhanced knowledge base whereby learning orientated organisations are aware of their strengths for competition, 2) have the capacity of continuous improvement and 3) are able to continuously challenge existing ways of doing things. Within a learning organisation, individual and team learning are equally valued and encouraged, hence Senge (2006) argues that organisations learn only through individuals, although individual learning by itself does not guarantee organisational learning.

CHALLENGES OF IHL IN BECOMING LEARNING ORGANISATION

Universities like any other organisations operate in an ever-changing and challenging environment. Such environment presents the institutions of higher learning with both opportunities and challenges. For higher education to be impactful in producing skilled, competent, analytical thinkers able to influence societal change, the sector has to learn both opportunities and challenges. From basic to higher education the apartheid system presented bottlenecks which hindered black South Africans to equally develop their intellectual capacity. Based on discriminatory policies of apartheid, education failed to play a national building and social cohesion where all South African citizens are given equal educational opportunities. Since the dawn of democracy in South Africa and in view of the challenges presented, the higher education sector is not learning fast enough to take advantage of the opportunities at its disposal. Structural restructuring imposed by the democracy euphoria which culminated in the adoption of national policy of 1997, which dictated the amalgamation of 36 higher education institutions into 23 including the funding model and access. Resistance to change by previously English and Afrikaans universities (UCT, Wits, Free State, Rand Afrikaans University, Rhodes, Natal, Stellenbosch, etc) left a hostile environment for collective learning for these institutions. Historical perpetuation of policies of apartheid in general and Bantu education in particular, exclusion due to language, entry requirements continue to be the obstacles for effective learning.

Consequently, these challenges led to fragmentation, which according to Nakpodia (2009, p. 81) emanate from linear thinking, specialization, independent, warring fiefdoms. Universities are set to compete among each other based on categories such as research-intensive universities, comprehensive universities and universities of technology. The irony is that those universities never implicated through merger such as UCT, Wits, Rhodes, have high output of post-graduate students, top ranked nationally and internationally and more often attracted experienced and qualified researchers and professors. Despite the achievements attached to these institutions, the media and commentators criticised them for being elite with discriminatory elements against black lecturers and students as well as the administrators and general employees. As such, these knowledge-producing institutions are caught in a vicious cycle of recycling mediocre scholarship in the name of higher education transformation. Abundance of challenges and the failure by university management to deal with them decisively divert their attention away from unlocking human potential through creativity and innovation. Instead of drawing lessons from historical epochs of 1976 students' rampage against the apartheid imposition of Afrikaans as the medium of instruction (Brown, 2015), repeated incidents of 2015 & 2016 with student movement challenging tuition fee increment (Ray, 2016). Although these students led struggles created spaces for dialogue among higher education stakeholders and public, finger pointing and blaming preceded the opportunity for universities to strategize long-term planning based on holistic solutions to challenges besetting higher education sector. Without central and funded units, programme or directorate designated to run, manage and coordinate community engagement and service learning, individual disciples assume the role of running their own project-based service learning. Projects, which are short-term, have ramifications especially for communities suffering from historic injustices as they deprive both the students and organisations from building solid relationships. In this regard, Schenck et al. (2010, p. 131) are of the view that the foundation for any participatory change is the trustful relationships based on context in which people live. Nakpodia (2009, p. 81) warns that universities often times enter into competition, thus creating an environment in which looking good is more important than being good; measurable, short-term gains count more than long-term achievement, and problems are solved by individuals in isolation.

BUILDING BLOCKS FOR LEARNING BASED INSTITUTIONS OF HIGHER LEARNING

Peter Senge's book the Fifth Discipline (1990, 2006) presents the conceptual underpinning of the work of building learning organisations (Senge et al., 1995, p. 5). The author introduces five disciplines as the core of the learning organisation, as follows:

Personal Mastery

According to Senge (1990, p. 7), personal mastery is described as continually clarifying and deepening one's personal vision, focusing on one's energies, developing patience and seeing reality objectively. This is viewed as the essential cornerstone of the learning organisation. The author views people with a high level of personal mastery as having a special sense of purpose that lies behind their visions and goals, and who functions in a continual mode of learning. Senge (1990, p. 7) states that there are few organisations that encourage the growth of their people, resulting in vast untapped resources. In essence, "organisations learn through individuals who learn. Individual learning does not guarantee organisational learning, but without it no organisational learning occurs". Individual employees within higher education are motivated by various reasons. Some of the reasons include financial remuneration as top of their motivators, others value enabling environment and personal growth as the primary drivers for excellent productivity and higher performance. The table below depicts the situation of the employees within various categories as part of ranking in South African universities.

Table 1 reflects a dire need for university employees who are self-motivated in order for transformation to take place. With 20% as higher performers, such category of staff is likely to migrate to other lucrative jobs with market competitive environment within government departments or private sectors. Professors and senior professors are at the peak in terms of their academic careers and as such are expected to continue to provide leadership guidance to junior staff. Both category B and C share 40% of employees each, though different they have the common denominator for mediocre performance. 40% of the staff who are known for maintaining the status quo are equally responsible for most of the challenges betting municipalities. These are mainly those staff members employed through the policy of cadre employment, often without requisite skills and knowledge to do the required job. Considering that higher education institutions are created precisely to produce knowledge which is

Table 1. Category of employees and performance percentages

	Category	Performance	Percentage
A	Professor/Senior Prof	Established scholar & highly rated local and international	50%
B	Associate Professor	Entry into the professorship & expected to take a lead in terms of research	30%
C	Senior Lecturer	Matured lectured who are expected to balance their academic research and teaching	20%
D	Lecturer	Entry into academia	10%

Source: Author's analysis

consumed or used by society at large, gives them power and prestige. Fundamental outcome of such institutions is to produce skilled and competent, dedicated and motivated students capable of contributing to the development and empowerment of society.

Personal mastery is viewed as where people live in a continual learning mode (Senge, 1990, p. 142). Individual learning should be motivated by academics and non-academics staff to empower themselves and further contribute towards societal change. Throughout the history of South African universities, South Africans have taken the initiative to enrol themselves both for formal certificates, diplomas and degrees offered by various public and private institutions of higher learning to upgrade their skills and academic qualifications. Formal education and training, together with informal knowledge exchange engagement through either through workshops and academic excursions are key in a knowledge driven society (Castel, 2000). Staff development either through formal or informal training is aligned to the strategic and action orientated planning of the colleges and faculties. Strategic and action orientated planning within colleges and faculties which direct the development of curriculum of various disciplines. The central tenet of this belief is that no one can increase someone else's personal mastery; however, there can be conditions which can encourage and support people to increase their personal mastery (Senge et al., 1995, p. 197).

Mental Models

Mental Models are described as deeply ingrained assumptions, generalisation, or even pictures or images that influence the way we understand the world and how one takes action. People are not aware of the impact of mental models on behaviour (Senge, 1990, p. 8). For example, in a public sector organisation, employees can make assumptions that an African candidate for a senior post was not appointed on merit, which would result in people in the organization acting and behaving inappropriately. Senge (1990, p. 9) states that the discipline of working with mental models involves turning the mirror inward; learning to unearth our internal pictures of the world, to bring to the surface and hold them rigorously to scrutiny. Therefore, it requires the ability of one's own thinking. In order for academic staff and other employees such as school managers and administrators are required to embrace a paradigm shift in their thinking. For the university workforce to integrate their formal and informal education and training, an enabling environment is of paramount importance. Despite the academic qualifications (MAs & PhDs) demanded from those aspiring to be lecturers in the higher education sector, staff members embark on formal training and capacity building. Either in the form of short or long term modules and courses, academic and non-academic staff go through refresh workshops on new theories and methods including requisite skills and knowledge needed in the academia. For universities to model themselves on the path to learning organisations, addictiveness and openness should be part of individual and organisational structures and ethos (Higgs & Smith, 2015). This entails the ability of both employees and organisational structures to recreate themselves.

Mental models are fundamental in generalising the direction the university type of organisations. Mental models like any assumptions and human behaviours can be learnt or unlearned. Mental models can be either positive or negative. Positive mental models such as attitudes and relational behaviours are crucial among individual employees and are often cultivated through conducive environment, mentoring for personal and organisational growth, with grounded processes and systems. For example graduates who also happened to be staff members within universities, upon completing their degree qualification are eager to put their knowledge into public use. At the university level, this entails individual employees to be aware of their capabilities in their areas of expertise, which require strengthening and consolidation. Mental models have a negative side due to the absence of transformative leadership, hostile environment and lack of motivation, the workforce is prone to be unproductive. In most of the universities, learning and transformation is hampered by the mentality that subscribes to non-compliance especially by senior managers. Thus, people entrusted with positions of power to transform the universities are often caught in political-administrative dichotomy; hence, they are unable to fulfil their task professionally.

Building Shared Vision

The practice of shared vision begins with a viewpoint about an idea that has inspired leadership for thousands of years, that is, the capacity to hold a shared picture of the future the organisation wants to create (Senge, 1990, p. 9). Senge further elaborates that many leaders have a personal vision of the organisation that is not translated into a shared vision. To translate individual vision into a shared vision involves genuine commitment and enrolment rather than compliance (Senge, 1990, p. 9). Similarly to other institutions, universities are guided by visions and missions created to steer their strategic and operational functions. All universities are identified and differentiated through their visions and mission statements. Mazibuko, Chetty, and Mneney (2010, p. 73) add that these visions and mission statements are forged with the quest to create South African and African universities. For Moloi (2009, p. 59), building a learning organisation is a team effort with learning taking place through stakeholder participation.

Vision statements are pillars for any organisations including universities. By design these statements are symbolic of the commitment to build an African-centred institutions of higher learning capable of producing knowledge through research, teaching and community engagement hence critical thinkers. Within their geographical locations, universities take pride in graduating themselves from teaching to research orientated institutions of higher learning in Southern Africa and beyond.

Essentially, vision statements depict the (re)commitment of universities in advancing knowledge focussed and rooted on African experience. As reflected, such institutions entail the combination of research-intensive (UCT, Pretoria, UKZN, etc), comprehensive universities (Limpopo, Fort Hare, Mpumalanga, Walter Sisulu, Nelson Mandela) and finally the universities of technology such as CUT and CPUT. Essentially, universities are designed with shared visions that are supposed to inspire academic community, with the management governance structures being at the centred of excellent in terms of the core business of these institutions. The effective implementation of these visions demands the synergy and alignment of internal policies, organisational structures, strategic leadership, organisational purpose, operational systems, technical capacity and financial abilities (Palmer et al., 2017, p. 109). The repertoire of these skills lay a solid background instrumental in restoring the university organisational memory, increasing internal confidence for employees to be productive. Importantly, a shared vision implies 1) that conclusions are communicated to all those within the organisation who take decision, 2) involving in the planning process, both through consultation and through a proper mixture of top-down and bottom-up, 3) a strategy which is truly corporate, with meaning for everyone in the organisation (Smith, 1994, p. 19).

HEIs like any organisations are grounded and are based on university visions. Strategic management becomes efficient when the management team work towards a common shared vision and strategic goal. In addition to that, the team has to have a collective vision where all the strategic management team has consensus on a collective vision. A common and collective vision thus is key to strategic management as it brings solutions and change. Tesoriero (2010, p. 117) argues that a vision does not necessarily lead to goals being achieved. He states that a vision serves as a source of inspiration for change and as a framework for interpreting and seeking change from the perspective of medium- and long-term goals instead of purely being reactive. A vision allows one to seek an alternative paradigm, whereas purely reactive 'problem solving' and an insistence on being realistic mean being permanently imprisoned within the existing dominant paradigm (Tesoriero, 2010, p. 117). For universities to realise their vision, the McKinsey 7-S framework that include skills, strategy, systems, style, staff, structure and shared values (Smith, 1994: 86). According to Smith, this framework could be helpful in looking at the organisation's present position, help identify problems and weaknesses which require organisational attention.

Figure 1 reflects that a learning organisation is comprised of interwoven relationships, which links the organisation or university's vision, mission, values and behaviour to the desired outcomes (Govender, 2009, p. 375). For Pearn et al., (1995, p. 20), vision and mission of a learning organisation manifest themselves through appropriate values and behaviours.

There is link between mission, vision, values, strategy, behaviour and outcomes that underpins a learning organisation. The intrinsic synergy between all these elements as outlined by Carre and Peran (1992 in Pearn et al., 1995, p. 21). Thus, collective and shared vision and mission enable organisations such the universities to create strategic and operations objectives which are often expressed the professional and ethical behaviour and relationships. With skilled leadership and competent personnel, organisations through proactive planning reap desired outcomes within the timeframe.

Without ownership and collective participation of all stakeholders, visions are difficult to translate into actions and end up redundant. It is obvious that when citizens are excluded and marginalised from participating in contributing towards a vision of the municipality, they become what McKnight and Block (2010, p. 99) call 'rusty' because they fail to do what only themselves can do. A vision is strategically designed to 'give people hope, inspire and excite them' (van Rensburg, 2007, p. 17). A common vision thus unites people and becomes the driving force behind actions that awaken the latent potential in people to create a better issue (van Rensburg 2007, p. 17). Leaders including higher education management are aware of the effectiveness and success of a vision which is dependent on the people who are implicated and need to buy into it.

Team Learning

To practice the discipline of team learning requires members of the team to begin with dialogue, where the members argue through and discover insights that cannot be obtained as individuals (Hudson, 1999). The fundamental characteristic of team learning allows for the team to become more aligned as a commonality of direction emerges, and a resonance or *synergy* develop. Within universities as organisations, team learning has three critical dimensions. First, there is a need to think insightfully and together with all the powerful forces in the organisation, which arise from the intelligence of the teams. Second, there is a need for innovative and coordinate action. Third, team learning becomes a collective active, as learning teams continually learn from other teams by inculcating the practices and skills of team learning (Senge, 1990, pp. 10 & 234-237). Universities are structured with organisational composition including Colleges, Faculties, Departments and Disciplines. For the effective, efficient and productive functioning of these knowledge producing entities, various structures are encouraged to work within terms.

Within public organisations, universities included, all the relevant stakeholders are to contribute in order to build and forge local sphere as a learning organisation for its success, effectiveness and sustainability (Govender, 2009). Figure 2 depicts the four stages of learning as represented by the experiential learning cycle, the cycle encompasses concrete experience, observations and reflections, formation of abstract concepts and generalisations and finally testing implications of concepts in new situation (see Swart et al., 2004, p. 145). Viewed from concrete experience stage, managers may observe staff stationed in different departments and positions learning and working collaboratively within assigned teams. Accordingly, through dialogue, teams within organisations are able to promote and generate learning, and further unlock their potential as individuals and a group as a whole (Hudson, 1999, p. 348). Experiential learning is key for the transformation of universities, more particularly through reflecting on real and concrete experience. For Kolb's experiential learning cycle (in Govender, 2009, p. 370), it is only when people observe and reflect on their daily encounter with real world that both abstract and concrete ides, opinions and concepts or frameworks. Ideas and abstract concepts generated through dialogue further influence emancipatory action and knowledge for transformative praxis (Ledwith & Springett, 2010).

This requires universities through their departments and designated research units to strategically adopt and embrace the culture of learning as exposed by Kolb's experiential learning (Kolb, 1984). The fourth stage envisage the formation of abstract concepts and generalisations where both managers and team members reflect on strategies and skilled gained by figure out how effectiveness such skills and knowledge could be used improve their performance. The final stage dictates that all learning organisations such as universities with their respective teams and units have to put to test the concepts developed in the previous stage. This stage allows academic staff, students and managers from various faculties, colleges and departments are capable of working in diverse groups and teams. For example, the experience gained through community engagement informs the curriculum development and niche-areas for further empirical research. The deployment of senior staff and administrators in commissioned research projects have yielded results with collaborative work among staff, students projects managers. Inter-departmental and faculty initiated and managed seminars, colloquium and conferences have been dominant pathways to share knowledge and team learning. State funded knowledge-based institutions such as National Research Foundation (NRF), Human Sciences Research Council (HSRC) and latest the National Institute for the Humanities and Social Sconces (NIHSS) are instrumental in funding and providing academic support for intellectual debates and dialogue. For example, due to the shortages of PhDs holders especially in universities, NIHSS has not only funded PhD candidates, but also give registered PhDs the professional-academic support through aligning students with professors as supervisors and mentors. Over the years, NRF has rated scholars based on their niche research areas and expertise, establishment of various chairs with funding allocated for candidates to conduct robust research, fundamentally aimed at providing alternatives solutions to community-societal challenges. Since the formation of HIHSS, and awarding of PhD scholarships, the Institute managed to graduate 100 PhDs as part of its transformative agenda aimed grounding scholarship within humanities and social sciences. According to Professor Mosoetsa (2018, p. 36), the Director of HIHSS, highlighted that transformation in higher education could be advanced through 1) building the next generation of scholars, 2) ensuring that various project's collaborative effects take place in south Africa and on the continent through sharing expertise, resources and cultures as the foundation for a unified university system, 3) affording HIHSS funded graduates opportunities to explore inter/multidisciplinary research. In the case of HIHSS, Mosoata (2018, p. 36) adds that:

the Institute is not just a funder of catalytic research projects and doctoral studies. Through greater support, notably, by means of our mentorship programme-with initiatives such as Shup-Up and Write that provide doctoral fellows with the opportunity and space to think and express their unique ideas-we ae exhibiting exactly how, collectively. We can make Humanities and social Sciences more dynamic on our continent.

Evidenced from this deliberations is that team learning is key not only sharing knowledge, but also in experimenting with collective options based on evidence-based research.

Systems Thinking

System thinking theory forms part of the fundamental framework upon which higher education institutions (HEIs) could be grounded as a learning organisation (Bui & Baruch, 2011). Universities as learning organisations are centres of excellence, teaching, research and store houses of knowledge (Nakpodia, 2009). According to Stacey (1999, p. 276), this theory challenges the scientific management approach and its origin could be attached to the work of the German biologist Von Bertalanfy within his idea of organism and human organisations as open systems. Systems are differentiated by having various component sub-systems that are not only interrelated, but are interdependent on each other (see Nkuna & Sebola, 2015, p. 43). Similar to universities which are structured with a management structure led by the council, with faculties, departments and disciplines coupled by underlying policies, processes, systems and procedures created to guide the operation of these institutions. Thus, in the context of South African universities, since the higher education transformation and restructuring resulting into meagre of most institutions, there has been decentralisation of certain functions from faculties to respective schools. Considering the racial composition of higher education during the apartheid era, restructuring was imperative and as part of redress and democratising institutions of higher learning into inclusive education system (Manik, 2017). This requires the strategic alignment of universities' visions and missions with their operational programmes and projects.

Another complementary category crucial to function of the university is the administrative structure headed by the vice chancellor (VC). The structure is staffed by employees appointed based on merit, qualifications and experiences. Systems thinking is a conceptual framework where systems theory is integrated into the learning organisation, and where it integrates the disciplines of building a shared vision, mental models, team learning and personal mastery into a coherent body of theory and practice (Senge, 1990, p. 12). Systems thinking is viewed as the cornerstone of how learning organisations think about their world as there is a shift in thinking from seeing the whole, seeing people from being helpless reactors to.... active participants (Senge, 1990, p. 69). The five disciplines of the learning organisation are key in assisting public sector managers and head of departments within municipalities to identify and develop best practices and competencies geared towards building a learning organisation.

FUTURE RESEARCH DIRECTIONS

Institutions of higher education were discussed within their capacity and potential to learn by innovatively and creatively transforming information into ontological and epistemological knowledge systems. Academic institutions are knowledge actors who primordially created to generate and disseminate knowledge for public use towards the socio-economic development of nations. The concept of learning organization as advanced by Senge (1990) was used to assess the potential, role and challenges faced by institutions of higher learning. Due to persisting challenges faced and societal expectations placed on higher education sector, the following are suggested for future research:

1. A study focusing on how learning-based universities and the knowledge generated could be used to effectively to address challenges preventing African nations to be developmental states.
2. An investigation to be undertaken to advance knowledge as comparative and competitive advantate for universities especially those with limited infrastructural resources.
3. An empirical study on how the universities could transform their research outputs such as MA and PhD theses and dissertations into socio-economic projects and programmes for the benefit of communities and organizations.

CONCLUSION

The chapter has deliberated on the relevance of employing the notion of learning organisation within the context of transforming institutions of higher learning. Although learning organisation is more popular in organisational and management fields, it has emerged as a model to revive and activate university. The effective, efficient and proactive functioning of a university is dependent mainly on its ability to repair itself as part of addressing challenges faced. The notion of learning organisation is underpinned by the quality of the workforce and its ability to translate policies into tangible and implementable projects and programmes. Similarly to learning organisations, universities are institutions capable of expanding their capacity through creating the environment and results as planned.

It is undisputable fact that higher education institutions (HEIs), universities included are producers of knowledge (Soudien, 2016), but it does not automatically translate them into learning organisations. The adoption of learning organisation within the context of universities is a conscious decisions which requires the alignment of strategic visions and missions with operational plans at faculty, college, schools and departmental levels. As the chapter deliberated it is through the deployment and positioning of qualified, skilled and competent academic, administrative and management staff that could render these institutions their comparative advantage. For institutions to gain organisational effectiveness, excellent in core business of research, teaching and community engagement should be strengthened. The chapter has argued that institutions of higher learning are strategically positioned to transform themselves as learning organisations provided they take into consideration the socio-economic and political environment imposed by globalisation. Thus, learning organisation-based HEIs could be advanced by transmitting knowledge through teaching and learning, knowledge production through research and managing and disseminating knowledge through community engagement or service learning.

Through using Senge (1990)'s five disciplines to demonstrate individual, collective and institutional envision is key in elevating learning-based institutions such as universities. It through personal mastery based on mental models that shared visions are crafted with effective teams building and learning being created for operational functioning of higher education institutions-universities.

REFERENCES

Alexander, N. (2006). Language, Policy, Symbolic Power and the Democratic Responsibility of the Post-Apartheid University. In R. Pithouse (Ed.), *Asinamali: Understanding Struggles in Post-Apartheid South Africa*. Asmara: Africa World Press Inc.

Argyis, C., & Schon, D. A. (1978). *Organizational Learning: A Theory of Action Perspective*. Reading, MA: Addison-Wesley.

Ayres, J. S., & Silvis, A. H. (2011). Principles of Working Together: Developing Relationships that Support Community Development initiatives. Academic Press.

Balintulo, M. (2004). The role of the state in the transformation of South African higher education, 1994-2002: Equity and redress revisited. In P. T. Peleza & A. Olukoshi (Eds.), *African Universities in the twenty-first century*. Pretoria: UNISA Press.

Barnett, R. (2011). *Being a University*. London: Routledge.

Bender, G. (2008). Exploring conceptual models for community engagement at higher education institutions in South Africa. *Perspectives in Education*, *26*(1), 81–95.

Brown, J. (2015). *South African's Insurgent Citizens On Dissent and the possibility of Politics*. Sunnyside: Jacana Media Ltd.

Bui, H. T. M., & Baruch, Y. (2012, November). Learning organisations in higher education: An empirical evaluation within an international context. *Management Learning*, *43*(5), 515–544. doi:10.1177/1350507611431212

Castel, M. (2000). *End of Millennium* (2nd ed.). Oxford, UK: Blackwell Publishing.

Cebekhulu, E. (2013). *Umhlaba Uyahlaba: The World is Thorny. Wandsbeck*. Reach Publishers.

Chamber, R. (1993). Participatory rural appraisal (PRA): Analysis of experience. *World Development*, *22*(9), 1253–1268. doi:10.1016/0305-750X(94)90003-5

Chambers, R. (2003). *Whose Reality Counts? Putting the First Last. Warwickshire CV23 9QZ.* ITDG Publishing.

Chetty, N., & Merrett, C. (2014). *The Struggle for South of a South African University.* The University of KwaZulu-Natal-Academic freedom, corporation and transformation.

Higgs, P. (2003). African philosophy and transformation of educational discourse in South Africa. *Journal of Education, 30,* 5–22.

Hudson, M. (1999). *Managing without profit: Art of Managing Third-Sector Organisations.* London: Penguin Books.

Jeffery, A. (2010). *Chasing the Rainbow: South Africa's Move from Mandela to Zuma.* Johannesburg: South African Institute of Race Relations.

Kolb, D. (1994). *Experiential learning: Experiences as the sources of learning and development.* Englewood Cliffs, NJ: Prentice Hall.

Ledwith, M., & Springett, J. (2010). *Participatory practice: Community-based action for transformative change. Bristol BS8 1QU.* The Policy Press.

Manik, S. (2017). What Is Being done? 'Ubuntu' in Student Support Programs in Public Higher Education Institutions in South Africa. In M. Shaw & G. Whiteford (Eds.), *Bridges, Pathways and Transitions: International Innovations in Widening Participation.* Chippenham: Elsevier Ltd. doi:10.1016/B978-0-08-101921-4.00012-9

Margison, S., & Considine, M. (2011). *The Enterprise University: Power, Governance and Reinvention in Australia.* Cambridge, UK: Cambridge University Press.

Marquart, M. J. (2011). *Building the Learning Organisation: Achieving Strategic Advantage through a Commitment to Learning* (3rd ed.). Boston, MA: Nicholas Brealey Publishing.

Mazibuko, F., Chetty, D., & Mneney, E. (2010). Establishing a New Institutional Identity. In The Creation of the University of KwaZulu-Natal: Reflections on a Merger and Transformation Experience (pp. 73-93). New Delhi: Excel Books.

Minkler, M., & Wallenstein, N. (2003). Introduction to community based participatory research. In M. Minkler, N. Wallenstein, & B. Hall (Eds.), *Community-based Participatory Research for Health* (pp. 3–26). San Francisco, CA: Jossey-Bass Wiley.

Moloi, K. C. (2009). *The School as a Learning Organisation: Reconceptualising school practice in South Africa* (2nd ed.). Pretoria: Van Schaik Publishers.

Mosoetsa, S. (2018, November 9). Transformation taking place in the higher education system. Mail & Guardian, 36.

Nakpodia, E. D. (2009). Implications and Challenges of Nigerian Universities as Learning Organisations. *Academic Leadership Journal*, *7*(3), 1–8.

Ndlovu-Gatsheni, S. J. (2016). The Imperative of decolonised the Modern Westernised University. In S. J. Ndlovu-Gatsheni & S. Zondi (Eds.), *Decolonizing the University, Knowledge Systems and Disciplines in Africa*. Durham, NC: Carolina Academic Press.

Nkuna, N. W., & Sebola, M. P. (2015). Developmental Local government and the State of Public Administration: Theoretical Discourse in South Africa. In M. P. Sebola (Ed.), *Local Government Administration Post-Apartheid South Africa: Some Critical Perspectives. Polokwane*. Batalea Publishers.

Ramphele, M. (2012). *Conservations with my Sons and Daughters. Parktown*. Penguin Books.

Ray, M. (2016). *Free Fall: Why South Africa Universities are in Race Against Time*. Johannesburg: Bookstorm.

Ritkin, S., & Camphell, C. (2001). *Partners in Planning: Information, participation and empowerment*. London: TALC & Macmillan Education.

Rothblatt, S. (2006). *The Modern University and its Discontents: the fate of Newman's legacies in Britain and America*. Cambridge, UK: Cambridge University Press.

Rowntree, K., & Fox, R. (2017). Contributing to the agenda for sustainable development through North-South educational partnerships: An analysis of two Linnaeus-Palme staff-student exchanges between Sweden and South Africa. In Knowledge for justice: Critical perspectives from southern African-Nordic research partnerships (pp. 131-146). Cape Town: African Minds.

Schenck, R., Nel, H., & Louw, H. (2010). *Introduction to participatory community practice*. Pretoria: Unisa Press.

Sehume, J. (2018). Solving poverty, unemployment and inequality. *The Sunday Independent*, *24*(June), 15.

Senge, P. M. (1990). *Fifth Discipline: The Art & Practice of Learning Organisation*. Croydon: CPI Group.

Senge, P. M. (2006). *Fifth Discipline: The Art & Practice of Learning Organisation*. Croydon: CPI Group.

Skovdal, M., & Cornish, F. (2015). *Qualitative Research for Development: A Guide for Practitioners*. Practical Action Publishing. doi:10.3362/9781780448534

Soedien, C. (2016). Leading in the South African Higher Education. In Leadership: Perspectives from the Front Line (pp. 205-219). Ransburg: KR Publishing.

Stewart, P. (2007). Re-envisioning the academic profession in the shadow of corporate managerialism. *The Journal of Higher Education*, *5*(1), 141.

Stoecker, R. (2016). *Liberating Service Learning and the Rest of Higher Education Civic Engagement*. Philadelphia: Temple University Press.

Teferra, D. (2013). Introduction. In D. Teferra (Ed.), Funding Higher Education in Sub-Saharan African (pp. 1-12). London: Palgrave Macmillan.

Terreblanche, S. (2012). *Lost in Transformation: South Africa's Search for a New Future since 1986*. Johannesburg: KMM Review Publishing Company.

Thiongo, N. (2005). *Decolonising the Mind: The Politics of Language in African Literature*. Nairobi: East African Educational Publishers.

Van Rensburg, G. (2007). *The Leadership Challenge in Africa*. Pretoria: Van Schaik Publishers.

Van Rhyn, L., McMillan, G., & Ndlebe, J. (2016). School Leadership. In Leadership: Perspectives from the Front Line (pp. 189-204). Ransburg: KR Publishing.

Wells, G., & Edwards, A. (2015). Introduction: The Changing Face of Higher Education. In Pedagogy in Higher Education: A Cultural Historical Approach (pp. 1-17). Cambridge, UK: Cambridge University Press.

Yakubu, H. (2017). Higher Education for Innovation and Development. In Innovating University Education: Issues in Contemporary African Higher Education. Kampala: Fountain Publishers.

ADDITIONAL READING

Senge, P. M., Lichtenstein, B. B., Kaeufer, K., Bradbury, H., & Carroll, S. (2007). Collaborating for Systemic Change. *MIT Sloan Management Review*, *48*(2).

Serrat, O. (2017). *Building a Learning Organization*. Singapore: Springer. doi:10.1007/978-981-10-0983-9_11

Vernooy, R., Qiu, S., & Xu, J. (2006). The Power of Participatory Monitoring and Evaluation: Insights from South-West China. *Development in Practice*, *16*(5), 400–411. doi:10.1080/09614520600792275

Wotela, K. (2017). A proposed monitoring and evaluation curriculum based on a model that institutionalises monitoring and evaluation. *African Evaluation Journal*, *5*(1), 1–8. doi:10.4102/aej.v5i1.186

KEY TERMS AND DEFINITIONS

Community Engagement: It is one of the core university businesses to teaching and research and it is through community engagement or service learning that students are placed within organizations, government departments or community-based structures with the primary purposes of affording them to integrate theory into practice.

Institutions of Higher Learning: These are institutions created in order to offer higher level knowledge, skills, and competencies either through formal education or through placements and integrated education.

Knowledge Society: It is a society that values and acknowledges the impactful role and contribution of knowledge in pursuit of socio-economic development.

Learning Organization: It is an organization that is capable to acknowledge the knowledge, skills and talents possessed by its workforce and are used to transform organization to be effective, efficient, and productive.

University as a Learning Organization: A university that embraces tenets of a learning organization where knowledge, insight and skills embedded within its workforce is recognized and utilized for its competitive advantage.

University of Technology: Unlike the traditional and comprehensive university which focuses on the traditional fields such as sociology, anthropology, etc., university of technology is a university with technical and engineering related subjects as its fields of specialization.

Chapter 3
The Formation of Human Capital and Its Relationship With the Knowledge Society in Mexico

María del Rocío Soto Flores
Instituto Politécnico Nacional, Mexico

Ingrid Yadibel Cuevas Zuñiga
Instituto Politécnico Nacional, Mexico

Susana Asela Garduño Román
Instituto Politécnico Nacional, Mexico

ABSTRACT

The processes of economic globalization and accelerating technological change have led to changes in economic and social life at a global level. New technologies, such as the TICs, systems of artificial intelligence, scanning, connectivity, nanotechnology, and biotechnology, among others, have transformed the national productive structures and human capital that require technologies disruptive today. In this context, education has become the main element of the knowledge society and training of human capital that demands a knowledge-based economy. The objective of the chapter is to analyze the relationship between human capital formations in the construction of a society of knowledge in Mexico. The structure is organized in three sections: 1) an analysis of the knowledge society, 2) the formation of human capital and the institutions of higher education in the knowledge society, and 3) human capital formation and its relationship in the construction of a society of knowledge in Mexico.

DOI: 10.4018/978-1-5225-8461-2.ch003

INTRODUCTION

For some decades, planetary economies and global societies have witnessed multiple transformations associated with the emergence of a diversity of technologies, all of colossal complexity. This accelerated technological change has meant that organizations modify their traditional work schemes, to adapt to the new conditions required by a more informed society and productive processes specialized in advanced technologies that demand the formation of a highly qualified and specialized human capital in the management and control of these technologies.

In this narrative, UNESCO (2005) states that "the radical changes provoked by the third industrial revolution - that of new technologies - have in fact created a new dynamic, because since the mid-twentieth century, the formation of people and groups, as well as scientific and technical advances and cultural expressions, are constantly evolving, especially towards a growing interdependence." In this transformation, knowledge and new technologies are propagated as the main element of economic progress and development of the societies of the world. That is, knowledge and its rapid exploitation by economic and social agents, mainly from advanced economies, have generated greater divergences between rich and poor countries, which prevent prospering towards information and knowledge societies worldwide.

The objective of this chapter is to analyze the relation that the formation of human capital has in the construction of a knowledge society in Mexico. The structure of the chapter is organized into three sections: 1) A brief analysis of the Knowledge Society; 2) The formation of human capital and the Higher Education Institutions in the Knowledge Society and, 3) The formation of human capital and its relationship in the construction of a knowledge society in Mexico.

BRIEF ANALYSIS OF THE KNOWLEDGE SOCIETY

Different authors agree that the term knowledge society was used for the first time in 1969 by Peter Drucker (UNESCO, 2005; Casas, 2010).

Years later, in the nineties, the concept was deepened in other investigations such as Robin Mansell's or Nico Stehr's. The notion of knowledge society is also inseparable from the studies on the information society generated by the development of cybernetics and [telematics]. At the end of the nineties, the trilogy of Manuel Castells, devoted to the "information age", with its relevant analysis on the information society, synthesized in a certain way the transformations and tendencies described or glimpsed by the first precursors: penetration of power by technology, new economy of scientific knowledge, changes in work, etc. (UNESCO, 2005).

A central element of knowledge societies is the ability to identify, produce, process, transform, disseminate and use information with a view to creating and applying the knowledge necessary for human development. While the notion of the information society is based on technological progress, the concept of knowledge societies includes much wider social, ethical and political dimensions. The world information society only makes sense if it fosters the development of knowledge societies and is assigned as a purpose to go towards a development of the human being based on the rights of the latter (UNESCO, 2005). For Linde and Stock (2011, cited by Gremm et al., 2018), the information society represents, thereby the technical perspective of a society where innovations are based on information and communication technologies (ICT). A knowledge society goes even further by being an information society in which the information content becomes a priority, and knowledge will be available for everyone at any time and any place.

In this dynamic, Castells (1997) identifies the emergence of a new global economy, which he calls informational and global. "It is informational and global because, in the new historical conditions, productivity is generated and competitiveness is exercised through a global network of interaction. And because the revolution in information technology emerged in the last quarter of the twentieth century, provides the material basis for this new economy. The historical link between the knowledge-information base of the economy, its global reach, and the revolution in information technology is what gives birth to a new and distinct economic system". In another of his works (Castells, 2010), he states: "Nowadays, knowledge has become the dominant factor that not only determines the economic sector—where finding employment is getting better and better for knowledge workers that arise from premium knowledge institutions".

In knowledge society discourse, everything related to knowledge and knowledge production can be included and interconnected, regardless of whether it concerns individuals, organizations or entire societies (Latour, 1988, quoted by Välimaa & Hoffman, 2008).

According to Bell (1973, quoted by Välimaa & Hoffman, 2008), post-industrial society can be characterized as a knowledge society in a double sense: ''first, the sources of innovation are increasingly derivative from research and development (and more directly, there is a new relation between science and technology because of the centrality of theoretical knowledge); second, the weight of the society - measured by a larger proportion of Gross National Product and a larger share of employment - is increasingly in the knowledge field.

The above responds to the progressively rapid rise of organizations based on new technologies, which also demand the incorporation of highly qualified personnel in specific areas of knowledge.

In fact, the OECD and UNESCO recognize that information is fundamental for economic and social development. In the first instance, to favor the exchange of goods and services, either by promoting the technological and productive growth of companies, training and innovation, or because information is constituted as a good in itself; and secondly, because access to information allows to raise the educational level of the people, empower them to create social welfare, help defend their identity and culture, and ultimately, promote the integral creation of human capital (Casas, 2010), as a determinant factor in the construction of a knowledge society.

The revolution of new technologies has meant the entry of information and knowledge in a cumulative logic that Castells, cited by UNESCO (2005), has defined as "the application [of knowledge and information] to the procedures of creation, processing and dissemination of information in a loop of cumulative feedback between the innovation and its practical uses. For Castells (1997), "the generation, processing and transmission of information become the fundamental sources of productivity and power" in the information and knowledge society.

The coincidence of the rise of the Internet, as well as of mobile telephony and digital technologies, with the third industrial revolution – which, at first, caused the migration of a considerable part of the active population towards the service sector in the developed countries - has radically modified the situation of knowledge in societies. The birth of a global information society as a consequence of the revolution of new technologies should not lose sight of the fact that it is only an instrument for realizing knowledge societies (UNESCO, 2005). It is a fact that knowledge and new technologies, especially information and communication technologies, have revolutionized the societies and economies of the world, since they have become the center of gravity of the economic progress of the nations that exploit them with celerity.

HUMAN CAPITAL FORMATION AND THE KNOWLEDGE SOCIETY

For decades, the formation of human capital has become the preponderant factor in the generation of knowledge and the construction of a knowledge society on a global scale. However, this technological revolution, expressed mainly by information and communication technologies, has established new scenarios and needs for training and learning, which is why education plays a central role in the formation of human capital in the context of the knowledge societies.

Education (OECD, 2004) has always been related, by definition, to knowledge; nonetheless, knowledge has played an ambiguous and imperfect role in improving the effectiveness of education systems. Advances in science and information and computing technology have allowed scientific knowledge to develop and spread at an accelerated pace. In certain cases, new information and communication technologies drive innovation, but more importantly, they provide the means to develop a variety of interactions that make new types of innovation possible.

These developments represent an immense opportunity for educational systems, even if they do not produce a model of innovation that is tailor made and totally transferable. There are many peculiarities in sectors such as microelectronics and biotechnology or applied sciences, which are not shared by the education sciences. Nevertheless, those responsible for educational policies can learn a lot by observing how innovation occurs and how those sectors are transformed into more knowledge-intensive areas of the economy (OECD, 2004).

Education is a link (Carreón & Melgoza, 2012), which articulates the different objectives of development, changes in university institutions and national science and technology systems. These, in turn, condition the way to face their reproductive role of human and cultural capital that demands an economy and knowledge society and an industry focused on the use of advanced technologies.

In this new paradigm, there is an interrelation (Madrigal, 2009) between the economy based on knowledge, education, knowledge, science and technology; which induces, that the engine of the development of a country, at present, are the ideas and the application of technology on skills, learning and human capital. The cornerstone of this economy and knowledge society is human capital, that is, the knowledge, skills and abilities that each person possesses, develops and accumulates.

An economy based on knowledge is supported in its human capital, in the use of ideas more than in the use of physical skills, in the applications of technology rather than in the transformation of raw materials or the exploitation of labor. The knowledge economy demands new skills linked to the needs of society, it involves the learning capacity of national institutions, the productive and academic sector, as well as the generation of inter-institutional networks for the solution of problems, and the intensive use of knowledge in the social space (Madrigal, 2009).

The changes associated with the knowledge society affect all levels of the activities of individuals and companies in their multiple spheres. Therefore, the learning and training processes become dynamic and conditioned by the own transformations of society (López & Leal, 2002); new technologies, the globalized economy and the new productive structures, demand a highly qualified human capital.

In fact, since the end of the twentieth century, Peter Drucker, in his work Post-capitalist Society, in which he develops an interesting analysis of the dramatic changes that the economies of the world, industries and companies have witnessed since the beginning of the seventies, derived from the appearance of a cluster of new technologies that altered and put pressure on the productive, social and labor structures, advanced "that the greatest need for employment in the coming decades will be" technicians "; and those technicians not only need a great skill, but they also need a high degree of conventional knowledge and, above all, a high capacity to learn and acquire additional knowledge [...] knowledge has become the key resource of all work "(Drucker, 1998).

In another of his writings, Drucker (2006) emphasizes the role of human capital and human resources management, stating that "the task of management is to train people to perform together, to make their strengths effective and their weaknesses irrelevant. As Davenport says: "having more human capital means also greater employment opportunities", and, also, he points out that "human capital includes skills, experience and knowledge" (Davenport, 2000). That is, individuals with the skills and knowledge demanded by organizations that work in an economy based on knowledge and information are needed.

It is important to acknowledge that today, the disruptive change in the technologies affecting the world economies, requires new jobs generation, according to the new technological progress including, the tendency in a new future, is to displace many of the current positions. In a recent study by the World Economic Forum (2016), it is affirmed that "in many industries and countries, the most in-demand occupations or specialties did not exist 10 or even five years ago, and the pace of change is set to accelerate. By one popular estimate, 65% of children entering primary school today will ultimately end up working in completely new job types that don't yet exist". Meaning, we find ourselves before a fast-evolving labor market, where the universities would have to quickly adapt to the new needs of human capital training demanded by future positions from a knowledge-based society and the new technologies.

On the same tenor, Graham (2017), refers to a study made by the firm McKinsey & Company published in 2017, revealing that almost 30% of the tasks in 60% of professions will be computerized. The same author, mentions that, in 2016, the chief economist of the Bank of England, declared that "80 million of American employments and 15 million of English employments could be robotized". This information confirms the tendency and the disruptive power that new technologies bring along and that will have in the future of the economic activities and the whole society.

THE FORMATION OF HUMAN CAPITAL AND THE HIGHER EDUCATION INSTITUTIONS IN THE KNOWLEDGE SOCIETY

For UNESCO, higher education institutions are destined to play a fundamental role in knowledge societies, in which the classical schemes of production, dissemination and application of knowledge will have undergone a profound change.

Although there is no single organizational model, it is important to ensure that the emerging higher education systems possess a sufficient level of quality and relevance and a degree of international cooperation, so that they can fully play their role as pillars in the construction of knowledge societies (UNESCO, 2005). Knowledge and information in all its forms has increasingly become the most valuable intangible resource, in which investments in R & D and education as a percentage of GDP have grown rapidly in developed economies for several years.

The growing importance of knowledge, research, innovation and evolving perspectives on expertise are changing the social role of universities in the globalized world. One of the most popular concepts used to approach these changes is the Knowledge Society together with a number of other conceptualizations (like Knowledge Economy, Information Society, Learning Society) aiming to illuminate the nature of societal change (Välimaa & Hoffman, 2008).

Higher Education Institutions are the source of production of human capital that will nourish the knowledge society. According to the OECD (2007), human capital is defined as "the knowledge, skills, competences and attributes incorporated in individuals that facilitate the creation of personal, social and economic well-being". And as Schultz said in 1961, "economists have long known that people are an important part of the wealth of nations." What several economists pointed out, including Schultz, is that "a modern economy cannot grow without an educated workforce", namely, it requires a highly skilled and specialized human capital that contributes to the economic growth and the scientific and technological development of a country. In this context, "Universities and other institutions of higher education are the building stones of a knowledge society, since they qualify the future knowledge workers" (Gremm et al., 2018).

As suggested by UNESCO (2005), it is worth remembering that the progress made by some countries is largely the result of decades of patients and concerted efforts in areas such as education at all levels, the recovery of technological backwardness in strategic sectors, the scientific research or the creation of high-performance innovation systems [...] the liberalization of trade has considerably modified the very nature of economic competition, which requires rapid and profound changes in national policies of higher education and scientific research.

Although, just as a good supply of well-educated workers can help the growth of the economy, their absence can be an obstacle [...] Education fosters change and, in turn, responds to social, economic and cultural change. Societies that fail to take advantage of talents and skills will increasingly polarize and create communities that are excluded from the economic and social benefits of globalization and the knowledge economy (OECD, 2007). In this panorama, higher education institutions have an unquestionable commitment and responsibility in the formation of quality human capital that a knowledge society demands.

Knowledge society discourse is also rooted in the fact that higher education institutions are more important than ever as mediums in global knowledge economies. In the age of globalization, higher education institutions are integral to the continuous flows of people, knowledge, information, technologies, products and financial capital (Marginson, 2006, quoted by Välimaa & Hoffman, 2008).

In addition, higher education institutions face great challenges, because as Clark points out (1983, quoted by Välimaa & Hoffman, 2008), the main source of social dynamics in higher education is the expansion of knowledge. Following the reasoning of Clark, the expansion of knowledge leads to new research fields creating a demand for new chairs and professorships to be established for emerging fields of research and disciplines. It also creates the need to establish new training programs and new higher education institutions. To put it shortly, the logic of expansion both in research based knowledge, the number of students, staff, and higher education institutions, is creating a situation in which this expansion changes the social dynamics of the higher education institutions, national systems of higher education and relationships between national higher education systems.

The importance of education and the critical spirit highlights that, in the task of building authentic knowledge societies, the new possibilities offered by the internet or multimedia instruments should not make us disinterested by other authentic instruments of knowledge... Before computers and internet access, most of the world's populations need the books, textbooks and teachers they lack (UNESCO, 2005). To cope with the changes that have taken place, higher education institutions must transform at the speed demanded by accelerated technological change where the main characteristic is linked to the emergence of increasingly sophisticated and more complex technologies, which, at the same time, demand for their management, people prepared with quality and specific skills. In this sense, higher education institutions play a preponderant role in the formation of the human capital that a true knowledge society demands.

THE FORMATION OF HUMAN CAPITAL AND ITS RELATIONSHIP IN THE CONSTRUCTION OF A KNOWLEDGE SOCIETY IN MEXICO

In the case of Mexico, in order to prosper towards a knowledge society, it is necessary to articulate a series of policies that link efforts from the point of view of the economy or the development of the information, communication and telecommunication industries, as from the actions that should be undertaken in the field of education and culture. A comprehensive and articulated vision is also needed, linking information and communication policies in different areas, in order to move the country in the direction of an authentic knowledge society (Casas, 2010).

The traditional policies and higher education institutions in Mexico show weaknesses to train people in scenarios such as globalization, artificial intelligence, digital technology and information and communication technologies; so the importance of these changes, requires higher education institutions to introduce a radically new approach to the processes of human capital formation that will contribute to the construction of a knowledge society.

In this sense, the OECD suggests that information and communication technologies can play an important role in supporting citizens as a requisite for training and education. This implies that Mexican higher education institutions must improve their learning processes through the rapid and efficient incorporation of information and communication technologies as instruments to support education, in order to expand their coverage to all the areas of the population and to advance with firm steps towards a more educated society, that produces knowledge and that supports the economic development of the country.

The ability to develop knowledge has to do with the access to information in the first place, but also with the resources that the State can grant in order for the country to develop research in science and technology. This implies the need to structure a strategy that links scientific and technological development with those of higher education, so that the research work contributes to generating the necessary knowledge to solve the specific problems that the country requires (Casas, 2010) to move towards a knowledge society. Unfortunately, the Mexican government allocates a percentage of the Gross Domestic Product for science and technology, well below what other countries of the world channel; in 2016, according to data from the National Council of Science and Technology, Mexico's research and development spending was only 0.53% of its Gross Domestic Product.

Actually, several international organizations point out that it is necessary to attack the enormous gaps that separate the countries of the world in the application and use of new technologies, their scientific and technological development, and the formation of quality human capital, if we aspire to be part of a global knowledge society.

Ergo, the knowledge society for Latin America and specifically Mexico, should be one that will privilege the educational and training processes - not only in the school setting but throughout life - to use them as a driving force for the application of theoretical knowledge in all areas of life, that is, to solve specific problems of daily life, but also of far-reaching, and at the same time, to allow individuals to have a better understanding of the world (Díaz, 2011). But those educational and training processes must be based on quality educational institutions that adapt quickly to the changes and needs demanded by a global economy and a more dynamic society. In this context, the formation of highly specialized human capital that higher education institutions are able to offer, will allow for better results for Mexico to advance towards a knowledge society.

Casas points out (2010) that, according to some researchers, the location of Mexico in the knowledge society can be seen from two points of view: on the one hand, the country suffers from a significant backwardness in research and development processes that have not managed to be properly linked to the three fundamental agents of knowledge development that are the government, the universities and the industries. On the other hand, the country registers a certain advance in the economic processes that are related to the electronic-computing sectors and the telecommunication services industry in which the private initiative takes the lead, which denotes a lack of government coordination to promote the relationship between the productive sector with equity, education and knowledge.

One of the characteristics of the knowledge society (López & Leal, 2002) is the new role acquired by the learning processes and the educational and training systems. In this new society, training, in particular, is not limited to specific moments of the person's life or restricted to certain areas. One of the most relevant characteristics of the knowledge society is that learning leaves formal formative frameworks, in which it was located in the industrial society, and diffuses, into non-formal and informal spaces. One learns constantly and in any circumstance.

The future society will be a knowledge society and, in that society, "education and training will be, more than ever, the main vectors of identification, belonging and social promotion. Through education and training, acquired in the institutional educational system, in the company, or in a more informal way, individuals will be the owners of their destination and will guarantee their development "(Commission of the European Communities, 1995, cited by López & Leal, 2002).

That's why, if Mexico aspires to move forward a knowledge society, it is needed, as indicated by the European University Association "to have a university consolidated organization on their different levels: at a higher level promoting an efficient work, and at a system level, through excellence with the stakeholders and their interconnected activities" (European University Association, 2003).

The World Bank (2008), in its publication entitled "Mexico's transition to knowledge-based economy", is convincing when affirming that: To tap the potential of new knowledge and accelerating technical change, an educated and skilled work force is needed. Ensuring that expenditures on education are allocated efficiently and that the entire population can participate in the knowledge based economy requires particular attention. Why: Because education is the basis for creating, acquiring, adapting, disseminating, sharing, and using knowledge. A country's institutions, rules, and procedures affect how it acquires, creates, disseminates, and uses knowledge. Today, the bulk of technical knowledge is produced in developed countries. The disparity in the production of technical knowledge per capita between developed and developing countries is even greater than the disparity of income.

According to the OECD, Mexican SMEs suffer from shortage of human capital, inadequate use of technology (organizational capital), and lack of access to networks (external capital). Their development is further hampered by weak tangible and intangible capital and limited access to finance (OCDE, 2007, quoted by Daou et al., 2014). This implies that Mexico and its higher education institutions and business organizations, face great challenges in reversing technological lag, on the one hand, and on the other, satisfying the needs of human capital demanded by a society that aspires to generate and use the knowledge as a means to solve the problems of poverty, inequality and inequity, among others.

CONTRIBUTION

The document analyzes the decisive role of higher education institutions in the development of a nation's science and technology. It reflects on the importance of education in the generation and accumulation of scientific knowledge and the formation of human capital as key elements for the construction of a global knowledge society. Another important aspect of the document is the reflection that is made in relation to the place that Mexico occupies in the knowledge society and the problems that the government faces in order to integrate citizens in the current context of an economy of information and knowledge, based on the generation of knowledge, new technologies and human capital as key elements towards a knowledge society.

FINAL REFLECTIONS

The notion of knowledge societies cannot be reduced to an exclusive vision of the countries of the North since it also seems to be a new development approach relevant to the countries of the South (UNESCO, 2005). Therefore, the accelerated emergence of knowledge and new technologies requires constant adjustments in the education system as a whole of each country in order to move towards a knowledge society.

In the economic and knowledge society, the human capital is a determining factor to generate science and technology knowledge and skills. In that tenor, the study of human capital and its relationship with the knowledge society has great relevance, since the advanced economies, to keep their growth, have bet on the knowledge accelerated incorporation and embrace. However, in the less industrialized countries, the human capital deficient development, holds back the capacity to create new knowledge, the absorption of new technologies and the advance towards a foolproof knowledge and information society, that is why, like in the Mexican case, the Higher Education Institutions would have to strengthen and reverse the technological stagnation, and also, they would need to satisfy the human capital demand from a society that aspires to generate and use the knowledge as means to solve poverty, inequality and inequity problems.

Mexico presents strong lags in the advance towards a knowledge society. In order for it to channel the population towards the accumulation of knowledge, it needs its citizens to have "access to information through the appropriation and guarantee of the use of new information and communication technologies" (Casas, 2010). In addition to integrating new technologies in all areas, it is necessary to strengthen the educational level and skills of the individuals that will integrate the human capital that a knowledge society demands.

The technological backwardness of Mexico is related, on the one hand, to the scarce investment that the government makes in research and development, a figure that reached only 0.53% of the gross domestic product in 2016, while similar economies such as Brazil, invested 1.1% of their GDP. On the other hand, and as the World Bank points out, Mexico must expand and modernize its education system, in addition to investing more in hiring academics, mainly doctors of science in all areas of knowledge; only then, the country will be able to train with quality the people that an economy that requires inserting itself in a global knowledge society demands.

Given the importance of the formation of human capital in the information and knowledge society, it is urgent that the Mexican government invests a greater amount of resources in the education of Mexicans and promotes an educational policy of national scope, ensuring that resources reach to the classrooms and fulfill their objective of building a system of quality education and oriented to promote national scientific and technological development.

Given that the analyzed topic in this chapter has various edges and complexity in the information treatment, it is proposed to take other researches related to the problems faced by the developing economies to move towards a knowledge society; as well as to go deep on the relationship between the Higher Education Institutions and the human capital training for a knowledge society.

REFERENCES

Adhikari, D. R. (2010). Knowledge management in academic institutions. *International Journal of Educational Management, 24*(2), 94–104. doi:10.1108/09513541011020918

Banco Mundial. (2008). Mexico's transitions to a knowledge-bases economy. Challenges and opportunities. Washington, DC: Author.

Bell, D. (1973). *The coming of post-industrial society*. New York: Basic Books.

Carreón y Melgoza. (2012). México: Hacia una sociedad del conocimiento. *Noésis (Pau), 21*(41).

Casas, P.M. (2010). México: sociedad de la información o sociedad del conocimiento. *Virtualis, 1*.

Castells, M. (1997). *La era de la información. La sociedad red* (Vol. 1). Madrid: Alianza Editorial.

Clark, B. R. (1983). *The higher education system*. Berkeley, CA: University of California.

Comisión de las Comunidades Europeas. (1995). *Libro Blanco sobre la educación y la formación. Enseñar y aprender. Hacia la sociedad del conocimiento*. Luxemburgo: CCE.

CONACyT. (2016). *Informe general del estado de la Ciencia, la Tecnología y la Innovación*. CONACyT.

Daou, Karuranga, E., & Su, Z. (2014). Towards a better understanding of intelectual capital in Mexicans SMEs. *Journal of Intellectual Capital, 15*(2), 316–332. doi:10.1108/JIC-08-2013-0092

Diaz, E.A. (2011). Información y sociedad del conocimiento en América Latina. *Biblioteca Universitaria, 14*(1).

Drucker, P. (1969). *The Age of Discontinuity. Guidelines to our changing societies*. New York: Harper & Row.

Drucker, P. (1993). *Post-Capitalist Society*. New York: Harper Business.

Drucker, P. (2006). *Drucker Para todos los días*. Bogotá: Ed. Norma.

European University Association. (2003). *Response to the communication from the commission. The Role of the Universities in the Europe of Knowledge*. European University Association.

Graham, B. M. (2017). *L'Éducation et la quatriéme révolution industrielle*. Paris: Prépare pour Groupe Média TFO.

Graue, A. (2009). *Fundamentos de Economía*. Pearson.

Latour, B. (1988). *The pasteurization of France* (A. Sheridan & J. Law, Trans.). Cambridge, MA: Harvard University Press.

López, C., & Leal, D. (2002). Cómo aprender en la sociedad del conocimiento. Barcelona. *Gestion.*

Madrigal, T.B. (2009). Capital humano e intelectual: su evaluación. *Revista Observatorio Laboral, 2*(3).

Margison, S. (2006). Putting "public" back into the public universities. *Thesis Eleven, 84*.

OCDE. (2004). *Innovation in the Knowledge Economy: Implications for Education and Learning*. Paris: OCDE.

OCDE. (2007). *Insights Human Capital: How what you know shapes your life*. Paris: OCDE.

Real Academia Española. (2017). *Diccionario de la lengua española*. Madrid: RAE.

Schumpeter, J. A. (1964). *Business Cycles*. New York: McGraw Hill.

UNESCO. (2005). *Toward knowledge societies. UNESCO world report*. UNESCO.

Välimaa, J., & Hoffman, D. (2008). Knowledge society discourse and higher education. *Higher Education, 56*(3), 265–285. doi:10.100710734-008-9123-7

World Economic Forum. (2016). *The future of Jobs. Employment, skills and workforce strategy for the fourth industrial revolution*. WEF.

Chapter 4
Ecological University for Transformative and Critical Intellectual Capital Advancement and Scholarship in South Africa

Ndwakhulu Stephen Tshishonga
University of KwaZulu-Natal, South Africa

ABSTRACT

This chapter interrogates an ecological model of university as a framework to understanding evolving roles played by institutions of higher learning, particularly universities, thus including their implications for a wider society transformational change. Barnett has explored various models ranging from the metaphysical, scientific, entrepreneurial, and bureaucratic to liquid, therapeutic, authentic, and ecological models. The author further argues that being and becoming ecological is a huge project, as it takes the university into a new order of being. A university within this model becomes an entity that constantly engages with itself and its adjacent environment in order to remain relevant and be part of the solutions to the societal challenges. In this chapter, case studies from the South African universities were used as the research technique, including selected interviews with key stakeholders in the higher education sector.

DOI: 10.4018/978-1-5225-8461-2.ch004

INTRODUCTION

Institutions of higher learning are challenged to transform themselves to play a decisive role in an ever-changing environment (Rugunanan, 2015). Globalization and global restructuring of economies have a major effect on how the institutions of higher learning function, more particularly in the emergence of a knowledge-based economy (Moja, 2004). Globalization expects higher education systems to play an active role in social and economic development in the 'knowledge society' (Castle, 1998). The demand for intensive labour with high-level skills has place high a demand on the universities as institutions of higher learning to train and produce a professional and competent workforce. The higher education system is charged with the responsibility of expanding the production of highly skilled professionals and further enhance the innovative capacity of the nation (NDP, 2011: 263). The developed nations compared to their developing counterparts have managed to benefit from the globalized economy, by taking advantage of their highly competitive higher education systems.

Thus, assessed from an open system theory, these institutions like any other organization are compelled to discover, contextualize and employ appropriate and deliberate strategic planning, management and tools to address the needs and aspirations imposed by their environments. The environments within which institutions of higher learning, especially the universities, operate have become the determinants for either their success or failure in executing their mandate. With the global demand for universities to provide diverse solutions to multiple challenges confronting societies, more particularly in the developing nations, these institutions are compelled to configure, revisit their role and models for them to impact positively on their immediate and wider stakeholders. Thus, the existence of universities as social institutions Teferra and Altbach (2003), compels them to transcend their traditional role of teaching and learning, research and community engagement to using knowledge as a social tool to transform society. However, due to the encroachment of neo-liberalism and managerialism, universities are run or expected to run like businesses-based on bureaucratic structures (Muller, 2016).

In an attempt to reclaim their identities and development role, universities have configured themselves and assume different responsibilities in response to multiple societal needs and challenges. Through globalisation and internalization, universities are compelled to experiment with various models, which are categorised as being: 1) the metaphorical university, 2) the scientific university, 3) the entrepreneurial university and 4) the bureaucratic university. The secondary category falls within those 'becoming possible' universities as: 5) the liquid university, 6) the therapeutic university, 7) the authentic university, 8) and ecological university (Barnett, 2011). The focus of this chapter is based on ecological model of university, including its strategic and operational mechanism to navigate pressures imposed by both the immediate and broader environment. How does embracing the ecological university model impact on the core functions viz. teaching, research and community engagement? What capacity does university need to have to be active in advancing the ecological university model?

This chapter argues that being and becoming a functional and a developmental university within the context of the ecological framework requires all is a huge project, as it takes the university into a new order of being, thus inhabiting 'a new ecology, at once applied and theoretical, ethno-political and aesthetic' Guattari, 2005: 67). The ecological model poses challenges for modern universities to cease operating as ivory towers amidst societal misery, gross underdevelopment and injustices. A university within this model becomes an entity, which constantly engages with itself and its adjacent or broader environment in order to remain relevant and be part of the solutions to societal challenges. The ecological model of universities, as discussed in this chapter, is deliberated within its potential to embrace social and scientific as well as emancipatory knowledge aimed at advancing intellectual capital. In this chapter, case studies from the South African universities are used as the research technique, including selected interviews with key stakeholders in the higher education sector.

CHALLENGES FACING SOUTH AFRICAN UNIVERSITIES

Anderson (2016, p. 157) highlights the crisis in the education system in South Africa. Anderson writes that South Africa is criticised for having one of the worst education systems in the world for the past twenty years. History however tells us that the crisis has its roots in apartheid education which was deliberately designed to privilege white and disadvantage blacks. Rugunanan (2015, p. 283) reports that higher education is scathed by apartheid. Although the post-apartheid education system is based on equality, regardless of race and gender, Anderson (2016, p. 163) notes that higher education is still faced with many challenges. The author reports that huge inequalities continue in educational institutions. The National Development Plan (2011, p. 18) states that the country's higher education system contributes to economic and social progress but its performance is mediocre. South African universities especially the larger middle and comprehensive categories (Sutton & Giddens, 2013) are the victims of transformation itself. Most of them are still labelled as either 'bush; or historically disadvantage universities such as the University of Venda, University of Zululand, University of Limpopo including the previous technicons who were renamed through the meagre as universities of technology (e.g. Mangosuthu, Durban University of technology, etc). Since 1994, these universities have witnessed a massive of influx of students from the previous disadvantaged background, yet without adequate resources and infrastructure to accommodate them. For previously white universities, such as UCT, Stellenbosch, Rhodes, University of Johannesburg, Wits and University of Pretoria the challenges was moving from being elite to mass institutions. Despite the efforts to make universities accessible to most of the black students, the challenges accompanying Tefera and Altbach (2003) this transformation were funding and inadequate resources. One of the participants highlighted that:

the gradual opening of doors for black students, specially ill-prepared students due to Bantu education, led to resistance by these institutions. Thus, language such as English and Afrikaans, has been used as a barrier to prevent black students in particular from accessing previously white-only universities.

Mainly, the Afrikaans dominated universities such Pretoria, Stellenbosch, former Rand Afrikaanse University, renamed University of Johannesburg (UJ), were implicated in their refusal to embrace bilingualism or English as a main language for academic engagement. In this context, racially and ethnically based universities failed to develop as integrative institutions with common vision and one education system. Apart from the language issue, funding became a problem for most of the students from low-income household. The Fees-Must-Fall campaign is testimony to the financial struggle faced by students in tertiary institutions in South Africa. In its report the Heher Commission, established by President Zuma in 2017 to investigate the feasibility of free higher education in South Africa, states that poor education increases the cost of producing graduates and a relatively small number of black student graduates from universities. However, in his book titled 'Democracy & Delusion-10 myths in South Africa Politics', Mpofu-Walsh (2017) argued for the debunkment of the myth that free higher education cannot be achieved. Some European countries were cited to advance the notion of free higher education and its benefit to students. It included the Scandinavian countries where higher education is not only free, but students are paid to attend universities.

In general South African universities are faced with disproportionate level of access and opportunities for staff and students across race, gender, class and even geographical locality. The massification of education in higher education has proven to be complex due to the lack of the lack of capacity and infrastructure especially at former white universities. Universities are unable to address past inequalities and have limited resources which lead to higher fees which in turn put barriers on the poor from accessing higher education. Rugunanan (2015, p. 286) notes that the massification of higher education put additional demands on an already pressured higher education system. Lecture theatres were meant to accommodate fewer students but now have to accommodate more students, who often times sit on the floor because of lack of space.

GROUNDING THE UNIVERSITY ON MODELS

This section of the paper investigates a variety of models experimented with by institutions of higher learning to get to grips with evolving roles which universities are faced with, including their implications for a wider transformed societal change. These models range from the metaphysical, scientific, entrepreneurial and bureaucratic to liquid, therapeutic, authentic and ecological models (Barnett, 2011). Within a single university, the research university, the entrepreneurial university, the bureaucratic university and even the corporate university have presence and influence. The four models of a university viz. the metaphysical, scientific, entrepreneurial and bureaucratic are used aptly to understand and analyse the existence of the university in a contemporary world, while the other categorized sets such as the liquid, therapeutic, authentic and ecological models are projecting the possibilities of the university.

The first model, the metaphysical university, is informed by the ideas emanating from university engagement with the universe or the world. Through the metaphysical approach, the university enlightens and socialises individuals in knowledge transference with the possibility of producing new individuals. Metaphysical ideas, though abstract, have images of new relationships that transcend the immediate world. For Audi (1999, p. 563), the metaphysical university is open to the world and its affinity to the universe enables it to investigate the nature, constitution and structure of reality. Barnett (2011, p. 13) argues that university boundaries are constantly widening and becoming even more open to negotiation, and according to the author, the idea of a university encompasses knowledge, truth, discussion, inquiry, authenticity, care, understanding, veracity, application, persons, critique, development and action. The notion of a metaphysical university is intrinsically linked to the ecological model of university as both are anchored in developing critical intellectual capital by exposing students to the broader environment. One of the academics reiterated this point by saying that:

the 21 century requires higher education institutions to be open systems not only by facilitating access to previously disadvantaged students, but also broadening their horizon by collaborating with other international institutions.

Taking a lead in the fourth industrial revolution, African universities would require academics and produce students who are capable of thinking outside the box.

Secondly, the scientific university, emerged post the abandonment of the metaphysical university. The scientific university resembles the research university with a bias towards what Barnett (2011, p. 21) calls 'hard science' or knowledge produced within the 'natural sciences', especially engineering and medicine. This model is influenced by a knowledge society underpinned by a strong connection with the state and industry. Compared to the humanities, natural sciences have a bigger share of a university budget hence; the value for money is intrinsically linked to technological applications and economic growth. Universities of technology such as Durban University of Technology, Tshwane University of Technology, Free State University of Technology, Mangosuthu University of Technology are exemplars of scientific institutions with a strong affinity to industries through their integrated work learning programmes (Maake, 2011). Most South African institutions of higher learning proclaim to be research universities and that has become their measure for being rated nationally and internationally. Epistemologically, research universities are identifiable through their pursuit of research reflected in academic journals. Barnett (2011, pp. 31-32) categorizes knowledge into four quadrants; knowledge-for-itself, knowledge-in-itself, knowledge-in-the world and lastly, knowledge-for-the-world. Barnett (2011, p. 31) has presented the university and knowledge grip with A) ivory tower reflective of the interface between knowledge-for-itself and knowledge-in-itself. B) category being the professional university with the knowledge-for-itself interfacing knowledge–in-the-world while category C depicts the entrepreneurial model of university with knowledge-in-itself and knowledge–for-the–world. D category according to Barnett (2011) is developmental university which is differentiated from other categories due its reflection of knowledge-in the world and knowledge-for-the-world.

The knowledge grid according to Barnett has four quadrants. Quadrant (a): knowledge-for-itself/knowledge-in-itself depicts the ivory tower university where pure knowledge is produced apart from the world hence, its utility is considered. Quadrant (b): knowledge-for-itself/knowledge-in-the world is reflective of a professionalized university which is rooted in the world and professional knowledge related activities to advance the university's own interests. Quadrant (c) is knowledge-in-itself/ knowledge-in-the world represents the entrepreneurial university and knowledge and its products in this form are largely produced apart from the world, either to be applied or sold to the world for profits or economic returns (Barnett, 2011, p. 32). The last Quadrant (d) is knowledge-in-the world/knowledge-for-the world, and is unique in the sense that the university is active in the world and knowledge is generated by engaging in the world-embedded activities. The primary purpose of this

Figure 1.

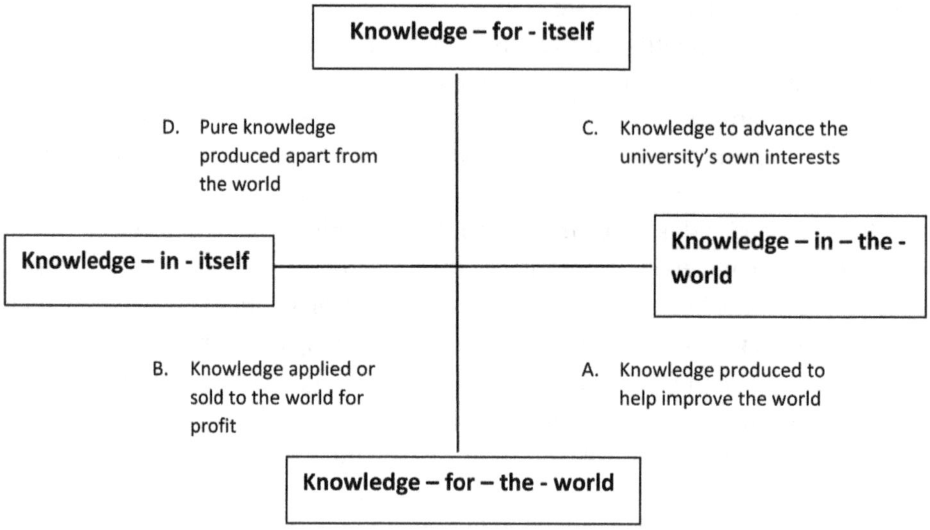

Quadrant is to help improve the world; hence, knowledge production is actualised to work for-the-world.

The third model is the entrepreneurial university as proposed by the work of Clark (1998, 2004). It is argued that due to financial constraints and financial hardships experienced by students, universities are forced to consider entrepreneurialism as the pathways of their sustenance. From the entrepreneurial model, a university is perceived as a set of spaces and it enters into spaces of an entrepreneurial ethos and its practical manifestations (Barnett, 2011, p. 36). Entrepreneurship within universities differentiates hard and soft models. Hard models fall within those forms of entrepreneurship with definite intention to secure an economic return while the soft models are those forms not driven primarily by income generation. From the Barnett (2011) perspective, hard entrepreneurship in the context of higher education borders regulated and unregulated market with unintended consequences such as unbridled and curtailed nature of business endeavours. On one hand, the radical advancement of hard entrepreneurship has the potential of breeding corruption and unethical conduct among the academic staff and university administrators. While on the other hand soft entrepreneurship could promote both civic and restrained entrepreneurism. Due to financial constraints, most universities have opted for hard entrepreneurship with hired professional managers charged with fundraising and running tailor made programmes and projects targeting either the government employees or the corporate sector. Yet extra finances generated through these designated units and programmes were primarily earmarked for research and infrastructural development.

The financial dependency of universities to the state and private sector has led to a managerialism approach to governing these entities. Managerialism according to Maake (2011) is the new jargon of higher education which mirrors the private sector unleashing and entrenching some oppressive culture. The repercussions for such dependency have resulted in the demise of academic freedom and lack of autonomy. Through entrepreneurialism, universities encourage their staff, especially academics and income units to get involved in ventures and programmes aimed at maximizing profit within and across disciplines. Entrepreneurial universities by their nature avoid using their capital for unproductive use hence; they are more prone to generate some of form of returns for their own efforts. Entrepreneurial branded universities invest through their capital hence, their quest for capital growth and expansion of intellectual capital (Barnett, 2011, p. 34). Despite the economic return attached to entrepreneurial activities, universities embark on such ventures to profile themselves for their image, reputation and positioning in the outside world.

The university as a bureaucracy is the fourth model and is often associated with the corporate nature of a university. Through a bureaucratic university, institutions of higher learning are run resembling businesses with bureaucratic procedures and processes imposed on academic life. Some of these procedures entail student admissions, the appointment of staff, and the balance of academic activities, examinations, research applications, curriculum structures, recording of research activities and publications, teaching hours and meeting with research students (Barnett, 2011, pp. 45-46). The expansion of these bureaucratic procedures saw the regulation of academic activities by non-academic staff who happened to be administrators and managers constructing such procedures.

The university in 'becoming possible' is categorised within the following set of models such as the liquid university, the therapeutic university, the authentic university and the ecological university. The liquid university is fluid hence; it continues to unfold for future possibilities. Epistemologically, Barnett (2011, p. 110) equates a liquid university with an amoeba and the argument is that such a university is always on the move and it interacts with its environment. This model of university is described by a never-ending succession of shapes and is not shapeless. Accordingly, a liquid university is always on the pathway to a continuous process of assimilation and accommodation. In becoming a university, it presents itself with new income opportunities from the state agency, changes in a funding stream and students' expectations. These elements interact dynamically in an environment that is complex enough hence, adaptable to move through the processes of assimilation. Universities also have to modify themselves to stay relevant to their call of duty. Despite the assimilation process, institutions of higher learning have to accommodate the changing environment and this entails being proactive in responding to the funding deficiencies faced by students. For example, the recent Fees-Must-Fall campaign staged by South African students was based on a lack of funding for students to access quality education.

Another model is a therapeutic university and this version of a university according to Bahti (1992, p. 68) resembles an injured modern university with a need for therapy. According to Barnett (2011:120), a therapeutic university has a caring element, especially for human beings and caring for the university community thus i.e. its staff and students. The author places this model within marketization of higher education where students are located and underpinned by a market relationship with their institutions. Almost all universities have units and programmes that offer psychological services to students who face some trauma and hardships at both an educational and personal level. Uniquely, due to some challenges students encounter traditionally, the University of KwaZulu-Natal (UKZN) decided to establish indigenous services in 2007 within the UKZN community thus, staff and students are afforded an opportunity to consult a traditional healer or sangoma. Mkhize (2017), a woman in charge of providing indigenous counselling highlighted during an interview that:

The indigenous services are offered to all, especially the students who encounter challenges beyond what Western medical doctors and student psychological counselling could provide.

However, the therapeutic university creates both ontological and epistemological uncertainties. Ontologically, students are exposed to a changing world which causes insecurities pertaining to who exactly they are and what they are. One post-graduate student lamented that:

Without prospects for securing a job in the labour market, universities have become the breeding ground for producing unemployed graduates. Without tangible skills and competencies relevant to the workforce, students turn to become wasted resources with degrees which cannot enable them to be employed or self-employed.

Thus, universities are caught between advancing intellectual scholarship and offering marketable skills and knowledge for their students to be employable or create their own jobs once graduated. On the idea of graduate students creating their own jobs, Rudigi (2018) in a seminar hosted by the UKZN Centre for Civil society, entitled ‘Entrepreneurship through research - converting research into community projects’ argued that:

While the role of universities is to transfer knowledge and prepare graduates for the labour market, I argue that this role should also be of shaping the labour market by entrenching new ideas and innovations. In essence, universities should play the role of creating jobs rather than just creating job seekers.

He further asserts that:

This can be achieved by ensuring that graduates are equipped with necessary knowledge and skills beyond producing academic work. This approach could create an enabling environment for graduates to identify and close the gap between knowledge and socio-economic problems. It means graduates should have first-hand experience in advancing and experimenting with new knowledge produced through research. They should also be equipped to see problems in their communities and be able to come up with viable lasting solutions.

Therefore, according to Rudigi (2018), it is crucial for newly registered students to develop critical analytical skills, self-awareness, and to socialise themselves through various engagements in the university environment.

The third model is the authentic university model which is an idealist one, which strives to comprehend its place in a multi-layered world. For Barnett (2011, p. 135), an authentic university projects itself into future possibilities and as such, it lives in the past, the present and the future all at once. Since this university is not in existence yet, the context, proposed enquiry and learning, the envisaged responsibilities and conditions are some of the core ingredients for an authentic version of the university. The university which is authentic is aligned with its own responsibilities with categories a) and b) bordering authentic and non-authentic models of universities. On the contrary, c) and d) categories are reflective of authentic and in-authentic with responsibility at the centre (Barnett, 2011, p. 103).

An authentic university is a model, where learning and enquiry are driven and inspired by the purposes of understanding, reflection and inquiry across society assisting itself to have a better grasp of the real world (Finnegan 2005; Barnett, 2011). Barnett (2011, p. 132) identified four conditions under which the authentic university is created. Firstly, are the contingent-and-general conditions, where being part of a global learning economy; universities subject themselves to similar callings and subjugations. Secondly, are the contingent-and-particular conditions which compel universities to position themselves, thus considering the markets, income flows, reputation, mix of teaching and research and their epistemologies. Thirdly, are the specific value conditions regarding the precariousness of the authentic university, thus, based on the space and responsibility, universities are able to forge their own value position and such value position has to be sustained. Lastly, are the general value conditions. However, the difficulty is for universities to live up to the expectations of being part of the global family of universities (Barnett, 2011, p. 132). For an authentic university to be actualised, it should be rooted in the real world with its own self-image navigated through forces and expectations of it. In addition, Barnett (2011, p. 135) argues that an authentic university could realize its authenticity through: 1) a grasp of the level of the world; 2) a sense of the complex interplay of factors affecting it; 3) a crystallisation of its own hopes and self-image; 4) an ethical undemanding of itself reflecting on a value position and 5) time as authenticity is realised over time and through time.

ECOLOGICAL MODEL OF UNIVERSITY

An ecological model of university emanates from the ecological system theory. The ecological system theory makes intrinsic connection between the person and the environment. This theory was developed by Urine Bronffenbrenner who advocated that a person's development is greatly affected by everything in their surrounding environment. In the context of the universities, the ecological system theory illustrates how the university's environment affects how students grow and develop emotionally and intellectually (Bronfenbrenner, 1917 – 2005). Within the ecological model, family together with physical, social/emotional, language collectively form important components of early childhood development not only for the child's survival, but also for opportunities for learning experiences and life-long well-being (Germann et al., 2018, p. 42). Bronffenbrenner (1979 & 1994) is convinced that a child's development is shaped by the microsystem underpinned by the child's environment, where the environment influences the child and the child influences the environment (Krishnan, 2010). Thus, people are able to develop themselves not in isolation, but within their interaction and in relationship especially the family and society (Germann et al., 2018, p. 43). An ecological approach focusses on child development where social environment, including household, play a vital role in shaping children environment. Through adopting an ecological system, the researcher was able to situate the role individual or a child, family and society play in the holistic development of children. For Betancourt et al. (2018, p. 165), ecological systems entail microsystem, mesosystem, ecosystem, macro system and chrono system, thus reflecting the interaction between individuals, their family units and their societies. Ecological system is essential in helping university stakeholders to understand the social context in which students, teaching and learning take place; thus opportunities and challenges faced by universities across the globe and South Africa in particular.

The notion of ecologic is centred on the wellbeing and interconnectedness of the environment, with care for environment being the central framework (Barnett, 2011, p. 139). The ecological university is rooted on real urgency towards the world and its ethical responsibility. Such a university comprehends itself as having a responsibility towards networks and interconnections (Guattari, 2005, p. 34). Thus, a university which is ecologically grounded has the capacity to promote understanding through learning and inquiry. The ecological model of university is a radical shift from other models where traditionally, the university places emphasis of on enquiry based on the advancement of scientific scholarship. Unlike the other models, the ecological version of a university according to Barnett (2011) calls for 'an openness of mind and open society'. The ecological university is rooted on a real urgency towards the world as its ethical responsibility. Such a university comprehends itself as having a responsibility towards networks and interconnections (Guattari, 2005, p. 34). Thus, a university which is ecologically grounded has the capacity to promote understanding through learning and inquiry. The ecological model challenges modern universities to cease operating as ivory towers amidst societal misery, gross underdevelopment and injustices. A university within this model becomes an entity, which constantly engages with itself and its adjacent environment in order to remain relevant and be part of the solutions to societal challenges. Davids and Waghid (2018, p. 27) designates an ecological university to be a university that:

[h]as spaces of agency and remains on the look-out for large deficiencies in its own research and in the wider world. It has an ethical concern to promote democratic interests to help people to understand one another, coexist and make sense of the world in which they live.

Accordingly, the entrepreneurial type of university has the potential of entering into a dialogue and the pursuit of its core business to advance intellectual scholarship anchored on robust teaching and learning, research and community engagement (Buber, 1958). The philosophy of dialogue encourages the university to create a dialogical environment upon which people embrace their co-existence as people are able to relate to each other in seeking alternative remedies to their challenges (Buber, 1958).

The ecological university and its quest for dialogical engagement distances itself from the relationship based on the dichotomy of 'I' and 'it' as a separate entity. For instance, research is engaged for mere purposes of gathering information, for grounding concepts and proving or disproving set hypotheses (Davids & Waghid, 2018). This created dichotomy dictates a university to be understood as a place where only knowledge is produced, thus expanding a gap between the researcher and knowledge within the 'I-it' relationship. Contrary to the forged 'I-it' relationship, is the 'I-thou' relationship which unfolds through a university's encounter with the world and its humanity in full integration. This co-existence is reflective of the philosophy of Ubuntu, which is underpinned by a Nguni phrase 'I am because you are'. The university operating within the context of Ubuntu does so integrally and in concert through people's collective action and solidarity (Msila, 2015).

EMBRACING THE ECOLOGICAL MODEL FOR UNIVERSITY TRANSFORMATION

Universities operate in a complex environment and with a multiplicity of stakeholders with unique needs and challenges to which these institutions are expected to react and respond. These environments present universities with both challenges and opportunities. Despite the restructuring of higher education since the dawn of democracy in 1994, universities in particular are still confronted with challenges. The persistence of these challenges undermines higher education institutions efforts to become centres of excellence and robust scholarship. In order for universities to serve as a platform for human and intellectual development (Cebekhulu, 2013), radical and holistic transformation is imperative. In part the privatisation of higher education (Sutton & Giddens, 2013) and has led to elitist institutions with ivory tower syndrome and enclave, and only the selected few could be privileged enough to attend such institutions.

Universities have opportunities to transform themselves despite numerous challenges to forge their identity and renew their mission to serve humanity through the advancement of development.

GROUNDING AN ECOLOGICAL UNIVERSITY

The world has moved on and education has changed drastically. The university has also changed and moved on with the times. Critics of the old style university now call for an ecological university which encompasses the world in which it exists. Barnett (2011) an advocate of ecological university argues that the university should not remain an island but has to be interconnected with the world. There are types of university that are no longer fit for purpose in the 1st century. Historically the university was only a place of learning, a liquid university with no sense of direction where research, goals and knowledge transfer moves in many directions as described by Deleuze and Guattari (2004) and losing direction along the way. The university was also therapeutic and seen as one that seeks to avoid and minimise risk to itself. It is not only in the UK as mentioned by Barnett (2011) that universities develop systems to assess risk and do self-audit on all actions that might be considered risky. Similar to other universities in the world, South African universities use risk assessment processes in order to control issues such as student protests, and other risky incidentals. Therapeutic universities give degrees to students as a panacea to generate an educated and disciplined society. In the South African context it is through publication and recruitment of post-graduate students at both Masters and PhD that universities are incentivized by the department of higher education and training. Ecclestone and Hayes (2009 cited in Barnett 2011) criticise the therapeutic university as near abusive as university falls short of its true destiny of producing graduates that embrace the world in its totality. Rather it is accused of mollycoddling students and focusing on their wellbeing while neglecting its primary functions connected with critical appropriation of knowledge.

Another university that needs to move towards the ecological university is the authentic university. Unlike the therapeutic university, the authentic university, as its name suggests, tackles issues without mollycoddling. Barnett views this type of university as one that is moving towards connectedness as it is a networked university. He however points out the problems with the authentic university. For example, Cooper (2002 cited in Barnett, 2011) cites that it tries to sort out what a disencumbered position might look like such that it can offer the prospects of authenticity. Its other problem is holding on to being in a position of a university, a sense of entitlement. The authentic university thus builds up itself as a place of enquiring minds of a particular community for academics and students while undermining students' abilities to become consumers of self-knowledge and self-understanding. Evidence shows that an enquiring mind fits into that of an authentic university a position taken by some universities in South Africa.

SUSTAINABLE DEVELOPMENTAL UNIVERSITY

Venetoulis (2001) assessed the ecological impact of a university and found that universities and colleges had made great strides in making universities greener. Similarly to Barnett's (2011) argument, Venetoulis argues that communities which pursue environmental sustainability do not exist in and of themselves. The author adds that in the same vein college campuses do not exist in and of themselves. This means sustainability will not happen in and of itself. Smith (1993) also notes that since the 1960s the college and university communities are taking action planting trees using less waste, recycling, preserving energy leading to the decline of toxic products and other gas emissions. There have been many activists like Dr Mathaai Wangari of Kenya among others who have mobilised communities to plant trees in order to create a sustainable environment for future generations. Dr Wangari managed to plant over half a million (500 000) since the 1970s. Her actions went beyond the borders of Kenya but influenced many other communities such as universities to work on developing and managing the environment and sustaining it.

In his study on the ecological footprint for the University of Redlands in The United States of America (USA) Venetoulis (2001) argued that the success of linking sustainability concerns with campus ecology is to some extent dependent on how the campus is conscientized about problems and commitment to enhance understanding through aspirations and desires of the university campus community. The point of Venetoulis' study was to find out how the campus' ecological footprint was impacting on the environment. His study found that in its effort to sustain the environment the university had reduced its consumption, toxic waste and emissions. The university under study through its Environmental Design Studio has also helped to guide the initial development of several alternatives that would move it towards sustainability by changing the design of some buildings. For example, the University of East London with the aid of its architecture students in the 1990s designed sustainable buildings on brown land thereby reducing waste and maintain the ecological structure along River Thames where it is located.

THE ECOLOGICAL UNIVERSITY: THE IDEAL PLACE OF LEARNING IN THE 21ST CENTURY

In order to move to the higher echelons of learning it is high time that universities embrace and become ecological universities. Davids and Waghid (2018) inform us that an ecological university is one that has space of agency and remains on the look-out for large deficiencies in its own research and in the wider world. It is a university that seeks to interconnect with the world in which it exists. Davids and Waghid (2018) state that the ecological university has an ethical concern to promote democratic interests to help people to understand one another, coexist and make sense of the world in which they live in. According to Barnett's (2011), prediction an ecological university is already emerging through the idea of students as global citizens for example. Global citizens and students are concerned about the world and not their university communities as in other types of universities. The students and global citizens are aware of the world's challenges. They connect with each other as they strive to understand the world around them and making sense of it while contributing to the world particularly in the developing world and extending knowledge and capability which Sen (1999) views as the best thing to ever happen within a university. Nixon (2011) adds that the ecological university produces individuals who develop around public goods where students are encouraged to engage in civic associations.

The ecological university cannot only be seen as a place where only knowledge is produced (Davids & Waghid, 2018) but a place where students and academics network with the wider society and through those networks availing their knowledge resources (Barnett, 2011). For universities to stay relevant to the 21st century demands which are global in nature, democratising knowledge by being flexible to other knowledge systems is imperative. Ecologically, critical analysis of the immediate and broader environment not only renew the vision of university to be the leader in knowledge production and providing conducive environment for such knowledge to be utilised for national development. This implies universities investing in research and development especially in science related field. Since a direct interest in building the knowledge base of society is a shared responsibility with global organisations such as UNESCO, World Trade Organisation, the World Bank, National Research Foundation, and universities could benefit enormously by expanding their research base through developing knowledge networks. Universities as knowledge organisations are challenged to be at the forefront of the fourth industrial revolution and knowledge economy. One way of doing this is through the development of scientific and innovative solutions to global challenges. Via the production of intellectual capital and technological applications (Stone, 2012, p. 343), the ecological model could provide a basis for universities to inform and interrogate developmental alternatives. Thus, by building coalitions based on knowledge networks, universities could be assisted in redefining their role beyond their elite and privileged status as ivory towers. The ecological model in this context demands institutions of higher learning to advance their social responsibility variably through community-based learning, academic conferences and more importantly via knowledge-based networks and research collaboration. These spaces become the forums to produce, disseminate, collaborate and utilise knowledge produced for the common good of society.

FUTURE RESEARCH DIRECTIONS

Institutions of higher learning especially universities throughout the world have been evolving to embrace new roles depending on the models adopted. The models deliberated in this chapter are fundamental not only in shaping the visions of these institutions, but also challenges them to adapt for purpose in the contemporary society. Based on university models as espoused by Barnett (2011), the adoption of models such as the metaphysical, the scientific, entrepreneurial, the bureaucratic including the ecological one are survival mechanisms in the world that is knowledge based and is fast moving toward the fourth industrial revolution. Considering that universities are public institutions created to advance scholarship and educate society, these institutions cannot afford to operate as ivory towers detached from the reality of poverty and underdevelopment.

Through embracing an ecological model, university could be in a better position to harness intellectual capability of stakeholders such as indigenous communities and transform such experiences into tangible solutions to socio-economic and political challenges. While community-based engagement or service learning is part and parcel of the core business of universities, rigorous research is however needed, where experiences obtained through engaging communities and organisations are documented. That would include the implications of the ecological university model on teaching and learning. Importantly, such research could be enriched by tapping into Senge's (2006) learning organisation theory, Kretzmann and McKnight (1993) asset-based approach by and Ubuntu embedded principles of caring, solidarity, sharing, humanness, respect and compassion by Broodryk (2002), Mbigi and Maree (2005).

CONCLUSION

This chapter outlined the many types of university and how many have moved beyond the echelons of learning and production of knowledge and research, and have moved into the 21st century model of the ecological university. The university has moved from being a community in itself to a community within others by interconnecting with the rest of the world. The ecological university is one that transforms the way education, knowledge and its transference has to be done in the 21st century. The chapter argues that the transformed university works actively with the world in which it exists; helping to bring a sustainable world which not only looks at the environment but also personal and social well-being including the physical material such as sustainable buildings and accepting its responsibility in terms of reducing consumption, toxic waste and other emissions that damage the environment. The chapter also reiterates that the ecological university transforms intellectual capital which has to be shared with the wider world while at the same time advancing scholarship.

REFERENCES

African National Congress (ANC). (1994). *The Reconstruction and Development programme (RDP): A Policy framework*. Johannesburg: Umanyano Publications.

Anderson, B. (2016). Education: With emphasis on South Africa. In Sociology: A South African Perspective (pp. 156-176). CENAGE Learning.

Bahti, T. (1992). The Injured University. In R. Rand (Ed.), *Logomachia: The Conflict of the Faculties*. London: University of Nebraska Press.

Balintulo, M. (2004). The role of the state in the transformation of South African higher education, 1994-2002: Equity and redress revisited. In P. T. Zeleza & A. Olukoshi (Eds.), *African Universities in the twenty-first century* (pp. 441–458). Pretoria: UNISA Press.

Barnett, R. (2011). *Being a University*. London: Routledge.

Booysen, S. (Ed.). (2016). *FeesMustFall: Student Revolt, Decolonization and Governance in South Africa*. Johannesburg: Wits University Press.

Borrdryk, J. (2002). *Ubuntu: Life Lessons from Africa*. Pretoria: Ubuntu School of Philosophy.

Brink, C. (2016). Two tales of quality and equality. In *Reflections of South African university leaders*. Cape Town: African Minds.

Buber, M. (1958). *I and thou* (2nd ed.; R. G. Smith, Trans.). New York, NY: Charles Scribner's Sons.

Castle, M. (1998). The Information Age: Economy, Society and Culture: Vol. 111. *End of Millennium*. Oxford, UK: Blackwell.

Cebekhlu, A. (2013). *Unhlaba Uyahlaba: The World is Thorny. Wandsbeck.* Reach Publishers.

Chetty, N. (2009, June 1). Intellectual freedom the lifeblood of universities. The Mercury.

Chinnia, B. (2018). Importance of education. *The Glenwood Weekly Gazette*, *22*, 9.

Commonwealth Expert Group Report. (1991). *Human resource development for a post-apartheid South Africa*. London: Commonwealth Secretariat.

Crossman, P. (2004). 'Perceptions of 'Africanisation' or 'Endogenisation' at African Universities: Issues and Recommendations. In P. T. Zeleza & A. Olukoshi (Eds.), *African Universities in the twenty-first century* (pp. 319–340). Pretoria: UNISA Press.

Davids, N., & Waghid, Y. (2018, April 6). Embrace the ecological university. Mail & Guardian, 27.

Deleuze, G., & Guattari, F. (2004). *A thousand plateaus: Capitalism and schizophrenia*. London: Continuum.

Dipholo, K. (2010). *Universities in transition: From Ivory Towers to People-centred Institutions*. Paper presented at the 9th PASCAL international Observatory Conference, Gaborone.

Du Plessis, H., Sehume, J., & Martin, L. (2011). The Concept and Application of Transdisplinarity in Intellectual Discourse and Research. Johannesburg: Mapungubwe Institute for Strategic Reflection (MISTRAN).

Ebong, M. B. (2004). University Industry relations in Nigeria. In African Universities in the Twenty-First Century: Vol. 2. Knowledge and Society (pp. 555-570). Dakar: CODESRIA.

Ferreira, G. (2008). Collective Bargaining and the public sector. *Journal of Public Administration, 43*(2), 191-202.

FitGerald, P., & Seale, O. (2016). Between a Rock and a Hard Place: University Management and the #FEESMUSTFALL Campaign. In Fees-Must-Fall: Student Revolt, Decolonization and Governance in South Africa (pp. 235-255). Johannesburg: Wits University Press.

Freire, P. (1972). *Pedagogy of the oppressed*. Punguin Books.

Guattari, F. (2005). *The three Ecologies*. London: Continuum.

Jeffery, A. (2010). *Chasing the rainbow: South Africa's Move from Mandela to Zuma*. Johannesburg: South African Institute of Race Relations.

Johnson, K., & Jacobs, S. (Eds.). (2012). *Encyclopedia of South Africa. Scottville*. University of KwaZulu-Natal Press.

Johnson, P. (2013). The passive revolution and the post-apartheid university-Black Skin, White Masks. In Beyond the Apartheid University: Critical voices on Transformation in the university sector (pp. 55-68). University of Fort Hare Press.

Kretzmann, J. P., & McKnight, J. L. (1993). *Building Communities from the Inside Out: A Path toward finding and Mobilising a community's asset*. Chicago: ACTA Publications.

Maake, N. (2011). *Barbarism in Higher Education: Once Upon a Time in a University*. Johannesburg: Ekaam Books CC.

Makgoba, M. W., & Chetty, C. (2010). The History and context of Higher Education in South Africa post-1994. In The Creation of the University of KwaZulu-Natal: Reflections on a Merger and Transformation Experience (pp. 1-23). Excel Books.

Mamdani, M. (1989). *Social movements and constitutionalism in the African context.* Centre for Basic Research Working Paper 2, Centre for Basic Research.

Marwala, T. (2018, March 25). The fourth industrial revolution. *The Sunday Independent*, p. 17.

Marwala, T. (2018, June 24). Will AI affect our standard of living. The Sunday Independent, p. 15.

Mbigi, L., & Maree, J. (2005). *Ubuntu: The Spirit of African Transformation Management*. Randburg: Knowres Publishing.

Minogue, K. (2005). The concept of a university. Transaction.

Mpofu-Walsh, S. (2017). *Democracy & Delusion: 10 Myths in South Africa Politics*. Cape Town: Tafelberg.

National Development Plan (NDP). (2011). *National Development Plan; Vision for 2030*. Pretoria: National Planning Commission.

Nengwekhulu, R. H. (2009). Public service delivery challenges facing South African public service. *Journal of Public Administration.*, *44*(20), 341–363.

Noxon, J. (2011). *Higher Education and the Public good: Imagining the University*. London: Continuum.

Picard, L. A. (2005). *The State of the State: Institutional Transformation Capacity and Political Change in South Africa*. Johannesburg: Wits University Press.

Pillay, P. (2016). Financing of Universities: Promoting Equity or Reinforcing Inequality. In S. Booysen (Ed.), *Fees Must Fall: Student Revolt, Decolonization and Governance in South Africa* (pp. 256–268). Johannesburg: Wits University Press. doi:10.18772/22016109858.17

Ramphele, M. (2008). *Laying Ghosts to rest in South Africa: Dilemmas of the Transformation in South Africa*. Cape Town: Tafelberg.

Sehume, J. (2018). Solving poverty, unemployment and inequality. *The Sunday Independent*, *24*(June), 15.

Sen, A. (1999). *Development as freedom*. New York: Albert Knopf.

Senge, P. M. (2006). *The Fifth Discipline: The Art & Practice of the Learning Organisation*. London: Random House Business Books.

Stone, D. (2012). Agents of Knowledge. In D. Levi-Faur (Ed.), *The Oxford Handbook of Governance* (pp. 338–352). Oxford, UK: Oxford University Press.

United Nations Development Programme (UNDP). (1990). *The Nature of States Parties Obligations*. Oxford University Press.

United Nations Development Programme (UNDP). (2000). *South Africa: Transformation for Human Development*. Pretoria: UNDP.

Uys, L., De Kadt, E., Bawa, A., & Mazibuko, F. (2010). 'Core business (Teaching/ Research /Community Engagement). In M. Makgoba & J. C. Mubangizi (Eds.), *The Creation of the University of KwaZulu-Natal: Reflections on a Merger and Transformation Experience* (pp. 177–198). New Delhi: Excel Books.

Venetoulis, J. (2001). Assessing the ecological impact of a university: The ecological footprint for the University of Redlands. *International Journal of Sustainability in Higher Education*, *2*(2), 180–196. doi:10.1108/14676370110388381

ADDITIONAL READING

Barnett, R. (2015). *Understanding the University: Institution, idea, possibilities* (1st ed.). London: Routledge. doi:10.4324/9781315678245

Barnett, R. (2017). *The Ecological University: A Feasible Utopia* (1st ed.). London: Routledge. doi:10.4324/9781315194899

Barnett, R. (2017). *Thinking and Rethinking the University: The selected works of Ronald Barnett* (1st ed.). London: Routledge.

Barnett, R., & Napoli, R. D. (2009). *Wisdom in the University* (1st ed.). London: Routledge.

KEY TERMS AND DEFINITIONS

Developmental University: A university that orientated on development in its approach especially when executing its core business of teaching and learning, research and community engagement or community service.

Ecological University: It is a university that embraces changes exerted by immediate and broader environment for it to stay relevant and further respond to the needs arising from such environments.

University of KwaZulu-Natal: It is a South African university which comprises of five campus and has been created in 2004 after the merger between the former Universities of Durban Westville and Natal.

University of Technology: It is not a conventional university, but a university that offers technological career directed educational programs, focuses on innovative problem-solving research, and engages with government/business/industry with communities as end users.

Chapter 5
The Knowledge Society and Entrepreneurship Within the Higher Education Institutions in Mexico

Miguel Angel Mendoza Pérez
https://orcid.org/0000-0002-4409-3312
Instituto Politécnico Nacional, Mexico

Ingrid Yadibel Cuevas Zuñiga
Instituto Politécnico Nacional, Mexico

María del Rocío Soto Flores
Instituto Politécnico Nacional, Mexico

Susana Asela Garduño Román
Instituto Politécnico Nacional, Mexico

ABSTRACT

Knowledge has been an implied part of all social organizations, since it allows the progress and the discovery of new techniques and technologies to put up new activities that are not easily replicated by rivals. The chapter aims to show that institutions of higher education support the society of knowledge in Mexico for entrepreneurship through an analysis of the programs that are taught in the two public universities in the country. The structure of the chapter will be organized into three sections: 1) the knowledge of society and its relation with institutions of higher education, 2) the generation of entrepreneurship in higher education institutions, and 3) the society of knowledge and entrepreneurship in institutions of higher education in Mexico.

DOI: 10.4018/978-1-5225-8461-2.ch005

INTRODUCTION

The term "knowledge society" was first used in the United States of America and in the European Union (Breton, 2005). These countries were pioneers in evolving from an information society into a knowledge-based society using the technoscience as the tool to produce and disseminate information.

Knowledge is managed through the intellectual capital: acquired knowledge, competencies and aptitudes. It is obtained by means of training and education within the Higher Education Institutions (HEI), which are a key element to support the knowledge society, as they are equipped to produce, transmit, disseminate, and build upon knowledge.

According to Roca (2010), intellectual capital "is the combination of resources and human, organizational activities, and the relationships within an organization. Including knowledge, capabilities, experiences and employees' abilities, R&D, organizational practices, processes, systems, data bases, and the company's intellectual property rights; and all resources linked to the society's external relationships. This mélange of resources and intangible activities allows an organization to transform a mix of material, financial and human resources into a system capable of creating value to the stakeholders. The intangible, to become part of the intellectual capital, should be part of the internal organization".

Knowledge has been an implicit part (Dinu, 2005) of all social organizations, it facilitates progress through the discovery of new technology and techniques to perform activities difficult to replicate by competitors. The knowledge society is formed when an economy and its activities take awareness, including knowledge, as part of a strategy, favoring the intellectual capital and all it represents, leading to a new development adaptation resulting in the Forth Industrial Revolution. To accomplish this, knowledge management "is one of many components of good management in the knowledge-based society" (Adhikari, 2010).

According to Adhikari's work (2010) the responsibility to produce new knowledge, to train, and to transfer experience to all the society components, as well as to manage knowledge (intellectual capital and technology) belongs to the Higher Education Institutions.

The same author explains that there are two types of knowledge: the explicit and the tacit. The former is expressed in numbers and words and is easy to transmit; the latter includes intuitions and hunches, acquired skills and 'know-how', that can be more difficult to communicate. The universities maintain a responsibility towards the society, for which they need to:

- Have long term goals promoting the critical reasoning and diversity of thought through education and research;

- Promote the role of university autonomy in research to guarantee academic freedom, high quality teaching, improvement of abilities, and transmission and dissemination of knowledge;
- Consolidate alliances with other stakeholders;
- Strengthen local and regional bonds in betterment of society (European University Association, 2003).

According to the EUA, the universities in Europe are essential to achieve a knowledge-based continent, captured in the 'Lisbon Strategy', seeking to make their society "the most competitive and dynamic knowledge-based economy in the world, capable of sustainable economic growth with more and better jobs and greater social cohesion" (European Commitee of the Regions, 2018).

Thus, these institutions play a key role in the development of a society, forming quality intellectual capital by educating students, who are a key factor in knowledge production. In addition, they are sources of motivation for the learners to take advantage of this knowledge and increase the entrepreneurship index based on intellectual capital with a direct and positive impact in the society (Adhikari, 2010) using new technologies, ideas, and techniques to obtain an economic growth in a society.

The acquired knowledge (Carreon & Melgoza, 2012), "creates continuous innovation and permits to develop competitive advantages." These two concepts encourage the entrepreneurship and new forms of doing business, generating new products, new ways to solve problems, by taking the base of new learned experiences and the information received through the universities.

However, the innovation index in Latin America and the Caribbean shows a delay in this area. The Economic Commission for Latin America and the Caribbean (ECLAC) published that the delay is due to the lack of technology as consequence of the economic structure in the region, but it also mentions that there are other factors that limit innovation such as the scarce participation and performance of academic institutions (Rivas & Sebastian, 2014).

That is why developing countries choose to form alliances with other institutions to promote the production, transmission, dissemination and exploitation of knowledge, in order to have a sustainable impact in the society, the economy and the natural environment. In Mexico, a key ally for the academic institutions is the National Council for Science and Technology (abbreviated CONACYT), which serves as a responsible agent to champion science and technology policies in the country (SEGOB, 2018).

It should also be mentioned that in developing countries, like Mexico, even when they lag behind OECD (Organization for Economic and Co-operation Development) members regarding their capabilities to introduce innovation in the markets, they have had a significant growth in the entrepreneurial dynamism in the last decade.

In the frame of a renewed interest in the knowledge production and exploitation, and the innovation and creation of innovative startups with high growth potential (OCDE, 2015), Mexico has been formulating strategies to disseminate knowledge to support the economic growth and the construction of a knowledge-based society.

In this sense, the Higher Education Institutions have driven the entrepreneurship in the teaching and motivating students to create their own businesses in which they could apply the knowledge acquired during their education. For entrepreneurs (World Economic Forum, 2014), "there are three pillars to be considered as the most important to obtain growth: accessible markets, human capital and labor, and financing". One of these "most important pillars", human capital and labor, has its foundation in the acquired training in the classrooms of a HEI, where the knowledge that nourishes the knowledge-based society is produced.

This chapter proposal has as objective: to study the Higher Education Institutions in Mexico that cultivate the knowledge-based society in Mexico and aim for increased entrepreneurship, by analyzing the programs taught in the two main public universities in the country. The chapter structure will be organized in three parts: 1) The knowledge-based society and its relationship with the Higher Education Institutions; 2) the production of entrepreneurship within the Higher Education Institutions; and 3) the knowledge-based society and the entrepreneurship in the Higher Education Institutions.

THE KNOWLEDGE-BASED SOCIETY AND ITS RELATIONSHIP WITH THE HIGHER EDUCATION INSTITUTIONS

The different societies developed around the world change, adjust, and evolve according to the needs they face on a daily base, and it is reflected in the culture, in the economics, in the goods and services, in the technology, in the information and in the knowledge, which characterize and give life to a society. Each change, and social evolution is named "revolution", and each one takes different tools to transform the primary resources into benefits. It is recognized the agricultural, industrial, information and knowledge revolution, the latter resulting in a system known as "Knowledge Society" (KS).

To define the KS the platform Complexity Lab (2018) uses the frame DIKW (Data, Information, Knowledge, and Wisdom), which is a pyramid that upwards results in wisdom or knowledge application, and downwards analyzes each component of the pyramid.

Saša Baškarada and Andy Koronios (2013) make an analysis to define this frame and they conclude that "wisdom is the ability to increase effectiveness, intelligence is the ability to increase efficiency, knowledge is the know-how, and it allows the transformation of data into instructions, the information provides responses to questions such as: who, what, where and when, and the data are symbols representing properties of objects, events, and the environment, product of observation"

In their article there is an argument about the meaning of knowledge and it is mentioned that "it is tacit, subjective and it involves a person (with knowledge), and anything that could be articulated or become tangible out of the human mind is just information"; in other words, "a bookcase or a computer may keep a lot of information without knowledge" (Baškarada & Koronios, 2013).

Knowledge represents part of a context that can be applied to achieve goals based on information. Breton (2005) defines the knowledge society as "the production, dissemination, and use of knowledge, competences, and cognitive practices, dominated by social groups that recognize and claim them (through research and development, services, tech professionals, etc.) to yield an individual or collective, economic, social and cultural performance".

Each person, as part of the society, is fundamental to make a KS a real thing, without it, it's only possible to have information; at the same time the individual is the engine of knowledge and competences as an asset and primary resource for a social and economic development (Lovece, 2009). Lovece (2009), defines the KS as the society "that provides stimulus and allows its members, groups and institutions to continuously improve their knowledge, abilities and behavior. The education is anchored to the culture as main condition of existence, and it is considered important in the social institutions' programs. Further to the educational systems, other agencies are involved such as the massive media, syndicates, industries, commerce, sanitary services, and others".

The sectors that strengthen the KS are:

1. Research and Development of new technologies and products.
2. Education.
3. Royalties and licenses.
4. Advisory and strategic management.
5. Business services.
6. Financial services.
7. Computer services.
8. Communications (development and commercialization).
9. Personal, cultural and leisure services.
10. Design (Leal, Úbelis, & Berzina, 2015).

The World Bank (2008) considers that the KS in Mexico is a paradox; on one side, the country has grown at a technological level and obtained high productivity through transnational enterprises and matured industries based on knowledge, technology and infrastructure transfer; and on the other side, this progress has few links with the rest of the economy. There is knowledge, however, it is not available for everyone.

Adhikari (2010) alludes that the responsibility to create new knowledge, train and transfer experience to the society agents, as well as to be the manager of knowledge (intellectual capital and technology) falls on the Higher Education Institutions (HEI), and Mexico has a week educative performance compared to the OECD members and a lower graduated rate from the HEI than Argentina (40%), Brazil (57%), and Chile (35%) (Kuznetsov & Dahlman, 2008).

With that said, it is inferred that the KS in Mexico is less developed than it is in countries where graduated students from a HEI rate is higher, and it can be confirmed through the knowledge economy index, affirming that there is an essential relationship between knowledge production and the universities to develop a KS. Governments are financing the "national prosperity by promoting new lucrative technologies along with the universities to become an economic, social and cultural engine in the regions" (Välimaa & Hoffman, 2008).

Individuals as part of the society, are in charged of analyzing the available information and build upon knowledge. To complete this task the HEI offer the required tools and environment to produce, transmit, disseminate, and spread the knowledge and competences via a good knowledge management, even though it is discussed that these institutions don't keep the sole right on the management; knowledge can have origin from different organizations and institutions, the way it happens in a triple helix interaction: universities, government and industry (Välimaa & Hoffman, 2008).

A good knowledge management by the HEI implies supplying technological tools to analyze, research and spread information, in addition of the accurate training to handle and complement its application to achieve knowledge. Referring to the KS, this knowledge application should have a favorable impact in all members of a society and be available throughout the information society.

In order to boost the KS, there should be a strong university organization at different levels: at the upper level, promoting efficient operation; and at the system level, working with the stakeholders with whom they are interconnected (European University Association, 2003).

Every institutional mission should be differentiated through specialization within each HEI, offering various quality programs to students, keeping a complementary network on research and teaching, which will result in more university enrollment for a bigger part of the population, resulting in an advancement towards a mature KS.

The individuals of a society acquire tools and develop knowledge by enrolling to a HEI, and in exchange the institutions make knowledge part of an economy and part of the social strategic activities; they contextualize knowledge by adapting them to the needs of a society gaining a competitive advantage in return.

THE PRODUCTION OF ENTREPRENEURSHIP WITHIN THE HIGHER EDUCATION INSTITUTIONS.

According to the Swedish publication on "Entrepreneurship, Innovation and Economic Growth. Past Experiences, Current Knowledge and Policy Implications" (2010), there isn't a specific definition for the word "entrepreneurship" for what it becomes subjective, however it meets certain characteristics such as the embrace of market (and/or social) opportunities to satisfy needs implementing new, or different, actions to achieve goals, which doesn't always mean creating but designing or using the tools in inventive ways; with an uncertain rate of risk that can be measure as activities move forward; by means of the application of cognitive skills and by using the creativity of the individuals.

Same story happens with the definition of the word "entrepreneur". "Everyone is an entrepreneur only when they actually make new technic and activity blends, and this characteristic is lost as soon as a business is created, established, and handled as any other person would do it" (Braunerhjelm, 2010). An entrepreneur shows characteristics like: a) innovative, finds and create new opportunities; b) works under uncertainty and fulfills planning, production, management, and marketing processes without carrying for the risk undertaken, which doesn't mean it isn't considered; and c) seeks profitability in the economic markets.

Entrepreneurship is born based on pillars that shape the suitable ecosystem for opportunities exploitation. The main pillars are: accessible markets, human capital and labor, and financing (World Economic Forum, 2014). In order to increase and develop the mentioned entrepreneurship and entrepreneur characteristics, the knowledge management institutions and any other institution that boost an efficient macro-economic frame and that stimulate the human behavior (entrepreneurial spirit), are part of the entrepreneurial scenario (Braunerhjelm, 2010).

Knowing this, the HEI generate a significant impact as they are cognitive abilities and knowledge management institutions aiming for entrepreneurship. In Mexico two of the most important national public HEI are: The Instituto Politécnico Nacional (abbreviated IPN) and The Universidad Nacional Autónoma de México (abbreviated UNAM). For both institutions the entrepreneurial matter is relevant, for what they manage programs and areas to promote it: The Technology-based Enterprise Incubator Center (abbreviated CIEBT) and the PoliEmprende program, both from the IPN; and the entrepreneurs and innovation program from the Innovation and Development Coordination (abbreviated CID) from the UNAM.

In Table 1, it is shown the different program characteristics with entrepreneurial approach from the mentioned institutions in Mexico. It is detailed the objective of each program and the corresponding body coordinator. It includes the services offered and the sub-programs in which the entrepreneurs could enroll, as well as the web sites of each party.

In the Table 2, there is a list of remarkable successful cases from the business incubator created by the entrepreneurship and innovation programs, taken from the web sites of each institution (CIEBT, IPN) (CID, UNAM).

In 2018 Samsung along with the CIEBT from the IPN organized the second edition of the 'Polytechnic Entrepreneurship Award' "with the purpose of boosting and recognizing entrepreneurial talent within the education institution" (Samsung NewsRoom Mexico, 2018). The paradox is that from the participating and winning institutions at high educations and postgraduate level, 90% were represented by engineering, meaning there is an important work to do within the institutions with administration and social approach.

The entrepreneurship generation in the HEI should keep the goal of creating a productive entrepreneurial system, with a real impact in the society, in the economy and in the natural environment of a country, making it possible through the students (future entrepreneurs) exploring new opportunities and adding more value to new products and services (Stam & Spigen, 2016).

In an entrepreneurial ecosystem the HEI are part of the fundamental institutions that strengthen the human capital and the entrepreneurial culture, at the same time, these two items support the HEI growth and development. However, what really matters is the students and their creativity to contribute with new ideas and increase the intellectual capacity in a community (Manson & Ross, 2013).

The effort and aim of the entrepreneurial programs from the IPN and the UNAM reinforce these premises, motivating the students to be creative end express their ideas to build upon business opportunities. Each institution is a cornerstone for this possible technology-based entrepreneurship.

Table 1. Characteristics of programs with entrepreneurial approach from the public institutions in Mexico

HEI	IPN	UNAM
Entrepreneurship body	The Technology-based Enterprise Incubator Center (CIEBT)	Innovation and Development Coordination (CID)
Objective:	Create and consolidate innovative polytechnic enterprises with social and economic impact, resulting from the academic work by strengthening the entrepreneurial culture.	Generate bigger development opportunities for the university community through the creation of enterprises and new business development.
Services:	• Business plan creation advisory. • Management advisory. • Marketing advisory. • Graphic and industrial design. • Productive process advisory. • Final good development advisory. • Financial advisory. • Technology connection. • Training. • Legal advisory. • Intellectual property. • Financing resources links. • Informatic and computer services. • Administrative services.	• Training. • Technology-based enterprises incubator. • InnovaUNAM. • Support programs. • Entrepreneurs magazine. • CDE-CANACINTRA. • Business plan creation advisory. • Legal, financial and fiscal advisory. • Graphic and industrial design, marketing, management, strategic planning, production process advisory. • Business plan presentation development to investors training. • Financing and business resources links. • Business hosting. • High-Tech installations and specialized labs links.
Programs:	• Entrepreneur. • Business person. • Investor. • Ally. • Mentor. • Innovative PoliEmprende. • Engineer Entrepreneur. • Ideas Lab. • Poli incubator route.	• Entrepreneurs. • Business incubator. • Applied research and technology development. • Test, analysis, and lab use. • Process development.
Addressed to:	Polytechnic community.	University community.
	Transversal and vertical system addressed to all educational levels: medium-high, high and postgraduate.	
Web site:	https://www.ipn.mx/CIEBT/Paginas/Inicio.aspx	http://www.innova.unam.mx/

Source: Self-elaborated based on the information available on the web sites: CIEBT (IPN) and CID (UNAM)

Table 2. Successful cases from business incubators

Successful Cases	
IPN	**UNAM**
JuluMed aka FixYouMx Personalized method to correct cranial deformations on babies. Design cranial orthoses.	**Bleps Vision** Research and development, and commercialization of technology for visual health.
Child Alert Portable device to alert and to supervise minors through an app.	**Medi Print** Creation of personalized medical devices through 3D printing.
Renovart Herbalist oil to facilitate cartilage restoration on joints.	**Inmersys** Software developer of augmented reality.
Mecatronica Voxel Design and develop devices and software for 3D printing.	**Virmagyx** Visual tools by implementing 3D printing. 3D environments.

Source: Self-elaborated based on the information available in the CIEBT (IPN), the CID (UNAM) (JuluMed, 2018), (Medi-Print, 2018), (Inmersys, 2018)

THE KNOWLEDGE-BASED SOCIETY AND THE ENTREPRENEURSHIP IN THE HIGHER EDUCATION INSTITUTIONS.

Most of the technological achievements and advancement on the last decades, besides being remarkable and be followed by economic growth, have a relation "knowledge-growth" and "entrepreneurship-growth" keeping a perception of the correlation entrepreneurship, innovation, and knowledge (Braunerhjelm, 2010).

This technological progress is linked to "unprecedented and simultaneous advances in artificial intelligence (AI), robotics, the internet of things, autonomous vehicles, 3D printing, nanotechnology, biotechnology, material science, energy storage, quantum computing and others are redefining industries, blurring traditional boundaries, and creating new opportunities. We have dubbed this the Forth Industrial Revolution, or the industry 4.0, (Brown-Martin, 2017) and it is fundamentally changing the way we live, work and relate to one another" (Skilton & Hovsepian, 2018)

This Industry 4.0 can be nourished in the interconnection between KS, entrepreneurship, and HEI, deeming that without the human capital, there wouldn't be any kind of relationship, nor knowledge creation or innovation. Knowledge is produced, disseminated, applied, and spread in the HEI, and they are the institutions that train, educate, and boost students as future entrepreneurs.

The HEI are knowledge managers and provide the needed tools to boost a KS spreading skills, reasoning, know-how, and information to obtain better performance and cultural, economic and social improvement. It's within the HEI where the social and market opportunities make the most of them to achieve entrepreneurship.

The tools provided by the HEI activate the creativity on the students to apply it in different ways from the traditional encouraging innovation, moving forward to an industry revolution.

And even when the universities don't act in solo to promote the entrepreneurship and knowledge, but they are supported by the government and the industry, it is there where the human capital with potential is found and where the tools are ready to be used by their imagination and allow growth and development by means of knowledge and entrepreneurship.

It's a real thing to say that in Mexico there is a lack of continuous work and effort to disseminate the student's knowledge and encourage them to provide ideas and to participate actively in the entrepreneurship and innovation programs that already exist; however, the successful cases start to be numerous and to be recognized national and world wide. For instance, the Instituto Politécnico Nacional has created a National Lab for Water Treatment (LNAgua) in order to R&D technology for water source systems, water collection, treatment and purification (Instituto Politecnico Nacional, 2019). And students from the same institute have eliminated the 100% of the human papillomavirus on 29 patients in Mexico City (El Economista, 2019)

Additionally, it is important to increase the graduated rate from the HEI to let more curiosity be part of the new business entrepreneurship, and make the students feel confident when completing the knowledge generation and application process. "The institutions and knowledge that govern the dissemination and knowledge maintenance, seems to be the most representative aspect of innovative entrepreneurship. The individuals with certain abilities and characteristics tend to be more committed in an entrepreneurial process distinguished by research, uncertainty and randomness. A highlight is the involvement of individuals in continuous experiments, consenting to try different ideas and models before finding the right one" (Braunerhjelm, 2010).

This experimentation is important in all education levels and in the knowledge areas, to vary the entrepreneurship in different subjects, industries, sectors, and knowledge. That's how the supportive programs add strength to the entrepreneurial ecosystem in Mexico and readiness for future jobs carried out by the new industrial revolution. According to an inform from 2016 by the Economic World Forum, 65% of children starting their education are being prepared for jobs that don't exist just yet. (World Economic Forum, 2016)

For the HEI it represents added value to have, keep, and develop spaces, programs, and workshops that allow the interaction between different bodies capable to create knowledge, and the exchange of ideas to appreciate different points of view and technic mélanges, and experiences and obtain a new or different result. And in the same way in which there is an inner interaction in the university, the interactions with all the external stakeholders gives an opportunity to entrepreneurship.

The entrepreneurial ecosystem matures according to a country's economic dynamism, universities, public policies, infrastructure, markets, and all services supporting the creativity application (Stam & Spigen, 2016). Developing an entrepreneurial culture will validate and boost the entrepreneurial ecosystem. Its creation and maturity depend on the institutions with access to knowledge.

The HEI have the faculty to encourage the students to question the social, economic, and environmental performance, to be able to give ideas and prove their results through research and development. Risk fear is an obstacle for the Mexican society. In Mexico, only 35 people out of 10 thousand of the economically active population follows a financial culture, which is a very low number in comparison to the 60 people out of 100 in the United States (CONDUSEF, 2018) and the culture fomented by the universities has the responsibility to change that behavior, and educate with fundamentals for the entrepreneurship adapting to the new demands and world necessities.

What is coming in Mexico is a "hard" and long way towards the KS. Height Education Institutions will need to provide the tools to adapt to new industrial revolutions in order to obtain real entrepreneurship, and to prepare the society for the new upcoming jobs to facilitate the betterment of the entrepreneurial ecosystem, otherwise the country will enter a technological stagnation.

Finally, from the analysis and literature revision on this work, it is inferred that the KS is moving on a delayed construction and spread over the world economies; for which the HEI will continue to maintain a prevailing role and a social responsibility as the main knowledge generators and human capital trainers, in order to achieve development and betterment of the KS. Thus, the Knowledge Society is imagined equitable, contributing to the creation of societies favored by the knowledge generation and dissemination, and the new technologies, to improve the economic and social progress, which unfortunately, is still unequal in the world societies.

CONCLUSION

The Higher Education Institutions are the managers that allow the knowledge creation, transmission, dissemination and application; in addition, they train the human capital that use the knowledge to build upon entrepreneurship and, given access to a worldwide knowledge society.

The knowledge society is strengthened by the results given by the HEI and by the knowledge application to obtain new sources of information and successful experiments for the entrepreneurship, and by the participation on the Industry 4.0 development. The HEI encourage and have a catalyst role for entrepreneurship managing business incubator programs and business bodies, like the CIEBT from the IPN and the CID from the UNAM. They also reinforce their structure with the relations negotiated with third parties like the industry, the government, and the society, for instance, the work done by the IPN and Samsung during the project "Polytechnic Entrepreneurship Award".

This award made visible the commitment that the Institution needs to obtain more participation from all the knowledge areas and not only from engineering. Moving forward in the entrepreneurship subject, the universities will favor the knowledge society maturity in Mexico, motivating the students and encouraging an entrepreneurial culture for the knowledge application at an economic, social, cultural, and environmental level for the human benefit.

REFERENCES

Adhikari, D. R. (2010). Knowledge management in academic institutions. *International Journal of Educational Management, 24*(2), 94–104. doi:10.1108/09513541011020918

Baškarada, S., & Koronios, A. (2013). Data, Information, Knowledge, Wisdom (DIKW): A Semiotic Theoretical and Empirical Exploration of the Hierarchy and its Quality Dimension. *AJIS. Australasian Journal of Information Systems, 18*(1), 5–24. doi:10.3127/ajis.v18i1.748

Braunerhjelm, P. (2010). *Entrepreneurship, Innovation and Economic Growth. Past experiences, current knowledge and policy implications*. Stockholm: Swedish Entrepreneurship Forum and The Royal Institute of Technology.

Breton, P. (2005). La "société de la connaissance": Généalogie d'une double réduction. *Education et Societé*, 45–57.

Brown-Martin, G. (2017). *L'education et la quatrième revolution industrielle*. Ontario: Groupe Média TFO.

Carreon, H., & Melgoza, R. (2012). México hacia una sociedad del conocimiento. Nóesis. *Revista de Ciencias Sociales y Humanidades, 21*(41), 122–135. doi:10.20983/noesis.2012.1.5

CID. UNAM. (2018). *Innovación UNAM*. Retrieved from http://www.innova.unam.mx/

CIEBT. IPN. (2018). *Incubadora de empresas*. Retrieved from https://www.ipn.mx/CIEBT/Paginas/Inicio.aspx

Complexity Labs. (2018). *YouTube*. Retrieved from Knowledge Society Explained: https://www.youtube.com/watch?v=mU3pvZHv-dE

CONDUSEF. (2018). *Pierde el miedo*. Retrieved from Condusef: https://www.condusef.gob.mx/Revista/index.php/inversion/otros/303-pierde-el-miedo

Dinu, M. (2005). *What is knowledge society?* ResearchGate.

El Economista. (2019, Feb 4). *Científicos del IPN eliminan 100% del virus del papiloma humano*. Retrieved from https://www.eleconomista.com.mx/arteseideas/Cientificos-del-IPN-eliminan-100-del-virus-del-papiloma-humano-20190204-0058.html

European Commitee of the Regions. (2018). *The Lisbon Strategy in short*. Retrieved from Europe Monitor 2020 Platform: https://portal.cor.europa.eu/europe2020/Profiles/Pages/TheLisbonStrategyinshort.aspx

European University Association. (2003). *Response to the Communication From the Commission, The Role of the Universities in the Europe of Knowledge*. European University Association.

Inmersys. (2018, Oct 13). *Inicio*. Retrieved from https://www.inmersys.com/

Instituto Politecnico Nacional. (2019, Feb 15). *Pone en marcha IPN primer laboratorio nacional del agua*. Retrieved from https://www.ipn.mx/CCS/comunicados/ver-comunicado.html?y=2019&n=18

JuluMed. (2018, Oct 13). *Inicio*. Retrieved from http://julumed.com/nuestrocasco

Kuznetsov, Y., & Dahlman, C. (2008). *Mexico's transition to a knowledge-based economy. Challenges and opportunities*. Washington, DC: The International Bank for Reconstruction and Development / The World Bank.

Leal, F. W., Úbelis, A., & Berzina, D. (2015). *Sustainable development, knowledge society and smart future manufacturing technologies*. Springer.

Lovece, S. (2009). *E-Learning e società della conoscenza*. Bologna: Università di Bologna.

Manson, C., & Ross, B. (2013). *Entrepreuneurial Ecosystems and Growth Oriented Entrepreuneurship*. The Hague: OECD LEED Programme and the Dutch Ministry of Economic Affairs.

Medi-Print. (2018, Oct 13). *Inicio*. Retrieved from https://mediprint3d.com.mx/

OCDE. (2015). *Start-up America Latina. Construyendo un futuro innovador*. París: OCDE.

Rivas, G., & Sebastian, R. (2014). *Nuevas instituciones para la innovación: Prácticas y experiencias en América Latina. Santiago de Chile: CEPAL; Alis*. Cooperación Alemana.

Ronca, C. (2010). *Società della Conoscenza, sviluppo locale e competitività delle imprese. Modelli e metriche di valorizzazione degli intangibili di impresa*. Roma: Fondazione Adriano Olivetti.

Samsung NewsRoom Mexico. (2018). *Samsung y el IPN presentan la edición 2018 del concurso Soluciones para el Futuro*. Retrieved from https://news.samsung.com/mx/samsung-y-el-ipn-presentan-la-edicion-2018-del-concurso-soluciones-para-el-futuro

SEGOB. (2018). *El Conacyt.* Retrieved from Conacyt: https://www.conacyt.gob.mx/index.php/el-conacyt

Skilton, M., & Hovsepian, F. (2018). *The Forth Industrial Revolution. Responding to the impact of Artificial Intelligence on Business*. Palgrave Macmillan.

Stam, E., & Spigen, B. (2016). *Entrepreneurial Ecosystems*. Utrecht: Utrecht School of Economics.

Välimaa, J., & Hoffman, D. (2008). *Knowledge society discourse and higher education*. Jyvaskyla: Springer. doi:10.100710734-008-9123-7

World Economic Forum. (2014). *Entrepreneurial Ecosystems Around the Globe and Early-Stage Company Growth Dynamics*. Geneva: World Economic Forum.

World Economic Forum. (2016). *The Future of Jobs, Employment, Skills, and Workforce Strategy for the Forth Industrial Revolution.* Global Challenge Insight Report. Author.

Chapter 6
Towards Advancing Human-Centered Intellectual Scholarship Through University-Community Partnership

Ndwakhulu Stephen Tshishonga
University of Kwa-Zulu Natal, South Africa

ABSTRACT

This chapter explores the potential benefits and opportunities for institutions of higher learning (HEIs) to advance human-centered intellectual scholarship through institutionalizing university-community partnerships. The chapter argues that the success of these partnerships are not only depended on respect and mutual understanding but also on collective envisioning by all partners in forging both the strategic and plan of action. Paying lip-service to community-civil engagement or service-learning-deprived students, universities' and respective learning communities generate transformative knowledge and use knowledge as a strategy to deal with their problems. The chapter uses service learning or community engagement-related programs and projects from different universities as case studies in South Africa. Informed opinions from experts from academic institutions and students will be engaged to extract primary data.

DOI: 10.4018/978-1-5225-8461-2.ch006

INTRODUCTION

Community-university partnerships have emerged as vital arrangements for teaching, research and practice (Butterfiled & Soska, 2004). These partnerships emanate from increasing pressure for HEIs to assist in addressing challenges faced by communities through linkages. Institutions of higher learning have ceased to operate as ivory towers detached from reality. Through university-community partnerships, universities assume new public purposes with direct links to societal improvement and its transformation (Fisher, Fabricant, & Simmons, 2004). Within institutions of higher learning, partnerships take different forms, names and shapes. Depending on the institutions, the environment and the challenges at hand, phrases such as civic engagement, service learning, community engagement, HEIs social responsibility are fundamental. Apart from teaching and learning, and research, community engagement or service learning forms one of the core business of the university. Service learning is defined as a form of experiential education in which students engage in activities that address human and community needs together with structured opportunities intentionally designed to promote student learning and development (Jacoby, 1996; 5). Thus, service learning by its design involves partners within and across the institutions such as schools, government departments, CBOs and NGOs, private service providers and community members. Community-university-partnerships describe relationships that exist between universities and communities and such partnerships involve collaborative processes that enable engaged stakeholders to combine their knowledge, skills and resources for them to accomplish more together than they can individually (Jacoby, 2003).

This chapter argues that the successes of these partnerships are not only dependent on respect and mutual understanding, but also on collective envisioning by all partners in forging both the strategic and plan of action. Paying lip-service to community-civil engagement or service learning deprived students, universities and respective communities from learning from each other, generate transformative knowledge and use knowledge as strategy to deal with their problems. The chapter uses service learning or community engagement related programmes and projects from different universities in South Africa as case studies. Informed opinions from experts from academic institutions and students were engaged to extract primary data.

COMMUNITY-UNIVERSITY PARTNERSHIP

Community-university partnership interface the grounding concepts of community, university and the notion of partnership itself. The partnership arrangement consists of community and university as essential and integral concepts that warrant both theoretical and pragmatic explorations. In the context of this chapter, community entails an external physical entity geographically located outside the university community. Different fields of study have defined the concept of community in different ways. Geographers, traditionally view community as a geographical space occupied by people residing collectively in a particular area. This understanding of community subscribed to Tonnies's concept of 'Gemeinschaft' often found in traditional societies with natural affection and mutual respect as common features (in Heywood, 2000, p. 122). This definition conjures images of the traditional African village or the urban slum or squatter settlements (Midgley, 1986, p. 24). The concept of community has since evolved to include 'shared interests and needs or in terms of deprivation and disadvantage' (De Beer & Swanepoel, 2013, p. 49). In social terms, communities of interest are emerging dominantly, thus transcending those traditional communities defined graphically based on place-based location (Phillips & Pittman, 2015, p. 3). Togni (1996) underlines the concept of community with a cluster of people who interact daily in their place of residence, work and other primary activities. It is noted that either geographical or communities of interest, commonly share certain characteristics such as belonging, a recognisable community spirit, self-contained (Togni, 1996, p. 111), common identity based on bonds of comradeship, loyalty and duty (Heywood, 2013, p. 158). A plurality of interpretations has disrupted older definitions of community that once served as a powerful incentive for the building of strong social groups. (Tesoriero, 2010, p. 15). The chapter acknowledges that a community does not necessarily mean that the people share common values and characteristics or live in harmony. The notion of community can be misleading as there may be no consensus and those who have power may influence people's participation or lack of it (Tshishonga, 2018). Community can be an illusionary place which denies the collective experiences of other groups such as minority diasporic groups and groups of differing class, gender and sexual orientation which according to Swyngedouw (2011) can be considered exclusionary. As mentioned earlier, this chapter emphasises that community is not socially bound, nor is it contained in geographic units. It is not a homogeneous entity with a single and agreed interests. Thus, the chapter acknowledges that community is romanticised and can be a false reaction to uncertainties.

The second term that form part of the community-university partnership equation is the university. Universities are prevalently conceptualised as social institutions created with the core business of teaching, research and service. Universities both in the developed and developing nations assert themselves as agents in the business of knowledge production (Yakubu, 2017, p. 7). As institutions traditionally mandated to generate knowledge, researching and providing a variety of services to and in partnership with the community, Yakubu (2017) contends that universities should widen their mandate by translating such knowledge to benefit the society.

Universities are social institutions charged with the responsibilities of teaching and learning, conducting research and community engagement. Traditionally, these functions comprise of the core business of the university (Uys et al. 2010). Although teaching and research form the core business of the university, university are also expected to be responsive to the communities in its proximity. The trio functions of universities of teaching, research and community engagement underlie the traditional roles of universities. These functions help to define a university within the broader higher education institutions. From the developmental role, university is associated as auxiliary, self-governing institution, as instrument for development agenda and as engine of development (van Schalkwyk & Bailey, 2013, pp. 157-158). As such universities should be conceptualized as part of the broader institutions of higher learning designated to produce knowledge and disseminate such knowledge to a broader society. At the core of the notion of a university is the production of knowledge with scientific and scholastic rigour. In essence, a university is a community of scholars, people who apart from teaching and learning, they indulge in ground breaking research and further extend their scholarship through community or social engagement.

A university is an institution of higher learning where learning takes place (Brink, 2016: 115). Through institutions of higher learning, knowledge is generated and an environment for creativity and innovation is created to produce scholars and theorists. Marshall (1990: 1339) defines a university as an educational institution designed for instruction, examination or both, of students in many branches of advanced learning, conferring degrees in various faculties and often embodying colleges and similar institutions. Beyond being institutions of higher learning and custodian of knowledge, production and its dissemination, these knowledge-based institutions should also play an active role in helping individual citizens, governments and society as whole in their planning and managing of human capital. University is a community of students, academics and support staff with the core business of directly or indirectly engaging in the educational process (Mkhize, 2014, p. 108).

Historically, community-university partnerships variably manifested as 'service learning', 'civic or service engagement', 'community engagement', academic service learning or community-based learning, community service. For the purposes of this chapter and conceptualise community-university partnerships, some of the concepts warrant a theoretical exposition. More importantly, all these titles translate into collective engagement with communities, higher education institutions and service providers as partners in the delivery of service and knowledge production for the common good. Other institutions locate community-university partnership within the context of experiential learning such as 'out-of-class activities', volunteering, service add-ons, internships as fundamental components (Mooney & Edwards, 2001).

THE PLACE OF UNIVERSITIES IN SOUTH AFRICAN TRANSFORMATION AGENDA

In South Africa, universities are central in developing capable and committed human resources within the parameters of social transformation (Tshishonga, 2016). Higher education sector since 1994 was envisaged to transform itself in order to bring about broader societal transformation. As such, Ramphele (2008: 196) argues that higher education is the platform for the practice of high-level human and intellectual work and the training of current and future generations of professionals, scientists and technological experts. Universities are strategically positioned to advance human-centred intellectual capacity by imparting knowledge and educate society at large. Considering the discriminatory role the South African higher education played during apartheid, post-apartheid universities are challenged to offer transformed and competitive knowledge to all its students. This entails utilising education and institutions of higher education as part of redress, nation building and social cohesion through citizenship education. For this to happen, commitment to genuine transformation by all stakeholders would be needed. Students through #FeesMustFall campaign reminded South Africans that despite educational policies developed since the dawn of democracy, higher education institutions are still not accessible to the poor and disadvantaged (Mpofu-Walsh, 2017). For these knowledge-based institutions to contribute to knowledge economy and the fourth industrial revolution, Stone (2012, p. 347) argues that universities should be part of knowledge networks. Scholars such as Parmar (2002 cited in Stone, 2012, p. 347) views knowledge network as a system coordinated research, result dissemination and publication, intellectual exchange, and financing across national boundaries.

Universities and other tertiary institutions play a pivotal role in building the human resources and advancing knowledge and a responsible society. South Africa is still suffering from poor, unskilled and incompetent human resources despite twenty years of democracy. As evidenced through poor performance records regarding delivery of sustainable services, public sector is crippled by poorly skilled and incompetent civil servants. Nengwekhulu (2009, p. 351), however, notes that public service delivery failures should not be blamed only to skills deficiencies and shortages, but also to other critical factors. This situation is further aggravated by unfilled strategic posts across all the spheres of government which is also accompanied by a laissez faire type of leadership ill-equipped to take strategic decisions more particularly at managerial level. In this regard, Ramphele (2008) suggests that transformative leadership is crucial for the public sector to address the legacy of apartheid, service delivery backlogs, skills and state capacity constraints.

Human resource development aimed at empowering both the employees and the institution is essential since skilled and competent human resources become central in terms of bringing about lasting and positive changes. Human resource development in this context has the ultimate outcome of human betterment through achieving effective performance. Ferreira (2008: 204) advocates for a holistic approach towards the development of human resources that entail training, education, and staff rotation, attendance of workshops or conferences within a public sector. In addition, human resource development is associated with effective and efficient service delivery to the public and in particular poor communities who are wholly dependent on government institution (Ferreira, 2008: 205). This is in spite of the government public policies such as the Skills Development Act (1998) aimed at skilling the South African workforce. The white paper on Public Service Training and Education (1997) provides a policy foundation aimed at transforming the public service training and education into a dynamic, needs-based and proactive instrument which is still underperforming in South Africa.

Education as a tool for human development is fundamental to the South African society riddled by the dire need for skills, knowledge and competencies to run the country democracy and professionally. Given the Bantu history of apartheid, it is therefore no surprise that upon the advent of democracy as Picard (2005: 117) argues that 'Black people in the main were not equipped, either by education or by temperament for success in the new South Africa. Transforming higher education for human development rests on the imperative to 'enlarge people choices' and the process of enlarging people's choices according to UNDP (1990) but also entails empowering them to achieve their potential to lead fuller and more productive lives. Similarly to the human development paradigm to higher education transformation, the development of human capabilities and empowerment of people is central to participate in the development process (UNDP, 2000). According to UNDP (2000), transforming education for human development involves the creation and adherence of non-racialism, non-sexism, a unified system, democracy and redress. Education in this regard is linked to the broader transformative agenda of the South African society to enhance people's education for people's power.

More importantly, service learning has been elevated in the literature as pedagogical of tool and a teaching methodology that integrates academic learning's goals with a community experiences in order to produce community service (Robinsion & Green, 2011, p. 5). The authors identified three key characteristics, which underpin service learning, thus differentiating it from the traditional community service or volunteering. Firstly, service learning involves experiences aimed at meeting community needs. Second, service learning should benefit its stakeholders such as students by providing them with practical learning experiences. Through service learning intervention, students are afforded an opportunity to apply theories in a pragmatic manner. Third, the experiences gathered through service learning should enrich students' understanding of community life and its context.

INTELLECTUAL SCHOLARSHIP THROUGH TEACHING AND LEARNING

In higher education sector, teaching and learning remains one of the core functions. Through this noble function, universities impart knowledge by engaging students and other key stakeholders with concepts, ideas, theories and discourses. More often teaching is utilised as a pedagogical methodology to deliberate and share knowledge within higher education and beyond. Sharing through such engagement produce information and the data obtained is processed into knowledge. Facilitation of knowledge in the context of collaborative learning requires creative teaching strategies and learning methods with experiential and hands-on engagement (Jelier et al., 2005, p. 154).

In the teaching fraternity, teaching beliefs are an integral part of the teaching and learning philosophy. Interactive teaching breaks away with the traditional methods centred on lecturers' knowledge gate-keepers. It subscribes to the emancipatory and liberatory philosophy which is mainly influenced by the works of Paulo Frere (1979: 11). Accordingly, this philosophy is anchored on conscientisation and praxis, where students are made aware of their potential to tackle the socio injustices around them. Freire (1979: 13) argues that this philosophy has the power to transform reality. Hence, a classroom or theatre is transformed into a liberatory forum for both students and lecturers to enter into a dialogical engagement in the process of constructing knowledge based on praxis. Ife (1996: 230) associates praxis to embrace the involvement in a constant cycle of doing, learning and critical reflection. This philosophy is in line with the constructivist theory which places the onus of learning on the students. Thus students playing a central role on creating knowledge (Von Glaserfeld, 1995). Students could be resourceful in generating knowledge to be used for empowerment in their respective communities within an enabling learning environment.

Accordingly, this philosophy believes that teaching and learning should be interactive and engage students to unlock their academic potential. The potential of the interactive model is that it integrates theory and practice, thus affording both the students and the lecturer an opportunity to engage in the process of critical and collaborative learning from secondary sources as well as from each other. In order to benefit the students through the use of this liberatory teaching pedagogy, a lecture theatre no matter how it is designed and arranged should be an enabling and conducive environment created for students where they could engage constructively without fear of retribution or embarrassment. Through interactive and collaborative teaching model, one is able to integrate social, scientific and transformative knowledge by making use of mind-mapping, brain teasers such as controversial quotations, puzzles, short DVDs, games, short case studies and mini-presentations led by students (see Killen, 2013). Within this context, the classroom is transformed to explore social-

general knowledge which then becomes the basis for advancing proven scientific knowledge through engaging various theoretical discourses and their practicality in the real world situation. With the advancement of technology, innovative teaching methods are employed to stimulate information and knowledge sharing.

Teaching and learning is anchored on knowledge production and acquisition is value loaded. Values are like mission and vision statements that hold the Institutions of Higher Learning relevant to its core business of teaching and learning, research and community engagement (Uys et al., 2010). They seek to commit an institution to what is considered a high to excellence based on quality assurance; a conducive environment for academic excellence, personal growth, social responsibility. Such values are integrated in the academic curriculum and reinforce each other in producing students who are critical and competent in making a difference in their respective constituencies.

Grounding Human-Centred Scholarship Through Research

Through research, universities and other institutions of higher learning engage individuals, organisations and communities for research purposes. Lindsey et al., (2005, p. 108) argue that community-based research within academia is often closely related to paradigm of action research which is aimed at to develop solutions to practical challenges. Research is critical in not only generating vital information and knowledge which when disseminated to the public and within the private and civil society sectors, but generated knowledge could also be utilised by such sectors to make informed decisions. Research generated through human-centred scholarship labelled as community-based research and action research with its quest being to bring about community-based socio-economic and political change. Scholarship based on participatory action research is rooted on robust and transformative research where university community represented by students in collaboration with community representatives conduct research with the purpose of finding solutions to their problems. Leal Filho et al. (2017, p 1) argue for multi-, trans- and interdisciplinary research undertaken to jointly find solutions and strategies aimed at contributing to good lives of communities. Knowledge produced through collaborative research as Halvorsen et al, (2017) put it not only is non-hegemonic, but also allows both researchers and communities to be co-creators of knowledge. This type of collaboration underlies community engaged research, and research approach which radically moves away from traditional research agenda where researchers set the agenda to a new research paradigm where the agenda and questions are set by communities. Such community-based research is according to Lindsey et al., (2005, p. 108) informed by and initiated in response to priorities and needs identified by people with the communities. However, the challenge post-this stage of community-based research is often building trust and effective working relationship among collaborators.

Through community-engaged research, groups, communities or organisations enter into a collaborative relationship with professionals to identify issues, opportunities and find alternative solutions to collective identified challenges (Velthuizen, 2017, p. 78). As an inter- and trans-disciplinary approach (Nicolescu, 2005), community engaged research is centred on community-people's real issues, with solutions not imposed on them, but endogenously generated through deliberations and consensus. A typical example is the research conducted by the Institute for Dispute Resolution in Africa (IDRA) where the research team made use of Community engaged Participatory Research methodology to engage the San of Platfontein community as part of conflict resolution and management. The research was three-pronged phase 1) the Knowledge Discovery phase, 2) a Design phase and an Implementation Phase. The knowledge discovery phase was comprised of researchers laying the agenda upon which interviews were conducted by using; conflict mapping to process the wealth of information from communities. The Designed phase afforded the communities and researchers in planning solutions collectively where community leaders, scholars and practitioners from various disciplines managed to forge the way forward through a retreat or conference. The final phase was implementation which dispute resolution interventions in targeted communities such as Platfonteinies. Through this phase, the community was empowered to put the resolution into practice with the ultimate outcome of rediscovery the unique traditional forms of dispute resolution (Velthuizen, 2017, p. 81). Learning drawn from this research engagement fits well with mutual bridging meanings by Rogoff (1995) and the building of common knowledge by Edwards (2010). Through such research, Rogoff (2010) argues that value, history and practices embedded within communities are sustained with regular involvement. Thus, the interface of broader and university communities are blended through collaborative research across disciplines, faculties and university boundaries whereby memorandum of understanding are signed with communities, private organisations, civil society sector included (Kinti & Hayward, 2015).

From the open system perspective, universities are social institutions, sociologically created to play an active role in knowledge creation and transference. As a social system, higher education sector symbolically constituted and bounded entities produced through human communication and through such framework, stakeholders engaged in research are able to derive life-meaning (Scott, 2007). Thus, universities operate in an environment that is not only flexible, but also complex entities and for their survival have to depend on interactions with intermediate and wider environments. Like any systems, universities have campus, faculties, departments and disciplines, visions and mission, processes and procedures, most importantly the human resources. All these components are sub-systems essential for the effective, efficient and productive functions of higher education institutions. Universities are thus service-providing systems whereby their immediate and broader environments together with sub-systems are institutionalised to respond to the needs of a university community and broader society. Knowledge generated by these institutions is extracted from the public through the application of scientific research methods. In essence, communities and organisations are the custodians of knowledge. Universities exercise their social not doing communities favours, By engaging and investing in community service and community engagement, universities are able to exercise their social responsibility ither in the form of community development or project-based service learning via their faculties, disciplines or centrally co-ordinated community engagement.

Post 1994 agenda for transformation of higher education in South Africa saw the categorisation of this sector into research-intensive, comprehensive and universities of technology (Muller, 2016, p. xiv). Those universities regarded as research-intensive such as Wits, UCT, invested a lot of financial resources to staff who demonstrated the research potential to produce quality and internationally rated and cited articles, books and book chapters.

FORGING COMMUNITY-UNIVERSITY PARTNERSHIPS THROUGH COMMUNITY OF PRACTICE

Higher education institutions can be conceptualised and contextualised as communities of practice. The concept of communities of practice or community of practice ascended to academic and practical debate through the work of Lave and Wenger (1991). Wenger (1998 cited in Ledwith & Springett, 2010, p. 83) associates communities of practice (CoPs) as mutual engagement based on a shared practice with sharing of insights, gaining new knowledge, engaging in learning and creating new meanings through critical engagement. The concept was developed by Lave and Wagner (1991) as 'a group of people who share a concern, as a set of problems or a passion about a topic, and who deepen their knowledge and expertise by interacting on an ongoing process basis. The authors saw the acquisition of knowledge as a social process in which people participated in communal learning at different levels depending on their authority in a group such as new comers learn from old timers by being allowed to participate in tasks relating to the practice of the community (Kimble & Li, 2010). Within higher education, community engagement provides the space for students and lecturers to engage wider communities for reciprocal knowledge sharing and engagement. Since 1991 when the concept was developed it has incorporated various purposes which include the promotion of transference of knowledge into practice, improving knowledge management, encouraging and supporting professional development, promoting learning and information exchange and helping to promote and recognise both tacit and explicit knowledge.. Thus CoPs are meant to facilitate information sharing and knowledge translation, but they can also have multiple aims, including overcoming geographical and professional isolation and improving networking. Through established research networks and partnerships, universities have entered into collaborative scholarly arrangement for the purposes of undertaking research and transference of such knowledge to the general public. The concept has since been expanded to include a far wider range of definitions (Wenger 1998; Wenger & Snyder, 2000). Wenger (1998) asserts that CoPs arise from the need to achieve goals in an organisation and to provide learning avenues within, between and outside of that business. This means that a business or organisation is not an isolated community but a part of interrelated CoPs that can spread beyond the borders of the host organisation. This can be traced to the recent Arab Spring where the virtual community was used to spread information which moved outside the original place of strife; Tunisia to the rest of the Arab world.

Through communities of practice, individuals within the collective are able to unlock their human and institutional potentials (Tshishonga, 2017). Thus, communities of practice can be instrumental in developing human intellectual capital. Thus organisations and communities are positioned to expand their networks for the purposes of addressing socio-economic challenges exerted by both immediate and broader environments. These types of communities exist for a purpose and are charged with the sole mandate of achieving a shared vision. Maslow's (1943) hierarchy of needs are basic needs inclusive of physiological to self-actualisation hence such communities are mandated to meet these basic needs. MaxNeef (1991) points out that rearranged needs as 'wheel of fundamental human needs' which according to him are fundamental and essential with different satisfiers. At the centre of communities of practice are vital and fundamental needs in activating organisational strategic and pragmatic action into fruition. In the context of the quest to build sustainable and democratic communities capable of redressing socio-economic predicaments, engagement with primary and secondary stakeholders is paramount. At organisational level, Mupepi (2017, p. 433) argues that communities of practice could be deployed to understand the nature and description of the economic prevailing conditions. Hence as one of the democratic change management mechanism, community of practice could forge an interdependent environment whereby communities, state, government as well as private sector partners to bring about positive democratic change (Mupepi, 2017). Evidence from multiple studies show that CoPs have long and short term benefits. On one hand, short term benefits include rapid identification of skills within a workforce, knowledge sharing, provision of safe environments for sharing problems, capturing and reusing existing knowledge, improvement in topical knowledge and the rate of implementation of evidence-based practice. Other the hand, long term benefits include providing a forum for expanding skills and expertise, a network for current awareness and help to foster a sense of professional identity. It has also been found that CoPs information and sharing are key activities that contribute towards innovation and communication over geographical distances hence it is not a limitation that should bar people from participating in their own governance. Although CoPs are considered inexpensive methods of virtual meetings, in contrast to face-to-face meetings and effective ways to spread information and exchange information globally particularly in low resource setting, it is still however a challenge for citizens in developing countries like South Africa to access the internet and buy data which is still sold at exorbitant prices. CoPs meetings offer a learning experience for users to inform policy on governance but it normally takes place among citizens in the urban areas who can access the internet either through their cell phones or free Wi-Fi at city centres and libraries. CoPs limit the challenge of geographical distance but in the case of the rural residents it can be a challenge. However where it is possible people can hold meetings through teleconferencing cutting down on transport and other expenses. Virtual meetings can also improve the structure of meetings and discussions. There is no fear of being undermined as in the case of face-to-face meetings.

UNIVERSITY-COMMUNITY CASE STUDIES

This chapter make use of various case studies to demonstrate the beneficial opportunities and challenges embedded in community-university partnerships. The potential benefits and opportunities are explored with tangible outcomes and non-tangible such as social capital accrued because of university engagement with communities and organizations. Challenges of institutionalizing community-university partnerships are interrogated for individual partners and collective. Thus, for institutions of higher learning (HEIs) to advance human-centered intellectual scholarship, university-community partnerships become a platform upon which social responsibility is exercised for the benefit of partners involved. The adoption of university-community partnerships has reciprocal benefits. On one hand, universities are able to renew their commitment to share knowledge, skills and competencies in various fields while communities including Community Based Organisations (CBOs) and Non-Governmental Organisations (NGOs) enjoy academic-practitioners space for their own development an empowerment.

UKZN-Community-Based Learning (CBL)

Community-based learning is one of the experiential learning institutionalised to expose students into the real world. Community-based learning (CBL) is grounded as service-oriented service-learning module in most of the universities. Thus, service-orientated modules are designed to engage students in community service with support from module co-ordinators or lecturers for learning from such engagement (Petersen & Osman, 2013). Through CBL or service-orientated module, students are indulged into epistemological journey whereby they have the first encounter with communities and challenges. The study done by Eyler et al. (2001, pp. 1-2) on service learning highlighted some of the long-term student outcomes derived from engagement in service learning (SL). These outcomes include among others 1) student personal development (a sense of personal efficacy, personal identity, spiritual growth and moral development), 2) interpersonal development including the ability to work with others as well as leadership and communication skills), 3) reduction of stereotypes and facilitating cultural and racial understanding, 4) creating a sense of social responsibility and citizenship skills, 5) commitment to service and lastly 6) being associated with involvement in community service after graduation. Students' experiences become not only central in their learning, but also activate them to be knowledge producers and active citizens.

For Mbokazi & Matse (2018), the module serves as yet another opportunity to engage in university community partnerships to not only provide students with the necessary skills and knowledge, but also to assist in generating the cadre of development practitioners with a consciousness of social justice required for Africa's development. The key focus of this module is fittingly captured in the following quotation: "Before change agents can change others, they have to change themselves and their consciousness. They have to constantly try to shed their own

Table 1. Community-based learning-course description

Community-based Learning-Course Description **Lecturers: Dr Mbokazi & Dr Matse**
Welcome to one of the exciting final modules in your undergraduate studies – the Community-Based Learning (CBL)! This 32-credit year-long module is designed with an assumption that students already have a sound understanding of development theories, concepts and approaches. Thus, it acts as a capstone that brings all the learning together, without putting too much emphasis on teaching new content. The fundamental contribution of the module to learning rests in it providing a space for experiential learning within community settings. The course is coordinated with the assistance of community-based organisations (CBOs), schools and government departments in order to ensure that students who have grasped the theories, also have understanding of their social relevance.

Source: Mbokazi & Matse (2018)

contradictions, weaknesses, and prejudices" (Bhasin, 1990 cited in Burkey, 1993, p. 98). The module is primarily purposed to expose students to practical experiences in community development focusing specifically on the multi-dimensional nature of poverty and what communities are doing to address it. This purpose is advanced by 1) giving students an opportunity to experience community development through involvement with a community project or initiative; 2) inculcating a culture of reflection and learning, while nurturing the students to be critical, competent, empathetic and ethical; and 3) helping students to gain hands-on experience in a community context towards merging theory and practice. Through CBL, long lasting partnerships are created between, students, hosting organisation higher education institution. Each stakeholder plays a pivotal role in building partnership which includes benefits. While students benefit by experiential learning and integrate theory into practice, university is able to retain students, enhance community relations with host community or organisation being able to gain skills derived from collective knowledge production and utilisation for the benefit of the community. Through this module, is to instil self-responsibility among students by allowing them to organise organisations at their respective home towns while the second semester having CBL coordinators assuming the responsibility by arranging placements among CBOs and NGOs, municipal departments, public schools in vicinity of eThekwini Municipality (UKZN-CBL Course Outline, 2018).

UCT-School Improvement Initiative (SII)

The crisis in South African public schools has a direct impact on universities. Many learners who attend township and rural schools perform poorly in the matric examinations. This hampers their efforts to qualify for university. The quality of school education for the majority of South Africans needs to improve dramatically if we are to break this cycle of under achievement and failure. This is a monumental task and one that requires all stakeholders to get involved. This is why the Schools Improvement Initiative (SII) at the University of Cape Town came into being. SII is envisioned to develop strong and responsive university/school partnerships which contribute positively to long-term change in the classroom, the school and in the broader community.

The SII, UCT engages practically, developmentally and critically with the problems of schooling in this country. With a strong focus on interdisciplinary collaboration and school improvement, the programme draw on university-wide resources and initiatives – including academic staff and student service organisations. UCT is also committed to forging links by working in partnership with education-related groups outside of the university, in particular the province's Metropole East Education District. The SII focuses its interventions on schools in the township of

Khayelitsha in Cape Town Metropole. Whereas the core of their school improvement work is in three primary and two secondary partner schools, through the 100-UP university preparation programme, the SII works in all 20 secondary schools in the township. http://www.sii.uct.ac.za/sites/default/files/image_tool/images/271/SII/SII_BROCHURE_2017_HIRES.pdf

UCT is one of top performers academically both locally and in the African continent and is geographically located in a well-off province, Western Cape. Despite both province and UCT being well resourced entities (Tshiwula & Magopeni, 2014) UCT through its SII intervention to education in townships like Khayelitsha has been hailed an act of institutional exercise academic citizenship. South African youth are confronted by various factors hindering them from accessing tertiary quality education (Mlatsheni, 2012); however the role of higher education institutions like UCT via SII improves access by offering tuition to the township students and learners. Among the three categories of universities, UCT is regarded as the research-intense institution and it has inverted intensively on research and publications. Despite sticking to research and teaching, UCT has various programmes and engage in project-based community engagement, hence Sanders (2016, p. 12) said a lot of research work done at UCT has consequences for the communities around the university.

University of Pretoria's Community Enablement Programme

Community engagement by the University of Pretoria (UP) is embedded in the overall vision statement of the University which states that he University of Pretoria is committed to discharging its social responsibilities.

'Community Enablement' Through 'Community Participation', Designing Itself Away

Into this politically fractious patchwork of informal and semi-formal sectors and settlements comes another kind of 'community engagement', which I would include as a *fourth* kind of relation that the University has established with the City. It is one more firmly grounded in academic teaching - for instance in an Honours course spearheaded by UP's Department of Architecture (2015), on Human Settlement and Urbanism under the title 'Community enablement through the critical agency of spatial design', whose motto is 'community participation' (including 'community action planning', 'participatory Geographic Information Systems [GIS]', 'participatory research', 'social capital: networks'). The course outline demands 'community participation' in places where there is none to speak of, speaking of which it then makes its 'intervention'. Oblivious to structures of power and their bases and histories, of clientelism and patronage, the course outline enjoins the charting of 'sites of intervention' on a map that it comes to define, as if it were *terra nullius:* 'Key to this intervention method will be developing a response to the specific people that are identified as the proprietors of the nodal energy points, so that the collective *client* consists of the people representing that network' (University of Pretoria, Department of Architecture, 2015). This method is to be 'replicated in order to establish a basis for appropriate architectural strategies of intervention in various urban conditions' (University of Pretoria, Department of Architecture, 2015). However, this 'intervention method' has taken on board none of the lessons learnt in the immediate post-apartheid reconstruction period, principal among which is a 'scepticism, based on political principle' despite being academic.

University of Venda's Community Engagement

Unlike the other universities where community engagement is left to individual faculties, departments or disciplines, University of Venda (UNIVEN) institutionalised community engagement through the establishment of the Directorate Community Engagement in 2009. The Directorate strives for excellence in supporting interdisciplinary community engaged teaching and learning, community engaged research geared towards addressing community poverty-related challenges and development needs of the communities in the Limpopo Province and in SADC rural communities (http://www.univen.ac.za/directorates-centres/community-engagement). From the onset, a Directorate on Community Engagement (CE) was created to ensure that a qualitative, symbiotic and reciprocal relationship exists between itself and its community stakeholders – a relationship of mutual benefit. It is the intention of UNIVEN to excel in Community Engagement programmes that are both scholarship-based and community oriented, embedded in the academic work of the institution. UNIVEN sees community engagement as goal-orientated, reciprocal interactions between the university and the community, with the aim of establishing a win-win partnership, through collaborative projects. Netshandama (2018) defines community engagement in higher education as development of the scholarship of reciprocal knowledge and she further warns that community engagement should not be confused with community outreach, which often involves philanthropic deeds (in The Mercury, 2018). Over the past eight years UNIVEN has done well in scholarly engagement with our communities and we intend to build on this strong foundation for our future projects which will increasingly serve as a means of institutionalising engaged teaching, learning and research (Netshandama, 2018). These interactions serve as vehicles for increasing community awareness, social consciousness and active citizenship among our students. According to Netshandama (2018), community engagement related initiatives are integral part of already flagship community engagement projects for the purpose of enhancing those pockets of excellence. In line with national and provincial development initiatives, UNIVEN's community engagement takes the form of integrated initiatives to find solutions to societal challenges such as poverty, under-development, unemployment, inequality, and lack of relevant and appropriate skills. Community engagement at UNIVEN according to UNIVEN Strategic Plan (2018, p. 24) focuses on 1) building and maintain flagship community engagement projects, 2) building local-knowledge economy through science and knowledge outreach to local communities, 3) developing social consciousness and social enterprise among students and finally 4) developing work-integrated learning as an essential component of all career-focussed and professional programmes.

LEARNING OPPORTUNITIES THROUGH UNIVERSITY-COMMUNITY PARTNERSHIP

For Wiewel and Knaap (2005, p. 6), universities are mandated to educate students and the best preferred way to teach them is to get them engaged in in real-world problem solving. There are beneficiation opportunities attached to universities' commitment to university-community partnership. For higher education sector, community-based partnership provides a platform which they can reflect on the relevance of the institution as a whole and the applicability of their curriculum in practice. Universities by their creation are knowledge producing institutions and as such enjoy the status of being the custodian in the informational age and knowledge society. Through such partnership endeavours, universities expose their students to real-world, thus affording them experiential platform for them to integrate theory into practice with both tacit and explicit knowledge, skills and competencies to be gained. Maurrasse (2001), in his book titled 'Beyond the Campus: How Colleges and Universities form Partnerships with their Communities' has documented case studies that highlighted opportunities derived from community-university partnerships. Collaboration, creativity, stakeholder engagement and participation were found to be fundamental ingredients towards building effective community engagement based on mutual understanding of all partners. Institutions of higher learning entered into dialectic service learning with the primary purpose of maximizing the learning opportunities for their students (Stoecker & Tryon, 2009, p. 34). While partnership aligned communities and organisations attempt to maximise their capacity to impact their communities. In this regard, Bell and Carlson (2009, p. 20) identified four types of motives that organisations have, namely 1) the altruistic motive to educate the service leaners, 2) long-term moves for the sector and the organisation, 3) the capacity-building move and lastly, 4) the higher education relationship motive. Firstly, the altruistic motive to educate the service leaners is grounded on the organisational mission to help students. Second, long-term moves for the sector and the organisation geared toward long-term sustainability of their organisation. Third, the capacity-building move engages service learners to expand their organisational capacity. Fourth, the higher education relationship motive is anchored on organisations plan to build and strengthen connections with colleges and universities (Bell & Carlson, 2009, p. 20). Both organisations and communities alike could benefit from highly skilled and productive students especially when strategically deploying this cadre of students to fulfil certain organisational chores under the supervision of more experienced staff members. Learning from these community-university partnerships is not only for students but also benefits academic institutions and communities as well as local organisations. The study conducted by Vanessa Nichol (2010), regarding Community-Based Learning involving the School for International Training in Wentworth (Durban, South Africa), revealed that the programme led to substantive increase trust, goodwill and voluntarism among community members and their respective community-based organisations.

Based on sound and quality relationship developed between the universities and organisations, service learning students not only gained knowledge of how such organisations operate, but also share their theoretical know-how including case studies tested in other nations. Such multiple-network engagement exposes organisations and communities to various practices rooted on reflective social learning and instrumental learning as outlined by Gilardi and Radaelli (2012, pp. 156-158). These learning types are fundamental especially in engaging organisations through social interaction for governance and social learning and drawing lessons. As integral members of the community, higher education institutions utilise their spaces for engagements and skills and expertise accumulated from professionalised fields of architecture, urban planning, housing, social work, engineering including medicine and built environment.

CHALLENGES BESETTING UNIVERSITY-COMMUNITY PARTNERSHIP

More often partnerships are forged to optimise the strengths of each partner, partnerships similarly formed to mitigate the weaknesses of partners. Challenges faced by community-university partnerships range from expectations as each partner enters into the coalition which in most cases is marred by poor planning and the absence of clear vision and commitment to make shared vision a collective reality. The mentality that communities and organisations are dependent entities in need of help especially the universities to apply top-down and welfarist approaches (Fourie, 2006, p. 41). Emanating from this mind-set, is the undermining of community capacity to deal with their issues without outside imposed ideas and it could culminate dependency among communities. Thus, ill-planned especially among project-based service learning and community engagement have devastating results with unhealthy partnerships at the end. Building a healthy partnerships requires a change of mind-set from the side of higher education institutions. Thus, community-building based on effective partnerships demands a shift from the mentality that perceiving communities and local organisations as passive recipients with nothing to contribute. However, Maurrasse (2001, p. 5) through his effective involvement in community-college-campus partnership building in the United States has noticed that community partnerships are beginning to progress beyond the paternalistic approach of deciding what is best for communities without seeking local input.

The failure to create and build a learning culture, equality and openness (Simanowitz & Knotts, 2015, p. 76) inculcates stereotypes and misconceptions among stakeholders that widen the gap between communities and higher education institutions. In addition, the disconnections result into trust and communication deficits which underscore the principles of community-university partnerships. Both concrete and process indicators are fundamental in growing winning partnerships, however, the failure to invest time and effort on the process as opposed to output and outcomes have detrimental effects on the sustainability of partnership. The existence of university-based and community-based knowledge create inferior-superior, authentic-non-authentic, scientific-non-scientific dichotomies. The held view that community-based knowledge is inferior and it is without tested scientific methodologies led to devaluing of info and knowledge generated through community-based research engagement (Nyden, 2006). In this regard, Nuden (2006) further argues that by segregating organisations and networks that create knowledge from those that produce university knowledge could undermine society's capacity to understand and solve problems. The challenges in community-based research have to do with building trust and effective working relationship among collaborators (Lindsey et al., 2005, p. 108). Stakeholders constituting community-university partnerships are from diverse organisational backgrounds with differing values, ethics and principles, and reconciling all these elements become a contested and source of conflictual tensions. The mediocre status attached to partnership strangely among the research-intensive including comprehensive universities is due to poor financial allocation by universities despite their articulated in their mission statements. Comparatively, incentives for community engagement are far less or non-existent compared to teaching and research. Narrow adoption of community engagement as an add-on activity by universities especially academic staff and faculty administrators has contributed to the dislike and negative sentiments to community engagement or service learning.

FUTURE RESEACRH DIRECTIONS

The chapter was set to deliberate on the potential and benefits derived from grounding institutions of higher learning (HEIs) in advancing human-centered intellectual scholarship through institutionalizing university-community partnerships. Thus, universities as academic institutions are equally charged with the responsibility of contributing to societal development through third core function of HEI often known by different names such as community engagement, service learning or university-community partnerships. University-community partnerships differ from institution to institution however all have common purpose of empowering, sharing benefits and sharing risks among various stakeholders. University-community partnerships have emerged as vital arrangement for teaching, research and practice and their successes are depended on memorandum of understanding (MOU). This MOU should be based on Ubuntu values and principles in the form of respect, mutuality, solidarity and sense of collective purpose.

Based on these deliberations, further research is imperative on how hold communities and organization can make use of knowledge generated through university-community partnerships. Thus, such research should have a specific focus on how Community-university intellectual property could be preserved for sustainable and empowerment of partners involved. The purpose of such research should be anchored on the drive to restore knowledge to the people by transferring skills and knowledge for community empowerment and organizational development.

CONCLUSION

The chapter has deliberated the notion of community-university partnership within the higher education sector. Theoretical exposition of each concept was grounded for better conceptualization on how partnership functions and optimally benefit stakeholders involved. Potential benefits and opportunities for institutions of higher learning (HEIs) to advance human-centered intellectual scholarship through institutionalizing university-community partnerships. Although community engagement or service learning is often less prioritised compared to other core functions of higher education, the chapter perceived it to be vital for teaching and research. (Butterfiled & Soska, 2004). South African case studies were utilized to demonstrate the value embedded within community-university partnerships as mutually benefiting entities. It became apparent in these deliberations that the success of these partnerships not only depended on respect and mutual understanding, but also on collective envisioning by all partners in forging both the strategic and plan of action for the benefit of all stakeholders and the general community. Paying lip-service to community-civil engagement or service learning deprived students, universities' and respective communities from learning from each other, generate transformative knowledge and use knowledge as strategy to deal with their problems. The chapter uses service learning or community engagement related programmes and projects from different universities as case studies in South Africa. Informed opinions from experts from academic institutions and students were engaged to extract primary data.

REFERENCES

Bell, S. M., & Carlson, R. (2009). Motivations of Communication Organisations for Service Learning. In The Unheard Voices: Community Organisations and Service Learning (pp. 10-37). Philadelphia: Temple University Press.

Burkey, S. (1993). *Putting People First: A Guide to Self-Reliant Participatory Rural Development*. London: Zed Books.

Cebekhulu, E. (2013). *Umhlaba Uyahlaba: The World is Thorny. Wandsbeck.* Reach Publishers.

Edwards, A. (2010). *Being an Expert Professional Practitioner: The relational turn in expertise*. Dordrecht: Springer. doi:10.1007/978-90-481-3969-9

Gilardi, F., & Radaelli, C. M. (2012). Governance and Learning. In D. Levi-Faur (Ed.), *Oxford Handbook of Governance* (pp. 155–168). Oxford, UK: Oxford University Press.

Halvorsen, T., Ibsen, H., Evans, H. C., & Penderis, S. (2017). Introduction. In Knowledge for justice: Critical perspectives from Southern African-Nordic research partnerships. Somerset West: African Minds.

Kimble, C., & Li, F. (2010). Effective virtual Working through Community of Practice. In S. Dasgupta (Ed.), *Encyclopedia of Virtual Communities and Technologies*. IGI Publishing.

Kinti, I., & Hayward, G. (2015). Developing skills for Collaborative, Relational Research in Higher education: A Cultural Historical Analysis. In Pedagogy in Higher Education: A Cultural Historical Approach (pp. 181-197). Cambridge, UK: Cambridge University Press.

Lave, J., & Wenger, E. (1991). *Situated Learning: Legitimate Peripheral Participation*. Cambridge, UK: Cambridge University Press. doi:10.1017/CBO9780511815355

Ledwith, M., & Springett, J. (2010). *Participatory practice: Community-based action for transformative change.* The Policy Press.

Lindsey, G., Ottensmann, J., Palmer, J., Wilson, J., & Tutterrow, J. (2005). Encouraging Smart Growth in a Skeptical state: University-Stakeholder Collaboration in Central Indiana. In W. Wiewel & G. J. Knaap (Eds.), *Partnerships for Smart Growth: University-Community Collaboration for Better Public Places* (pp. 95–114). London: Routledge.

Maslow, A. H. (1943). A Theory of Human Motivation. *Psychological Review, 50*(4), 370–396. doi:10.1037/h0054346

Maurrasse, D. J. (2001). *Beyond the campus: How Colleges and Universities form Partnerships with their Communities.* New York: Routledge.

Max-Neef, M. A. (1991). *Human Scale Development: conception, application and further flections.* New York: Apex.

Midgley, J. (1986). Community participation: History, concepts and controversies. In J. Migley (Ed.), *Community participation, social development and the state.* London: Methuen.

Mlatsheni, C. (2012). The Challenges Unemployment imposes on Youth. In H. Perold, C. Cloete, & J. Papier (Eds.), *Shaping the future of South Africa's Youth: Rethinking post-school education and skills training* (pp. 31–41). Somerset West: African Minds.

Mooney, L. A., & Edwards, B. (2001). Experiential learning in sociology: Service learning and other community-based learning initiatives. *Teaching Sociology, 29*(2), 181–194. doi:10.2307/1318716

Mpofu-Walsh, S. (2017). *Democracy & Delusion: 10 Myths in South African Politics.* Cape Town: NB Publishers.

Mupepi, M. G. (2017). Developing Democratic Paradigms to Effectively Manage Business, government and Civil Society. In Handbook of Research on Sub-National Governance and Development (pp. 432-462). Hershey, PA: IGI Global. doi:10.4018/978-1-5225-1645-3.ch020

Nichol, V. (2010). *Exploring Community Benefits in Community-Based Learning: A Study of International Community-Based Learning Initiatives in Wentworth, Durban* (Master's thesis). University of KwaZulu-Natal.

Nicolescu, B. (2005). *Towards Transdisciplinary Education and Learning*. Paper prepared for conference on Science and Religion: Global Perspectives. Philadelphia: Metanexus Institute.

Robinsion, J. W., & Green, G. P. (2011). Developing communities. In Introduction to Community Development: theory, Practice and Service Learning. Los Angeles, CA: Sage.

Rogoff, B. (1995). Observing sociocultural activity on three planes: Participatory appropriation guided participation, and apprenticeship. In J. V. Wertsch, A. Alvarez, & P. De Rio (Eds.), *Sociocultural Studies of Mind* (pp. 139–164). New York: Cambridge University Press. doi:10.1017/CBO9781139174299.008

Scott, J. (2007). *Fifty Key Sociologists: The Contemporary Theorists*. London: Routledge.

Simanowitx, A., & Knotts, K. (2015). *The Business of Doing Good: Insights from one social enterprise's journey to delivery on good intentions*. Practical Action Publishing Ltd. doi:10.3362/9781780448640

Stoeker, R. (2009), Unheard Voices: Community Organisations and Service Learning. In The Unheard Voices: Community Organisations and Service Learning (pp. 10-37). Philadelphia: Temple University Press.

Stoeker, R. (2016). *Liberating Service Learning and the Rest of Higher Education Civic Engagement*. Philadelphia: Temple University Press.

Stone, D. (2012). Agents of Knowledge. In D. Levi-Laur (Ed.), *The Oxford Handbook of Governance* (pp. 339–352). Oxford, UK: Oxford University Press.

Tshishonga, N. (2017). Operation Sukuma Sakhe: A New Social Contract for Decentralised Service Delivery and Responsive Governance in KwaZulu-Natal. In Handbook of Research on Sub-National Governance and Development (pp. 304-323). Hershey, PA: IGI Global. doi:10.4018/978-1-5225-1645-3.ch014

Tshiwula, L., & Magopeni, N. (2014). A return to basics: selected views on factors preventing access to higher education in South Africa. In M. Speckman & M. Mandew (Eds.), *Perspectives on Student Affairs in South Africa*. Somerset West: African Minds.

Velthuizen, A. (2017). Engaging with the African ground: Towards a new research paradigm for conflict studies in Africa. In V. Msila (Ed.), *Decolonising knowledge for Africa's renewal: Examining African Perspectives and Philosophies* (pp. 73–86). Randburg: KR Publishing.

Wenger, E. (1998). *Communities of practice: Learning, meaning and identity*. Cambridge, UK: Cambridge University Press. doi:10.1017/CBO9780511803932

Wenger, E., & Synder, W. (2000). Communities of practice: The organisational Frontier. *Harvard Business Review*, 139–145.

Yakubu, H. (2017). Higher Education and Development. In J. Ssempebwa, P. Neema-Abooki, & J. C. S. Musaaki (Eds.), *Innovating Higher Education: Issues in Contemporary African Higher Education* (pp. 1–17). Kampala: Fountain Publishers.

ADDITIONAL READING

Field, J., Schmidt-Hertha, B., & Waxenegger, A. (Eds.). (2015). *Universities and Engagement: International perspectives on higher education and lifelong learning* (1st ed.). London: Routledge.

Jones, D. R. (2018). *The Origins of Civic Universities Manchester, Leeds and Liverpool* (1st ed.). London: Routledge.

Keith, N. Z. (2015). *Engaging in Social Partnerships: Democratic Practices for Campus-Community Partnerships* (1st ed.). London: Routledge. doi:10.4324/9780203805374

Marginson, S., & Consdine, M. (2011). *The Enterprise University: Power, Governance and Reinvention in Australia*. Cambridge: Cambridge University Press.

Seepe, S. (Ed.), *Towards African Identity of Higher Education. Pretoria*. Vista: Skotaville Media.

KEY TERMS AND DEFINITIONS

Learning Organization: An organization that has the potential to acknowledge the skills, knowledge, and competencies of its workforce, and is able to utilize such abilities and capabilities towards the empowerment of members and organizational development.

Service Learning: It is one of the core business functions where university students are placed within communities, organizations and the primary purpose being for students to learn from the community-organization context by putting theory into practice.

University: It is an institution where intellectual scholarship is debated, and knowledge-based discourses are advanced through teaching, research, and community engagement.

University-Community Partnership: It is a partnership that is formed between university and Communities with the primary purpose of undertaking collective research for knowledge generation and utilization for community development and empowerment.

Chapter 7
#FeesMustFall Campaign and the Quest for Accessible, Quality, and Decolonized Higher Education in South Africa

Ndwakhulu Stephen Tshishonga
University of KwaZulu-Natal, South Africa

ABSTRACT

This chapter is framed within the broader context of the transformative agenda of higher education sector in post-apartheid South Africa. The #FeesMustFall campaign started late October 2015 and the entire 2016 and has grown to become one of the biggest movements ever witnessed in the history of South African student politics. Similarly to the struggle waged by 1976 youth against the dominance of Afrikaans as the medium of instruction, FMF challenges the current government and universities to provide free, quality, and decolonized higher education. The slow pace of transformation, inaccessibility institutions due to fee increment, and Eurocentric curriculum, among others prompted the students to demand accessible financial inclusion and education relevant to their needs and reality. The chapter makes use of qualitative approach with both secondary and primary data extracted from books, accredited articles, and empirical data from selected participants.

DOI: 10.4018/978-1-5225-8461-2.ch007

INTRODUCTION

Formal education in Africa and particularly in South Africa has a protracted history dating to the colonial and apartheid period. Castell (2001, p. 212) asserts that universities in particular are rooted in a colonial past. Unfortunately, formal education in most African countries was introduced during colonial times and was an instrument used by colonisers to train low-level clerical staff (Nshemererwe, 2016, p. 9). Similarly, education in South Africa has colonial-apartheid baggage with social, economic and political implications. Higher education is recognised as a major resource, especially for national development and knowledge production, however, it was also noticed that its structure and capacity was dented by apartheid's inheritance (ANC, 1994). Education in general and higher education in particular was pursued and encouraged for a domestication agenda as opposed to developing analytical and independent African thinkers and scholars. In essence, colonial education, borrowing from the Brazilian scholar, Freire (1993), highlighted that 'banking' education was designed to domesticate rather than 'problem-posing' aimed at liberating students. Freire further argues that the education system became a weapon of oppression and those who ran it were the oppressors. However, the attainment of independence saw the exodus of Africans to overseas universities and colleges to acquire education and training. The hunger for knowledge was prompted by these African scholars to assume leadership positions in government and educational institutions in post-colonial period. The crisis in education is fueled by the disconnection between education and employment coupled by a lack of resources for young people to acquire technical and vocational training demanded by the work force (World Bank Group, 2018). Honwana (2013, p. 39) argues that educational systems in Africa are unable to provide youth with the tools they need to compete in a labour market which requires high levels of specialised technical skills. However, in the African continent, the quest for accessible and quality education was reiterated by policy articulations and numerous struggles waged by students across the continent (Luyat, 2003). Despite the commitments shown by African governments through policy promulgated and signatories geared towards improving education sectors at all levels, Africa's education remains poor compared to their counterparts in the world. More than two decades of democratic governance as part of redress has seen the opening up of previously only white institutions (English and Afrikaans) such as Pretoria, Stellenbosch, Free State, Rand Afrikaanse (now University of Johannesburg) for black students for the first time.

Education remains one of the contested sectors and obstacles for South Africa's integrated development. With its central role in developing a skilled and competent work force, higher education is challenged to offer relevant and competitive education.

The so called decolonised education has resulted in restructuring dynamics which forms this type of education. For many students around the globe, higher education is recognised as an engine of national economic growth, a provider of the opportunities and prosperity given to Teferra and Altbach (2003) individuals (Johnstone, 2003). These students strongly believe that higher education which is free could be an instrument of social justice, excessively reducing the stigma attached to the poor standards of living, while increasing growth externalities for all irrespective of ones' economic status (Wangenga-Ouma, 2012). With that being said, the following study intends to examine the history of the FeesMustFall movement, the implications associated with the campaign as well as the stand in which the government took in response to the demands of furious students who ultimately fuelled most of the universities with violence.

BACKGROUND

Internationally, education is held as the key to development and a prosperous society. In Africa, following decades of the legacy of the colonial-apartheid rule, education is considered the pathway out of socio-economic challenges and underdevelopment. In order to break the cycle of underdevelopment in Africa, national investment by African governments, according to Mangcu (2017, p. 9) is fundamental to developmental progress. This essence has demanded the transformation of the higher education sector, especially universities offering access to quality education. Transformation in the context of Eurocentric educational dominance necessitates a move away from such education to a more Afro-centric system of education. Given the colonial and apartheid history particularly in South Africa and the African continent in general, dismantling of colonial, apartheid Bantu Education and Eurocentric education systems should embrace a competitive Afrocentric education system (Makhanya, 2017, p. 5).

Similarly, in South Africa, black students were subjected to Bantu Education which was not only inferior, but it was the education system which prepared young people to be subservient in the labour force (Cebekhulu, 2013; Ramphele, 2008). At a basic education level, the separate education system was based on the Bantu Education Act of 1953 while higher education was regulated by the 1959 Extension of University Act (Johnson & Jacobs, 2012, p. 31). The latter policy framework became the basis upon which institutions of higher education were established racially and ethnically across the country. Black students were relegated to universities such University of Venda, University of Transkei and Fort Hare, Indian students had to attend at University of Durban Westville while the University of the Western Cape was designated for 'coloured' students. English students were accommodated at the universities of Cape Town, Rhodes, Natal and Wits with Afrikaans speaking students having to attend at University of Pretoria or Rand Afrikaanse University (Maake, 2011). The University of South Africa was the only university in South Africa which was accessible to all races and ethnic groups; black students who wished to attend white universities had to be granted special permission from the Minister of Education. Although such discriminatory education was challenged by students in 1976 (Duncan, 2015; Dayile, 2017), its legacy has continued in the post-apartheid era.

While the 1976 Student Uprising was triggered by the imposition of the Afrikaans language as the medium of instruction, the 2015-2016 revolution under the auspices of #FeesMustFall was triggered by increasing tuition fees at tertiary institutions (Chikane, 2018). Without affordable and accessible quality and transformed education despite the legislative promises, students grew resentful and #FeesMustFall was born. For Godsell and Chikane (2016, p. 55), a transformed society should be based on a post-colonial university underpinned by fairness, equality, equity and social justice. Through FMF, students in their different formations challenged the university management and the government to keep its promise to open the doors of learning (Chikane, 2018). Student representative bodies (SRCs) were however born on the terrain of struggle and have been central to transformation and academic freedom (Ngcaweni & Nkuna, 2018). FMF was the direct reaction by student protestors of the financial exclusion and unaffordability of higher education (Modupe, 2018). Broadly, the continual lack of transformation in higher education has contributed to the alienation of students especially those from poor background. (Maneta, 2018), but also financial exclusion has mainly affected students from poor and low socio-economic households. Considering the prevalence of poverty, unemployment and inequality, higher education can not only be the key to national development, but be an instrument to inefficiencies through imparting marketable skills and knowledge (World Bank Group, 2018).

HISTORICAL PROFILE OF HIGHER EDUCATION IN (SOUTH) AFRICA

World-wide knowledge acquisition is advanced through formal education at schools, colleges and universities. Sociologically, these institutions have been constructed and came to be known for developing scholarship in various fields of study including mathematics, engineering, sciences, accounting, planning and law. Higher education institutions, universities in particular, emerged attracting men and women with intellectual ability to enter into an epistemological and ontological journey in search of and advancing knowledge through teaching and research. It is through the quest for knowledge and scholarship that international universities such as the Massachusetts Institute of Technology (MIT), Oxford, Harvard, Cambridge, Yale, Princeton and London are recognised for academic production. In Africa, high ranking universities include UCT, Wits, the University of Cairo, and the American University of Cairo, Nairobi University, Rhodes, University of Johannesburg, Stellenbosch, and UKZN amongst others. The ranking of these institutions has been undertaken by reputable groups such as The Times Higher Education and Russel Groups for the British universities. Ground-breaking researches with tangible and innovative solutions to societal challenges are among the criteria used to rank these institutions. The ranking of universities including other institutions of higher learning has not only earned them scholastic prestige, but also their capacity to influence policy across the globe. With the advent of information age and knowledge society (Castell, 2003), institutions of higher education, especially research-intensive universities are resourceful as knowledge producers and disseminators. Based on their strengths, universities have been categorised into a three-tier systems At the apex of this system are the research-intensive universities which not only do well in research output, but also ranked top in the world. Above being research-orientated (Holmwood, 2010), these institutions have attracted academically talented scholars and competent administrators to run their programmes. Their intake is always a small number of academically ready students, whom the majority are from wealthy families capable of paying exorbitant tuition fees imposed upon them. The second tier is predominantly teaching only universities with low production of research. According to Giddens and Sutton (2013; p. 908), universities in this category struggle for their survival academically. More often than not their capacity is undermined by factors which entail massification, poor infrastructure, students from poor academic schools, low-economic families and incompetent teaching staff and administrators. The third category of universities is depopulated, and due to their mediocre status, attract students and staff who are academically incompetent. The panacea to their challenging situation results in either a merger or closure as part of saving public resources (Giddens & Sutton, 2013; p. 908). Interestingly, the economic survival of universities depends on their interactive engagement and contribution to the wider society including governments and industries which their funding is derived from (Castells, 2001). As public institutions are funded from the public budget, these entities are required as Cloete et al. (2011) highlighted, should balance the outward looking and inward-looking. This implies that in their drive to excel in research and innovation, they should be balanced with fostering teaching community engagement equally as a core function of any university (van Schalkwyk, 2013).

In Africa, the history of education and higher education in particular is complex and for decades has suffered colonial and apartheid blows. Despite the growing number of academic institutions in the post-colonial era, the marginalisation of the higher education sector as knowledge creators continue to be a reality. Within the continent, education whether basic or tertiary was strategically utilised and abused as a weapon to colonise and domesticate Africans, thus denying Africans educational opportunities to develop intellectually. More brutally, the imposition of Western education systems based on who has colonised which African country, remains critical in the development of Africa socially, economically and politically. Colonisation and apartheid governance systems were entrenched in the African mind with the existence of an identity crisis and undermining of African Indigenous Knowledge (AIK) and its systems as the outcomes. As African intellectuals and scholars such as Ngugi wa Thiongo have noted, Africa would not fully develop unless she claimed unapologetically her educational and cultural inheritance. These scholars have over the decades joined the academic chorus through their writings and became critics of the perpetual imprisonment of Africans through the dominance of Western knowledge systems and also demonstrated the power of knowledge in liberating the mind and advancing Africa's development. The imposition of Western-European knowledge as the only legitimate and scientific system had negative consequences for the development of African human capital. Most of the challenges faced by higher education institutions in Africa emanate from both the former coloniser through their international agencies and African governments themselves. Political interference by governments with unwarranted government interference and abuses of academic freedom undermine the authority and quality of the institutions of higher learning (Teferra & Altbach, 2003, p. 11). The higher education sector is considered to be an excellent centre of knowledge production and leaders in human capital development. However, Teferra and Altbach (2003) argue that most African governments are intolerant of dissent, criticism, nonconformity and free expression of controversial, new or unconventional ideas. These challenges are often exacerbated by Professor Patrice Lumumba's articulation that power to impact change rests with African leaders, yet ordinary people have ideas too. The failure to integrate power and ideas has resulted in the worst governance Africa has ever experienced.

Similarly, to the rest of Africa, higher education in South Africa has not escaped the colonial and apartheid enclave. Since the arrival of the Europeans, education has always been in the spotlight. Historically, the colonial and apartheid eras were notorious in reinforcing Western mentality that Black people are primitive and savages, who through embracing western modern practices and models can only be liberated. Hence, Africans had to replicate western models of education in order to be accepted.

CHALLENGES FACING HIGHER EDUCATION

Challenges facing the higher education sector are enormous and they range from policy related, access and massification without adequate financial and human resources, poor quality of education to politicisation of education, leadership and governance (Morrow, 2008). Most of the challenges inflicting education in general and higher education in particular, border on the legacy of Bantu education and inequality created through unmet promises by the democratic government. Policies enacted during apartheid, especially the Bantu Education Act of 1953 (in Rugunanan, 2015, p. 281), which gave birth to a Bantu education system, saw the separate schools and universities created for various races and ethnic groups. Apartheid education in general, was designed to keep black students in poverty and give them an inferior education and continue to deny them employment opportunities. For historically disadvantaged South Africans, the World Bank Group (2018, p. 68) argues that exclusion remains entrenched in the education system. Lack of quality education adds to the exclusion and marginalisation of most of the students from basic schooling to universities (Anderson, 2016). The structural inequality and poverty due to apartheid remains a reality in all sectors of society with education being the central sector that undermines South Africa's potential to be a developed nation. Education holds the key for most of the black majority to escape the persistent deprivation trap, however, the current nature and status of higher education remains in crisis. As such, DBSA (2008, p. 184) highlighted that the poor educational status does not equip previously disadvantaged children with competitive knowledge and skills not only to escape poverty and inequality, but also for them to contribute to national development. However, the dismal economic crisis together with over-subscription in humanities has resulted according to World Bank Group (2018), to unemployed and underemployed graduates. The unemployed graduates have multiplied and as such, are adding to the statistics of the growing number of unemployed youth in the country.

Most of the challenges besetting higher education, especially universities which are rooted within the weak and poorly managed basic education system which continue to inject ill-prepared learners for university. In the name of transformation, universities were forced to open their doors and relaxing the entrance requirements which not only saw an influx of students from the low-income families, but also students who cannot afford tuition fees including other necessities. Due to the persistence of poverty, unemployment and inequalities, most parents are unable to pay for their educational needs. The World Bank Group (2018, p. 69) attested to that despite South Africa being a middle income country with only 2 million students who can afford higher education. The low numbers of enrolment have been blamed on poor outcomes at lower levels of education where exclusion is entrenched. Currently, the World Bank Group (2018, p. 69) revealed that:

37 percent of the tertiary students are enrolled in universities, another 37 percent enrolled in TVET colleges, 17 percent are distance learners enrolled with the University of South Africa and the rest are enrolled in either community colleges or private higher education institutes.

Despite the improved access and support for black students since 1994 through the National Student Financial Aid Scheme (NSFAS), the above percentages demonstrate that the majority of students from poor backgrounds are still excluded (Bloch, 2009).

SOUTH AFRICA'S FEESMUSTFALL CAMPAIGN

FMF is a student initiated campaign staged to demand a decrease in university fees across South African institutions of higher learning (Gon, 2016). Since its emergence, FMF has received huge media attention and coverage and generated enormous writing and discourses in local, national and international newspapers and journals alike. All these non-academic and academic discourses were centered on the fundamental question which is, is FMF feasible amidst all the pressing priorities warranting public attention by both the government through the Department of Higher Education and Training and the universities respectively? The FMF campaign and later the movement is incrementally triggered by frustrated students, especially in predominantly black universities. The snail's pace of transformation, funding issues and governance embedded challenges became the boiling point for students and their student bodies to stage protests and demonstrations disrupting the operation of universities. Squally, (2015, 2016) were declared FMF, however Ray (2016: 329) traced the discontent among university students way back in 1999 more radically in the University of the North West, Mahikeng campus. SASCO was the vanguard of the campaign geared toward denouncing the lack of institutional transformation, the high fee structure and the university's drift to 'neo-apartheid'. The underpinning grievances of the students were succinctly captured by one student Madondo (in Ray, 2016: 330) who said:

We have been raising issues for years...five years of democracy had not changed the institutional and power structure of the campus. Issues of academic representivity and the democratisation of the council and the curriculum are much of the same.

Generally, transformation if any, took place under the guise of an institutional merger where 'bush or Bantustan' universities and technikons were forced into marriages of inconvenience with white and well-resourced universities (Yigezu, 2013). Despite the mergers of most universities, the institutional culture remains stubbornly unchanged with white Afrikaners and English academics still dominating the teaching staff and councils. Structurally, although some changes took place, these changes pay lip service to deeply rooted transformational inherited predicaments caused by racially and spatially segregated universities and tecknikons. Accordingly, restructuring the system of higher education without addressing the socio-economic challenges of those living in poverty and structural problems in education became a mockery to the previously disadvantaged families and students. However, it should be noted that this campaign is overloaded with demands that transcend the increment of tuition fees to include the entire transformation of the entire higher education system. The FMF should be understood as the microcosm of a variety of unresolved issues and challenges in post-apartheid South Africa. The protests regarding fees were also sported at universities such as Wits and Johannesburg in late 2007, and some demonstrations at the Durban University of Technology (DUT), Tshwane University of Technology (TUT) and the University of Limpopo (UL). Student activism in South Africa had died down but the emergence of FMF revived it. October 2015 has become the milestone for universities across campuses, particularly in student activism in garnering massive support among their fellow student's nation-wide and workers in general (Ray, 2016: 368). The students' alignment with university workers meant these cadres of students had to add demanding the scrapping of 'outsourcing' into their fees must fall demands.

Each university has its own story to tell from negotiating in good faith that their demands would be met to taking to the streets, university council meetings, and ultimately to Parliament. The march to Parliament was organized and joined by the students from Cape Peninsula University of Technology (CPUT), University of the Western Cape (UWC) and the University of Cape Town (UCT). Through FMF, students regardless of race, gender and socio-economic class demonstrated their mobilising skills and their resilience to survive confrontation and brutality in the hands of police and campus security guards' harassment and intimidation. Sit-ins, diplomatic negotiations through their respective SRCs with university councils, broadly with the Department of Higher Education through the Student Union, and demonstrations based on radical confrontation with police were some of the mechanisms utilized by student activists.

STUDENTS DEMAND FOR FREE EDUCATION

In defining free education, it is crucial to look at factors which contribute to the accessibility of education currently available for many students in South Africa. There are funding mechanisms of higher education which enable students to enrol in universities in most of South Africa. Such funding mechanisms are useful but do not cover all the financial barriers to opportunities of higher education, resulting in some students not being able to have access to higher education (Wangenge-Ouma, 2012). For this motive, some scholars argue that in order to fully address the funding issue, the mechanism being used for funding should also necessitate subsidised tuition fees, food, and accommodation (Phungo, 2015). The issue of students demanding free education is heard, nonetheless the majority of these students want free education for everyone irrespective of a students' status whether or not they are poor (Langa, Wangenge-Ouma, Jungblut, & Cloete, 2016; Parker, 2015). Irrespective of students' demands for free education, government officials proclaim that students who can afford higher education should cover their fees (SABC news, 2016). From a critique of government officials, scholars argue that the students' demands regarding free education for all would unreasonably benefit those who can afford the least percentage of fees (Wangenge et al., 2008). The demand for free quality education by students was based on the following as argued by one student interviewee:

As tertiary students, we decided to participate in the Fees Must Fall campaign because we were convinced that education, especially at a tertiary, was being commodified as if it was a product. This, in our view, was regressing some of the progress that had been made post-1994 and a break of promises that had been made by the ANC government to uplift the poor (8 March 2018).

Another student justified her standpoint by saying:

We understood that the majority of South Africans were poor and education was the greatest single asset which would take them out of poverty. Making education a product was never going to bring favour to those hoping to escape the scourge of poverty. Making education free for deserving students is key to progressing the country, in our view, and a necessity (28 June 2018).

Student pursuing free education for all had various reasons which contradicted those of the officials such as the Minister of Higher Education and Training and the Minister of Science and Technology who argue that free education would not be made available because if there was to be free education, no one would be responsible for the costs of that education (Smolentseva, 2015). The citizens of South Africa are already paying tax which enables students to enrol in different universities of their choices, hence the quest for free education will add the burden on tax payers (Moerane, 2015). The country is made up of numerous economists who evaluate issues to do with the capital of the country, hence they argue that free education currently being made available to students refers to students borrowing from the public. When these students get employed in the future, they pay the money thus enabling the future generations of students to enrol in university institutions (Vandenberghe, 2005).

In as much as government officials believe that higher education can never be free, protesting students emphasize that their battle for free higher education forms part of their human rights. They argue that free higher education is a human right and should be made available without requiring a certain amount of money (Moerane, 2015). In the European countries, students have benefited from freed education while in the Scandinavian countries students are even paid for gong to university (Mpofi-Walshe, 2017). Chiloane (2016) argues that if higher education is a human right, it should be made accessible. Scholars such as Acheampong and Kayange (2016) also assert that higher education is a human right and necessitates for it to be accessible to everyone irrespective of the economic status of the particular country.

QUEST FOR ACCESSIBLE AND QUALITY EDUCATION

Students claiming that education is part of their human right and should therefore be made freely available do not recall how that influences the type of education they will receive in return. Scholars like Cloete (2016) argue that education which is free will result into poor quality of education that the universities intend to offer students. Cloete (2016) further claims that in as much as a request for free education can be taken into account, and reduce some inequalities associated with it, the standard of that education provided will reduce while the inequality is done away with, hence Cloete (2016) argues that inequality and quality higher education cannot be achieved at once. Majozi (2016) agrees that if a price for goods and services were to be cut off, that would compromise the quality of those goods. In the favour of his example, Majozi asserts that the public service of health care in South Africa is poorly given to the public and the fact is that public health care service sets the standard at a very low level, not being able to give the best care to its' recipients as possible. In accordance, higher education being free will result in its' standard being very poor. Allen (2005) asserts that the priority for many university institutions is to offer education that is effective to those receiving it. A student highlighted that:

The FMF prioritized accessibility of quality education and access to experts who serve as part of the academic staff at many of the country's tertiary institutions, for all students. The clarion call was that making education freely accessible should not mean that education must be devalued. Students demanded free high quality tertiary education (28 October 2018).

One of the reasons why African education remains poor according to one academic is that free education does not equate to quality education. Quality education in South Africa could be compromised through inadequate funding and massification of unprepared students.

The Bill of Rights in the Constitution of the Republic of South Africa, 1996 is clear with regard to the privileges each citizen must be given. Despite being clear of the document containing the rights of each individual, shocking social differences amid the citizens of South Africa are taking place. The socio-economic disparities mostly favour certain minorities like the middle class, while those in the rural areas and townships form the majority of the disadvantaged. Spreen and Vally (2006) asserts that most of the statistics that make up university enrolment comes from the townships and rural areas. These scholars argue that most young people are not able to attain quality education at the tertiary level due to the backgrounds they come from as most of them come from poor families. Hence, these scholars argue that as much as the Bill of Rights permits access to education for all, the fact remains that students from poor backgrounds find it hard to access higher education. The massification also makes it hard for the state to provide quality higher education for most matriculants. Jansen (2004) makes reference to unlimited access to higher education, equal job opportunities as an ongoing quest that the country is still fighting to acquire.

TRANSFORMATION THROUGH DECOLONISED EDUCATION

There has been countless students' protest associated with the fees must fall movement, resulting in decolonised education in seeing the worst where busses were set alight and has also seen vehicles being stoned Teferra and Altbach (2003) as furious students ultimately spread the entire country with violence through fees must fall (Ngcobo, Manyathela, & Bateman, 2016). The student protests primarily evolved around the fees must fall movement, but it ended up seeing a host of other related consequences apart from the fee issue. Chiloane (2016) emphasises that the fees must fall movement ended up covering a wide range of factors which include the issue of facilities. Regardless of the fact that the issues that the students raised made sense, such a clash between students and the police and the way the violence contributed negatively to the struggling current economic growth of the country.

Decolonised and free education which students in the country fought for has seen some destruction of university property and this could force the staff to exit university offices (Chiloane, 2016). A closer glance at the demands of the students for the reduction of fees and decolonised education reveals that students no longer want a Western paradigm found in universities which neglects their culture (Manjra 2016; Pilane 2016). Some scholars claim that the antiquity of the FeesMustFall movement and service delivery protests replicate the 1970s and 1980s (Lodge & Nasson, 1991; Rhoads, 1998).

The learners of 1976 instigated protests due to the excessively oppressive educational system that existed during their time; as a result, they played a part in tackling the apartheid regime (Bernstein, 1994: xvii; Modise, 2000, pp. 36-7; Morrow, 1998:499). Similarly, the history of the student FeesMustFall movement is believed to be derived from the discontent that might relate to challenges that students face in universities, be it student acculturation, or cultural adaptation to universities (Everatt, 2016; Manjra, 2016; Pilane, 2016). Scholars believe that it is common of the students, who are familiar with their own environment, find it hard to amend to a new university culture. Such a phenomenon calls for knowledge which can be used to assist students to adjust effectively to the context of the university/ties. The knowledge does not only help students, but can help administrators to understand factors which shape the processes of acculturation, such as shared knowledge will enable students to receive the support that is effective in the process. Students view the current higher education sector as being overwhelmed with colonial pedagogy. This pedagogy is being pursued in repression of quality Afrocentric scholarship and seeks to produce a generation of colonised thinkers, who laud Western intellectuals' alternative to their own. Decolonisation of the curriculum was therefore a key issue in the FMF movement because students understood that it was important to validating black scholars and Afrocentric educational systems.

The FeesMustFall student movement resulted from the reduction of higher education institutions from 36 to 21 universities to these adjustments were made through a mechanism of mergers and the issue of funding post-1994 which caused violence during that era (Jansen, 2003a). For this reason, it can be argued that the issue of FeesMustFall is not new as evidence reveals that historically black universities have been characterised by violence due to student protests. To demonstrate, some history is demonstrated by scholars such as Marcia Vilakazi and Musawenkosi Malabela at the Tshwane University of Technology (TUT) and the University of Turfloop (University of Limpopo) regarding financial exclusion. Jansen asserts that the primary mergers of these universities intended to improve access to higher education for black minorities and financial support (National Commission on Higher Education, 1996). Jansen opposes the victory of these transformation mergers which are still marked by many disparities rather, material, cultural and social positions still separates these universities (Jansen, 2003a). To illustrate, TUT (Soshanguve Campus) experienced the negative merger with Technikon Pretoria, which is a historically white. The mergers post-1994 was part of the transformation of South African Higher education. Apparently, the merger of Cape Peninsula University of Technology (CPUT) with Cape Technikon, which was a former white institution, is experiencing strong inequalities between campuses are populated along racial lines. Hence, the FeesMustFall movement which was accompanied by violence is believed to have resulted from such disparities (Mamdani, 2003).

The FeesMustFall movement goes beyond the reduction of higher education fees. Although FeesMustFall was a priority other issues were factored into the protests including social and political issues; the land issue and ideological differences that exist between blacks and whites. During the protests, students pointed out the scarcity and recovery of their African-ness. Students felt that they could not access or restore their African-ness without having ownership of land. Hence, the history of FeesMustFall covers the issues of the curriculum and land. A focus group interview with PASMA and the Feminist group, (2015) stated that students shifted from the FeesMustFall movement to call for free decolonised education. Students articulated their grievances on broader social issues and structural transformation.

The FeesMustFall movement strived to remove the boundaries of power while risking arrest. Students were determined to bring change to the country and the belief of black liberation, as well as the attitude that will tackle the foundation of whiteness. Thus, the aforesaid evidence shows that the history of the FeesMustFall movement covers many factors. The imbalances of the past were highlighted by referring to the history of education in the country. At tertiary level, student movements have grown strong, rally around the issue of finance as well as broader political issues such as the role of Afrikaans as a language of instruction or the aim of interpreting South African history through an Africans lens (#FeesMustFall) (World Bank, 2018). The FeesMustFall movement raised numerous interesting issues other than the fees within spaces of universities; rather, it revealed profound, deeply seated alienation and frustrations of black protestors. Moreover, the aforementioned evidence reveals that black subgroups are still undermined and for this reason, the FeesMustFall movement did not evolve around the issue of fees only, but was rather shared black pain and rage over lack of higher education opportunities. Fanon (1952, p. 82) asserts that it does not bother a black man to be black; that is not the issue but rather, the black man is concerned about being black in relation to the white man. Hence, the issue of whiteness and blackness ought to be understood. Power dynamics of suppression need to be taken into consideration as they exist between these aforementioned groups. The issue of RhodesMustFall was due to the broader racial identities that existed in that institution (Bosch, 2017, p. 225). The FeesMustFall movement empowered activists to play a role in broader discussions regarding the issue of racial identity.

One of the students who protested reported that they joined the movement in order to bring free decolonised education. The PASMA-affiliated students (interviewed 2016) agreed that they joined the movement for change and that change had to do with free decolonised education. The argument evolved around the inclusion of black minorities in universities who argued that education granted to blacks should enable them to be empowered and thus ensuring black independency in terms of both doing and thinking (Crenshaw, 1989). Another issue that emerged was that of using black South African heroes such as Steve Biko and Chris Hani's names at universities rather than white names. Over and above the aforesaid arguments, students further argued that decolonisation should be about the composition of the academy, the symbols that are found in universities and the university architecture. Thus, students' movement for decolonised education was associated with dissatisfaction of Eurocentric knowledge which exists in South African universities. Gumede (2016, p 186) notes that South Africa's student uprisings have generally focused their anger at symbols of apartheid and colonialism. Gumede further states that the power structures of colonialism and apartheid are largely intact and that the symbols are stark reminders of lived racial, social and economic inequalities. Ndlovu-Gatsheni (2013, p 46) cautions that the renaming of previously dominant symbols that reveal Eurocentrism should be thought about very carefully.

Decolonisation of higher education has also to do with physical and social restoration of the university space. This covers radical and alternative ways in which the students learn. Nicolson (2015) argues that students complained about the issue of language politics which is particularly pronounced at historically white institutions. Students who were interviewed were against the notion of using Afrikaans which favours Afrikaner students at the expense of black students. Fanon (1964, p. 105) disagrees that true liberation that is dominated by the colonial elements but rather favours the demolition of the colonial system which covers the language issue, customs and images that belongs to the colonialists, and also the destruction of the exclusion which black students face. These students asserted that when they speak of decolonisation, they speak about the curriculum speaking to them, not to white people. They reported that they wanted to learn university modules in their own languages (Group interview, PSMA and Feminist participating students, 2016). These students felt that the African National Congress had failed to make meaningful changes after 1994. African communities are driven by their morals and values which are perceived to be norms among them. These still shape different societies in the African communities. Nyamnjoh, Holeta, Le Grange, Chemhuru, and Molefe

(2016) argue that many students when enrolling in universities of South Africa, tend to realise there are biased Eurocentric epistemological traditions which deviate from their perceived norms when they enrol at universities. When students enrol in different previously white dominated universities, they experience blackness in their own country and they perceive such as a site of perpetual suffering and oppression. Nyamnjoh et al. (2016) assert that these students believe that what belongs to them has deliberately been taken away from them. Fanon (1952) asserted that a black man's' destiny is to be white; nonetheless for these students the priority is to repossess the lost resources which will allow them to set new ways.

The FeesMustFall movement was inspired by the discourse of Black Consciousness, which called for blacks to thoroughly understand their situation and oppose the long domination of whites that has been in existence (Biko, 2015). Biko referred to Black being beautiful, hence the movement which Blacks initiated, forced them to stand against an inferiority complex and deliver themselves from the oppressive structures they had been frightened to oppose. Indeed, Altbach (1996) has a valid point when he asserts that protesting of students started as limited enthusiasm but ended up fuelling external issues which ultimately caused almost all universities to go on strike, resulting in excessive violence between students and the police. Concerns which also arose through the FeesMustFall movement were societal issues (Bond, 2015). The chapter notes that the primary factor of the student protests was about the issue of fees, but also went on to include other issues with regards to the apartheid era and the domination of a white culture in universities which oppresses black students.

VICTORIES GAINED THROUGH FMM CAMPAIGN

Students of the FeesMustFall movement were determined to raise their voices until they were heard (Burger, 2018). To argue in favour of the aforementioned thesis, evidence reveals that a total of 52 percent of the students were content about the Zero percent increase in tuition fees that were announced for the year 2016 (Bozzoli, 2015). In the dissimilar, a certain number of students were not certain whether or not to favour the rest of the students with regard to their response regarding the zero tuition fee increment, these 48 percent of students were worried about what they perceived could force university institutions to double up their costs if the university was not able to make up for the loss. Bazzoli (2015) reported that some of the student were against the idea of zero fee increment on the basis of economic situation. The interviewed student stated that the economy of the country was in bad state. The implication of free education could lead to competing prioritisation of resources including infrastructure. The adoption of free education could see some lecturers moving into the private institutions. Student interviewees highlighted that through

FMF, both university management and the Department of Higher Education were able to enter into dialogue with the outcomes such as higher education announced free for the poor and missing middle class students. The FMF campaign managed to push the authority under the leadership of the ANC to establish the Heher commission to specifically look at the feasibility of free education in the South African higher education sector. To attest to the above victories, one of the students stated that:

The FMF movement should be credited with creating a nationwide discourse on the state of higher education in the country. FMF should be credited with the Heher commission. It should be credited with the disbursement of NSFAS funding to many more students than in the previous years (28 November 2018).

Critically, one of the FMF student leaders added that:

To be honest, there weren't many victories in the FMF movement as the education system is still untransformed. Education is, still, unfortunately a commodity in our view – and because the state of basic education is wanting, many students from poor households are unable to access tertiary education (28 October 2018).

Seemingly, the FeesMustFall movement benefitted those conquered in it. The statement given by the government of South Africa, outlined that it can make free higher education available. Still, the majority of about 66 percent of students replied undesirably to the governments' response. Students realise that already the national budget that is addressed each year, fails to cover essential issues with the money. Moreover, it is believed that funding for higher education do not have access enough funding that will ensure that a student is sustainably supported. Cloete (2015) argues that percentages of the Gross Domestic Product (GDP) are constantly poor and it should be remembered that the GDP stabilises higher education since the budget that government allocates for higher education is currently taking strain. Indeed, students have won the struggle of the fees not increasing. Other students stated that the economy of the country will be easily affected due to the zero fee increment. Some students were opposed to the zero fee increment, fearing that it would result into high unemployment should higher education be made free.

As the former president, Mr Jacob Zuma had announced the zero fee increment on the 23rd of October 2015, some students were content about the decision (Cloete, 2015). Even so, evidence reveals that other students were against the decision and continued protesting (Moerane, 2015). Students who did not surrender were in quest for fee-free higher education for all. To criticise the idioms "fee-free higher education for the disadvantaged" and "free higher education for all" is fundamental; seemingly these two idioms do no convey analogous meanings hence, they ought to be examined (Cloete, 2015, p.2). Scholars criticise the notion of free higher education for all not being a good idea, Cloete (2016, p. 8) asserts that instead of stabilizing the poor, free-fee higher education has greater chance of generating harm to the poor than actually assisting them. North West University (2016) agrees with Cloete, and argue that free education has already resulted to numerous constraints of strengthening inequalities and poor political economies which cannot afford such education. The North West University raises its' critique on the basis that in order for economies to operate efficiently, they should call for growing resources to sustain education that embraces excellence.

Scholars such as Cloete (2016, p. 9) oppose the notion of fee-free higher education for all, reasonably proposes that there must be a mutual joint with regard to the costs, amongst all the stakeholders involved. In most cases, socio economic status oppress students, some who do enrol in university institutions are unable to cover all the essential costs, hence such stigma attached to them accelerate as a restriction. For this reason, Cloete continues to call for weakening the aforementioned restriction. Moreover, the life expectancy for graduates must be higher than of those who do not have qualifications, the life expectancy involves the period of time in which a graduate has to retire on. Finally, Cloete asserts that there should be longer public savings from the contribution to the system, and then later on those savings may be used for funding of public universities Cloete (2016). Thus, Cloete asserts that when graduates repay the money over a period of time, fee-free higher education stands excessive chances to be achieved.

COUNTING THE FINANCIAL COST

Students, in the quest for free higher education are not aware of the multiple problems that the economy of South Africa is in, these problems covers the issue of unemployment which is excessively high, the schooling systems which are drastically poor as well as the inequality of society (Acheampong & Kayange, 2016; Zusman, 2005). Looking at the GDP of the country, suppose government intended to at least spend 1 percent of the gross domestic product of the country, on higher education to be precise, the overall costs would make the sum total of R41 billion. Still, Acheampong et al. (2016) assert that in the year 2015-16, the budget that was made for higher education amounted to R30 billion in the financial year of those two years. The only difference that was seen from the spending on higher education over the past years was between 0.68 percent and 0.72 percent as asserted by Cloete (2015). South Africa seems to have less expenditure when relatively compared to other countries. Brazil seems to have spent 0.95 percent on higher education, followed by Senegal and Ghana which spent about 1.4 percent (Cloete, 2015). South Africa funds closely to 12 percent on higher education while Brazil funds about 20 percent for higher education. This evidence shows how South Africa is struggling to cover funding costs for universities in the county. The only way South Africa could enable many students to enrol in university institutions is by increasing funding to a more levels compared to that of the international 1 percent of the GDP (Cloete, 2015). Arguably, one of the students said:

The financial cost of FMF must be credited on government, which refused to create an enabling environment for discussions and dialogue to take place. Students are of the view that it did not have to take students to march in the streets for government to even consider transforming pedagogy and create access for the poor or even establish the Heher Commission (28 November 2018).

There are other alternative ways that the government can use to alleviate the stigma associated with the shortage of funding for higher education. Teferra (2016) states that the South African government can switch to the raising revenues by raising existing taxes or by borrowing money at a cost that is high. Nonetheless, Moerane (2015) asserts that it should be taken into account that tax payers are already burdened by tax which is straining them. Moerane further asserts that some of these tax payers earn a very small income but still have to subsidise education which highly favours the rich (Cloete, 2016). These scholars contend the notion of paying tax due to the fact that some of these tax payers will not have access to higher education but still have to contribute to the tax; an advantage of certain minorities who will benefit from such arrangement (Hull, 2015). Vandenberghe (2005) agrees with Cloete and Hull by saying that financing free higher education through the collection of income taxes throws the unethical burden to poor people. In essence, the zero fee increment has been a victory for many students as most the students come from poor families. Scholars revealed that free education will result in a wide range of factors associated with the quality of education. Hence, in as much as students' quest for free education and government surrendered to the students' demands, the government had to recollect and strategically think of the best way to provide free education while not suppressing the current economic growth which scholars discovered to be currently struggling as it has been assigned to stabilise higher education despite the crisis it already Teferra and Altbach (2003) faces. The current societal inequalities could be a barometer to gauge if whether or not free higher education is feasible. Considering other pressing issues that demand fiscal attention, would prioritising free education be wise? The announcement by former President Zuma, that education would be free, thus targeting poor and working class students with family income of less than R350,

000 per year in December 2017 (Word Bank Group, 2018, p. 69). On the contrary, the release of the Heher Commission Report stated that free university education is not feasible or unaffordable for government. As an alternative, the Report proposed the government-guaranteed loans, thus, increasing public funding thereby reducing inefficiencies in resources use.

FUTURE RESEARCH DIRECTIONS

The chapter interrogated FMF as an expression of students' quest for accessible, quality and a decolonized higher education post-apartheid South Africa. In the context of reluctant higher education transformation FMF as a student led campaign depicted unfinished business within the sector. It became apparent in this campaign that financial accessibility for students does not resolve all the challenges engulfing the higher education sector. Equally important in the transformation agenda is the overhaul of curriculum which is still dominated by Eurocentric knowledge systems. Having highlighted these daunting challenges, more research is needed with particular focus on student leadership and its impact on higher education governance and management. This premised on the discourse that students together with their student movement have to take a responsible leadership which is more influenced by students' inspirations as opposed to party political influences. More research is also needed on educational policies.

CONCLUSION

This chapter deliberated on the FMF campaign staged by tertiary students between 2016 and 2017 from the context of higher education transformation. The chapter has wrestled with conceptual, definitional and operational issues underpinning FMF from the political economy perspective. FMF is understood to be part of political-educational demands framed to transform the higher education system for accessibility, affordability and quality. Since the dawn of the democratic order, issues pertaining to accessibility, affordability and quality have been conflicting hence; Ramphele (2008: 196) argues that excellence was compromised over equity by the political elites. This has dire consequences directly linked to some of the FMF's demands to have justice in terms of access and quality and, institutional and curriculum development that responds to the needs of local people. However, this call questions the relevance of universities in post-apartheid South Africa beyond being ivory towers for the privileged few.

While the demand for free education was viewed as politically appealing by tertiary students and the general public, the author argued that its economic feasibility could be a distance dream provided there is long term planning. Considering the existing economic pressures and dwindling economic growth, the quest for free education remains at the peripheral of national priorities. Despite the available funding solicited primarily from private foundations and public funding through NEFSAS, Ikusasa Student Financial Aid Programme (ISFAP) and the annual budget, universities and students' needs exceed financial resources. From the deliberations in this chapter, it is apparent that the FMF campaign is not a linear encounter, but a series of demands evolving under the guise of no-fee increment at tertiary institutions. Thus, FMF epitomises the endured struggle for democratizing the education system for a democratized South Africa in a post-apartheid era.

REFERENCES

Acheampong, P., & Kayange, J. J. (2016). University education in Ghana: A privilege or a right? *International Journal of Research Studies in Education*, *6*(3), 17–25. doi:10.5861/ijrse.2016.1563

Allen, W. R. (2005). A forward glance in the mirror: Diversity challenged – access, equity and success in higher education. *Educational Researcher*, *34*(7), 18–23. doi:10.3102/0013189X034007018

Altbach, P. G. (1996). Students and politics. *Comparative Education Review*, *10*(2), 175–187. doi:10.1086/445214

Amtaika, A. (2013). *Local Government in South Africa since 1994: Leadership, Democracy, development and Service Delivery in a Post-Apartheid Era*. Durham, NC: Carolina Academic Press.

ANC. (1994). *The Reconstruction and Development Programme: A Policy Framework*. Johannesburg: Umanyano Publications.

Anderson, B. (2016). Education with Emphasis on South African Education. In Sociology: A South African Perspective (pp. 156-171). Hampshire, UK: Cengage Learning EMEA.

Bernstein, H. (1994). *The Rift: The exile experience of South Africans*. London: Jonathan Cape.

Biko, S. (2015). *I write what I like: Selected writings*. University of Chicago Press.

Bloch, G. (2009). *The toxic Mix: What is Wrong with South African Schools and How to Fix It.* Cape Town: NB Publishers.

Bond, P. (2015). Student protesters win as race and class fused in epic battle. *Green Left Weekly, 1075*, 3.

Bosch, T. (2017). Twitter activism and youth in South Africa: The case of #RhodesMustFall. *Information Communication and Society, 20*(2), 221–231. doi: 10.1080/1369118X.2016.1162829

Burger, P. (2018). *Getting it Right: A New Economy for South Africa.* Sandton: KMM Review Publishing.

Castell, M. (2001). Universities as dynamic systems of contradictory functions. In Challenges of Globailisation: South African database with Manuel Castells (pp. 206-224). Cape Town: Maskew Miller Longman.

Castell, M. (2003). *Conversations with Manuel Castells.* Oxford, UK: Polity Press.

Cebekhulu, A. (2013). *Unhlaba Uyahlaba: The World is Thorny. Wandsbeck.* Reach Publishers.

Chikane, R. (2018). *Breaking a Rainbow, Building a Nation: The Politics behind #FeesMustFall Movements.* Johannesburg: Picador Africa.

Chiloane, M. (2016). Wits workl 22rd dies after inhaling extinguisher fumes set off during protest. *Eyewitness News.* Retrieved from http://ewn.co.za/2016/09/26/Wits-worker-dies-after-inhaling-extinguisher-fumes

Cloete, N. (2016). *The flawed ideology of "free higher education".* Retrieved from http://www.universityworldnews. com/article.php?story=20151104111825416

Crenshaw, K. (1989). Demarginalising the intersection of race and sex: A black feminist critique of antidiscrimination doctrine, Feminist theory and antiracist politics. *University of Chicago Legal Forum, 140*, 139–167.

Dayile, A. (2018). Aryan Kaganof's Decolonising Wits: A film analysis. In We Are No Longer at Ease: The Struggle for #FeesMustFall (pp. 73-80). Sunnyside: Jakana Media Ltd.

De Gayardon, A., & Bernasconi, A. (2016). *Chilean Universities: Not so tuition-free after all.* Retrieved from http://ejournals.bc.edu/ojs/index.php/ihe/article/view/9372

Everatt, D. (2016). *What must fall: Fees or the South African state?* Retrieved from https://www.enca.com/opinion/whatmust-fall-fees-or-the-south-african-state

Fanon, F. (1952). *Black Skin, White Masks*. London: Pluto Press.

Fanon, F. (1964). *Toward the African Revolution: Political Essays*. New York: Grove Press.

Freire, P. (1993). *The Pedagogy of the oppressed*. London: Penguin.

Giddens, A., & Sutton, P. W. (2013). Sociology (7th ed.). Malden, MA: Policy Press.

Godsell & Chikane. (2016). The Roots of the Revolution. In S. Booysen (Ed.), *FeesMustFall: Student Revolt, Decolonization and Governance in South Africa* (pp. 54–73). Johannesburg: Wits University Press.

Gon, S. (2016). Fees can Fall, But First.... Johannesburg: South African Institute of Race Relations (IRR).

Higgins, J. (2013). *Academic Freedom in a Democratic South Africa: Essays and Interviews on higher Education and the Humanities*. Johannesburg: Wits University Press.

Honwana, A. (2013). *The Time of Youth: Work, Social Change and Politics in Africa*. Boulder, CO: Kumarian Press.

Hull, G. (2015). *Free university education is not the route to social justice*. Retrieved from http://theconversation.com/free-university-education-is-not-the-route-to-social-justice-49755

Jansen, J. (2003). Changes and continuities in South Africa's higher education system, 1994–2004. In L. Chisholm (Ed.), *Changing Class: Education and Social Change in Post-Apartheid*. Cape Town: HSRC Press.

Jansen, J. D. (2004). Changes and continuities in South Africa's higher education system, 1994–2004. In L. Chilsholm (Ed.), *Changing Class: Education and Social Change in Post-Apartheid* (pp. 293–314). Cape Town: HSRC Press.

Johnson, K., & Jacobs, S. (Eds.). (2012). *Encyclopedia of South Africa. Scottsville*. University of KwaZulu-Natal Press.

Langa, P., Wangenge-Ouma, G., Jungblut, J., & Cloete, N. (2016). *South Africa and the illusion of free higher education*. Retrieved from http://www.universityworldnews.com/article.php?story=20160223145336908

Luyat, Y. G. (2003). The Development of Higher Education in Africa: A Historical Survey. In D. Teferra & P. G. Altbach (Eds.), *African Higher Education: An International Reference Handbook* (pp. 15–43). Bloomington, IN: Indiana University Press.

Maake, N. (2011). *Barbarism in Higher Education: Once Upon a time in a University*. Johannesburg: Ekaam Books CC.

Majozi, P. (2016). *Quality education isn't free. Expect a fallout, either way*. Retrieved from http://www.biznews.com/thought-leaders/2016/09/28/phumlani-majozi-quality-education-isnt-free-expect-a-fallout-eitherway

Maneta, R. (2018). 2015, the year of the student: A personal account. In We Are No Longer at Ease: The Struggle for #FeesMustFall (pp. 125-127). Sunnyside: Jakana Media Ltd.

Modupe, T. (2018). What does a revolutionary look like? In We Are No Longer at Ease: The Struggle for #FeesMustFall (pp. 121-124). Sunnyside: Jakana Media Ltd.

Moerane, B. (2015). *SA far from free tertiary education: Economist*. Retrieved from http://www.sabc.co.za/news/a/76b40b004b239e5bbb38fb445cadceaa/SA-far-from-free-tertiary-education:-Economist20153112

Morrow, S. (2008). Race, Redress and Historically Black Universities. In A. Habib & K. Bentley (Eds.), *Racial Redress & Citizenship in South Africa* (pp. 263–288). Cape Town: HSRC Press.

Ndlovu-Gatsheni, S. (2013). Decolonising the university in Africa. *Think*, *51*, 46–51.

Ngcobo, Z., Manyathela, C., & Bateman, B. (2016). *FeesMustFall protests turn violent, bus set alight in Jhb CBD*. Retrieved from http://ewn.co.za/2016/10/10/Bus-set-alight-during-Wits-protests

Nicolson, G. (2015). Luister: The viral film exposing South Africa's ongoing racism problem. *TheGuardian*. Retrieved from https://www.theguardian.com/world 2015/Sep/07/luister-south-Africa-film-racism-Stellenbosch

Nyamnjoh, F. (2016). *RhodesMustFall: Nibbling at Resilient Colonialism in South Africa*. Bamenda, Cameroon: Langaa Research and Publishing Common Initiative Group.

Phungo, R. (2015). *University fees: Free higher education is possible in South Africa*. Retrieved from https://www.dailymaverick.co.za/article/2015-10-21-university-fees-free-higher-education-ispossible-in-south-africa/#.WRG5qOWGPcs

Ramphele, M. (2008). *Laying Ghosts to rest in South Africa: Dilemmas of the Transformation in South Africa*. Cape Town: Tafelberg.

SABC News. (2016). *Free education for all not feasible: Manana.* Retrieved from http://www.sabc.co.za/news/a/cd65af004c50f448a2cdbe8be7d9f0df/Free-education-for-all-not-feasible:-Manana20160407

Smolentseva, A. (2015). *Will there be free higher education in Russia?* Retrieved from https://ejournals.bc.edu/ojs/index.php/ihe/article/viewFile/7485/6680

Spreen, C. A., & Vally, S. (2006). Education rights, education policies and equality in South Africa. *International Journal of Educational Development, 26*(4), 352–362. doi:10.1016/j.ijedudev.2005.09.004

Teferra, D. (2016). *Why free education is a folly in an unequal society.* Retrieved from http://theconversation.com/whyfree-education-is-a-folly-in-an-unequal-society-54515

Teferra, D., & Altbach, P. G. (2003). Trends and Perspectives in African Higher Education. In D. Teferra & P. Altbach (Eds.), *African Higher Education: An International Reference Handbook* (p. 314). Bloomington, IN: Indiana University Press.

Van Schalkwyk, F. (2013). Beyond Engagement: Exploring tensions between the academic core and engagement activities at Nelsomn Mandela Metropolitan University. Academic Press.

Vandenberghe, V. (2005). *Free higher education. Regressive transfer or implicit loan?* Discussion Paper 31. UC Louvain, Department des Sciences Economiques.

Wangenge-Ouma, G. (2012). Tuition fees and the challenge of making higher education a popular commodity in South Africa. *Higher Education, 64*(6), 831–844. doi:10.100710734-012-9531-6

World Bank Group. (2018). *An Incomplete Transition: Overcoming the Legacy of Exclusion in South Africa.* Cape Town: UCT Press.

Yigezu, M. (2013). Funding Higher Education in Ethiopia: Modalities, Challenges, Opportunities and Prospects. In D. Teferra (Ed.), *Funding Higher Education in Sub- Saharan Africa* (pp. 38–71). Basingstoke, UK: Palgrave Macmillan. doi:10.1057/9781137345783_3

ADDITIONAL READING

Nash, A. (2006). Restructuring South African universities. In R. Pithouse (Ed.), *Asinamali: University struggles in post-apartheid South Africa* (pp. 1–10). Eritrea: Africa World Press Inc.

Ntsebeza, L. (2012). African Studies at UCT: An Overview. In T. Nthlapo & H. Garuba (Eds.), *African studies in the Post-colonial University* (pp. 1–22). Cape Town: University of Cape Town.

Soudien, C. (2004). Constituting the class: an analysis of the process of integration in South African schools. In L. Chisholm (Ed.), *Changing class: Educational and social change in post- apartheid South Africa* (pp. 89–114). Cape Town: HSRC Press.

KEY TERMS AND DEFINITIONS

1976 Student Revolt: It is known to be the revolution waged by both the secondary and tertiary students fighting against the imposition of Afrikaans as a medium of instruction and broadly the discriminatory and exploitative apartheid regime.

Decolonized Education: It is the education system with curriculum that is not influenced by Western knowledge systems and curriculum, language, cultural background.

Eurocentric Curriculum: It is an educational curriculum that is dominated by Eurocentric or Western knowledge systems.

FeesMustFall: It is a campaign or movement initiated between 2015 and 2016 led by South African tertiary students demanding free, quality, and decolonized education. This campaign was triggered by increasing tuition fees for 2016 as well as incomplete higher education sector.

Higher Education: It is an education that is provided mainly for universities, college, or post-schooling students at institutions of higher learning, be they public or private.

Ikusasa Student Financial Programme: It is a funding model for poor and middle-income students proposed by government that advocate for the contributions from donors, private, and public sectors.

National Student Financial Aid Scheme (NSFAS): It is a financial scheme for needy tertiary students established through the National Student Financial Aid Scheme Act of 1999 which provide students with bursaries and loans to cover tuition fees, accommodation and food allowances.

Quality Education: It is an education in which its curriculum is of great quality and designed to impart relevant skills, knowledge enabling students to gain academic competencies for socio-economic survival.

Chapter 8
(Un)feasibility of FeesMustFall Campaign From a Political Economy Perspectives

Ndwakhulu Stephen Tshishonga
University of KwaZulu-Natal, South Africa

ABSTRACT

The FeesMustFall campaign since October 2015 has grown to be one of the biggest movements ever witnessed in the history of South African student politics. Similarly to the struggle waged by 1976 youth against the dominance of Afrikaans as the medium of instruction, FMF challenges the current government and universities to provide free, quality, and decolonized higher education. Considering the slow pace of economic growth, the realization of free and quality education might be an impossible dream. Thus, dropping the fees seems to be a financial relieve to the poor students, but not the panacea to challenges faced by institutions of higher learning. FMF movement challenges both the government and ANC leadership to walk the talk by implementing policies and resolutions taken to transform higher education from declining. The question is, What are the costs and benefit of free education as advocated through FeesMustFall campaign? Can South Africa afford sustainable free education without compromising other areas of need?

INTRODUCTION

Higher education in (South) Africa has a long history. This history is linked to the decades of imperialism, colonialism and apartheid. Higher education in Africa is traceable to the pyramids of Egypt, the obelisks of Ethiopia and the Kingdom of

DOI: 10.4018/978-1-5225-8461-2.ch008

Timbuktu (Teferra & Altbach, 2003, p. 4). These academic centers of higher learning since disappeared, hence the adoption of Western models tradition and learning. Common to colonial higher education were its limited access, imposition of the language of the colonizers, limited academic freedom and limited curriculum (Teferra & Altbach, 2003, p. 4). These factors became the basis for sustenance of the legacy of colonial higher education in Africa. In South Africa, formal education goes to the opening of first school by the Dutch East Indian Company in 1658 for the children of the settlers (Johnson & Johnson, 2012). Since then the education has undergone through changes from 1910 Opinion of South Africa where white children were afforded an educational opportunity to the reinforcement of apartheid education in 1953 through the establishment of Bantu Education. It was the introduction of Bantu Education Act in 1953 under the Afrikaner-led National Party that the root of segregatory education based on racial and ethnicity was sown.

However, despite the progress made, the 8 percent fee increment in 2017 by most of the universities has angered the students who declared 2017 'the year of free education' (Fengu, 2017: 9) or 'freed education in our lifetime' (Maseremule, 2016, p. 19) and vowed to intensify the campaign until their demands are met. The SA Union of Student has committed itself to a mantra that says 'no academically serving student will be excluded on the basis of their financial status' (Fengu, 2017, p. 9). Additionally, the student bodies have warned that protests could begin as the first week of the academic year if students are excluded on the basis of affordability (City Press, 2017, p. 2). However, London (2017, p. 9) warns against 'big bang' type of the solution to the challenges raised by the students and for the progress to be made in this regard, he proposed three mindset changes to take place. These changes entail focusing on what is possible in education, thus viewing real learning as a product of creative and constructive engagement from multiple viewpoints. Second, mindset should take place especially in understanding that any good educational system should be inherently developing. Third, mindset should not only embrace learning as the product of creative and constructive engagement, and evolving educational system, but also that education and learning should be incremental, thus work in progress. This chapter therefore interrogates the feasibility or non-feasibility of free education by narrating the implications of political rhetoric on the economy. The chapter begins by grounding the state of higher education in South Africa. The historical background is followed by theoretical exposition on the political economy as the conceptual framework guiding the chapter. A brief explanation and its genesis of #FeesMustFall campaign is traced followed by the political grounding informing the campaign.

STATE OF HIGHER EDUCATION IN SOUTH AFRICA

Higher education in (South) Africa has a long history (Johnson & Jacobs, 2012). This history is linked to the decades of imperialism, colonialism and apartheid. Higher education in Africa is traceable to the pyramids of Egypt, the obelisks of Ethiopia and the Kingdom of Timbuktu (Teferra & Altbach, 2003, p. 4). These academic centers of higher learning since disappeared, hence the adoption of Western models tradition and learning. Common to colonial higher education were its limited access, imposition of the language of the colonizers, limited academic freedom and limited curriculum (Teferra & Altbach, 2003, p. 4). These factors became the basis for sustenance of the legacy of colonial higher education in Africa. In South Africa, formal education goes to the opening of first school by the Dutch East Indian Company in 1658 for the children of the settlers (Johnson & Johnson, 2012). Since then the education has undergone through changes from 1910 Opinion of South Africa where white children were afforded an educational opportunity to the reinforcement of apartheid education in 1953 through the establishment of Bantu Education. It was the introduction of Bantu Education Act in 1953 under the Afrikaner-led National Party that the root of segregatory education based on racial and ethnicity was sown (Johnson & Jacobs, 2012). Unfortunately, formal education in most African countries was introduced during colonial times and was an instrument used by colonisers to trained low-level clerical staff (Nshemererwe, 2016, p. 9). Higher education is recognized as a major resources especially for national development and knowledge production, however, it was also noticed that its structure and capacity was dented by the apartheid inheritance (RDP, 1994, p. 66). Thus, education was pursued and encouraged for domestication agenda as opposed to developing analytical and independent African thinkers and scholars. In essence, the colonial education borrowing from a Brazilian scholar, Paulo Freire, highlighted that 'banking' education was designed to domesticate rather than 'problem-posing' aimed at liberating the students. In this context, Banking education has resemblance with Bantu or Inferior Education imposed by the Nationalist Party in 1953, which was extended to universities through the Education Act of 1959 (Johnson & Jacobs, 2012). Freire further argues that the education system became the weapon of oppression and those who run it are the oppressors.

Since 1994, higher education has undergone tremendous transformation including the development of educational policies and their amendments. The outcomes of higher education transformation led to the merging of various institutions resulting in 23 academic institutions being formed (Mpofu-Walsh, 2017). Since the merger, two additional universities were built, one in Mpumalanga and the second one at Kimberly in the North West Province culminating into 26 universities (Mpofu-Walsh,

2017). Thus, in a democratic dispensation, and as part of redress, restructuring of higher education saw the opening up of previously only white institutions (English an Afrikaans) such as Pretoria, Stellenbosch, Free State, Rand Afrikaanse (now University of Johannesburg) for black students for the first time (Maake, 2011). However, the paradox of this transformation resulted in massification and flooding of students academically unprepared to survive in the institutions of higher learning. The consequences of massification coupled with lack of funding in higher education has led to high drop outs and degree incomplete. Under-resourced universities especially the previously marginalized and Bantustan institutions, continue to struggle to transform themselves into academically credible entities. Under-resourced universities in particular funding is not only a South African challenge but a wide spread in African higher education institutions. In Africa, with challenges such as fiscal constraints, demand for access, the legacy of colonialism and long-standing economic and social crises (Tererra & Altbach, 2003, p. 3), higher education remains unfinished business. These challenges together with state bureaucracy not only drive away highly qualified and trained experts and academics. Attest to these challenges were unearthed by students' protests demanding for institutional transformation and quality free higher education through FMF movement (Mzileni, 2018).

In South African Institutions of Higher Learning, the last quarter of 2015 and the entire 2016 was branded by student discontent and demonstrations through the Fees Must Fall campaign (Olalde, 2017: 9). Through this campaign, the students went on rampage to demand not only free education, but also transformation of universities and decolonized curriculum at universities. The campaign was graduated into a full-fledged movement led by students in various campus throughout the country and such it was captured by the media as the most popular and widely written about. Unfortunately, similarly to any other struggles waged in South Africa, FMF had victories and casualties. Through the resilient of the students and their student bodies, the FMF managed to push both the government and university councils to enter into negotiations. Emanating from such negotiations, special through the South Africa Union of Students, an apex body representing students, a Fees Commission was set to look into the challenges and funding for tertiary students (Mpofu-Walsh, 2017). Prior to the release of the Commission report, former President Zuma prematurely pronounced free education for poor and working class students from the families earning less that R350,00 per year. This decision generated widespread criticisms especially from academics and higher education official was was contradicted by the findings of Heher Fee Commission. On the contrary, the Commission suggested that free university education would not be unaffordable to government. Further, the Report proposed government-guaranteed loans and advise an increment for tertiary education funding from 0.6 percent of GDP to 1 percent (World Bank Group, 2018,

p. 69). Essentially, government was advised to assess the actual cost of free education for the poor and working class with the primary purpose of searching for strategies to mobilize sufficient additional public resources to cover the new financing needs (World Bank Group, 2018). For tertiary education institutions, the Commission suggested ways to be found to reduce inefficiencies especially in resources utilization. The perseverance of the students has paid off as additional funding has been allocated through the national Minister of Finance's medium budget speech. This allocation is a top-up to the normal portion of funding through the national budget from the Treasury. However, the FMF protests became violent resulting into fierce clashes with police and security companies hired by the universities and as a consequence some of the students were incarcerated. Academically, the strikes and demonstrations were so destructive and radical, and the presence of police, universities witnessed the 'militarisation of campuses' and closer was panacea to curl down the students' anger and frustrations.

POLITICAL ECONOMY FRAMEWORK

The chapter make use of political economy to gauge the (un)feasibility of providing free education at higher education as demanded by the students. For free and quality higher education, political decision through public institutions such as the parliament should be aligned to the economic growth and resource distribution. Schoeman and Graham (2017, p. 243) define the political economy of a country to designate the way in which the production, distribution and consumption of wealth are organised within that society. Through political economy, politics and economics converged to forged a developmental state capable of intervening in the planning of the economy. It is 'how politics determines aspects of the economy, and how economic institutions determine the political process' as well as 'the dynamic interaction between the two forces (Martin Staniland cited in Handleman, 1996, p. 216). It is the way in which production in a country is distributed and consumption of wealth is organised within a society (Staniland, 1985). Thus, political economy is essentially about the state capacity to balance the market forces and meeting people needs, hence politics play a determinant role in regulating the economic growth and development of any given society (Handelman, 1996). Political economy is thus the role and domain of the state, however, in the case where the state has adopted liberal economic policies underpinned by free-market systems, the state is limited in playing a meaningful role (Schoeman & Graham, 2017, p. 243). The link between politics and economic compelled the state to exercise its leadership and coordination role especially in developing and growing the economy.

The South African stark reality is that in 1994 political freedom was won enabling all citizens regardless of race, gender and ethnic groupings can vote, however the economic emancipation remains a challenge. Schoeman and Graham (2017, p. 5) highlighted the paradox of attaining political freedom on one hand while on the other hand the economic exclusion and marginalisation based on racial lines and apartheid historical legacy of socio-economic and political discrimination. The persistent of poverty, unemployment and inequality paints a gloomy reality faced by the majority who happened to be blacks. The inherited capitalist economy from apartheid continues to reproduce poverty, inequality, unemployment and uneven development (Dexter, 2017, p. 3). Thus, the continuous reproduction of economic underdevelopment has been blamed on the adoption of neoliberal economic policies manifesting through poor leadership and widespread corruption both in public and private sectors. The existing socio-economic challenges debilitate the democratic strides made since 1994 due to what Fukuyama (2011, p. 80) calls 'tolerance for economic inequalities'. Ntsaluba (2017, p. 15) adds that these challenges have manifested themselves through an increasing fiscal burden and a widening current-account deficit as the country grapples with competing needs.

Since 1994, South Africa experimented with various economic policies such as RDP (1994), GEAR (1996), ASGISA (2006) and currently its comprehensive development plan (NDP, 2011). All these policies were aimed at boosting the economic growth, however, the reality is its failure reach 6 percent as predicted by GEAR as South African economic policy. Donnelly (2017, p. 21) came to the conclusion that South African limping economy has slowed down due to low growth and investment. Thus, South Africa remains a country of vast contrast, with wealth siting side by side with abject poverty and underdevelopment and could be best described by a two-nation thesis as exposed by the former President Thabo Mbeki depicting the co-existence of first and second economies. Thus, the 'two nation' thesis describes the co-existence of the first and second economies. Mbeki (2004, p. 29) contends that the first economy, on the one hand, is modern, produces the bulk of the country's wealth and is integrated within the global economy. The second economy (also known as the marginalized economy) on the other hand, is characterized by under-development, contributes little to the Gross Domestic Product (GDP), contains a big percentage of our population, and incorporates the poorest of our rural and urban population. Thus, the second economy is structurally disconnected from both the first and global economy, and is incapable of self-generated growth and development (Mbeki, 2004, p. 29). This metaphor of 'two economies' echoes the apartheid description of South Africa's two worlds, the first and the third worlds. The first world being reflective of the market economy while the third world reflects second and survivalist economy (Hallowes & Munnik, 2006, p. 121).

This situation is exacerbated by the adoption of the liberal constitution of 1996 which Kondlo (2017, p. 4) argues has provided many political rights, but left numerous grey areas pertaining to economic equality. As such, Ntsaluba (2017, p. 5) likened South Africa as an uncut diamond with its share of rough edges, a country with the glaring structural challenges of high poverty levels, widening inequality, high levels of unemployment and an ongoing education crisis. These issues continue to undermine efforts to redress the injustices of the past and ultimately rendering South Africa a stressed society. A stressed society according to Pather (2017, p. 18) is the one unable to realise a united, prosperous and democratic nation where higher food prices, few jobs and more poverty can be a history. Political economy in the context of South Africa is underpinned by inequalities in wealth distribution and creating opportunities for participation in the economy (Schoeman and Graham, 2017, p. 251).

The current 'radical economic transformation' by President Zuma has been dismissed by political scientists and commenters as a political rhetoric without any concrete plan how such transformation will be achieved (Mckaiser, 2017, p. 23). Emanating from its 53rd national conference, radical economic transformation articulated to mean the 'fundamental change in the structure, systems, institutions and patterns of ownership, management and control of the economy in favour of all South Africans, especially the poor; the majority of whom are Africans and females' (in Pillay, 2017, p. 18).

GENESIS OF FEESMUSTFALL CAMPAIGN

FMF is a student initiated campaign demanding the decrease in university fees across South African institutions of higher learning. Since its emergence in 2015, the FMF has received huge media attention and coverage and generated enormous writing and discourses in local, national and international newspapers and journals alike. All these non-and academic discourses were centered on the fundamental question if FMF is feasible amidst all the pressing priorities warranting public attention by both the government through the Department of Higher Education and Training and the universities respectively. FMF campaign and later the movement is incrementally triggered by frustrated students especially in predominantly black universities. Snail pace of transformation, funding issues and governance embedded challenges became the boiling point for students and their student bodies to stage protests and demonstrations disrupting the operation of universities. Squally, 2015 and 2016 were declared FMF, however Ray (2016, p. 329) traced the discontent among university students way back in 1999 more radically in the University of North West, Mahikeng campus. SASCO was the vanguard of the campaign geared toward denouncing the lack of institutional transformation, the high fee structure and the university's drift to 'neo-apartheid'. The underpinning grievances of the students were succinctly captured by one of the student Madondo (in Ray, 2016, p. 330) who said:

We have been raising issues for years…five years of democracy had not changed the institutional and power structure of the campus. Issues of academic representavity and the democratisation of the council and the curriculum are much of the same.

Generally, transformation if any took place under the guise of institutional merger where 'bush or Bantustan' universities and technikons were forced into marriages of inconvenience with white and well-resourced universities. Despite the mergers of most universities, the institutional culture remains stubbornly unchanged with white Afrikaners and English academics still dominating the teaching staff and councils. Structurally, although some changes took place, these changes pay lip service to deep rooted transformational inherited predicaments caused by racially and spatially segregated universities and tecknikons. Accordingly, restructuring system of higher education without addressing the socio-economic challenges of those living in poverty and structural problems in education became a mockery to the previously disadvantaged families and students. However, it should be noted that this campaign is overloaded with demands that transcend increment of tuition fees to include the entire transformation of the entire higher education system. The FMF should be understood as the microcosm of the variety of unresolved issues and challenges in post-apartheid South Africa. Apart from the demand for free tuition in North-West in 1999. The protests regarding fees were also sported at universities such as Wits and Johannesburg in late 2007 and some demonstrations at the Durban University of Technology (DUT), the Tshwane University of Technology (TUT) and the University of Limpopo (UL). Thus, October 2015 has become the milestone for universities across the campuses more particularly in student activism garning massive support among their fellow students nation-wide and workers in general (Ray, 2016, p. 368). The students' alignment with university workers meant these cadres of students had to add demanding the scrapping of 'outsourcing' into their fees must fall demands.

Each university has its own story to tell from negotiating in good faith that their demands would be met to taking to the streets, universities council meeting and ultimately to Parliament (Ngcaweni & Ngcaweni, 2018). The march to Parliament was organized and joined by the students from Cape Peninsula University of Technology (CPUT), University of the Western Cape (UWC) and the University of Cape Town (UCT). Through FMF, students regardless of race, gender and socio-economic class demonstrated their mobilizing skills and their resilience to survive confrontation and brutality in the hands of police and campus security guards' harassment and intimidation. Sit-ins, diplomatic negotiations through their respective SRCs with university councils, broadly with the Department of Higher education through the Student Union, demonstrations based on radical confrontation with police were some of the mechanisms utilized by student activists.

POLITICAL GROUNDING BEHIND FMF

The Freedom Charter differentiated basic education from higher education and technical training (Congress of the People, 1955). The former articulate that 'education shall be free, compulsory, universal an equal for all children while the latter higher education and technical training is to be open to all by means of state allowances and scholarships on the basis of merit (in Polley, 1988, p. 135). State allowances and scholarships are not a free ride hence merit is one of the criteria for students to access such funding opportunities. Campaign for a free education in South African universities is complex beyond the political rhetoric either spearheaded by the Freedom Charter, the ANC sloganeering resolutions and the FMF movement itself (Maxwele, 2017). Thus, the discourse underpinning FMF talks directly to the sluggish and unfinished transformation agenda in the institutions of higher learning. Thus, the FMF movement is a stark reality of unfinished struggle first waged by 1976 students against Bantu education in secondary and higher institutions of learning (Brown, 2016). Currently, the FMF demanding not only for no fees increment to guarantee access and quality education, but also structural transformation of these institutions and curriculum development. Politically, prior to the democratic dispensation ushered in 1994, the commitment to transform education in general and higher education system is rooted in the Freedom Chapter. Freedom Charter has become the foregrounding document to influence the democratic Constitution and its adoption in 1996 as the supreme law of the Republic of South Africa.

Post-apartheid era saw the promulgation of various legislative frameworks and policies which touch on basic education and high education. Central to these policies is the 1996 Constitution which without specifics laid the ground for a transformed South Africa with education being one of the pillars of forging a democratic, none-racist and none-sexist society. However, the White Paper on Higher Education (1997) was bold in identifying three transformational pillars underpinning higher education such as 1) increased and broadened participation to accommodate a diverse student population; 2) responsiveness to societal needs at national and global levels; and 3) partnership in governance between the state, institutions and civil society aimed at creating an enabling educational environments that are culturally sensitive. Attempts to resolve the pandemonium brought through the fees must fall campaign, a Fees Commission was set to look at the feasibility. The mandate of this Commission was welcomed by some and dismissed by other who argued that it is misnomer since FMF is a political economy question rather than a legal quest. Instead of reacting to demands made by the students across the universities and political spectrum, A National Education Crisis Convention (NECC) headed by the retired Deputy Chief Justice Didgang Moseneke was initiated to engage various stakeholders in order to address the higher education crisis. Unlike the Fee Commission which was mandated to interrogate the feasibility of free higher education, the NECC was initiated as a dialogcal forum to engage student leadership, university councils and society at large in finding sustainable solutions to the education issues (Mazwele, 2017, p. 17). Demanding no fee increment by the students is far from resolving deep rooted challenges confronting the higher education sector which is mostly anchored on the legacy of Bantu education and transformational reluctance of higher education post-Apartheid era.

Thus, a fee challenge is just one of piece of the puzzle toward transforming institution of higher learning. As such Kgosiemang (2018) challenges the stakeholders in the higher education sector to re-imagine university transformation. Since the FMF campaign started in 2015, its expansion transcended to include demands for no fee increment, quality and access, institutional transformation and curriculum development. The reality is that access by itself does not guarantee quality or job opportunity. The ANCYL in its submission to the Fees Commission outlined five elements to underpinned free education (Selapisa, 2017: 2). These components include tuition and accommodation fees, books and study materials as well as travelling from residence to campus. In this regard, the SA Qualification Authority revealed shockingly that despite that higher education qualification tripled from 1995 to 2014, thus from 70 020 to 202 653, most of the graduate remain unemployed (in Gumede, 2017, p. 4). Yearly, this figure continues to add to the already swelling ground for the unemployed graduates languishing in the streets without employment or job opportunity. The growing rate of unemployed graduates remains discouraging especially for those who aspired to further their education up to the university level.

ECONOMIC (IN)FEASIBILITY OF FMF

Political rhetoric for free education as propagated by the ANC resolutions has been part of the electioneering which is not aligned to the economic reality. Such political decision either articulated along party resolutions or hinted through official government policies has economic implications both in short and long term (Habib, 2019). Thus, political and economic non-alignment pushes the President and the Treasury to make reckless decisions without considering the sources of financial resources to fund free education. Economically, South Africa depends on taxes an issue further complicated by the reality that most of its citizens are unemployed leaving few economically active people responsible for paying taxes. While the general populace is in agreement that FMF is a noble cause especially for academically deserving students, economists cite the heavy burden on the fiscus and heavy taxation on the few economically active people.

The feasibility of FMF has economic implications considering that the South African economy is not growing fast enough to accommodate the multiple demands such as poverty, unemployment, inequality and housing. The legitimacy of investing more on higher education was questioned by Habib (2019) who argues that the majority of youth are either outside the institutions or are unemployed. The FMF not only put exert pleasure on the dwindling budget of the country, but also made South Africa to think hard on the substance of such political decision. Considering the demand for financial assistance to cover not only tuition, bust also accommodation and subsistence, the rolling out of the compressive free education would be extra-economical for South Africa (Habib, 2019). In order to sustain free education, the government will be obliged to seek between R40-billion and 60 billion a year, translating to the equivalent between 3% and 5% of government spending. The implementation of comprehensive cover for free higher education according to Habib (2019, p. 8) would demand the state to have additional cost of 143bn per annum. An increasing number of unemployed graduates made one to question the economic value for education more in particular the higher education in South Africa. The Department of Higher Education and Training's Report of the Ministerial Committee for the Review of the Funding of Universities poor students who are poorly prepared for higher education studies (DHET, 2013, p. 2). These students are mostly dependant on National Student Financial Aid Scheme (NSFAS) funding to access higher education, and therefore adequate levels of NSFAS funding are vital to ensure that no student is excluded from higher education on the basis of its affordability.

POLITICAL RHETORIC VS ECONOMIC REALITY

Political scholars and commenters used both the Freedom Charter and the Constitution to dismissed the notion of free education in higher education. The narrative for free education at university level was dismissed as 'twisted' (Maseremule, 2016,

p. 19) and as such has 'failed the test' (Maseremule, 2016: 9). Free education was hailed as a noble move, however it was criticized for lacking political backing by the political and business elites as a policy directive. It is undeniable fact that as stated by the Freedom Charter, 'the door of learning and culture shall be opened' and emphasis was placed on extending free education as far as the basic education. On the contrary, the delivery higher education was to be realized 'by means of state allowances and scholarship'. Similar to the Freedom Charter, the Constitution (1996) declares education as a right hence it states that 'everybody has the right to a basic education including adult basic education; and to further education'. However, this right was to be realized gradually and through reasonable measures and within available resources and on the basis of merit. Unfortunately, as Ramphele (2008, p. 198) argues that equitable access to opportunities through higher education led to mediocrity as opposed to meritocracy. The carefully crafted Freedom Charter and the Constitution linked the delivery of education either basic or higher education on the basis of reassures availability and planning. Maseremule (2016, p. 9) traced the problem of the promise for free higher education to the ruling ANC party resolution passed in its 52nd national conference where 'free higher education was promised to the poor'. Through this resolution, the party committed itself to progressively introduce free education for the poor until undergraduate level. Within this narrative, the promise of free higher education is according to Maseremule (2016) a construct of the ANC's rhetoric and populist policies. Thus, the notion of free higher education is not only a misnomer, but is part of seductive political language of 'free this, free that' (Maseremule, 2016, p. 9).

MODELS FOR FUNDING FREE HIGHER EDUCATION

Ishengoma (2013, pp. 227-234) explored various higher education funding models. These models range from cost-sharing; full government-funding to donor support model. The cost-sharing model according to Ishengoma (2013, p. 227) is aligned to the entrepreneurial university model an is mainly implemented through the higher education's student loans and revenue diversification where public universities are allowed to raise funds to supplement inadequate government budgetary allocations. Through the full government-funding model, government fund both public and private universities especially through the national budget where higher education is allocated its own budget. The third model is donor support where indirect aid from donors contributed to capital development expenditure and support research and training in public universities (Ishengoma, 2013, p. 231).

Higher education in South Africa is funded from different sources, such as individual sources. (Godlimpi, 2018; Habib, 2019). These include private funding mainly solicited from family trust and foundations attached to prominent politic figures, namely Nelson Mandela Children Funds, Thabo Mbeki Foundation, Ahmed Kathrada Foundation, Jacob Zuma Foundation and many others. Another source of funding is derived from business foundations such as the Motsepe Foundation and others. These foundations contribute towards education, tertiary education include where through their corporate social responsibility where bursaries are either offered to the poor or academically bright students to access tertiary education. However, this sources of funding fit acutely with the 'donor support model' as outlined by Ishengoma (2013) above. Despite these multiple sources, the students' quest to enter TVET and universities often outnumber the available financial resources. Governments use different approaches to allocate funding to higher education institutions and programmes. DHET (2013, p. 117) explored three different funding approaches such as a) incremental funding; b) formula-based funding; and c) performance-based fundi. The incremental funding as one of the higher education funding approaches make use of incremental or subtractive adjustments to the previous year's allocation (DHET, 2013, p. 117). Formula-based funding and funding is made available through formulas aimed to distribute appropriations to individual higher education institutions. According to DHET's Report, the finding formulas are often based on factors such as historical data, enrolment and graduation data, anticipated trends, research out output and negotiated political agreements (DHET, 2013, p. 118). The third funding model is performance-based funding and is anchored on the performance of higher education institutions. Performance of these institutions is basis for funding allocation and improved efficiency, accountability and quality are the criteria (DHET, 2013, p. 119).

Despite the NSFAS's student funding scheme has being hailed as progressive towards funding poor students in accessing higher education. Since 2013, 415901 students were funded, 2014, 414792, 2015, 414949 while 2016, over 4000 000 students were assisted with funding. Overall, the number of students funded since 2013 were over 2 million and unsuccessful applicants for 2017 academic year were 53043 (Selapisa et al., 2017, p. 2). However, the administration of NSFAS remains a huge challenge hence the scheme was reported to be fraught with controversy and corruption. In some universities like the Tswane University of Technology (TUT), it has been reported that students turn NSFAS boo cards into 'spaza vouchers' by sitting outside bookstores selling the textbook allowances they received as part of their NSFAS aid parkages (Selapisa et al., 2017, p. 1). FMF pushed both the Department of Higher Education and the SA Union of Students to come up with various funding models. One such model is the Ikusasa Student Financial Aid

Programme (ISFAP) proposed by Higher education department with a target of R200 million in aid for2000 students from the combination of public and private funding (Olalde, 2017, p. 9). The second funding model is the one proposed by the FMF movement called the Lesedi Education Endowment Fund and the this Fund relies heavily on reinstating state subsidy to 50 percent and financial participation of the private sector especially through corporate taxes (Olalde, 2017, p. 9).

COST BENEFIT ANALYSIS

Costs for Free Higher Education

Free education as propagated by students is not only costly, but also burdens the national fiscus. Since the emergence of the protest through FMF campaign, both the President and the Minister of Finance through his 2016 Medium Term Budget Policy Statement Speech, uuniversities were apportioned an additional R9 billion for the National Student Financial Aid Scheme over the period ahead, raising its funding by over 18 percent a year. However, the former Finance Minister Gordham (2016: 16) emphased that expanded opportunities in South African universities cannot rely on government funding alone. Public expenditure on post-school education and training has in fact grown considerably faster than other budget allocations in recent years, and this will continue. Attest to that is the actual allocation of R16 billions for higher education with R9 billion added during the medium term budget. At the heart of the issue is that access has expanded faster than resources. As a result, many students face financial hardships that undermine their ability to succeed academically. Thus, the remedial measure to address students' predicament pertaining to fee exorbitant increment, over R8 billion to meet the costs of fee increases for students from households with incomes up to R600 000.

There are parallel arguments put forward by various sectors including Student Union, youth movements and universities themselves pertaining to the economic implications embedded through free education. One of the participants highlighted that:

Free education would be too expensive for the government which is already burdened by social services expenses. Let us consider that Health is free, Basic education and Social Grants are also free, considering the limited tax payers which is further exacerbated by stubbornly rising of poverty, unemployment and income inequality.

An educator commented that:

NEFSAS on its own is a very huge government contribution towards education. The problem gravitating most of the South Africans is the culture of entitlement which leads to the syndrome of dependency has killed the spirit of self-reliance. The economy is badly performing and uninformed South Africans have developed an impression that anything can be provided for free.

Contextualising FMF and the feasibility or non-feasibility of financing free quality education in a country like South Africa is complex. The complex nature of higher education is rooted in the failure by both political and economic elites who in the name of productivity have pushed universities to operate as extension of the private sector. Nkondo (2017, p. 19) calls this the marketization of universities with the tendencies of abusing public institutions for private gains. The author blamed academic capitalism for the woes inflicting universities which emphasises the utility of higher education to markets and its movement from basic research to academic capitalism. Thus, academic capitalism was also reinforced by the National Development Plan (2011) where universities are integrated into broader government planning with the focus on economic development, industrialization and technological advance. Through academic capitalism, political economy becomes an instrument that connects corporate and government to universities through the curriculum, funding of research and other collaborative public-private-university endevours. This partnership has given rise to entrepreneurial universities where students are trained to turn their research papers into business ventures (Musau, 2017, p. 16).

The Benefactors and Losers in Free Education

Political economy framing of FMF has three questions, namely who gains, who losses and how. Students in most universities sacrificed their academic year and risk even going to prison in their quest for free, quality and decolonized education. However, Buccus (2016, p. 9) is of the opinion that free education is misguided and he argues that only the poor students should get free education, modest fee for the middle class and the rich are obliged to pay high rate. Fundamental narratives to the FMF campaign is for the South African society and students to ask hard questions as to who are the benefactors and the losers of this radical demand. FMF was crafted to benefit the student from the poor and the disadvantaged background, who happen to be blacks. Admittedly, for the poor and middle-class South Africans, higher education is perceived as the only ladder into the affluent middle class (Cloete, 2016, p. 10). Although from its original conceptualization FMF was generally embracive of all the students, be they rich, middle class or poor students. As the struggle for FMF intensified, it became clear that the financially non-affording students and the missing middle are the targets for fee remission at their respective universities. From the onset, FMF should not be categorized into losers and benefactors. Thus, placing benefactors and losers of free education at the same equation is not only divisive but also undermines the quest for accessible, quality and transformed higher education system in South Africa. This is not to discard the historical inequalities created by Apartheid and the Bantu Education system with mainly the Blacks having suffered heavy blows. Hicks and Buccus (2016, p. 109) argue that apartheid has afforded black students poor quality education and continue to close spaces for dialogue. However, the FMF should not be used as a blanket approach hinting that South Africa in its current economic difficulties can afford free higher education for all students. Various commentators have alluded that for academically deserving students, free education is possible; however, Cloete (2016, p. 10) warns that much of subsidy in public universities accrues to students from middle and high-income families. In providing direction regarding the fees, the Minister of Higher Education and Training, Blade Nzimande, introduced an approach which demarcate those who are eligible to benefit or not from free education. The categories include the following: first, the poor from families earning below R120 000 will not pay fees but be subsidied through loans. Second, a middle class whose families earn between R120 000 and R600 000 will pay fees but will not be required to pay new fee increases for 2017. Third, the affluent middle class/rich, who will be required to pay fees in addition to any increase in 2017 academic year (in Cloete, 2016, p. 10).

However, in essence, targeting the poor and the missing middle is part of the redress of the imbalances of the past. It goes without saying that access to quality education, more particularly higher education, is the pathway towards eradicating poverty, unemployment and inequality. For South Africa to be competitive nationally and internationally, conscious investment in both basic and tertiary education should be prioritized to develop human and intellectual capacity. In this regard, Ramphele (2008, p. 196) argues that 'in the 21st- century knowledge economy, competitiveness is enhanced by the quality of a country's human and intellectual capital'. Understanding the interdependence of equity and excellence, competitive societies have invested in greater access to higher education and also improved quality' Without sustainable funding, the most academic deserving students, especially from low socio-economic class become losers.

The Economic Benefits of Free Education

The feasibility of fees must fall is intrinsically linked to the nature and state of the South African economy. The economic growth per its expectation enables the government to meet the socio-economic priorities. In his Budget Speech delivered on the 22 Feb 2017, Finance Minister Gordhan (2017, p. 11) highlighted that a growing economy makes more rapid transformation possible, but it is the fiscal system that is the most direct vehicle for redistribution and inclusivity. Thus, the Finance Minister Gordghan reiterated the over competing issues that require the South African budget finances, namely the construction of houses and schools, the education of young people, care for the elderly and incomes of the most vulnerable. About two-thirds of the Budget is dedicated to realising social rights. Some of these programmes entail those building infrastructure, supporting new businesses, empowering small farmers, developing human capabilities and incentivising job creation. Through 2017, a huge budget has been directed at programmes with the hope of boosting the economy. R3.9 billion for small, medium and micro enterprises and cooperatives; R4.2 billion for industrial infrastructure in special economic zones and industrial parks; R1.9 billion for broadband implementation; R3.9 billion for the Council for Scientific and Industrial Research (Gordhan, 2017, p. 6). An additional R494 million for tourism promotion with an additional R266m to support the aquaculture sector and realise the goals of the Oceans Economy Phakisa Operation and spending on agriculture, rural development and land reform amounting to nearly R30 billion by 2019/20. Gordhan (2017, p. 6) argues that 'effective implementation of these and other programmes and initiatives would set government on a higher growth trajectory than currently projected. Progress in engagements between government, the business sector and social stakeholders is imperative.

FUTURE RESEARCH DIRECTIONS

Higher education sector African scholars have over the decades pointed out the challenges facing the sector with the students bearing the brunt. Depending on the higher education policies and socio-economic and political environment as well as the governments' commitment to invest in education, funding, access, limited infrastructure, political interference, academic freedom and autonomy are among some of the challenges confronting the tertiary sector. Similarly to South Africa, the legacy of fragmented Bantu education and the sector reluctant transformation have rendered the education system one of the weakest economic link post-apartheid era. Therefore, #FMF campaign has emerged as a reaction to many struggles faced by students and student representative councils (SRC) or organizations in their quest for a transformed, decolonized and democratized education system. The chapter acknowledged the legitimacy of the demand for quality and affordable education especially for financially and academically deserving students. However, it joined the other scholars who argued that despite the free education rhetoric as propagated by students, someone or an institution has to pay for it.

The chapter has used a political economy framework to understand and analyse the #FeesMustFall campaign. #FMF as deliberated in this chapter has both political and economic implications for a middle income country like south Africa with burdens of poverty, unemployment and inequality. Legislative pronouncements (Freedom Charter and Constitution) to offer free education in its loose articulation got stuck with economic reality of slow economic growth and jobless growth. It has become apparent in this chapter that financial investment in higher education does not solved inherited educational problems. Solid foundation from the basic and secondary levels is required to deal with challenges besetting education in general. Failure to consolidate and balance between basic and higher education will continue to produce unemployed graduates with no or little technical and entrepreneurial skills, knowledge and competencies for the labour market or self-employability. FMF should understood as a mirror through which stakeholders in the education fraternity could do an introspection for radical redress. For education sector to be transformed and lesson to be drawn from FMF movement, more research is needed reflecting on student leadership and skills accumulated from the campaign across various institutions. Such research could benefit university management by incorporating the repertoire of leadership styles and skills for effective and ethical governance of high education institutions. Political interference through student organizations' affiliation to political organizations is another area of research interest worthy to be undertaken.

CONCLUSION

The chapter has wrestled with conceptual, definitional and operational issues underpinning FMF from the political economy perspective. FMF is understood to be part of the political-educational demands framed to transform higher education system for accessibility, affordability and quality. Since the dawn of the democratic order, issues pertaining to accessibility, affordability and quality have been conflicting hence Ramphele (2008, p. 196) argues that excellence was compromised over equity by the political elites. This has dire consequences directly linked to some of the FMF's demands to have justice in terms of access and quality, institutional and curriculum development that responds to the needs of local people. However, this call questions the relevant of universities in post-apartheid South Africa beyond being ivory towers for the privileged few.

While the demand for free education was viewed as politically appealing by tertiary students and the general public, the author argued that its economic feasibility could be a distance dream provided there a long term planning. Considering the existing economic pressures and dwindling economic growth, the quest for free education remains at the peripheral of the national priorities. Despite the available funding solicited primarily from private foundations and public funding through NEFSAS, Ikusasa Student Financial Aid Programme (ISFAP) and annual budget, universities and students' needs exceed financial resources. From the deliberations in this chapter, it is apparent that FMF campaign is not a linear encounter, but a series of demands evolving under the guise of no-fee increment at tertiary institutions. Thus, FMF epitomizes the endured struggle for democratizing education system for a democratized South Africa in post-apartheid era.

REFERENCES

African National Congress (ANC). (1994). *The Reconstruction and Development Programme: A Policy Framework.* Johannesburg: Umnyano publications.

Brown, J. (2016). *The Road to Soweto: Resistance and the Uprising of 16 June 1996.* Johannesburg: Jacana Media Ltd.

Buccus, I. (2016, October 6). The crisis at universities is escalating. The Mercury, p. 9.

City Press. (2017, January 15). #FeesMustFall: Cool heads are now needed. City Press, p. 2.

Cloete, N. (2016, September 29). No such thing as 'free higher education. The Mercury, p. 10.

Department of Higher Education and Training (DHET). (2013). *Report of the Ministerial Committee for the Review of the Funding of Universities.* Pretoria Department of Higher Education.

Dexter, P. (2017, April 23). Shared economic growth is the only way to go. *City Press*, p. 3.

Donnelly, L. (2017, April 21). Limping economy faces uphill. Mail & Guardian, 21.

Fengu, M. (2017, January 15). Protest loom over Bursary Funds. City Press, p. 9.

Godlimpi, Z. (2018). The rise and fall of higher education cost: How 'free' of government's free education policy? In We are No longer at Ease: The Struggle for #FeesMustFall (pp. 182-194). Sunnyside: Jakana Media Ltd.

Gumede, M. (2017, March 26). Curro' tertiary plan just for job. *The Sunday Times*, p. 4.

Habib, A. (2019). *Rebels and Rage: Reflecting on #FeesMustFall*. Johannesburg: Jonathan Balls Publisher.

Habib, A. (2019, March 18). Free higher education a vehicle for class mobility. *The Star*, p. 8.

Hallowes, D., & Munnik, V. (2006). *Poisoned Spaces: Manufacturing wealth, producing poverty*. Pietermaritzburg: Groundwork.

Handleman, H. (1996). *The Challenge of Third World Development*. Simon & Schuster.

Hicks, J., & Buccus, I. (2016). Public participation in South Africa: Strengthening state accountability in a dominant party system. In State, governance and development in Africa (pp. 100-122). Claremont: UCT Press.

Ishengoma, J. M. (2013). Funding Higher Education in Tanzania: Modalities, Challenges, Prospects and a Proposal for New Funding Modalities. In D. Teferra (Ed.), *Funding Higher Education in Sub-Saharan Africa* (pp. 214–246). New York: Palgrave Macmillan. doi:10.1057/9781137345783_9

Johnson, K., & Jacobs, S. (Eds.). (2012). *Encyclopedia of South Africa. Scottsville*. University of KwaZulu-Natal.

Kgosiemang, M. L. (2018). University transformation re-imagined: Discourses resulting after the Fallist movement. In We are No longer at Ease: The Struggle for #FeesMustFall (pp. 167-174). Sunnyside: Jakana Media Ltd.

Kondlo, K. (2017). The context of South African government and politics. In C. Landsberg & S. Graham (Eds.), *Government and Politics in South Africa: Coming of Age* (5th ed.). Hatfield: Van Schaick Publishers.

London, T. (2017, January 15). Education inherently evolves. Saturday Star, p. 9.

Maake, N. (2011). *Barbarism in Higher Education: Once Upon a time in a University*. Johannesburg: Ekaam Books CC.

Maseremule, M. H. (2016a, November 4). Narrative of free higher education has been twisted. *The New Age*, p. 19.

Maseremule, M. H. (2016b, November 3). Free higher education fails to test. The Mercury, p. 9.

Maxwele, C. (2017, March 26). Campaign for a free education. *The Sunday Independent*, p. 17.

Mbeki, T. (2004). Meeting the Challenge for the Second Economy. *New Agenda: South African Journal of Social and Economic Policy, 14*.

Mpofu-Walsh, S. (2017). *Democracy & Delusion: 10 Myths in South African Politics*. Cape Town: NB Publishers.

Musau, Z. (2017, March 28). Universities fund entrepreneurial graduates. The Mercury, p. 16.

Mzileni, P. (2018, September 21). Sasco must introspect to succeed. Mail & Guardian, 34.

Ngcaweni, W & Ngcaweni, B. (2018). *We are No longer at Ease: The Struggle for #FeesMustFall*. Sunnyside: Jakana Media Ltd.

Nkondo, M. (2017, April 23). Academic capitalism and state capture in higher education. The Sunday Independent, p. 19.

Nombembe, P. (2017, January 15). Blade's plan falls flat with #FeesMustFall. *Sunday Times*, p. 8.

Nshemererwe, C. (2016, November 4). Transforming from oppressed to truly liberated. *African Independent*, p. 9.

Ntsaluba, S. (2017, April 23). Rating downgrade has to be taken very, very seriously. *Sunday Times*, p. 15.

Olalde, M. (2017, January 14). Education funding riddle. *Saturday Star*, p. 9.

Pather, D. (2017, April 23). Why SA is a stressed society. *Sunday Tribune*, p. 18.

Ramphele, M. (2008). *Laying Ghosts to Rest: Dilemmas of the Transformation in South Africa*. Cape Town: Tafelburg.

Ray, M. (2016). *Free Fall; why South African Universities are in a Race Against Time*. Johannesburg: Bookstorm Ltd.

Republic of South Africa. (1997). *White Paper on Higher Education and Training*. Pretoria: Department of Education.

Schoeman, M., & Graham, S. (2017). The political economy of south Africa in a global Context. In C. Landsberg & S. Graham (Eds.), *Government and Politics in South Africa: Coming of Age* (5th ed.). Hatfield: Van Schaick Publishers.

Selapisa, L. (2017). Free education must have 5 components. *The NewAge*, *23*(March), 2.

Selapisa, L., Tshikalange, S., & Mahlo, A. (2017). Students turn NSFAS book cards into 'spaza vouchers. *The New Age*, *22*(May), 1.

Staniland, M. (1985). *What is political economy: A study of social theory & underdevelopment*. New Haven, CT: Yale University Press.

Tererra, D., & Altbach, P. G. (2003). Trends and Perspectives in African Higher Education. In African Higher Education: An International Reference Handbook (pp. 3-14). Bloomington, IN: Indiana University Press.

ADDITIONAL READING

Chetty, R. (2014). Class Dismissed? Youth Resistance and the Politics of Race and Class in South African Education. *Critical Arts*, *28*(1), 88–102. doi:10.1080/02560046.2014.883692

Chikane, R. (2018). *Breaking a Rainbow, Building a Nation: A Politics behind #MustFall Movements*. Johannesburg: Picador Africa.

Habib, A. (2019). *Rebel and Rage: Reflecting on #FeesMustFall*. Johannesburg, Cape Town: Jonathan Ball Publishers.

Jansen, J. (2017). *As By Fire: The End of the South African University*. Cape Town: NB Publishers.

Luescher, T. M., Klemencic, M., & Jowie, J. O. (Eds.). (2015). Student Power in African Higher Education. Journal of Student Affairs in Africa.

Naiker, C. (2016). From Marikana to #FeesMustFall: The Praxis of Popular Politics in South Africa. *Urbanisation and Health Newsletter*, *1*(1), 53–61. doi:10.1177/2455747116640434

Ngcaweni, W., & Ngcaweni, B. (Eds.). (2018). We Are no Longer at Ease: The Struggle for #FeesMustFall. Sunnyside: Jakana Media Ltd.

Pinhouse, R. (2006). *Asinamali: University Struggles in Post-Apartheid South Africa*. Africa World Press.

KEY TERMS AND DEFINITIONS

#FeesMustFall Campaign: It is a campaign organized and led by university students demanding for free: quality education as well as decolonized curriculum and transformed higher education.

Apartheid Education: It was a South African education system which was based on racial and discriminatory laws of apartheid and it was notorious for offering gutter or inferior form of education or schooling to Black learners and students.

Decolonized Curriculum: It is an educational curriculum that is not dominated by Western forms of education or curriculum that is not entirely Eurocentric and the one which embrace Afro-centric approach to education and learning. Such curriculum does not only focus on content, but also on the language as the medium of instructions at tertiary level.

Free Education: An education system in which students do not have to pay tuition fee for them to study or advance their studies.

Heher Commission: It was the commission set in 2016 by the former South African president, Jacob Zuma, to investigate the feasibility of free education and based on its findings make recommendations relating to the relevant funding model(s) to financially assist the deserving and needy students.

National Student Financial Aid Scheme (NSFAS): It is a South African financial scheme introduced in 1998 by the South African education department, especially to assist students from the low economic households with tuition fees, accommodation, and food allowance.

Political Economy: It is a system whereby the adopted policy system has an impact on the economy and the economic system equally has an influence on the political decisions taken by a country.

Chapter 9
Development of Competences Through the PBL and the Use of Technology

María Elena Zepeda Hurtado
Instituto Politécnico Nacional, Mexico

Yarzabal Coronel Nashielly
Instituto Politécnico Nacional, Mexico

Pérez Benítez Alma Alicia
Instituto Politécnico Nacional, Mexico

ABSTRACT

The objective of this chapter is to present a case study in the National Polytechnic Institute, which is focused on two aspects: 1) to know what kind of educational practices are implemented in the classroom and how ICTs are used and 2) to analyze the impact of project-based learning (PBL) in the Oral and Written Expression Learning Unit I to know what competences such as creative thinking, improving motivation, and meaningful learning are developed, as well as the use of ICT for research, analysis, experimentation, simulation, and socialization, in such a way that, during the application of the PBL methodology in conjunction with ICT, skills that are required throughout life are developed, both in academic, scientific, and occupational fields.

DOI: 10.4018/978-1-5225-8461-2.ch009

INTRODUCTION

To be at the level of the requirements of the knowledge society and to contribute to the student's development, it is necessary to invest in education and in a training that guarantees graduation profiles according to a work performance and skills that society requires in different areas: personal, academic and professional. Once the problems, needs and qualities of performance in society have been determined, in a second moment, it is about identifying the learning, which includes knowledge, skills and attitudes (elements that make up a competence) to contribute to its development from the classroom to its strengthening in other learning environments.

The National Polytechnic Institute offers technical careers in the upper middle, upper and postgraduate levels. At these levels, care has been taken to ensure that the profiles of graduates are complementary, sequential, and in line with the megatrends: computerized societies, globalized economies, use of ICT, use of scientific and technical knowledge in a changing and increasingly complex environment; in general, the student is prepared for a knowledge society in which the development of human capital has as its origin, and at the same time also as an end, the development and use of knowledge.

The OECD (1998: 22) states "that human capital is defined as the knowledge that individuals acquire during their life and that they use to produce good services or ideas in the market or outside of it," so education is one of the essential variables in the development of skills that result in the autonomous search for knowledge: learning to learn, search, motivate, investigate, undertake.

To meet these skills, it is necessary to create teaching spaces with a different educational framework from the traditional and incorporate methodologies that give the student active participation spaces, encourage collaborative work, identify and provide solutions or proposals for solving real problems. In this process of renovation and updating of the performance in the classroom, methodologies, strategies and activities focused on the performance of the student have been implemented, one of them is Problem Based Learning (ABP or PBL in English), considered as a methodology used and adaptable in different educational levels; its use has been generalized in a great variety of disciplines (Medicine, Law) as well as in Technical education.

The PBL, begins with the approach of a problem to be solved that implies the acquisition of knowledge, application and transfer in other contexts and circumstances, besides that basic skills are developed which will later serve for the development of others of greater complexity and that are used in their professional careers, considering Paredes (2016) the PBL allows greater autonomy in the process of student learning. Likewise, research, inferences and sample of findings interpreted individually and in groups to solve a research question were favored, where students were the protagonists of this process (p.21)

The PBL, begins with the approach of a problem to solve that involves not only the acquisition of knowledge but the application and transfer in other contexts and circumstances, in addition to developing skills for solving problems, which will later serve for the development of others of greater complexity and that are used in their professional careers.

Thus, the PBL allows the acquisition of knowledge, skills and generic skills that are characterized by being: key (applicable in various contexts and throughout life), cross-cutting (permeate other academic disciplines and learning outside the classroom) and transferable (necessary to acquire other competences: generic, disciplinary or professional), which gives a plus to the student training and refreshes the teacher's performance "whose principles should allow tutors to display didactic actions that strengthen the autonomous learning of students, build knowledge from the analysis and solution of real problems involving cognitive resources from the individuality of each person. (Hernández, 2016, p.171)

The implementation of different methodologies, in support of them and in favor of improving the quality of education, of students' attention, of teaching updating and of contributing to education in spaces outside the classroom, is not enough. The use of ICTs play a key role as tools that facilitate the instrumentation of new methodologies, as well as the development of research and communication skills, mainly. Casillas (2016) affirms that "the information society implies an intensive use of electronic media. Computers, mobile phones and their connection to the Internet are indispensable resources for the new global economy "(p.26) since now the criteria for use have changed, predominating previously the use of email and chat for productivity and school to the use of communication, recreational and ludic.

In this sense, in the school environment, there has been a struggle for the use of ICT and active educational practices where the student is the center of learning, to develop intellectual capital through the development of key or generic, disciplinary and professional competences. On the other hand, the use of ICTs as necessary tools for communication, research, analysis, experimentation, simulation and socialization of learning is also disclosed in such a way that during the application of the PBL methodology in conjunction with ICTs, skills that are required throughout life, both in academic, scientific and work are developed. Considering Mas – Torelló (2016):

Professional competences are more than the reserve of contents (knowledge), they also include skills (know-how), attitudes and values (know-how and being) that are demonstrated in a work context to optimally solve situations and / or problems of their own role, function or professional profile. Before attempting to define the profile of any professional, one cannot avoid establishing their three distinct but intimately interconnected and interrelated professional performance scenarios: the micro context classroom, the institutional and social contexts. (p.197)

ICTs enrich the development of the project in its different stages due to the diverse characteristics and flexibility they offer; they facilitate the performance of work individually or as a group, even asynchronously, through different technological devices, as well as the unlimited resources online and the widely used social networks, which allow the student to manage their own knowledge, developing a sense of responsibility and remaining motivated in the project.

In this way, the research presents a case study in the Higher Secondary Level (HSL) of the National Polytechnic Institute (IPN), which focuses on two aspects: the study of the impact of Project-Based Learning (PBL) in the Learning Unit of Oral and Written Expression to determine what are the competences that it develops, how it favors the creative thinking and the improvement of the motivation in the student, so it considers the stages of the PBL, such as planning, implementation and evaluation.

This work is organized as follows: the description of the PBL in the context of the HSL of the IPN; the second section, consists of the description of the planning and evaluation of the PBL in a case applied in the HSL, specifically in the CECYT 11 Wilfrido Massieu; the third section, focuses on the characterization of ICTs in the CECyT 11: availability and employment by the student and student teacher; the fourth section, discloses the results of the implementation of the PBL and; finally, reflections and limitations of the use of PBL are integrated.

The study shows that young people's interest in technology can be taken advantage of, as well as the advantages that this new era offers to generate greater learning or interest in the areas that they do not enjoy today; for this reason, the union of PBL and ICTs have been an appropriate combination for this time where young people need to learn actively through appropriate strategies and in accordance with the available resources, in order to support the teaching-learning process.

The results revealed that with the implementation of the PBL with ICTs, more and different competences were developed than those planned, mainly, the generic ones. In addition to the fact that the implementation of these strategies and resources are of interest to students, it promotes meaningful learning and maintains motivation.

DEVELOPMENT OF HUMAN CAPITAL AND EDUCATION

The importance of education for the development of a nation has been recognized in the sense that as investment in education increases, the earnings in the development and living standard of a country grows; wealth is focused on knowledge that the individual possesses, as a consequence, the way of acting and living of a society changes.

Under the context of globalization, education focuses on the development of skills, on the use of knowledge, techniques or procedures and attitudes for the solution or proposal of solving a real problem, under this paradigm, education has an impact and favors the economic growth when it meets graduation profiles that are consistent with what society demands through research, innovation, entrepreneurship, creativity, etc.

To achieve this end, in Mexico, the Competency-Based Human Resources Training Program (CBHRTP) is implemented at the Higher Secondary Education level in the technical education, vocational training and job training subsystems, to strengthen the development of the human capital closing the gap between skills acquired in school and the requirements of the productive sector, starting with CBHRTP (SEP, 2010):

> (i) the development of significant learning and competences that serve students in their work and throughout their lives; (ii) the strengthening of technology-based careers and training for work; (iii) greater linkage between education and the productive sectors; and (iv) the establishment of a teacher professionalization system (p.1)

In the same CBHRTP (SEP, 2010), three problems are identified in terms of the quality and relevance of the educational offer: curricular relevance and effective teaching methods, little connection with the productive sector, teacher's training and profiles. To counteract these problems in the Upper Middle Level, actions are put in place to develop the continuous training model:

1. strengthening the link with the productive sectors (educational planning and learning opportunities in the plant);
2. the standardized evaluation of young people's competences;
3. the strengthening of schools (adaptation of spaces and equipment) and their staff through new tools to improve student learning and enhance their transition from school to work;
4. the extension of the scope of the teacher training and professionalization actions; and
5. the reorientation and strengthening of the National Competency System (NCS) (p.2)

The deficiencies in education are limiting to be at the level of the demands, not only of a globalized world, but of the development of the country; as mentioned by CBHRTP (SEP, 2010), "communicate in an efficient way, work as a team, solve problems, use the information technologies effectively to adopt superior processes and technologies, as well as to understand the environment in which we live and be able to innovate."(p.1), that is, to guarantee the development of competences according to the graduation profiles.

These competences are directly related to the classification established by Lozano and Herrera (2013) cited by Zermeño and Lozano (2016), who establish that competences can be classified into:

1. labor and professional;
2. soft and hard;
3. generic and specific;
4. teachers and
5. basic, depending on the field where they are to be used, that is, not only work performance is enough, but at the beginning transversal competences are developed that are acquired outside the workplace, are transferable, applicable and demanded by different areas of knowledge (p.179)

Through education, knowledge is generated. The knowledge that is currently required can be developed through methodologies and strategies different from the traditional ones, which focus mainly on two edges: on identifying the learning that the student has to incorporate new ones and increase the existing, and in the same way, on developing and increasing specialized learning in the development of disciplinary and professional competences.

As we have seen, the development and investment in human capital needs to be strengthened by establishing a close relationship with the productive sectors, providing learning opportunities in a workplace, and in the classroom with equipment, materials, methodologies and strategies to develop and strengthen the generic, disciplinary and professional competences.

Another type of close relationship is established between the middle and upper level, as a way to give continuity and support to the skills developed in the students, that is, the upper middle level develops skills that at the higher level will be strengthened through training that combines theory and practice based on scientific and technological foundations under the reference of the reality of the professions or areas of knowledge that facilitate the acquisition of tools for life and the profession.

The upper and upper middle level establish specific objectives of each subsystem, but at the same time they are sequential since they are developed and complemented both curricularly (curricular maps, plans and study programs) and in the implementation, both subsystems recognize the development of competencies acquired at school and within the framework of work experience.

The PBL is a work strategy that adapts to the current contexts, the areas of training, modalities and levels, to give continuity between educational levels that work as links to promote lifelong learning, habits and attitudes for a successful work practice for professional development.

IMPLEMENTATION OF TEACHING STRATEGIES AND THE USE OF ICTs

ICTs provide increasing possibilities for teaching-learning processes and innovations to conventional classroom systems. "The introductions of these strategies produce improvement, changes that respond to a planned, deliberate, systematized and intentional process". (Salinas, 2004, págs. 3-4).

It is imminent to obtain better results in education, so we must aim to achieve meaningful learning. When this condition is met, the subject finds meaning in what he studies, understands it and can achieve meaningful learning.

Significant learning must have, on the part of the object, a logical organization that makes it comprehensible and, on the part of the subject, elements and background that allow it to learn it. In addition, the subject must know how to apply what he has learned when circumstances demand it, that is, learning must be functional. (Beciez, 2009, pág. 3)

Meaningful learning is achieved through activities that the student can perform and that provide some satisfaction when they are done, but above all that, related to what the student learns and his own experience, they integrate learning experiences. The learning that educates, requires the activity of the subject, he is the one who must carry out the process of relating the object and the new material to his previous experiences, to incorporate it into his mental structures, his habits, abilities, attitudes and values, as well as having reasons to do it (motivation).

To promote meaningful learning, some characteristics must be considered, such as: (Ontoria, Gomez, & Molina, 2000, pág. 55) "an affective implication in establishing this relationship between prior knowledge and new concepts, since it shows a positive disposition before learning ".

Meaningful learning is achieved in three stages; in the initial one, where simple forms of learning occur, it is resorted to previously conceptually isolated knowledge, which allows to pass to the intermediate stage, where we start with the formation of structures, reflect, understand and organize new information up to achieve analogies; finally, in the third stage, the structures and schemes are integrated, achieving learning, as the levels of relationship between knowledge increase. (Díaz Barriga, 2000, pág. 42).

So it is essential to use strategies that demand action from the student, according to the Doctor (Pimienta, 2012, pág. 127) "the active strategies are: a series of methodologies that allow to develop competences, which means putting skills, abilities, knowledge and attitudes at stake in a given situation and in a given context."

The strategies must be seen in an integral way, not as activities to reach an objective, nor are they lists of tasks to be carried out, there is a new vision where the aspects that affect their performance must be considered, according to (De la Torre, 2008, pág. 11) "the strategies have eight dimensions that are: preconceptions, context, organization, teacher role, mentee role, resources, climate and evaluation". Just to mention some examples of active methodologies, according to (Pimienta, 2012, pág. 128): "Generative topic, Simulation, Project, Case study, Problem-based learning, In situ learning, ICT-based learning, Learning based on service, Research with tutoring, cooperative learning, Webquest ". In this same sense, humanity has undergone great changes, reason why it has been chosen to call it the information society that will give life to the knowledge society, as (Bozu & Canto Herrera, 2009, pág. 88) explain below:

It should be noted that the knowledge society is not something that currently exists, it is a final stage of an evolutionary stage towards which society is heading, a subsequent stage to the current information age, and towards which it will be reached through the opportunities that represent the information and communication technology (ICT) of current societies. The name given to this society has been based on the amount of information that individuals have access to every day.

In the educational field, the term Educational Technology was established according to the (Association for Educational Communications and Technology, 2008, pág. 1) as: "... the study and ethical practice of facilitating learning and improving performance by creating, using and administering appropriate technological processes and resources."

The challenge that education systems are facing around the world is to use the new ICTs to promote to students the tools and knowledge needed for the 21st century. According to (Torres Gastelun & Moreno Coatzozón, 2013, págs. 48-65) "The incorporation of technologies in the university classroom requires a great effort from teachers and students in understanding the ways in which technology can support the teaching-learning process."

The task of using new technologies effectively is more than just having machines or software, you have to know how to use and integrate them properly in order to support the teaching-learning process and achieve success. According to another expert (Sunkel, 2006):

The educational policies that involve ICTs in educational establishments -and their effective use, both in the teaching/learning processes and in the organization of the teaching task- are a way of responding to the challenges. Therefore, they are not a simple fashion or sophistication, but respond to the development needs of our countries and their insertion in the globalized world (p.140).

Likewise, it is essential to consider what the Spanish professor in Educational Technology points out (Area Moreira, 2009, pág. 198). What is relevant should always be the educational, not the technological. Therefore, a teacher, when planning the use of ICTs, should always keep in mind what students will learn and to what extent the technology serves to improve the quality of the teaching process. Based on (Chávez Márquez & Gutiérrez, 2015), "Information and communication technologies (ICTs) are today a necessary tool in many areas, and are fundamental as a complement to quality education at all levels".

On the one hand, students guided by teachers have access to different materials, resources and sources of information such as databases, multimedia programs, electronic documents, library catalogs, consultation with experts, etc. from which they build their own knowledge autonomously according to their skills, knowledge, and interests.

Having distinctive characteristics such as motivation, independence and self-sufficiency, (Meyer, 2002) typical of this era.

The physical spaces where the teaching-learning process takes place find new training environments which will be more interactive and dynamic than the current ones, since students will not be passive recipients of information, but will have to make different decisions in this regard; the above, places management in a vital role to become a critical variable for the functioning of the quality of the system, in which all actors interact in teacher-student-management.

The challenge will be to articulate changes in the roles of students and teachers, in which:

The technology will allow the establishment of multimedia resource centers where information is freely accessible and circulated through the network; and three, that the information will be free and will circulate through the network, leading the school to transform into new environments by modifying its space for the transformation of the classroom into the life of cyberspace (Avedaño, 2007, pág. 45)

According to (Cabero, 2007), the use of ICTs contributes to the teaching incorporation and the creation of innovative contexts for training with advantages in the expansion of the information offer, creation of flexible environments for learning, elimination of space-time barriers, increase in educational modalities, enhancement of interactive environments. These technological changes are nuanced by (Punie, 2007, pág. 187) for whom technological changes are specifically affecting the ways in which we conceive learning in the knowledge society, this generates strategies that must be developed to improve the teaching-learning process. This research allows identifying technological resources, materials and didactic strategies to strengthen the teaching-learning process through the use of ICTs.

ICT Availability and Employment in the CECyT 11 Wilfrido Massieu

As mentioned by (Hernández, Fernández, & Baptista, 2009 p.184): "What is done in non-experimental research is to observe phenomena as they occur in their natural context, and then analyze them." This is the case of the research carried out, which is located as a cross-sectional study, because it is intended to measure variables at a given time.

The study population corresponded to the CECyT 11, made up of students whose ages range between 14 and 21 years, of medium and low socioeconomic level, coming from the different delegations and the metropolitan area. The study sample was random, 33% corresponded to women and 66% to men. The instrument used for the data collection was the questionnaire; the results obtained are exposed below.

In terms of the most used materials: the forms (guides, problems, use of books) with 56% and 24%, the use of the internet (only in reference to information search), followed by the use of scientific models with 15% and with 5% of digital interactive materials as can be seen in Fig. 1.

In the dimension of strategies used, the results obtained can be seen in Fig. 2. They show that traditional strategies reach 59%, these include: Brainstorming, teamwork, synthesizing information, mapping, exposure of students, among others; the active strategies reach 36% within which they are considered: Search of information and elaboration of works through Internet sources, solution of cases, roll playing, mini-projects among others. And with 5%, visits in which attendance at exhibitions, museums and conferences are considered.

Regarding the resources used in class, they are shown in Fig. 3, which highlights the use of the Internet for research and publications with 44%, the use of social networks reaches 20%, didactic materials such as simulators with 13%; the use of blogs where students interact with the teacher 8%, the use of videos, podcast or

Figure 1. Used materials
Source: Own elaboration

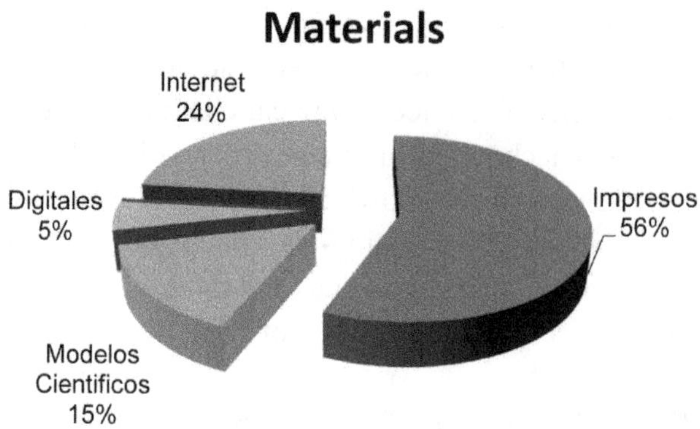

Figure 2. Strategies used in the classroom
Source: Own elaboration

movies with 7%, the use of email 6%; however, within the resources less used in the class are employment of programs or specialized software (2%).

As part of the changes required in the knowledge society, there are new approaches focused on learning, which make a difference in relation to the passive model of teaching and knowledge transmission, to a model in which the student is the manager of knowledge and information. Despite living in a highly technological age, it is observed that ICT is not used optimally in the classroom even though it is within the reach of students.

Figure 3. Resources used in the classroom
Source: own elaboration

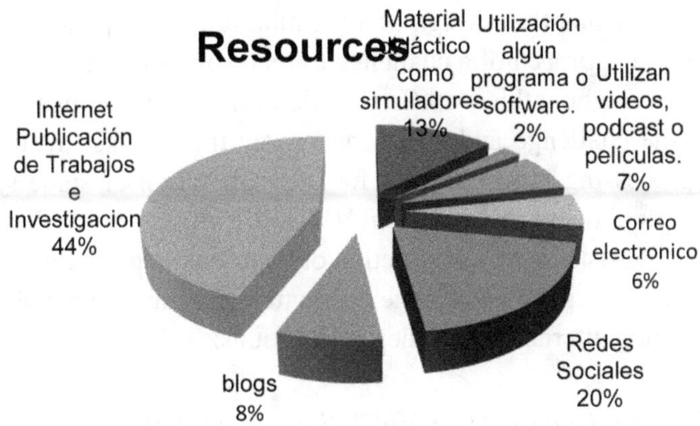

The PBL in One Case in the CECYT 11 Wilfrido Massieu

There are precedents in the search for solutions to improve the teaching-learning process, achieve significant learning and integrate ICTs for the development of skills and human capital.

In the Upper Middle Level of the IPN, the so-called Classroom Project was established in 2004, as a first approach for the application of innovative strategies in the classroom and as a way to ensure the development of the various competences: generic, disciplinary and professional that together, will promote others at the same time, mainly the investigation for the solution of problems, which complexity of the investigation depends on the level that the students take considering their antecedents, reason why the procedure goes from "basic investigation (documentary and field) and subsequently (levels 3, 4, and 5) projected in the technological research (induction, application, innovation or continuous improvement), to finally transfer and integrate what was learned in a terminal project (sixth level)" (IPN, 2010, pág. 2)

The research findings on the use of ICTs make it possible to determine the need to be reflective about the imminent need for a performance in the classroom different from the traditional one, using methods, strategies, tools, current and diverse materials, such as PBL, that is, the acquisition of competences through active and collaborative learning strategies make the student more responsible and aware of their self-learning. However, certain limitations of active methodologies and their application through ICT must be taken into account. The most important thing is that being requires a high motivation of both the student and the teacher. (From Lucas-Santos, 2017, p.255)

The PBL is considered a methodology, where, in a collaborative way, a problem is solved or solution alternatives are given for the product or products elaborated by the group; we quote that the "design of a learning project responds to a workflow that goes from the approach of a challenge to its resolution and the dissemination of the project. Throughout this workflow, students have to perform a series of tasks to respond to the challenge and in a generic way these tasks involve managing information, processing it and using it for the elaboration of some type of final product as a result of the work carried out" (INTELF, 2018, pág. 3). Problem-based learning (PBL) consists in the construction of solutions to problems based on real life in order to activate prior knowledge and in turn generate a dialogue that allows critically evaluating alternatives. Núñez defines it as:

It is a student-centered approach, in which students learn about a topic by working in groups in order to solve an open problem. Group learning facilitates not only the acquisition of knowledge, but also various other desirable attributes, such as cationic skills, teamwork, problem solving, independence, responsibility to learn, share information, and respect for others. (2017, p.260)

The table, that is shown below, is structured in three columns, the central column is the one needed to define the lateral elements, it starts by planning challenges, tasks and work teams to relate both vertically and horizontally; in the right column, to define competences, learning and evaluation goals, as well as in the left column, to define the human resources, equipment and materials that will be used, ICT tools and finally how to disseminate it. These same elements were considered as a guide to design the project, from them is how they have defined the planning and implementation of PBL as can be seen in Table 1.

The topic and challenges of this project were defined through the interests of the students, considering that, currently, the concept of sustainability is more than a concept, a process of growth, related to the care and protection of the environment, so it becomes a necessity to be aware of the wear and abuse that the human being with its economic, technological and social growth has generated over time on the environment; on the contrary, it requires awareness and actions that impact the environment favorably. These arguments are what gave rise to both the magazine and the presentation of the news.

Table 1. Planning and execution of the PBL

Elements	Characteristics	Planning
1.The competences to develop	What are the competences that are strengthened or developed?	Elaborates expressive messages orally and in writing by using the resources of literature in diverse contexts. Presents topics or issues considering the qualities of oral expression and the various communicative situations.
2.The learning goals	What are the goals to achieve?	Choice of thematic axis on which the process and the thematic product will focus: Sustainable development. To know the generalities of the types of sustainability and develop disciplinary competences of EOYE II and generic competences
3.Evaluation methods	What are the evaluation techniques and the instruments that will be used?	Checklist, rubrics and observation guide
4.Challenges and final product	What are the challenges for the students that will lead them to a final product?	**Challenges:** disciplinary integration, collaborative work, development of generic and transversal competences, promotion of research. **Questions:** Is it necessary to be aware of the abuse on the environment that the human being with its economic, technological and social growth, as well as the consequences that have generated over time? How and through what means can actions that impact the environment be favorably disseminated? **Final products:** by team: Electronic magazine about some kind of sustainability. Presentation of a newscast.
5.Tasks	Through which learning experiences will the tasks be carried out?	• Group assembly for the choice and delimitation of topic • Team division and distribution of sustainability types • Identify in each learning unit their contribution for digital magazine • Documentary research of each of the topics indicated in the learning units • Delivery and review of the progress of documentary research • Self-assessment of the structure of a scientific dissemination magazine to identify and develop a draft, continuous reviews and corrections as a team • Co-evaluation • Newscast script design considering the structure itself • Presentation
6.Work teams	How will the teams be integrated?	The group, consisting of 44 students, was divided into voluntarily teams composed by 7 or 8 participants.
7.Resources	What are the resources: human, material and technical?	The master teachers of the Learning Units who provided guidance from their specialty to inform or advise on any activity were integrated into the work. No specialized material was necessary
8.ICT tools	What ICT to use and for what?	Tools used: internet (documents, videos, movies, podcast, etc.) to carry out investigations. For publications: social networks, blogs and use of email
9.Dissemination	What actions to take for dissemination?	Preparation of the journal and publication in networks, as well as the presentation of the news

Source: Own elaboration

RESULTS OF THE IMPLEMENTATION OF THE PBL

After the implementation of PBL in the case of a group of HSL, which had as objectives to achieve significant learning and integrate ICTs in the development of various competences, in the application of measuring instruments (surveys and interviews) to the participating students, the results found identify:

The need to work with the use of ICTs as resources for research, dissemination of results and impact on broad communities for awareness and community actions; Derived from this point, the need was expressed for the selection of consultation sources that have validity and reliability.

The development of generic competences that the PBL implied for its execution, development of tasks, elaboration and presentation of final products: Organization and teamwork to deal with problems and reach the established objectives, elaborate through different means, codes and resources, messages in and for different contexts, it supports a personal stance before a challenge, respects others' points of view, and considered as one of the main contributions: learning by initiative, continuous and systematic.

Within the components of the competences, are the values and attitudes, the ones which were strengthened and/or developed were: responsibility, creativity, punctuality in the delivery of advances, critical, systematic, motivated to learn, satisfaction of what was learned.

As strengthened knowledge of theoretical and factual types: Sustainability (causes and consequences), characteristics of the sources, valid information, characteristics and structure of a magazine and a newscast.

Among the skills developed or strengthened are: Learning to operate programs to create documents, take order and systematize, extract relevant data: analysis, summaries, textual citations, synthesis; others: written and oral communication, use of language at different levels according to the context and recipients, such as colloquial and technical or scientific, as well as its variations.

Reflections and Limitations of the Use of PBL

In the same way, the students express the need for more time since the results are definitely satisfactory, which were replaced with spaces outside the classroom.

As the coordinator of this project, the reflections are based mainly on the fact that the development and/or strengthening of the teacher's own competences is required, such as: willingness to learn, in two senses, one that has to do with practices in the classroom other than the traditional, the other on the use of ICT tools and resources, in addition to equipment and materials available.

The OECD (2015b) has just published a report in which it performs an international analysis comparing the digital skills of students and their learning environments. The report notes that there is no direct and causal relationship between the availability and accessibility of technologies and their pedagogical use in the classroom, but rather notable variations and intensities in their use depending on the personal characteristics of the teacher, contextual factors derived from the educational policies implemented, and organizational-institutional factors.

Regarding different teaching practices in the classroom, they also require ongoing training and updating processes that give meaning to the teaching-learning process, to the role of the teacher and the student, strengthening the development of knowledge, skills and attitudes to advance in the construction of autonomous and collaborative learning experiences for the construction of meaningful learning. It is suggested to continuously monitor the individual tasks and equipment, as well as the deliveries of partial products because there is a risk of not reaching the work rate to finalize the final product in a timely manner. In this sense, Ramírez and Navarro (2015), state that PBL is a way to generate knowledge from the discussion and guidance of teachers who build critical thinking ... promote renewal in curricula that adapt to social changes and the needs of 21st century students (p.329)

Teaching practices different from the traditional ones have implications on information, tasks, evaluation of the students and on the teacher, implies a series of progressive and continuous challenges.

Recognize the use of ICTs as a support for the design, implementation and evaluation of work methodologies that do not substitute the teacher's own work and that do not magically build knowledge in the student; the use of ICTs is a technological tool that facilitates communication, research, and mainly, the process of student training, without forgetting the difficulties of access, the OECD (2015b) has just published a report in which it carries out an international analysis comparing the digital skills of students and their learning environments. The report notes that there is no direct and causal relationship between the availability and accessibility of technologies and their pedagogical use in the classroom, but rather notable variations and intensities in their use depending on the personal characteristics of the teacher, contextual factors derived from the educational policies implemented, and organizational-institutional factors.

FUTURE RESEARCH DIRECTIONS

Given the results found on the lack of use of ICTs and strategies that allow the development of human capital in the formation of competencies in the classroom, it can be deduced that the type of practices that dominate are characterized by fragmented contents of the teacher's domain, which in many cases the teacher is overwhelmed by the student in terms of the use of technology and devices, the lack of confidence to implement innovative practices and that in the same way that the student, the teacher requires accompaniment.

Therefore, it is evident that there are not enough processes of training and teacher updating in any of its modalities: courses, workshops, diploma courses, seminars, among others require to implement other actions: give the opportunity to the teacher to live to build learning experiences, but on the other hand, it also provides accompaniment for the implementation in the classroom, that is, recovering the academic life where performance is planned, implemented and evaluated, a continuous work among teachers is involved to improve strategies and methodologies, develop collaborative work and the use of resources.

On the other hand, it is necessary to consider if the graduation profiles of upper secondary students of the bivalent modality are sufficient and pertinent to be inserted in the workplace and / or continue at a higher level.

SOLUTIONS AND RECOMMENDATIONS

Regarding the problems presented for the implementation of PBL and the use of technology, it is clear that traditional strategies have yet to be replaced in the classroom by active, printed materials by the use of technological resources: simulators, specialized programs. The topics proposed for future studies are those related to: 1) education by competencies, the development of human capital according to the profiles demanded by today's society, the promotion of soft skills, such as: creativity, innovation, entrepreneurship, adaptation of collaborative work, etc., 2) formally know the relevance of technical and professional careers as well as the technical-pedagogical support that supports plans and programs of study in theory and in practice 3) identify teaching performance depending on their soft skills developed 4) identify the technological resources available in the classroom and the teaching skills for their use 5) Sequence and continuity between the upper and upper middle levels.

CONCLUSION

To increase the skills to communicate, work as a team, solve problems and efficiently use ICTs are requirements of every area of the productive sector, the challenge of education is the same, to close the gaps that exist between what is offered and what is needed, to close the gap between educational, industrial and social sectors.

Encourage and give continuity to academic work through active methodologies and the use of ICTs between the medium upper, upper and postgraduate levels facilitates the continuity of integral training, the empowerment of competences, the relationship from one level to another, the integration of new forms of work and technology.

To achieve the incorporation of new forms of work such as PBL and technological tools, there are challenges that must be solved, such as the will and effort to develop the competences that correspond to the teacher through systematic and continuous training and education, the commitment and the will of the student to play an active role, of the corresponding instances to acquire and provide the resources and technological means, that is, to undertake new forms of performance.

Prepare the student for job skills and develop human capital from the classroom can be emphasized in the knowledge of techniques, strategies and the use of ICTs, regardless of the lack of curriculum relevance, because these deficiencies can be overcome with effective teaching methods that will form the basis of the model of continuous training and skills of young people.

School or institutionally, there are also areas that can be improved that directly impact teachers: adaptation of spaces and equipment, use of new equipment and tools, expansion of training actions and teacher professionalization.

Specifying what and how to achieve the joint needs and actions of the productive and educational sectors is not an easy task, but it is necessary for the development of human capital, the PBL has advantages in the solution of complex problems of the real world.

The value of the contributions of this chapter are varied: they show the reality of the forms of teaching and learning, the limitations in terms of the availability and use of ICTs, which affect the results of the students' training, at the same time they are background between educational levels and previous knowledge: knowledge, skills and attitudes insufficient for the requirements between educational levels, personal and work performance.

This chapter offers the analysis of areas of opportunity to integrate ICTs in teaching-learning processes, strengthen teaching performance with strategies focused on the student and with the use of other modalities, the development of educational resources that renew work in the classroom and allow the construction of content, of knowledge in an autonomous and conscious way that does not result in the opposite direction, as distractors, loss of time or that encourage superficial learning.

ACKNOWLEDGMENT

The authors thank Dr. Edgar Oliver Cardoso Espinosa for his support and the sponsorship granted by the National Polytechnic Institute through the Research and Postgraduate Secretariat to prepare and present the chapter of the book derived from the researches whose registration numbers are: 20171952 A gamified environment for written communication, 20170619 Greek etymology: a tool for understanding information, and 20171093 Inductive process in understanding texts in contextualized problems.

REFERENCES

Area Moreira, M. (2009). *Introduccion a la Tecnología Educativa* (E. Universadad de la Laguna, Ed.). Recuperado el 12 de mayo de 2016, de http://bibliotecadigital.org/bitstream/001/415/5/Introducci%C3%B3n%20a%20la%20tecnolog%C3%ADa%20educativa.pdf

Association for Educational Communications and Technology. (2008). Definition. In Educational technology: A definition with commentary. New York: Lawrence Erlbaum Associates.

Avedaño, F. (2007). *Cómo gestionar el cambio tecnológico.* Barcelona: Paidós.

Beciez, D. (2009). *Obtenido de Curso AIU Estrategias de Enseñanza Aprendizaje.* Retrieved from http://cursos.aiu.edu/Estrategias%20de%20Ensenanza%20y%20Apredizaje/PDF/Tema%201.pdf

Bozu, Z., & Canto Herrera, P. J. (2009). El profesorado universitario en la sociedad del conocimiento: Competencias profesionales docentes. *Revista de Formación e Innovación Educativa Universitaria, 2*(2), 87–97.

Cabero, J. (2007). *Novas Tecnologias na educaión.* Coruña: SecretariaXeral de Análise e Proxeccion de la Xunts de Galicia.

Calderon, E., Flores, F., Gallegos, L., De la Cruz, G., Ramirez, J., & Casteñeda, R. (2016). Laboratorios de ciencias en el bachillerato: Tecnologías digitales y adaptación docente. *Apertura (Guadalajara, Jal.), 8*(1), 1–11.

Casillas, M. y. (2016). *La integración de México a la sociedad de la información.* UNAM.

Chávez Márquez, L., & Gutiérrez, M. d. (2015). Redes sociales como facilitadoras del aprendizaje de ciencias exactas en la educación superior. *Apertura (Guadalajara, Jal.)*.

De la Torre, S. C. (2008). *Estrategias didácticas en el aula. Buscando la calidad y la innovación.* Madrid: Universidad Nacional de Educación a Distancia.

Díaz Barriga, F. (2000). *Estrategias Docentes: Para un Aprendizaje Significativo.* Mcgraw-Hill Interamericana.

Granada, U. d. (2018). *Conecta 13. CANVAS para el Diseño del Entorno de Aprendizaje de una Organización.* Obtenido de Tomado de: http://conecta13.com/canvas/

INTELF. (2018). *MOOC Aprendizaje Basado en Proyectos.* Obtenido de http://docentesinnovadores.perueduca.pe/?get_group_doc=104/1498096235-aprendizaje-basado-en-proyectos.pdf

IPN. (2010). *Manual: Operatividad del proyecto aula.* IPN.

Mas-Torelló, O. y. (2019). El Profesor universitario en el espacio europeo de educación superior: La autopercepción de sus competencias docentes actuales y orientaciones para su formación pedagógica. *Revista Mexicana de Investigación Educativa*, 437–470.

Meyer, K. (2002). *Quality in diistance education. Focus on On-line learning.* Hoboken, NJ: Academic Press.

Nuñez, S. A. (2017). The developmente of critical thinking abilities in university students by means of problem-base learning. *Revista iberoamericana de educación media superior*, 84-103.

OECD. (2015a). *Students, Computer y Learning: Making the conection PISA.* Obtenido de http://goo.gl3X8cam

OECD. (2015b). *Teaching with Tecnology. Teaching in Focus Report.* Obtenido de http://goo.gl/NgxYKy

Ontoria, A., Gomez, J., & Molina, A. (2000). *Potenciar la Capacidad de Aprender y Pensar.* Madrid: Narcea, S.A. de Ediciones.

Paredes, R. (2016). Una estrategia de enseñanza de educación ambiental, en estudiantes de un liceo municipal de Cañete. *Revista electrónica educare*, 1-26.

Pimienta, P. J. (2012). *Estrategias de Enseñanza Aprendizaje docencia universitaria basada en competencias.* Pearson Educación.

Punie, Y. (2007). Learning Spaces: An ICT-enabled model of future learning in the Knowledge-based Society. *European Journal of Education*, *42*(2), 187. doi:10.1111/j.1465-3435.2007.00302.x

Ramírez, O. y. (2015). El aprendizaje basado en problemas y su utilidad en el desarrollo de las ciencias de la salud. *Revista de la Facultad de Medicina (Caracas)*, *63*(2), 325–330. doi:10.15446/revfacmed.v63n2.49171

Ruiz Ortega, F. (2007). Modelos didácticos para la enseñanza de las ciencias naturales. *Revista Latinoamericana de Estudios Educativos, 3*(2), 41-60.

Salinas, J. (2004). Cambios metodologicos con las TIC. *Estrategias didacticas y entornos virtuales de enseñanza-aprendizaje, 56*, 3-4.

SEP. (2010). *Programa de Formación de Recursos Humanos Basado en Competencias.* Cd.de México: SEP.

Sunkel, G. (2006). Las tecnologias de la información y comunicación (TIC) en la educación en America Látina. Una exploracion de indicadores (Serie de Politicas Sociales ed.). Santiago de Chile: CEPAL UNESCO.

Torres Gastelun, C., & Moreno Coatzozón, G. (2013). Inclusión de las TIC en los escenarios de aprendizaje universitario. *Apertura, 5,* 48-65.

ADDITIONAL READING

Flores-Fuentes, G., & Juárez Ruiz, E. L. (2017). Aprendizaje basado en proyectos para el desarrollo de competencias matemáticas en bachillerato. *Revista Electrónica de Investigación Educativa*, *19*(3), 71–91. doi:10.24320/redie.2017.19.3.721

Galán, J., Ivette, Y., & Jaime, H. Josefina, & González, Marko Alfonso. (2013). Competencias profesionales en la educación superior: justificación, evaluación y análisis. Innovación educativa (México, DF), 13(61), 45-65. Recuperado en 07 de febrero de 2019, de http://www.scielo.org.mx/scielo.php?script=sci_arttext&pid=S1665-26732013000100004&lng=es&tlng=es

García, J., & Pérez, J. Aprendizaje basado en proyectos: método para el diseño de actividades. núm. 10 (mayo-agosto 2018, pp. 37-63). Recuperado 20 de enero de 2019 de www.tecnologia-ciencia-educacion.com CEF

García-Varcálcel Muñoz-Repiso, A., & Basilotta Gómez-Pablos, V. (2017). Aprendizaje basado en proyectos (abp): Evaluación desde la perspectiva de alumnos de educación primaria. *Revista de Investigación Educacional, 35*(1), 113–131. doi:10.6018/rie.35.1.246811

Guerrero, S., González, S., Matos Chamorro, A., & Picón Ventocilla, E. (2015). Desarrollo del Capital Humano y su impacto en el Desempeño de Una Institución Microfinanciera no regulada del Perú. *Apuntes Universitarios. Revista de Investigacion, V*(1), 51–68.

Padilla, Z., María, A., & Rodríguez, L. Armando. (2016). Desarrollo de competencias interpersonales en ambientes virtuales. *CPU-e. Revista de Investigación Educativa*, (22), 176-199. Recuperado en 07 de febrero de 2019, de http://www.scielo.org.mx/scielo.php?script=sci_arttext&pid=S1870-53082016000100176&lng=es&tlng=es

Ramírez Ospina, D. (2015). Capital humano: Una visión desde la teoría crítica. *Cadernos EBAPE.BR, 13*(2), 315–331. doi:10.1590/1679-395114754

Torres, I. (2017). La implicación de las TIC en la educación: Alcances, Limitaciones y Prospectiva. *RIDE Revista Iberoamericana para la Investigación y el Desarrollo Educativo, 8*(15), 861–876. doi:10.23913/ride.v8i15.324

KEY TERMS AND DEFINITIONS

Competences: It is the integration and use of knowledge, skills and attitudes to solve a problem in a specific real or simulated context.

Didactic Materials: Also known as auxiliary or media, is any resource used to support and/or facilitate the teaching-learning process, used by the teacher or student.

Entrepreneurship: Word of origin in the business field. It is considered as the action of making changes with the intention of improvement for which creative and innovative talent applies.

Human Capital: Knowledge that a person acquires throughout his life formally or informally to perform in diverse contexts through the contribution of a service or the contribution of ideas.

Information and Communication Technologies (ICTs): IT tools or technological resources that facilitate the communication, emission, access and treatment of information.

Project-Based Learning (PBL): Learning methodology in which a problem to be solved is proposed through research, collaborative work, and dissemination of results.

Significant Learning: The subject of learning is the one who relates previous experiences, the object, and the new material to incorporate it into his mental structures; it occurs first in an isolated way until it is integrated into a structure and complex thought patterns.

Chapter 10
The Training of Intellectual Capital in the Tourism Sector Based on the Development of Professional Skills

Rosa María Rivas García
Instituto Politécnico Nacional, Mexico

Jésica Alhelí Cortés Ruiz
Instituto Politécnico Nacional, Mexico

Sandra Viridiana Cortés Ruiz
Instituto Politécnico Nacional, Mexico

ABSTRACT

The objective of this chapter is to offer an approach to the generation of competitive advantage in the tourism industry based on the definition of intellectual capital and its relationship with professional competences in tourism, which is why the topic of educational competences in higher education is described, since professional skills are achieved through these. Subsequently, the exploration of the intellectual capital concept and the conception of tourism is presented. Finally, the relation of the thematic axes of this chapter is presented to incorporate the conclusion that describes that the educational competences in higher education applied by professionals in the tourism industry will result in the productivity and profitability of the organizations known as intellectual capital.

DOI: 10.4018/978-1-5225-8461-2.ch010

INTRODUCTION

The dynamism in the tourism industry as well as the evolution and progress of science and the information and communication technologies have modified society from the social and economic approaches, therefore the development of concepts and theories that try to show a perspective of economic and financial management in the tourism sector and requires an advance of the theoretical postulates on which knowledge, educational competences, knowledge management, intellectual capital, among others, is based.

The training, production, adaptation, use and evaluation of new knowledge are a factor of increasing strategic management in the levels of competitiveness in organizations. The identification of intangible assets that must be directed to strengthen competitive advantage has led to the emergence of knowledge management and the measurement of intellectual capital. Currently, knowledge is a key element in the creation and generation of competitiveness and heritage in organizations. Human capital based on its competences and capabilities as an intangible resource of an organization has developed its importance to become the main generator of value. In this context, the central theme of this chapter is based on the conceptual confluence of professional skills and intellectual capital within the framework of the tourism industry.

In order to specify the thematic axes of the chapter, it is necessary to describe the perceptions of educational competences in higher education and intellectual capital in order to frame them in the professional training in tourism. As the tourism industry evolves, it tends to the effects of globalization and the innovation of tourism products; in addition, these changes impact the human capital of the industrial sector.

EDUCATIONAL COMPETENCE IN HIGHER EDUCATION

Initially, the concept of educational competences will be described. Because of the polysemic nature of the word "competence", this text will address the conceptualization -Peritia, aptitude, and suitability to do something or intervene in a given matter-. By virtue of which the Royal Spanish Academy (2018), considers different meanings for the word in question.

competence[1]

From lat. *competentia;* cf. *to compete.*

1. f. Dispute or contention between two or more people about something.
2. f. Opposition or rivalry between two or more people who aspire to obtain the same thing.

3. f. Situation of companies that compete in a market offering or demanding the same product or service.
4. f. Person or rival group. It has gone to THE competition.
5. f. Am. Sports competition.

competence[2]
From lat. *competentia;* cf. *competent.*

1. f. incumbency.
2. f. Expertise, aptitude or suitability to do something or intervene in a certain matter.
3. f. Legal scope of attributions that correspond to a public entity or a judicial or administrative authority.

Based on Table 1, when addressing the subject of Educational Competences, the extent of the material that the various authors have developed to explain this subject is identified; therefore, some of the classifications adopted to raise the issue of educational competences will not establish any aspect, terminology or specific points of view of any author; since each degree develops competences; some own or specific to the corresponding degree, while others are transversal or shared with other degrees.

- Specific competences, which are specific to a field or degree and are aimed at achieving a specific profile of the graduate (a). They are close to certain training aspects, areas of knowledge or groupings of subjects, and usually have a longitudinal projection in the degree.
- Generic (or transversal) competences, are common to most of the degrees, although with a different incidence, and are contextualized in each of the degrees in question. Within this block we find personal competences such as time management and the responsibility of learning itself; interpersonal skills, working as a team, leading or negotiating; competences related to information management, languages, computing, etc., these latter competences are under the denomination of instrumental.

According to the Education and Competency Evaluation Bulletin: a challenge for the Latin American Laboratory for Assessment of the Quality of Education (LLECE) of UNESCO - UNICEF (2008); the conception of education is being challenged by a combination of factors of change and unexpected crises: socio-demographic changes; the growing youth unemployment; the widening of gaps between and within the countries of the region; the challenges to food security and nutrition caused by

Table 1. Main definitions of the term educational competence

Authors	Educational Competence
McClelland (1973)	The competences are linked to a way of evaluating what "really causes a superior performance in the work", and not "to the evaluation of the factors that reliably describe all the characteristics of a person, in the hope that some are associated with performance at work".
Chomsky (1985)	Based on the theories of language, he establishes the concept and defines competences as the capacity and disposition for performance and for interpretation.
De Ketele (1996)	Organized set of capacities (activities) that are exercised on the contents of learning, and which integration allows solving the problems that arise within a category of situations. Set of tasks more or less of the same type, within a family of situations.
Roegiers (2000)	The competence is the possibility that an individual has to mobilize in an internalized way an integrated set of resources -of knowledge, of schemes, of automatisms, of capacities, of "know/do" of different types- in order to solve a family of problem situations. Knowledge that refers to complex situations that lead to managing heterogeneous variables and that allow solving problems that escape the epistemologically related situations with a knowledge discipline.
European Comission (2004)	The term "competence" refers to a combination of skills, knowledge, aptitudes and attitudes, and to the inclusion of the willingness to learn, in addition to knowing how. Key competences represent a multifunctional and transferable package of knowledge, skills and attitudes that individuals need for their fulfillment and personal development, inclusion and employment.
Perrenoud (2007)	The ability to mobilize a set of resources (knowledge, skills, information, etc.) to effectively solve a series of situations connected to cultural, professional and social conditions.
SEP (2011)	A competence is the ability to respond to different situations, and involves knowing-how (skills) with knowledge, as well as the assessment of the consequences of that doing (values and attitudes)".
OECD (2013)	A competence is more than knowledge and skills. It involves the ability to respond to complex demands, using and mobilizing psychosocial resources (including skills and attitudes) in a particular context.

Source: Own elaboration based on data from the cited authors

climate change; the increasingly frequent disasters; the depletion of natural resources; lifestyles and patterns of unsustainable production and consumption; the crises and volatility; as well as the issues of governance, migration, mobility and urbanization; the continuous acceleration in the production and circulation of knowledge; as well as the great development of new information and communication technologies.

All these factors are imposing new challenges and demands on education and education systems in the region (Latin America) and the world. The mission of most of the institutions in most countries is now to teach the basic disciplines to a lesser extent and offer more vocational training programs where emerging economies need trained specialists to perform scientific and technical professions and strong leaders with general knowledge, that are creative, adaptable and capable of addressing social advances from a broad ethical perspective. With the intention of addressing the challenges explained above, educational projects have adopted and adapted the concept of "competence", first arising in the labor area. The competency orientation is possibly an approximation for equal opportunities through the educational tool.

Based on the above, educational competences in higher education are defined below and are developed from the knowledge and discipline of each degree and which are the following:

- **Knowledge Competences:** Cognitive. Disciplinary. Conceptual.
- **Knowing How Competences:** Procedural. Instrumental.
- **Competences of Being:** Attitudinal. Valuable.
- **Generic Competences:** Transversal

INTELLECTUAL CAPITAL

The concept of intellectual capital specifies a perspective of generation of competitive advantage, because it is a non-transferable intangible asset that generates capital in an organization thanks to the combination of elements of intangible nature, as well as its human and structural resources, allowing to capitalize experiences, and transforming knowledge.

Based on Table 2, it is established that valuable intangible assets for an organization, established in knowledge as a capital producer, outline the concept of intellectual capital. Through an explanation supported by the valuation concepts of an organization in the market; based on the knowledge and professional competences of the collaborators.

In this way, intellectual capital is the set of intangible assets based on knowledge and access to the evolution of resources in a system of value creation, through the achievement of sustainable competitive advantages.

TOURISM

The following points are described with data from the UNWTO International Tourism Outlook (2017), which outline tourism activity as a key to development, prosperity and well-being;

- A growing number of destinations around the world have opened up to tourism and invested in it, making it a key sector for socio-economic progress, through the creation of jobs and businesses, the generation of income from export and infrastructure execution.

Table 2. Main definitions of the concept of intellectual capital

Authors	Intellectual Capital
Galbraith (1969) Quoted by Haghshenas and Barzegar (2014)	Galbraith believed that intellectual capital is an ideological process and consists of intellectual process. Before identifying, managing and measuring the intellectual capital, we need to understand the concept it has.
Steward (1998)	Intellectual material, knowledge, information, intellectual property, experience, which can be used to create value, wealth is the product of knowledge. This and the information have become the fundamental raw materials of the economy and its most important products.
Edvinson and Malone (1999)	Set of non-material contributions, which in the information age are understood as the main asset of the companies of the third millennium. It is the possession of knowledge, applied experience, organizational technology, relationships with clients and professional skills that give the company a competitive advantage in the market.
Bradley (2003)	Ability to transform knowledge and the rest of intangible assets into resources that generate wealth, both for companies and for nations.
Bueno, Salmador, and Merino (2008),	Indicates the value of accumulated wealth derived from knowledge or a set of assets of an intangible nature. It combines assets of an intangible nature, which create new knowledge, and this is transformed into business skills or the creation of competitive advantage. It generates value to the company and represents the new wealth of organizations and nations. It is not usually reflected in the financial statements of a company.
Rivero (2009)	Synergy of all the knowledge that an organization gathers, all the experience accumulated in its members, their abilities, skills, motivation and commitment, values, etc., applied to work. Everything it has achieved in terms of relationships, processes, discoveries, innovations, presence in the market and recognition in society.
Sarur (2013)	Intangible asset and is represented by the worker's competences at any hierarchical level or position; that is, what knowledge he has, what skills he has developed and what attitudes reflect in his work performance for the benefit of the organization.

Source: Own elaboration based on data from the cited authors.

- Tourism is an important category of the international trade of services.
- International tourism accounts for 7% of world exports of goods and services, after rising one percentage point from 6% in 2015. Tourism has grown faster than world trade during the last five years.

From Table 3, it is important to underline the importance of the elements that are common to all of them. There is a physical movement of tourists who, by definition, are those who move outside their place of residence. The stay in the destination must be for a certain period of time, not permanent. Tourism includes both the journey to the destination and the activities carried out during the stay. Whatever the motivation to travel, tourism encompasses services and products created to meet the needs of tourists.

Table 3. Main definitions of the term tourism

Authors	Definition of Tourism
Glucksmann, Schwinck or Bormann (1919-1938)	Tourism, as a matter of university research, begins to interest in the period between the two great world wars of this century. During this period, European economists begin to publish the first works, highlighting the so-called Berlin school.
Burkart and Medlik (1981)	The short and temporary displacements of people to destinations outside the place of residence and work, and the activities undertaken during the stay in those destinations.
UNWTO (1994)	Tourism includes the activities carried out by people during their trips and stays in places other than their usual environment, for a consecutive period of less than one year for leisure, business and other purposes.
UNWTO (2014)	Tourism is a social, cultural and economic phenomenon related to the movement of people to places that are outside their usual place of residence for personal or business / professional reasons. These people are called visitors (who can be tourists or hikers, residents or non-residents) and tourism is related to their activities, which involve a tourist expense.

Source: Own elaboration based on data from the cited authors

COMPETENCES OF THE PROFESSIONAL IN TOURISM

Tourism requires certain elements that are closely linked and that constitute it as a functional system, because each one has a specific function and 000contributes significantly to the activity to take place; therefore, when pointing out the element of human capital in the tourism industry a priori, the Majó table (2005) is presented, in which it lists the best valued competences in the Tourism Sector.

TRAINING OF INTELLECTUAL CAPITAL IN THE TOURISM INDUSTRY BASED ON EDUCATIONAL COMPETENCES

Considering the positive characteristics of tourism, the formation of competent human capital is essential to generate effective solutions to the needs raised by tourism activity, highlighting that approaches and researches will be described on the professional training in tourism in the global parameter in the range of educational competences and their relationship with the formation of intellectual capital.

With the purpose of contributing to a voluntary standardization in the treatment of quality problems in education and tourism training, the World Tourism Organization has developed the methodology TEDQUAL (Tourism Education Quality), in which it is pointed out that the best form of collaboration between the training center and the tourism industry will be the development of professionalism understood as a training for employability and as the ideal means to achieve professional excellence

Table 4. Best valued competences in the tourism sector

Academic Officers	Tourism Sector	Graduates in Tourism
• Work in English as a foreign language. • Targeted service orientation towards the client. • Use and analyze ICT in the different areas of tourism. • Manage communication techniques. • Understand the principles of tourism.	• Targeted service orientation towards the client. • Work in English as a foreign language. • Define objectives, strategies and commercial policies. • Use and analyze ICT in the different areas of tourism. • Manage communication techniques.	• Work in English as a foreign language. • Communicate orally and in a written way in a foreign language. • Lead and manage the different types of tourism entities. • Targeted service orientation towards the client. • Evaluate tourism potentials and prospective exploration analysis.

Source: MAJÓ, J. (2005). Competencias o capacidades profesionales que deben aportar las nuevas titulaciones al Sistema Turístico en Armonización de los estudios de Turismo en el Espacio Europeo de la Enseñanza Superior. XL Congreso Nacional e Internacional de Escuelas de Turismo. Universidad Europea Miguel de Cervantes. Valladolid. pp. 61-86.

based on the capacity for adaptation and intelligent realization of a relatively wide range of productive functions; the knowledge and the knowing-how will not be enough to achieve that professional excellence, so it is also necessary to know how to be. The education and training of human resources in the tourism industry is a key factor in a world where information, creativity and knowing-how are configured as the most important source of value creation. But, in turn, education and training are not free from the rules of the game of competitiveness: they cannot be developed apart from the needs and expectations of users and they have to optimize the use of their resources. (UNWTO Foundation. Themis, n.d.).

From the perspective of the Organization for Economic Cooperation and Development in relation to education and human resources strategies in the tourism sector, the OECD makes recommendations to member countries through the OECD Tourism Trends and Policies publication (2018) in which it points out that public policies on the supply side to improve competitiveness include the promotion of investments and the simplification of commercial regulations; however, it is recognized that it may be necessary to expand and clarify regulations in emerging areas such as informal tourist services promoted through electronic platforms. It is recognized that a key aspect for many countries is the need to resolve the shortage of personnel and skills in the sector, which requires work to improve the dissemination and attractiveness of careers in the tourism sector and the availability of relevant training.

Intellectual capital is established as an intangible asset and is represented by the worker's competences at any hierarchical level or position; that is, what knowledge he has, what skills he has developed and what attitudes reflect in his work performance for the benefit of the organization (Sarur, 2013).

After the review of information related to the business theory of knowledge management and its link with intellectual capital, it is necessary to establish the importance of this intangible asset, relevant in the achievement of goals of the organizations, since the human resource is considered as the most relevant in a company when contributing to the fulfillment of strategic objectives.

FUTURE RESEARCH DIRECTIONS

Derived from the fact that the concept of intellectual capital presents the characteristic of "intangible value", it is necessary to develop exploratory and descriptive research with a qualitative approach to the subject to demonstrate the importance in the preparation, growth and investment of this asset; this together with the relationship of educational competences, by virtue of the fact that human capital is capable of developing a competitive advantage based on professional training. In this case, future research is recommended especially in the tourism industry companies since, according to the UNWTO International Tourism Outlook (2017), as a category of world export, tourism ranks third, only behind the chemicals and fuels. In many developing countries, tourism is the main category of exports. And it is a key sector for socioeconomic progress through the creation of jobs.

CONCLUSION

Educational competences in higher education (knowledge, skills and attitudes) applied by professionals in the context of the tourism industry, for the fulfillment of organizational objectives in companies in the sector will redound in the productivity and profitability of the corporation denominated as intellectual capital, considered as an intangible asset, which consequently generates competitive advantage. And it must be evaluated quantitatively and qualitatively to establish the value it represents in tourism companies. Since as it was described, the tourist activity is of main importance from the economic approach to occupy the third industrial position worldwide.

ACKNOWLEDGMENT

This research was supported by Instituto Politécnico Nacional, Mexico. (SIP 20181155).

REFERENCES

Bradley, K. (2003). Intellectual capital and the new wealth of nations II. Business Strategy Review, 8(4), 33-44.

Bueno, E., Salmador, M., & Merino, C. (2008). Genesis, concept and development of intellectual capital in the knowledge economy: A reflection on the Intellectus Model and its applications. *Applied Economics Studies, 26*(2), 43-63. http://hdl.handle.net/10486/669095

Burkart, A., & Medlik, S. (1981). *Tourism: past, present and future* (2nd ed.). Heinemann.

Chomsky, N. (1983). Language and unconscious knowledge. In *Rules and representations*. FCE.

De Ketele, J. (1996). School Performance Evaluation: What? Why? For what? *Tunisia Journal of Science Education, 23*, 17-36.

Edvinson, L., & Malone, M. (1999). Intellectual capital: how to identify and calculate the value of the intangible resources of your company. Barcelona: Management 2000.

European Commission. (2004). *Key competences for lifelong learning. A European frame of reference.* Implementation of the Education and Training work program 2010. Work group B. Key competences. European Commission. General Directorate of Education and Culture. Retrieved from http://www.educastur.princast.es/info/calidad/indicadores/doc/comision_europea

Haghshenas, H., & Barzegar, G. (2014). *Intellectual Capital and Knowledge Assets for Value Creation M.A.* Islamic Azad University, South-Tehran Branch. Faculty Member at University of Mazandaran. Retrieved from http://zolcat.com/press/journal/sn/vol3/no1/sn.3.1.5.pdf

Majó, J. (2005). Skills or professional skills that new degrees must provide to the Tourism System in Harmonization of Tourism studies in the European Higher Education Area. In *XL National and International Congress of Tourism Schools*. European University Miguel de Cervantes.

McClelland, D. C. (1973). Testing for Competencies rather than intelligence. *The American Psychologist, 28*(1), 1–14. doi:10.1037/h0034092 PMID:4684069

OECD. (2013). *Panorama of education 2013 Indicators of the OECD*. Santillana.

OECD. (2018). *OECD Tourism Trends and Policies 2018*. OECD Publishing; doi:10.1787/tour-2018-

OMT. (1994). *Introduction to Tourism*. Retrieved from https://pub.unwto.org/WebRoot/Store/Shops/.../1128/9284402697.pdf

OMT. (2014). *Understanding tourism Basic Glossary*. Retrieved from http://media.unwto.org/en/content/entender-el-turismo-glosario-basico

OMT. (2017). *OMT panorama of international tourism. Edition 2017*. Madrid: World Tourism Organization. Retrieved from https://www.e-unwto.org/doi/pdf/10.18111/9789284419043

OMT Themis Foundation. (n.d.). *UNWTO Certification System*. TedQual. Madrid: OMT. Retrieved from http://themis.unwto.org/en/content/sistema-de-certificacion-unwtotedqual

Perrenoud, P. (2007). *Ten new competences to teach* (4th ed.). Barcelona: Graó.

RAE. (2018). *Spanish dictionary. Edition of the Tercentenary*. Madrid: Royal Spanish Academy. Retrieved from http://dle.rae.es/?id=A0fanvT|A0gTnnL

Rivero, D. (2009). *Conceptual model for the measurement of intellectual capital and a procedure for its implementation. Hospitality Case* (PhD thesis). Matanzas, Cuba: University of Matanzas.

Roegiers, X. (2000). *The future of competitions*. Brussels: De Boeck.

Sarur, M. (2013). The importance of intellectual capital in organizations. *Administrative Sciences*, *1*, 39–45.

SEP. (2011). *Generic competences that express the profile of the graduate of upper secondary education*. Retrieved from https://www.uv.mx/dgdaie/files/2013/09/COMPETENCIAS-GENERICAS-QUE-EXPRESAN-EL-PERFIL-DEL-EGRESADO.pdf

Steward, T. (1998). *The new wealth of organizations: intellectual capital*. Granica.

UNICEF. (2008). *Education and evaluation by competences: a challenge for the Latin American Laboratory for the Evaluation of the Quality of Education (LLECE)*. Retrieved from http://www.unesco.org/new/es/santiago/press-room/newsletters/newsletter-laboratory-for-assessment-of-the-quality-of-education-llece/n12/education-and- assessment-by-competences /

ADDITIONAL READING

Bernárdez, M. (2008). *Creation of intellectual capital.* Spain: Editorial Global Business Press.

Bueno, E., Salmador, M., & Merino, C. (2008). Genesis, concept and development of intellectual capital in the knowledge economy: A reflection on the Intellectus Model and its applications. Applied Economics Studies, 26 (2), 43-63. http://hdl.handle.net/10486/669095

European Comission. (2004). Key competences for lifelong learning. A European frame of reference. Implementation of the Education and Training work program 2010. Work group B. Key competences. European Commission. General Directorate of Education and Culture. Retrieved from http://www.educastur.princast.es/info/calidad/indicadores/doc/comision_europea

Haghshenas, H., & Barzegar, G. (2014). Intellectual Capital and Knowledge Assets for Value Creation M.A. Islamic Azad University, South-Tehran Branch. Faculty Member at University of Mazandaran. January 2014 3 (1): 21-25. Retrieved from http://zolcat.com/press/journal/sn/vol3/no1/sn.3.1.5.pdf

López, V. (2008). Synthetic indicator of intellectual capital. Eure Magazine (Vol. XXXIV, No. 101), pp. 45-70. Santiago, Chile, April 2008

OECD. (2018). *Education Policy Outlook 2018: Putting Student Learning at the Center.* Paris: OECD Publishing.

OECD. (2018). *Preparing Our youth for an inclusive and sustainable world. The OECD PISA global competence framework Paris.* OECD Publishing.

KEY TERMS AND DEFINITIONS

Educational Competence: Complex development processes which are suitable in set contexts, by integrating different knowledge (knowing how to be, knowing how to do, knowing to know, knowing how to live with), in order to do activities and/or solve problems with a sense of challenge, motivation, flexibility, creativity, understanding and undertaking, within an approach of meta-cognitive thinking, ongoing improvement and ethical commitment, which are aimed at contributing to personal development, the construction and strengthening of the social networking, the continuous search of a sustainable economic and business development, and the care and protection of the environment and the living organisms.

Intellectual Capital: Set of intangible assets based on knowledge and access to the evolution of resources in a system of value creation, through the achievement of sustainable competitive advantages.

Professional Competence: The degree of utilization of knowledge, skills, and the good judgment related to the people's profession, and in correspondence with all the situations that can be lived in the exercise of professional practice.

Tourism: A social, cultural, and economic phenomenon related to the movement of people to places that are outside their usual location of residence for personal or business/professional reasons. While these people are called visitors (which may be tourists or excursionists; residents or non-residents), tourism is associated with the people's activities and, therefore, implies tourism expenditure.

Tourism Industry: The term tourism industries include the factory complexes that regularly produce tourism products, and it is one of the most colloquial terms used in the tourism sector.

UNWTO: The World Tourism Organization (UNWTO) is the United Nations agency responsible for the promotion of responsible, sustainable, and universally accessible tourism.

Chapter 11
Incorporating Indigenous Knowledge in the Higher Education Sector for the Advancement of African Scholarship

Ndwakhulu Stephen Tshishonga
University of KwaZulu-Natal, South Africa

ABSTRACT

This chapter argues that IKS could be used as a framework upon which African scholarship could be claimed and advanced without overlooking the importance and relevance of other knowledge systems. This framework can break superior-inferior, developed-underdeveloped binaries while keeping in mind the core mandate of education, especially in producing skills and a competent and knowledge-based society capable of dealing with both local and international challenges. The academic socialization on IKS would rather require an integrated approach to research which is also interdisciplinary in nature and aimed at interfacing other knowledge systems. This chapter is based on IKS case studies drawn from South African universities. Data obtained from interviews with experts and practitioners in the IKS sector will be engaged to enrich the debates in this chapter.

DOI: 10.4018/978-1-5225-8461-2.ch011

INTRODUCTION

Over the last decade, the academic and pragmatic discourses on indigenous knowledge systems have generated raging debates and contestations among scholars and practitioners alike. These debates often border the dichotomy between western and indigenous systems of knowledge production and application in real life situation. Academically, few scholars have focused on the integration and synergy between the two knowledge systems as opposed to their differences, weaknesses and independent existence (Agrawal, 2022; Grange, 2007). On one hand, Western knowledge has been categorized as more scientific, advanced and modernized, open and is regarded as authentic knowledge (Higgs & Smith, 2015). On the other hand, indigenous knowledge is seen as primitive and backward, underdeveloped, generalized (Barnhardt, 2007; Grange, 2007). The dichotomy between these knowledge systems or worldviews especially the Western dominance of knowledge production creates a false and fragmented base for integration to take place. Despite the criticisms leveled against the indigenous forms of knowledge, proponents of indigenous knowledge or indigenous people's knowledge such as Breidlid (2008), Grange (2007), Nataka (2002) argue that it is important for personal development. In South Africa, in the institutions of higher learning academics have been accused for recycling western models and theories with little or no relevance to the local situation. Western or Eurocentric models and discourses are dominant knowledge systems and they have an impact not only on institutional governance, but also in curriculum development in the higher education sector. Colonialism for example was instrumental in labelling indigenous knowledge as inferior and non-scientific hence not competitive to the rest of the Western knowledge systems. In this regard, Ngubane (2017: 13) state that colonialism is characterised by dichotomy of superiority and inferiority, dominant and dominated, oppressed or marginalised. Afrocentric knowledge is perceived as 'primitive' and backward hence the FMF students started to question the relevance of Western based knowledge.

This dominance left the indigenous forms of knowledge being disregarded and relegated to the periphery of knowledge production and dissemination. This hegemonic display of power on the part of Western/Eurocentric knowledge system has certain consequences for indigenous African knowledge systems. These consequences according to Higgs and Smith (2015) include 1) the erasure of the rich knowledge legacy of African people. Western knowledge systems are perceived as 1) authentic knowledge. 2) the forged hegemonic discourse perpetuated propaganda based on an unequal relationship between what was referred to as 'developed 'and 'underdeveloped' countries. 3) The claim by Western/Eurocentric hegemonic discourse that progress is only achieved through the advancement of Western/Eurocentric science. The holders of these views not only dichotomise the world into 'First World' and 'Third World', but continue to instil the mentality that knowledge derived from African people was non-scientific. Emanating from this fragmentised and psychologically damaging foundation, scholars such Hoppers (2001, p. 74) concluded that Africans have lost self-confidence and academic stamina to engage radically against systems designed to downgrade and marginalise them. Exclusion of indigenous African knowledge systems is not accidental, but a deliberate scheme to keep the African people on the periphery of socio-economic and politico-governance debate critical to western world-view based on neo-liberalism. The culture of silence; as Freire (1972) postulates can change or be challenged by self-reflected critical awareness which Freire was convinced to be through a process of conscientisation.

The renewed debates on indigenous knowledge and its relevance across sectors such as medicine, health, education, climate change, agriculture, epistemology, and food security have resulted in research-based papers, articles and books (Buthelezi & Hunges, 2014; Nyong et al., 2007; Ngulube & Lwong, 2009). In order to dispel the myth that indigenous knowledge systems is fragmented and non-scientific in nature, Higgs and Smith (2015) argue that that African indigenous knowledge systems present holistic knowledge with physical, spiritual, emotional and intellectual dimensions. The scientific nature of indigenous knowledge systems according to Higgs & Smith is triangulated through multiple sources upon which knowledge and its use is subjected to rigorous testing. Ancestral wisdom from one generation to another is exposed empirically through critical observation with spiritual guidance (Higgs & Smith, 2015). Based on this background, this chapter investigates the possibilities of incorporating indigenous knowledge systems (IKS) in the higher education curriculum. The institutionalization of IKS will not only serve to balance the dominance of Western knowledge system, but also to restore and inculcate among academics and students the value of indigenous ontologies and epistemologies based on African knowledge systems, values and principles.

BACKGROUND

Knowledge Systems: Eurocentric Versus Indigenous

The world-over knowledge systems are embedded in people's culture and tradition, language, religious backgrounds, proverbs, folklore, mythology and such systems differentiate one nation from the other. At the centre of these knowledge systems is the cultural practices and languages as a means upon which knowledge is passed from one generation to the other. Traditionally, societies were educated through indigenous knowledge systems with oral discourses and debates were used a means of inferring historical and new knowledge. The indigenous people are the custodians of indigenous knowledge systems and practices and time immemorial such knowledge was utilised in local decision making as mechanism in the fields such as agriculture, health, natural resources management, traditional hearing. Contrary to the indigenous knowledge and its orality, the Western or Eurocentric knowledge system is anchored on European methodologies and systems and is presented in the written form. Falsified elevation and categorisation of Western knowledge as more scientific, advanced and modernized, open and being regarded as authentic knowledge (Higgs & Smith, 2015) have led to the underdevelopment of indigenous knowledge systems. Decades of colonialism, imperialism and apartheid systems have treated indigenous knowledge and viewed as primitive and backward, underdeveloped, generalized (Barnhardt, 2007; Grange, 2007). Lebakeng (2016: 60) puts it aptly that indigenous knowledge systems are not compatible with progress, modernization and development. The dichotomy between these knowledge systems or worldviews especially the Western dominance of knowledge production creates the false and fragmented base for integration to take place. The dominance of Western knowledge including the imposition of European languages led to most African universities relying on knowledge system conceived, developed and organized from the west with western ideologies and discourses (Teferra & Altbach, 2003: 13). Globally, the World Bank (1998: i) highlighted that IK is an underutilized resources especially in cross-cultural environment and sustainability of development.

Despite the criticisms leveled against the indigenous forms of knowledge, proponents of indigenous knowledge or indigenous people's knowledge such as Breidlid (2008), Grange (2007); Nataka (2002) provide academic and practical value attached to indigenous knowledge systems. Indigenous knowledge manifests itself through community practices, institutions, relationships and rituals and prevalent uses has been mainly in medicine, agriculture and traditional practices such as circumcision and marriages. Indigenous knowledge scholars such as Higgs (2002, 2008) envisaged this type of knowledge system being based on African knowledge with the potential to provide a vital philosophical framework. An empowering philosophical framework could be used to activate African people and their communities in partaking in their own educational developmental. Higgs (2002, 2008) assertion is based on the legacy of colonial domination and hegemony and its implications on the African education ways of knowing. Indigenous knowledge in the context of coloniality and the quest for African renewal through the process of Africanisation of knowledge, African identity and nation-building (Msila, 2007). This knowledge takes cognizance of the diversity, acknowledges the lived experiences and wisdom and more often has being exhumed to challenge the dominance of Western-Eurocentric forms of epistemologies.

Valuing Indigenous Knowledge Systems

Knowledge, knowledge systems, knowledge management and knowledge network play a major role in advancing societies socially and developmentally. The socio-economic and balancing act of the world cannot afford to rely on one knowledge system in expense of the others. Production of knowledge is not enough unless such knowledge is disseminated and marketed across sectors and among key stakeholders such policy-makers, think-tank university centres and government agencies (Stone, 2012). In the modern world, the production and transfer of knowledge is often done through the information and communication technology (ICT). On the contrary, indigenous knowledge has been always passed from one generation to another orally. Story-telling, proverbs, folklore, have been used to create and share knowledge intergenerationally. Each society according to Higgs (2013), has its own unique indigenous knowledge which manifest itself through community practices, institutions, relationships and rituals. Although this type of knowledge is not easily codified, communities have always enjoyed the application of indigenous alternative strategies in dealing with day to day challenges.

Valuing African indigenous knowledge and its systems implies acknowledge the contribution made by local people in preserving knowledge from previous generation to the current generation (Saurombe, 2017). The realisation that indigenous people including their indigenous knowledge systems form both the cultural and socio-economic and political fabric of indigenous societies across the globe made scholars and research to invest time and expertise in researching them. This curiosity has seen African scholars and higher education sector establishing university-based units and programmes aimed at embarking on researches embracing fields such medicine, food, agriculture, climate change and bio-diversity (Agrawal, 2002; Buthelezi & Hughes, 2014; Mubangizi & Kaya, 2015; Nakata, 2002). Valuing and embracing African indigenous knowledge systems should be linked to broader philosophical and anti-colonial-apartheid framework aimed at liberating the scholarship. Ubuntu philosophy re-emerged as the alternative framework that acknowledges and centralises African knowledge as worthy academic pursuance. Such a framework according to Ndlovu-Gatsheni (2017) should be based on Africanisation and African renaissance for the restoration of indigenous people's humanity against the dehumanisation and alienation through foreign language imposition. Africanisation and African Renaissance could be expressed through the practice of Ubuntu as an African philosophy. Janz (cited in Msila, 2017, p. 23) defines African philosophy as a philosophy produced by African people, representing African worldviews with African themes of personhood, space and perceptions of time as paramount. Protracted decades under colonialism and apartheid have witnessed the erosion of indigenous ways of knowing, thus resulting African people disliking their own cultures and languages as inferior for academic work. Deliberately, African languages were not only neglected and as such starved of essential material and human resources to develop to be languages of power (Johnson & Jacobs, 2012, p. 171). This underlies the coloniality of power from the western perspective which according to Quijano cited in Seroto, 2018, p. 4), involves racial and epistemological hierarchies entangled within global capitalism. In order to reverse this situation, Ndlovu-Gatsheni (2013) argues for the need to revisit, imagine and redefine spaces where indigenous and non-indigenous people experienced colonialism, neo-colonialism and underdevelopment. In the context of South Africa, the Department of Arts and Culture since 1994 restructured itself to play a pivotal role in restoring all people's arts and culture as a vehicle to fight the legacy of colonialism and apartheid.

For the Africanisation and decolonisation project, rekindling African values and principles as enshrined in Ubuntu philosophy is the starting point towards liberating Africa. Mubangizi and Kaya (2015, p. 125) argue that Africa has rich traditions and knowledge systems founded on the principles of caring for one another and the spirit of mutual support embedded in the African philosophy of *Ubuntu*. The mastery of indigenous knowledge systems within the higher education sector should enable Africans especially those in academia to view the world through multiple lens and perceptions with the African lens being the critical one. Within the tertiary institutions, students through the FMF campaign demanded institutions of higher learning to decolonise curriculum. Due to colonialism and coloniality as the project aimed at subjugating African people, Seroto (2018, p. 1) argues that the call to decolonise university programmes, intellectual landscapes and infrastructure is imperative. The Ubuntu philosophy is underpinned by principles, values and norms, which serve as the formidable foundation upon which development practitioners and project managers could adopt to advance a holistic and integrated community development. Importantly, the philosophy of Ubuntu is based on a Sotho or Nguni phrase: '*Motho ke motho ka batho/ umuntu ngumuntu ngabantu'*, literally translated to 'a person becomes a person through other people' (also, see Letseka, 2000; Mbigi, 1991; Nafukho, et al. 2005, cited in Nafukho, 2006, p. 408). The Ubuntu concept has broad connotations but its basic tenets such as caring and sharing, respect and religiosity (spirituality), consensus building, dialogue, solidarity form the foundation for organisational success (Msila, 2015; Nafukho, 2006). Such tenets are applicable socially, in the economy, politics and in developmental projects aimed at addressing socio-economic challenges. The Ubuntu model in this chapter is contextualised and grounded on an indigenous social capital based of Ubuntu philosophy. Indigenous social capital of Ubuntu displays how African people indigenous origin is integrated and such could be merged and strengthened through pragmatic application of Ubuntu embedded principles and values in community development projects. The chapter argues that the convergence of both Ubuntu and African indigenous knowledge systems are critical towards understanding the integrated nature of African humanity. A participant reiterated the above assertion by adding that 'Ubuntu should be the basis upon which African people should derive their ontological and epistemological source of knowledge and interpreting the world (interview, December 2018). Above all, the higher education sector is anchored on indigenous knowledge systems is capable of navigating the human and organisational challenges for the benefit of all its stakeholders. In this context, IKS and its application form the basis for universities to instil humane and solid educated citizenry who by not only conscious of their individual academic achievements, but also thrives to plough back the acquired knowledge and skill back to the community. The philosophy of Ubuntu encapsulates 'self-knowledge' of project members in their quest to redefine 'who were are, where we come from and where we are going from here' (Motshekga, 2012, p. 7). Introspectively, Ubuntu and its philosophical values and principles can be used to ground higher education within the competitive world academic community. A well packaged curriculum, with academic flavour of both world knowledge systems could equip (African) students to play a meaningful role in advancing African development and scholarship.

Put this way, it is no wonder that African scholars argue that "Ubuntu can play a creative role in rebuilding social relationships in our racially and socially divided society. It plays a significant role in building a spirit of harmony and reconciliation," (Mbigi, 1997: 3). A possible explanation for this is that the concept "…is based on the African way of life with emphasis on communal harmony and learning from each other," (Nafukho, 2006, p. 412). Such emphasis on harmony and the need to learn from each other and to address racial and social divisions is critical towards offering solutions to centuries old problems plaguing South African communities and other African societies in terms of governance. In particular, emphasis on the principles of harmony in the community, family and amongst individuals could be useful in promoting peaceful resolution to conflict.

It could be argued that African societies, more than ever before, need to re-examine the values and principles of Ubuntu as part of their initiatives to promote sustainable development, peace and democratic governance in the continent. This is particularly in view of an observer's crude view that almost all of us experience "… a dearth of self-knowledge [which] has made us disrespectful of ourselves and of others. We consider human life to have no value, as being cheap. We enslave one another. We abuse women and children. We kill innocent people. We become addicted to drugs and alcohol," (Motshekga, 2012, p. 7). In this regard, the usefulness of the Ubuntu philosophical approach towards explaining Africa's contemporary problems has to be explored especially as Africans seek alternative explanations towards understanding the massive social challenges the continent faces. In the case of South Africa, in particular, the country is plagued by numerous social problems such as high crime rate, unemployment, poverty, child and women abuse and specifically rape which is often said to give a very negative label to South Africa as the 'rape capital of the world'. A recourse to the values, principles and philosophy of Ubuntu might help resolve some if not all of these social problems.

Indigenous Knowledge System and Curriculum Development

The call for free quality education by the FMF movement was also attached to the broader higher education transformation Through the call for decolonisation of curriculum by students, universities were caught in a conundrum of unfinished transformational agenda with their curricular still being dominated by western knowledge systems. The discourse underpinning the decoloniality of curriculum became an epistemological force to unravel the psychological damage done by the dominance of Eurocentric education system (Joseph, 2018). Although most of the students demanding decolonised curriculum never lived during the colonial period, they share the sentiments that the curriculum in most of the universities do not reflect the post-apartheid transformative agenda in higher education sector. Across the disciplines and universities, mainly the black students were angered by the fact that they are not only taught by lecturers who are in resistance of change, with text books prescribed dominated by Western writers and scholars. The exclusion of African scholars in the curriculum was viewed as deliberate sabotaged by those who are anti-transformation. However, it should be noted that decolonised curriculum does not necessarily mean prescribing African scholars but deep rooted transformation of their entire system that resulted in preference of one body of knowledge over the other. In order to achieve this gigantic goal, decolonisation of knowledge and curriculum respectively would require radical reappraisal of the damage caused by decades of colonial project. This includes an intellectual appreciative enquiry of what Africa has managed to achieve since independence from the colonial rule through the pursuit of African scholarship.

Considering the institutionalisation of colonialism and apartheid, the subject pertaining to the development of curriculum at the tertiary institutions remains a sensitive debate even in post-apartheid era. In essence, a curriculum is a mirror reflective of not only the combination of modules or courses for a particularly field of study, but also a culture that is inculcated through language. Thus, universities committed to excellency and quality education, invest in both language and curriculum development in order to instil the culture greater excellence and scholarship. Curriculum development is part of parcel of any educational system and its narratives cannot be divorced from the core business of the universities. Curriculum or curriculum development informs the teaching pedagogy and community engagement as the core business of tertiary institutions. Central to teaching and learning, research and community engagement, the contextual positioning of university is to provide societal solutions through their curriculum development.

The University of North West (UNW) is one of the few universities in South Africa which has managed to establish the Indigenous Knowledge Systems (IKS) Centre. The IKS Centre is one of the five consortium partner institutions making the Department of Science and Technology-National Research Foundation (DST-NRF) Centre in Indigenous Knowledge Systems (CIKS). The partner institutions are the University of KwaZulu-Natal (UKZN), North-West University (NWU), University of Limpopo (UL), University of South Africa (UNISA), and University of Venda (UNIVEN). The Centre strives to play a role in contributing towards the uplifting of community livelihoods through knowledge and products generated by unlocking the full potential of Indigenous Knowledge Systems (IKS) and promoting the recognition, development, protection and affirmation of indigenous knowledge in scholarship and social responsiveness relevant to the knowledge economy (http://natural-sciences.nwu.ac.za/indigenous-knowledge-systems-centre/about-us). The University of North West (UNW) is one of the few universities in South Africa which has managed to establish the Indigenous Knowledge Systems (IKS) Centre. Interestingly, the IKS centre launched the first SAQA accredited inter- and multi-disciplinary Bachelor of IKS (B. IKS) which is a four-year professional degree. The IKS Centre has three fundamental purposes. The first is to document indigenous knowledge (IK). Most of IK has been transmitted orally and through observation. Colonisation and globalization are the major culprits for displacing the channel through which this knowledge was transmitted, thus many knowledge holders go to their graves with vital information. Therefore the documentation of IK is an urgent task. The second thing done through IK is to research and investigate it. This is an attempt to explore the depth and breadth of IK, to make new observation and discover new ideas from it. Lastly IK innovated upon. IK is used to generate new products and services that can be used to meet contemporary needs. This helps to solve community problems, and may involve commercialization. Community engagement is an integral element of all the research, teaching and learning activities of the IKS Centre (B. IKS, Brochure, 2018). The programme curriculum has specialisation options in Agriculture, Science and Technology S&T), Health, and Ethnomedicine from where research programmes for both Master's and Doctorate degrees evolve. The IKS centre collaborates with the DST and SAQA on an initiative to champion the Accreditation of Traditional healers. The Centre hosts a NEPAD/SANBio Regional IKS ode and co-ordinates IKS network activities that are initiated and supported by NEPAD in the region. The centre implemented a NEPAD/SANBio project titled 'Integrating IKS in Biosciences-An Initiative for Capacity Building and Networking in the Southern African Region' which covered five countries in the region for the period 2010-2013. The centre is one of the five South African partner institutions forming the DST-NRF Centre in Indigenous Knowledge Systems. According to Kaya (2018), the centre allows students to study indigenous knowledge as local ways of knowing and innovating. It is envisaged that students will have opportunities to specialise in specific areas of indigenous knowledge like health, agriculture, arts and culture (including languages), science and technology and their management systems. Considering the lack of inclusion of indigenous knowledge in higher education (Mji et al., 2017, p. 36), the establishment of a degree with particular specialisation in indigenous knowledge was exploded for its academic enthusiasm.

The quest for a transformed and decolonised curriculum development in Africa and South Africa inclusive has a colonial-apartheid inclination. The demand for decolonised curriculum re-emerged radically during the students rampant for free education and institutional transformation in 2015 and 2016 (Ray, 2016). Although the FMF commenced with no fee increment as the central goal, gradually the movement added decolonisation, free education, institutional transformation, in-sourcesing/outsourcing among some of their demands. All these demands are competing goals which warrant individual and collective leadership especially among Department of Higher Education and Training, university management, students' bodies, civil society organisations and the broader South African community. According to Petersen (2017, p. 70), decolonisation of tertiary education should focus on the curriculum aimed at assessing the extent to which it responded to local and regional applicability. Petersen's (2017) assertion grounds the development of curriculum based on its capacity to meet the immediate needs of the people. The author defines decolonisation of education as part of introducing different perspectives and views aimed at enriching curriculum.

In the context of students' demand for institutional transformation, decolonised curriculum symbolises a radical shift from Eurocentric education to Afrocentric curriculum (Joseph, 2006). Accordingly, Eurocentric orientated curriculum is embedded within the socio-economic and political context and such curriculum has been influences by western literature and epistemological discourse. Essentially, the historical conquests through imperialism and colonialism have been associated with the introduction and marketization of colonial curriculum in the colonies. Thus, Afrocentric driven curriculum is informed, inspired and contextualised to address the needs and challenges faced by the African continent (Shava & Nkopodi, 2017). The curriculum developed by both colonisers and missionaries was not free from imposition and socialisation of western norms, values and ideas where Europe was paraded as more civilised, socio-economically advanced and politically superior than the South-based nations including the African continent. Decolonised curriculum is liberatory and is rooted within 'African humanism' (Togni, 1996, p. 5). In line with the liberatory curriculum, one of the post graduate students defines decolonised curriculum as 'a curriculum with little or no colonial inclinations. Colonial curriculum for Hopers (2001) still exert hegemony over African education systems and with implications for marginalising indigenous knowledge systems. In order to reverse the curriculum of misconceptions, misrepresentations and misappropriations of indigenous knowledge (Nymnjoh, 2012), the curriculum requires drastic transformation. Essentially, indigenising the curriculum would mean that education is not meant to instil or promote colonial policies or colonial intended goals (Interview, 2 April 2017). Since the colonial-apartheid legacy cannot be undone overnight, the student was quick to argue that the process of crafting curriculum relevant to the African situation should be through constant engagement with stakeholders in the education sector. Thus, higher education's central role in educating the society, curriculum should be equally empowering and based on independent unbiased models. Gumede (2017: 21) dismisses a narrow version of colonisation by advocating what he calls a 'true and real decolonisation' which enable Africans to access to better quality education, which draws from the best global content, whether from Africa itself, industrial countries and emerging power.

Advancing African Scholarship Through Indigenous Knowledge

Prior to advancing African scholarship, it is imperative to lay a theoretical exposition as to what African scholarship entails. In Africa, the quest for higher education transformation is linked to African scholarship which is often reflected in most universities' vision statements. In the recent wring by African-based scholars and those in diaspora, the advocacy for Afrocentric approach to intelligentsia with universities at the centre of producing good knowledge and constructive and proactive citizens (Chetty & Merrett, 2014). African scholarship is intrinsically linked to the broader conceptualisation of Africanisation, African Renaissance and Pan-Africanism as the epistemological foundation for rebirth of Africa. This implies forging African scholarship based on the Africanisation of African universities with interface of knowledge systems for Africa development. African scholars such as Nkoane (2006) and Ramose (1998) associate Africanisation with reddening of Africa-ness based on evidence-based knowledge production including acknowledging that indigenous knowledge as both the source and foundation of all forms of knowledge. Pro-scholars of Africanisation and African Renaissance such as Makgoba, defended the Africanisation of higher education based on its relevance towards addressing challenges faced by the continent. Based on the philosophy of African Renaissance as popularised by former South African President Thabo Mbeki, the concept came to be associated with critical introspection by African people for African development. African Renaissance emerged to denote social cohesion, democracy, economic rebuilding and growth and the elevating of Africa as an important player in the geopolitical affairs (Johnson & Jacobs, 2012, p. 7). From an intellectual perspective; African Renaissance came to be known as a philosophical and political movement with agenda to promote education and the reversal of the brain drain of African intellectuals (Johnson & Jacobs, 2012, p. 7). Thus, rekindling African Renaissance implies acknowledging and a continuous battle to dismantle the coloniality of knowledge that is still Eurocentric (Segalo, 2017).

Advancing African scholarship through indigenous knowledge is fundamental for Africa renewal and reclaiming heritage in all sphere of life. It is through the indigenisation of knowledge including culture, education, economic livelihoods of the people that formal education embraces the originality of the epistemology and ontology of knowledge. In the post-modern world where solutions to world challenges cannot be confined to linear frameworks or strategies, hybridity of both western and indigenous knowledge systems. Without singular solutions to modern challenges, Ndlovu-Gatsheni (2017, p. 29) argues that the struggle for decolonisation of the world system and the modern Westernised university. The hybridity has power of knowledge of which Halvorsen (2017, p. 13) holds the view that both the content and holders are able to influence social development. For the African people, formal and informal education as espoused by Rodney (2009) could be responsible for social change, more so in shaping and transforming society. Other scholars such as Msila (2017, p. 27) advocate for formal education based on African philosophy as a weapon to dismantle the colonial legacy with institutions of higher learning being central advancing African Renaissance in education. For the restoration of African Renaissance, African intellectuals are challenged to thrive towards bringing enlightment by reclaiming African potential and going back to roots (Msila, 2017, p. 28).

Benefits of Incorporating Indigenous Knowledge in Higher Education

Knowledge produced through the utilisation of Western approaches, processes and models as the sole knowledge producers and gate-keepers is challenged by the renewal indigenous knowledge scholarship. In developing society, knowledge acquisition plays a pivotal role not only in producing skilled and competent human force, but is also instrumental in producing active and responsible citizenship. In this context, Nussbaum (1998, pp. 9-11) outlines three core values associated with education. The first value is self-self-examination, thus demonstrating the ability to reasons logically. The ideal of world citizenship constitutes the second educational value where students transcend their local citizenship through embracing their beings within the broader context. The third value as exposed by Nussbaum is narrative imagination which compels student to emphasise by being intelligent reader capable of exercising emotional intelligence.

The IKS scholars advocate for the incorporation of indigenous knowledge systems (Msila, 2017, Ramose adds that it should not only be incorporated in the academia but in all facets of life. According to these African scholars, institutions of higher education which incorporate indigenous knowledge forge an academic foundation upon which students and academics are able to reflect on the value and relevance of other knowledge systems. The following comments attest to the following benefits for incorporating African indigenous knowledge systems:

It ground students in local and traditional technologies, philosophical ways of thinking which are spiritual and able Africans to live in harmony with nature. It teaches how African humanity emerged and how through decade of transmitting knowledge and wisdom transcended the limitations imposed through modern and post-modern world.

The renewal discourses on IKS has made intellectual liberated practitioners and academics to appreciate the multiple paths of knowing. The protection of knowledge systems of indigenous peoples and local communities according Khor and Lin (2001, p. 39). IKS is holistic in nature as it embraces the social, cultural, music, medicinal and religious dimensions of society. Mndende (2018) adds that could prioritised in academic departments such as Education, Music, Development, Religion and African Languages. However, she argues that Africans should be bold enough to reclaim their cultural heritage. Thus, the indigenous religious beliefs and practices of African peoples include various traditional religions. While generalizations of these religions are difficult, due to the diversity of African cultures, they do have some characteristics in common. Generally, they are oral rather than scriptural, including a belief in a supreme being, spirits and other divinities, veneration of ancestors, use of magic, and traditional medicine. The role of humanity is generally seen as one of harmonizing nature with the supernatural.

The Challenges of Incorporating Indigenous Knowledge System

The westernisation of most universities led to the reluctance by academics to incorporating aspects of indigenous knowledge systems in the curriculum. The consequences have been assessing knowledge based on Eurocentric lens with models and theories as the only pathway towards acquiring scholarship. Besides, across the faculties and disciplines, one hardly see Africa writers and scholars being prescribed for students to indulge, let alone the dominance of colonial languages such as English and Afrikaans enjoying the academic dominance. One of the contributory factors in excluding indigenous knowledge systems in curriculum is the stigma that labelled IKS as primitive and without scientific base. This together with other factors led to criticisms with critics dismissing African Indigenous Knowledge as baseless and further compounded by its limited effort to provide its own clear definition and understanding of the concept of 'knowledge' based on Africa's own rich history of ideas and intellectual development (Mubangizi & Kaya, 2017). This criticism is against the historical reality that Africa has contributed enormously to global intellectual development especially in science and technology related fields (Hountondji, 2002). Silvester (2007) views this as missed opportunity for Africa to have developed a theoretical framework based on African indigenous methodologies underpinned by African ways of knowing and knowledge production into the post-colonial education system – especially higher education. The response to this criticism – which is considered Eurocentric – is that it portrays western cultural and intellectual arrogance, including a lack of understanding of the holistic nature of AIKS. The latter does not separate theory from practice. It is submitted that one of the common criticisms of western education in Africa and higher education, in particular, is that it suffers from two acute limitations. It is both too foreign and too rationalistic. It is too foreign, because it emerged from foreign western educational and academic traditions, and because a high proportion of its promoters are still too western-orientated and too rationalistic for reasons connected with its western ancestry – i.e., putting a special premium on a form of rationality which aspires to neutral universalism, including freedom from external interference, especially from community engagement and political demands. Western knowledge perspectives tend to be too 'scholarly', 'scientific' and individualistic in nature. Mndende (2018) argued against Western-European centred knowledge as fragmented as opposed to holistic nature of African indigenous knowledge systems. Over the decades, developing nations, Africa in particular have been judged through Western models and ways of thinking. The upholding and marketisation of Western views in teaching and learning methodologies have contributed towards dehumanising indigenous practices as primitive and backwards. Thus, for example the naming of sometimes interchangeable and include a stance of detachment from community engagements and national socio-political aspirations. It is this alleged stance of social disengagement that has led to the controversial debate between post-colonial African governments and higher educational institutions on the role of academics in a developing society. Michael (2008) poses the question: Can a post-colonial or post-apartheid country characterised by immense poverty and social inequalities afford pure academia?

Towards a Hybridised Framework

Considering that all knowledge systems in both developed and developing have their own deficits and strengths in dealing with societal challenges. Institutions of higher learning operate in a diverse environment which can only be navigated through the hybridity of knowledge systems, those from the Western, African and in Asia. The Western nations have the decades manage to develop their knowledge systems and packaged it through scientific methodologies for world consumption. With colonialism and imperialism, the West and Europe manipulated and impose their knowledge epistemologies and ontologies as a measure for academic success in the developing nations. No nation can claim knowledge as if knowledge is the construct without interactive engagement of cultures across the globe. There are benefits of integrating two knowledge systems, traditional and scientific for application and scientific validation (Nakata, 2002, p. 282). Since all these knowledge systems individually have their own limitations of its own, hence the interface among different knowledge systems hybridity. Undertaking scholarly work on each knowledge system could assist in dispelling the myth that indigenous knowledge suffer from fixation while the western system is elevated as dynamic, scientific and scholarly. Scholars such as Breidlid (2009, p141) argues that the integration of indigenous knowledge could be instrumental in sustaining development especially in meeting human development.

CONCLUSION

This chapter has wrestled with the concept of (African) indigenous knowledge system as scientifically credit method for knowledge production and disseminations within higher education sector. Central to this chapter was the objective to explore the benefits derived from indigenous knowledge systems. The discourses that interface western-European-based knowledge and indigenous knowledge systems were explored with the primary purpose of democratising the harm that colonialism and apartheid have caused especially in undermining the indigenous knowledge and African epistemological pathways of knowing (Matolino, 2017). The arrival of Europeans saw the abuse of education as it was it was used to institutionalise racial and discriminatory practises that had and its legacy still exert negative influence to existence inequalities across sectors. Scholars assert that the systems of information that exist today in African continent, reflects the robust western supremacy (Zeleza, 2006, p. 196). Hence, these scholars argue that the supremacy of Western world knowledge has flooded the entire continent of Africa. Thus, the domain of the western countries was made possible spearhead through the provision of inferior education to the indigenous African people (Zeleza, 2006). Evidence from these deliberations, the dominance of Western-based educational systems and values contribute to the exclusion and marginalization of indigenous knowledge systems (Mji et al., 2017). The effects are overwhelming as students produced turn to be pro-Europe-Western as opposed to embrace the philosophical framework of Ubuntu based on humanistic values and principles. The supremacy of collegiality has drastic effect on academic as most of the African institutions higher education became the extension of Western knowledge other than of African knowledge system framework.

Education mediate through various knowledge systems is more powerful in claiming African values and principles. The Chapter argues against the dominance of western knowledge system by further proposing cross-pollination of knowledge systems. Thus, the hybridity of both indigenous and western knowledge system has been framed within its potential to produce a well-balanced society grounded on traversal values principles. The possibility of incorporating indigenous knowledge in higher education was demonstrated by case studies

FUTURE RESEARCH DIRECTIONS

There is a wealth of knowledge generated on the importance and role of indigenous knowledge systems in sectors such as medicine, environment eg climate change. This chapter focused on indigenous knowledge within the context of the higher education sector. The dominance of Eurocentric knowledge systems has prompted African scholars and those in the diaspora to focus on indigenous knowledge systems as a source of advancing African scholarship. The chapter dismissed the created binaries that perpetuate superior-inferior, developed-underdeveloped advancing a framework that values knowledge across regions. Indigenous knowledge systems in the academia and beyond is acknowledged as a formidable force to reclaim African civilization. It is within the knowledge system that acknowledges positive African cultural and value systems. Hence further research is needed to explore how indigenous knowledge can be institutionalized and incorporated into the curriculum. The foundation of that knowledge should begin from primary to tertiary education.

REFERENCES

Breidlid, A. (2009). *Culture, indigenous Knowledge systems and sustainable development: A critical view of education in an African context*. Academic Press.

Chetty, N., & Merrett, C. (2014). *The Struggle for the South of a South African University: The University of KwaZulu-Natal-Academic freedom, corporatisation and Transformation. Scottsville*. UKZN Press.

eThekwini Municipality. (2010). *Innovations in Local Sustainability: good Practice from eThekwini*. Durban: eThekwini Municipality Corporate Policy Unit.

Freire, P. (1972). *Pedagogy of the Oppressed*. London: Penguin Books.

Grange, L. (2007). Integrated Western and Indigenous Knowledge Systems: The basics for effective science Education in South Africa. *International Review of Education, 53*(5-6), 577–591. doi:10.100711159-007-9056-x

Halvorsen, T. (2017). The Sustainable Development Goals, knowledge production and the global struggle over values. In T. Halvorsen, H. Ibsen, H. Evans, & S. Penderis (Eds.), *Knowledge for justice: Critical perspectives rom southern African-Nordic research partnerships*. African Minds.

Higgs, P. (2002). Indigenous knowledge as a System of African knowledge: An Educational Perspective. *Indilinga: African Journal of Indigenous knowledge, 1*(1), 27-36.

Higgs, P. (2008). Towards an Indigenous African Educational Discourse: A Philosophical Reflection. *International Review of Education, 44*(3,4), 455-458.

Higgs, P., & Smith, J. (2015). *Philosophy of Education Today: An Introduction*. Cape Town: Juta and Company Ltd.

Hoppers, C. O. (2001). Indigenous knowledge and academic institutions in South Africa. *Perspectives in Education, 19*(1), 73–85.

Johnson, K., & Jacobs, S. (2012). Encyclopedia of South Africa. Scottsville: University of KwaZuku-Natal.

Khor, M., & Lin, L. L. (2001). *Good Practices & Innovative Experiences in the South: Social Policies, Indigenous Knowledge and Appropriate Technology*. London: Zed Books.

Lebakeng, T. J. (2016). Reversing Epistemicide and the quest for relevant Social Sciences and Humanities. In Decolonizing the University, Knowledge systems and Disciplines in Africa (pp. 47-63). Carolina Academic Press, LLC.

Matolino, B. (2017). Return the Source? Challenges and Prospects. In P. Ngulube (Ed.), *Handbook of Research on Social, Cultural and Educational Considerations of Indigenous Knowledge in Developing Countries* (pp. 36–58). Hershey, PA: IGI Global. doi:10.4018/978-1-5225-0838-0.ch001

Mji, G., Kalenga, R., Ned, L., Alpersteisn, M., & Banda, D. (2017). Indigenous Knowledge Exclusion in Education Systems of Africans: Impact of Beingness and Becoming an African. In P. Ngulube (Ed.), *Handbook of Research on Social, Cultural and Educational Considerations of Indigenous Knowledge in Developing Countries* (pp. 36–58). Hershey, PA: IGI Global. doi:10.4018/978-1-5225-0838-0.ch003

Msila, V. (2007). From Apartheid Education to the Revised National Curriculum Statement: Pedagogy for Identity Formation and Nation Building in South Africa. *Nordic Journal of African Studies, 16*(2), 146–160.

Msila, V. (2017). Of African Philosophy and African Renaissance: Redeeming Education. In V. Msila (Ed.), *Decolonising knowledge for African's Renewal: Examining African Perspectives and Philosophies* (pp. 21–33). Randburg: KR Publishing.

Mubangizi, J., & Kaya, H. (2015). African Indigenous knowledge systems and Human rights: Implications for Higher Education, Based on the South African experience. *International Journal of African Renaissance Studies, 10*(2), 125–142. doi:10.1080/18186874.2015.1107985

Nakata, M. (2002). Indigenous Knowledge and the Cultural Interface: Underlying issues at the intersection of knowledge and information systems. *OFLA Journal, 28*(5/6), 281–291.

Ndlovu-Gathseni, S. J. (2013). *Empire, Global Coloniality and African Subjectivity*. New York, Oxford, UK: Berghahn Books.

Ndlovu-Gathseni, S. J. (2017). Foreword: The Case for a Decolonised/Africanised Africa. In V. Msila (Ed.), *Decolonising Knowledge for Africa's Renewal: Examining African Perspectives and Philosophies* (pp. x–xv). Randburg: KR Publishing.

Ndlovu-Gatsheni, S. J. (2017). The Imperative of Decolonizing the Modern Westernised University. In S. J. Ndlovu-Gatsheni & S. Zondi (Eds.), *Decolonising the university, Knowledge systems and disciplines in Africa* (pp. 27–45). Durham, NC: Carolina Academic Press.

Ngubane, S. (2017, June 2). Revolution or repression? Continent must choose. *Daily News*, p. 13.

North Western University. (2018). *Indigenous Knowledge Systems Centre Brochure: Reclaiming our Origin, Charting our Destiny*. Accessed from http://natural-sciences.nwu.ac.za/indigenous-knowledge-systems-centre/about-us

Nussbaum, M. C. (1998). *Cultivating humanity: A classical defence of reform in liberal education*. Cambridge, MA: Harvard University Press.

Nymnjoh, F. B. (2012). 'Potted plants in greenhouses': A critical reflection on the resilience of colonial education in Africa. *Journal of Asian and African Studies*.

Odoro-Hoppers, C. A. (2001). *Decolonising the curriculum, indigenous knowledge systems and globalisation*. Unpublished paper delivered at the Gauteng Institute for curriculum development.

Ramose, M. B. (2005). *African Philosophy through Ubuntu*. Harare: Mond Books Publishers.

Rodney, W. (2009). *How European underdeveloped Africa*. Panaf Publishing.

Saurombe, A. (2017). Towards a Regional Policy and legal Instrument for the Protection of Indigenous knowledge Systems in Southern Africa. In P. Ngulube (Ed.), *Handbook of Research on Social, Cultural and Educational Considerations of Indigenous Knowledge in Developing Countries* (pp. 16-35). Hershey, PA: IGI Global.

Segalo, P. (2017). Decolonising Social Psychology in Africa. In Decolonising the university, Knowledge systems and disciplines in Africa (pp. 165-178). Durham, NC: Carolina Academic Press.

Seroto, J. (2018). Dynamics of Decoloniality in South Africa: A Critique of the History of Swiss Mission Education for Indigenous People. *Studia Historiae Ecclesiastacae*, *44*(3), 1–14.

Shava, S., & Nkopodi, N. (2017). Indigenous the University Curriculum in Sothern Africa. In P. Ngulube (Ed.), *Handbook of Research on Social, Cultural and Educational Considerations of Indigenous Knowledge in Developing Countries* (pp. 80–91). Hershey, PA: IDGI Global. doi:10.4018/978-1-5225-0838-0.ch005

Stone, D. (2012). Agents of Knowledge. In D. Levi-Faur (Ed.), Oxford Handbook of Governance (pp. 339-351). Oxford, UK: Oxford University Press. doi:10.1093/oxfordhb/9780199560530.013.0024

Teferra, D., & Altbach, P. G. (2003). Trends and perspectives in African Higher education. In African higher Education: An International Reference Handbook (pp. 3-14). Bloomington, IN: Indiana University Press.

World Bank. (1998). *Indigenous knowledge for development: A Framework for Action*. Retrieved from www.Worldbank.org/afh/ik/ik.pdg

ADDITIONAL READING

Nuffic and UNESCO/MOST. (2001). Best Practices Using Indigenous Knowledge. The Hague: Nuffic, and Paris: UNESCO/MOST.

KEY TERMS AND DEFINITIONS

African Indigenous System: It is a knowledge system grounded on indigenous and local knowledge, experiences, cultural, and historical heritage of the African people.

African Renaissance: It is a philosophical and political movement which is used to denote social cohesion, democracy, economic rebuilding, and growth for Africa development.

African Scholarship: It is a scholarship derived from intellectual, social, economic, and political development of knowledge in Africa.

Eurocentric Knowledge System: Knowledge system that focusses primarily or exclusively on the European knowledge system and is advanced through ontological and epistemological disregard of other knowledge systems.

Higher Education: An education that is offered at post-secondary schooling and involve various academic institutions such as universities, community and technological colleges. It also includes both public and private academic institutions that generate and disseminate knowledge.

Indigenous Knowledge: It is the knowledge system that embraces community knowledge, skills, attitudes and technologies with a particular community. Its sources are intergenerational and is often derived from culture and history. Such knowledge reflects information and behaviors emanating from local knowledge and wisdom.

Indigenous Knowledge System: It is a universally accepted knowledge system that value and acknowledge generated through cultural, historical, and social interaction.

Ubuntu: It is a philosophical and indigenous term that depicts humanity and is embedded within the core values and principles of respect, sharing, love, solidarity.

Chapter 12
Proposal of Indicators for Intellectual Capital in Higher Education

Edgar Oliver Cardoso Espinosa
https://orcid.org/0000-0001-7588-9439
Instituto Politécnico Nacional, Mexico

ABSTRACT

The objective of the chapter is to provide a proposal of indicators of intellectual capital in higher education for the organizations that comprise it. The importance of valuing intellectual capital in educational organizations is to measure their contributions to society, which complement the financial landscape and allow comparison between similar institutions, in order to compare their performance. Therefore, the conclusion of carrying out this process in higher education is 1) providing adequate information on the value of HEIs to society, 2) assessing and directing the response capacity of the organization towards the needs of the productive and services sector (interest groups), 3) orienting the development of the components of intellectual capital towards a knowledge management that allows to solve in an efficient way the problems of the society, and 4) optimizing the human talent of the institution for the achievement of the organizational objectives.

INTRODUCTION

Economic globalization has established knowledge as a competitive advantage for any organization, so it has been oriented towards its management based on developing the skills that a person needs to acquire. Thus, the formation of human capital as

DOI: 10.4018/978-1-5225-8461-2.ch012

the main strategic resource that allows achieving productivity and profitability of organizations becomes relevant.

Also, as the environment evolved as a result of political, economic, social and technological transformations, organizations began to interact in a global, dynamic and competitive environment, where the only constant is change. In this sense, intangible assets have become relevant because they articulate, strengthen and stimulate internal processes, customer orientation and, as a consequence, an optimal financial result, which, depending on the capabilities and resources of the organizations, allow achieving competitive advantage (Silva, Barahona, & Galleguillos, 2014).

Given this panorama, higher education has acquired a transcendental role in the fulfillment of the training of human capital in the knowledge society. As pointed out by Molina, Arango, and Botero (2010): A key factor in generating competitive capacities of countries in their economic growth and in their social development is the improvement of formal education systems, so it is vitally important that the upper level transforms both its management models and its main teaching function. In this way, it is undeniable that educational institutions assume an important role in societies, becoming a key factor in generating competitive capacities of countries, in their economic growth and in their social development. Therefore, to compete in this scenario, it is necessary that the University as a formative entity of the intellectuality transforms its utopias and its management models.

Thus, higher education, aware of the value that knowledge has acquired worldwide, requires the integration and strengthening of information and communication technologies (ICT) together with the creation of knowledge networks that allow for their exchange (UNESCO, 2009). In this way, higher education is not immune to the changes produced by globalization or the value that knowledge has acquired for the improvement and growth of societies, so its priority function is the production and transfer of knowledge to achieve the transformation of society which allows the positioning of countries and regions in the geopolitical context (Arrieta, Gaviria, & Consuegra, 2017).

Therefore, the highly changing environment has impacted on the role of higher education institutions (HEIs) fostering an evolution from being closed systems to becoming open systems characterized by the generation and transfer of knowledge in connection with research and the main interest groups or "stakeholders". As mentioned by Etzkowitz (2003): HEIs have become an important economic actor, generating value beginning with their results based on the innovative capacity and the efficient use of investments in research and development (R & D) in the generation of knowledge, and its application for the solution of problems in the countries.

In this sense, Trillo and Fernández (2013) established that the benefits obtained from incentivizing investment in R & D are directly related to intellectual capital in higher education, so investment in innovation only becomes profitable through the increase in intellectual capital.

Consequently, as mentioned by Henao, López, and Garcés (2014), in the current knowledge economy, HEIs compete to lead scientific, technical and technological development, through the integral formation of trained professionals, and the promotion of research and innovation as determining activities of its competitiveness. In the search for higher quality standards, HEIs have focused on the task of improving their processes, permanently qualifying their staff, innovating, researching and producing basic and applied knowledge to improve the living conditions of society as a whole.

Faced with this situation, these organizations have to focus on managing intellectual capital, establishing as their main function the production of knowledge to fulfill its main mission of human capital formation that is capable of generating knowledge and disseminating culture, as well as optimizing the scarce resources that it has for the achievement of its organizational objectives (Bezhani, 2010).

In this way, the general objective of the chapter is to provide a proposal of indicators of intellectual capital in higher education for the organizations that comprise it.

BACKGROUND

As the chapter's object of study refers to intellectual capital, it is important to conceptualize this term. Edvinson and Malone (1999) define it as the possession of knowledge, applied experience, organizational technology, customer relationships and professional skills, which give a company a competitive advantage in the market.

On the other hand, Al - Ali (2003) mentions that this concept refers to the intangible resources and assets that can be used to create value through their conversion into new processes, products and services. These intangibles are the knowledge, experience and intellectual capacity of their employees, as well as the resources of knowledge, processes, culture and philosophy of an organization.

Additionally, Molina, Arango, and Botero (2010) define it as a set of intangible resources of a strategic nature that contributes to the creation of organizational value, even if it is not considered in its financial statements. Thus, this term is divided into human capital as the set of knowledge, skills, training, attitudes, abilities and experiences of the employees of the organization that make it possible to have the resources and the adequate capacities for the future. Structural capital, as the one that represents knowledge that has only been managed by members and that has been incorporated into organizational structures such as the organizational culture, policies and procedures. The relational capital, as the value of the relations of the organization with third parties, oriented to customers, suppliers and shareholders for what it considers the external perspective, that is, the organization with the environment.

Regarding the perspective of intellectual capital focused on the education sector, it is necessary to mention that HEIs produce knowledge as the main product derived from their substantive functions, either through the management of that knowledge or through teaching and productive relations with their interest groups (Ramírez & Santos, 2013). Among their most valuable resources are their teachers, researchers, administrative and service staff, as well as their students, along with their organizational processes and relationship networks, which is why both inputs and outputs are mainly intangible (Leitner, 2004; Cañibano & Sánchez, 2008).

Therefore, the term intellectual capital in higher education is used to name all non-tangible or non-physical assets of the institution, including its processes, innovation capacity, patents; the tacit knowledge of its members, their capabilities, talents and skills; the recognition of society, its network of collaborators and contacts, among others (Ramírez & Santos, 2013).

Regarding the components of intellectual capital in HEIs, it should be noted that it has been categorized into three dimensions, which are the following:

Human Capital, which refers to the set of explicit and tacit knowledge of the staff of the institution (professors, researchers, managers, students, and administration and services personnel) acquired through a formal and informal education and update processes included in their activities as detailed in Table 1 (Ramírez & Santos, 2013).

Structural Capital, as explicit knowledge related to the internal process of dissemination, communication and management of scientific and technical knowledge in the HEIs, so it is divided into: a) Organizational Capital: refers to the operating environment derived from the interaction between research, management and organizational processes, organizational routines, values and corporate culture,

Table 1. Components of human capital

Component	Characteristics
Formal education	Education received in educational institutions: bachelor's, master's and doctoral degrees
Training	Provide updated knowledge that the staff requires to carry out their work
Competences	Capabilities that allow performance in a work area
Experience	Capacities acquired in their professional work
Innovation and creativity	Capabilities to develop new ideas and design solutions for relevant problems

Source: Own elaboration

internal procedures, quality and scope of information systems, among others; b) Technological capital: refers to the technological resources available in the organization, such as bibliographic resources, documentaries, archives, technical developments, patents, licenses, software, databases, among others, as indicated in Table 2.

While Relational Capital comprises the set of economic, political and institutional relations developed and maintained between the organization and non-academic partners such as firms, non-profit organizations, public authorities, local government and society in general, it also shows how the University is perceived: its image, attractiveness, reliability, among others, as shown in Table 3.

Hence, Sánchez, Castrillo, and Elena (2006) define seven groups within relational capital: a) spin offs or companies that market the results of university research; b) research and development contracts and projects; c) transfer of knowledge through technology transfer institutions; d) transfer of knowledge through human resources;

Table 2. Components of structural capital

Component	Characteristics
Technological infrastructure	Series of technological tools that serve as support for the creation, communication and sharing of knowledge
Physical infrastructure	Set of assets that support the generation of knowledge in the organization
Organizational structure	Organizational chart of hierarchies and communication channels of the organization
Organizational culture	Set of norms, values and customs shared by the members of the organization
Intellectual property	Legal mechanism for the protection of assets of the organization

Source: Own elaboration

Table 3. Components of relational capital

Component	Characteristics
Student satisfaction	Level of opinion of the students about the educational service received
Linkage	Provision of services or consultancies to external organizations
Image	Accreditation of the programs of the organization
Networks	Working groups for teaching and research purposes at the inter and intra-institutional level
Mobility	Exchange processes of students, teachers and researchers with organizations
Suppliers	Subjects external to the organization that contribute to its institutional development

Source: Own elaboration

e) participation in political decision-making; e) participation in cultural and social life, and, f) public understanding of science. Thus, the HEI as the main generator of knowledge within society attracts, develops, and retains national and foreign professors and students, who in turn can be considered as users; while parents are interested in the quality of education received by their children, companies and the government sector are identified as applicants for professionals and research, and other organizations that fulfill the role of collaborators and competitors.

In the same way, it is necessary to mention the relevance of inter and intra-institutional work networks for the development of this capital, which are characterized by creativity, skills, innovative processes and internal motivation for work by the members of these networks, who, in turn, develop projects for the benefit of the country.

Therefore, for higher education, the components of intellectual capital are the following: Human capital is composed of the competences of teachers, researchers, students and administrative staff; the structural capital constituted by scientific production as publications, patents and developments; while the relational capital is represented by the link with other organizations, whether academic or the productive and services sector.

Similarly, Núñez and Rodríguez (2015) indicate that the management of intangible resources is the means to achieve the mission, which promotes the increase of their capacity for innovation and, accordingly, the generation of greater value for the HEI.

However, indicators focused on the measurement of intellectual capital have been created for organizations in the productive sector and not for higher education, which is why it has been presented that HEIs have adapted them to their context, which has not been optimal. The reason is that, for the productive sphere, the purpose is economic: to produce more and better to achieve the highest profitability by expanding the number of clients; while for the educational field the goal is social that is oriented towards the formation of human talent that responds to the needs of the context (Arrieta, Gaviria, & Consuegra, 2017).

This situation is confirmed by Nava and Mercado (2010) who consider that intellectual capital in HEIs has been little explored, so their practicality is still not appreciated: the generation of value.

PROPOSAL OF INDICATORS FOR INTELLECTUAL CAPITAL IN HIGHER EDUCATION

The Organization for Economic Cooperation and Development (OECD, 2009) states that it is advisable that HEIs and research centers improve the measurement of their contributions to society, which is why they must generate intellectual capital reports, which complement the financial panorama and that allow the comparison between similar organizations, in order to have parameters that allow to compare the organizational performances of this sector.

However, as Bautzer (2010) points out, educational institutions cannot be managed exclusively with traditional models of business management, due to their nature and the characteristic of the service they offer. Therefore, its managers are committed to developing organizational systems based on intellectual capital and, in this way, have tools that support their growth and enable alternatives in crisis situations. However, existing models have been created to respond to business needs and not to the needs of knowledge management and intellectual capital of higher education institutions.

In this sense, the construction of indicators of intellectual capital in educational organizations has been little investigated together with its measurement and impact on the generation of value. Nonetheless, and since the intellectual capital in public universities has been little explored in Mexico, it is still not appreciated that its practical meaning lies in the generation of value (Nava, Mercado, & Demuner, 2012).

Currently, HEIs are concerned with identifying adequate indicators to measure their intangible assets such as human capital (talents and skills of their employees), internal structural capital (administrative systems) and external capital (support and interest of their clients and suitability and speed of its suppliers). This type of capital is supported by tacit knowledge, talent management and essential and complementary skills (Bautzer, 2010).

In this way, the proposal of indicators for each one of the components that make up the intellectual capital of a HEI is presented.

Based on Table 4, it is presented that human capital is related to the knowledge, skills, experience, seniority and mobility rate of the entire management and staff of the organization. Thus, the institutional staff (professors, researchers, administrators, administrative staff and services) shows the sum of explicit and tacit knowledge, acquired through formal and non-formal education, and the updating processes that it includes in its activities.

From Table 5, relational capital implies ownership of the organization in systems, tools, operating philosophy, protected commercial rights, intellectual property, as well as it includes the structures and processes of the organization on which this internal capital depends.

While based on Table 6, relational capital encompasses the set of economic, political and institutional relations developed and maintained between the organization and non - academic partners such as companies, non-profit organizations, public authorities, local government and society in general; it also stores the way in which the university is perceived: its image, attractiveness, reliability. Thusly, this capital contributes to the dissemination of knowledge developed by teachers, researchers and students. In addition, it promotes the formal or informal active relationship with

Table 4. Components and indicators of human capital

Component	Indicators
Formal education	Number of professors with a degree Number of professors with a master's degree Number of professors with a doctorate degree Number of professors with a post-doctorate degree Proportion of full-time, half-time and part-time professors. Proportion of teachers with final appointment. Proportion of professors enrolled in the SNI. Years of service in the program Number of guided theses. Number of participations as synodal in the degree exams. Number of academic products produced by each professor. Number of books or book chapters published by professor. Number of educational research reports made by professor. Number of articles published in non-refereed and refereed journals in the area of education. Number of participations in national and international congresses on education.
Training	Number of institutional update courses Number of external update courses
Competences	Number of full-time researchers Number of part-time researchers Number of full-time professors Number of part-time professors Number of researchers belonging to the SNI Number of researchers belonging to a network
Experience	Average age of researchers Average age of professors Average age of support staff Years of work experience of researchers Years of work experience of professors Years of work experience of support staff
Innovation and creativity	Number of national publications Number of international publications Number of conferences Number of papers

Source: Own elaboration

businessmen, former students and diverse government agencies for collaborations of various types.

Thence, human capital and relational capital require structural capital to function so that these elements, as part of intellectual capital, interact together to create value for the organization.

Table 5. Components and indicators of structural capital

Component	Indicators
Technological infrastructure	Use of databases Measurement of connectivity bandwidth Type of software and hardware Software update
Physical infrastructure	Number of cubicles for professors Number of classrooms Number of documentation centers Number of laboratories Number of computers Number of classrooms for the delivery of the courses of the program. Number of cubicles for professors' use. Proportion of cubicles with computer for professor use. Number of computers in the computer center. Proportion of computers with legalized software. Proportion of computers with access to international networks in educational research. Proportion of computers with adequate maintenance. Number of audiovisual support resources in the program. Proportion of audiovisual support resources in optimal conditions. Number of spaces for conducting academic events and collegiate meetings. Number of titles that the library has in the educational field. Percentage of the stock that is updated. Percentage of the stock that is appropriate to the nature of the program. Percentage of the stock that is updated to the nature of the program. Number of titles held by the hemerographic library. Percentage of the hemerographic collection that is updated. Percentage of the hemerographic collection that is appropriate to the nature of the program. Percentage of the hemerographic collection that is updated to the nature of the program.
Organizational structure	Number of areas or departments Number of employees by department Number of professors per area Number of researchers per area Number of administrative support personnel by area
Organizational culture	Existence of the mission and vision statement Existence of the declaration of organizational values
Intellectual property	Number of patents Number of copyright registrations

Source: Own elaboration

FUTURE RESEARCH DIRECTIONS

In higher education, it is important to consider the standards of intellectual capital, in the aspects of human capital, structural capital and relational capital, in order to improve its creation and management. The measurement of intangibles continues to be a field that should be investigated in HEIs since their identification can become a source of value that is made known and that would generate greater importance to the institution.

Table 6. Relational capital components and indicators

Component	Indicators
Student satisfaction	Terminal efficiency Coverage Graduates Existence of modalities to attend the program. Existence of different schedules to attend the program. Existence of furniture for people with special educational needs. Existence of the infrastructure for people with special educational needs in the computing center. Existence of the infrastructure for people with special educational needs in the documentation centers. Existence of a program that allows determining the needs and expectations of the students before, after and upon graduation. Existence of a program focused on measuring the satisfaction and loyalty of students.
Linkage	Projects linking with companies, civil organizations or communities. Number of students working in the education area. Proportion of students that cover the program's graduation profile. Proportion of students that cover the requirements of the service sector. Proportion of agreements with organizations or institutions of higher education in the field of educational research. Number of educational researches carried out by the teaching staff with impact. Number of educational research carried out by the teaching staff with national recognition. Number of educational research carried out by the teaching staff with international recognition. Existence of a program focused on measuring the satisfaction and needs of the service sector.
Image	Position in the classification of organizations in higher education Terminal efficiency Reputation of graduates Citations of the organization Number of people who obtain the degree on the number of people who started the studies in each generation. Time to obtain the degree. Number of students who drop out of the program.
Networks	Number of participation in internal networks (intra-institutional) Number of participation in external networks (inter-institutional)
Mobility	Number of professors of the organization abroad. Number of external professors in the organization. Number of researchers of the organization abroad. Number of external researchers in the organization. Number of students in another organization. Number of external students in the organization.
Suppliers	Number of contracts. Number of agreements with publishing houses.

Source: Own elaboration

In the same way, HEIs need to integrate in their organizational strategy the design and implementation of knowledge management initiatives, measurement of intellectual capital and preparation of intellectual capital reports as relevant activities of the institution to carry out monitoring and evaluation of these processes that are so relevant today.

CONCLUSION

It should be noted that the knowledge society promotes the creation of knowledge related to the context, as well as the use of the benefits of knowledge, information, science and technology. Therefore, it is necessary to consider HEIs as fundamental organizations that enable the development of a country. Thus, the proposal of indicators of intellectual capital must be identified as part of the daily activities of the organization, as mentioned by Vallaeys, De la Cruz, and Sasia (2009).

In this sense, it is important to encourage the teacher to not only focus on teaching but also as indicated by Valencia, Estrada, Bedoya, Tuttle and Gaviria (2013) to get involved in carrying out research projects and exchanging information with other scientific networks, as well as elaborating and publishing articles, books and papers as knowledge dissemination strategies, which has an impact on the intellectual capital of the HEI.

Finally, the relevance of measuring intellectual capital in higher education is: 1) Providing adequate information on the value of HEIs to society; 2) Assessing and directing the response capacity of the organization towards the needs of the productive and services sector (interest groups); 3) Orienting the development of the components of intellectual capital towards a knowledge management that allows to solve in an efficient way the problems of the society and 4) Optimizing the human talent of the institution for the achievement of the organizational objectives.

ACKNOWLEDGMENT

This research was supported by the Instituto Politécnico Nacional, México [SIP number 20181014].

REFERENCES

Arrieta, N., Gaviria, G., & Consuegra, J. (2017). Papel del capital intelectual en la calidad de las instituciones de educación superior en Colombia. *Education and Educators*, *20*(3), 419-433. Retrieved from http://educacionyeducadores.unisabana.edu.co/index.php/eye/article/view/6823/4666

Bautzer, D. (2010). La gestión del capital intelectual y su impacto en la educación superior. *Educational Innovation*, *10*(51), 15–21.

Bezhani, I. (2010). Intellectual capital reporting at UK universities. *Journal of Intellectual Capital*, *11*(2), 179–207. doi:10.1108/14691931011039679

Cañibano, L., & Sánchez, P. (2008). Intellectual Capital Management and Reporting in Universities and Research Institutions. *Applied Economics Studies*, *26*(2), 7–26.

Edvinson, L., & Malone, M. (1999). *El capital intelectual.* Norma.

Etzkowitz, H. (2003). Research groups as 'quasi-firms': The invention of the entrepreneurial university. *Research Policy*, *32*(1), 109–121. doi:10.1016/S0048-7333(02)00009-4

Heinz, K. (2004). Intellectual capital reporting for universities: Conceptual background and application for Austrian universities. *Research Evaluation*, *3*(2), 129–140. doi:10.3152/147154404781776464

Henao, E., López, M., & Garcés, R. (2014). Medición de capacidades en investigación e innovación en instituciones de educación superior: Una mirada desde el enfoque de las capacidades dinámicas. *Framework*, *10*(1), 252–271.

Molina, P., Arango, M. & Botero, S. (2010). Análisis del valor agregado del conocimiento. Caso aplicado en una Institución de Educación Superior. *Journal Faculty of Economic Sciences: Research and Reflection*, *18*(2), 95 – 105.

Nava, R., & Mercado, P. (2010). Evaluación de la calidad métrica para indicadores de capital intelectual generados a partir de bases estadísticas. *The Journal of Higher Education*, *39*(155).

Nava, R., Mercado, P., & Demuner, M. (2012). Indicadores de capital intelectual para instituciones públicas de educación superior. In El capital intelectual en las organizaciones: una agenda de investigación. Universidad Autónoma del Estado de México.

OECD. (2009). *Education at a Glance 2009*. Paris: OECD. Retrieved from http://www.oecd.org/education/skills-beyond-school/43636332.pdf

Ramírez, Y., & Santos, J. (2013). Propuesta de un Informe de Capital Intelectual para las instituciones de educación superior españolas. *Applied Economics Studies, 31*(2), 525–554.

Sánchez, P., Elena, S., & Castrillo, R. (2006). The Intellectual Capital Report of Universities. Guidelines for disclosing IC information. Observatory of the European University: PRIME-OEU Methodological Guide, 223-251.

Silva, J., Barahona, P., & Galleguillos, C. (2014). Valoración prospectiva del capital intelectual de la Universidad de Atacama, mediante la técnica Delphi. *Ingeniare. Chilean Journal of Engineering, 22*(4), 567–574. Retrieved from https://scielo.conicyt.cl/pdf/ingeniare/v22n4/art12.pdf

Trillo, M., & Fernández, M. (2013). Caracterización de la innovación en Spin-Off de base tecnológica. *Industrial Economy, 388*, 67–78.

UNESCO. (2009). *World Conference on Higher Education 2009 Final Report.* París: UNESCO.

Valencia, M., Estrada, J., Bedoya, I., Tuttle, S., & Gaviria, F. (2013). Indicadores del capital intelectual en el área de ingenierías de una universidad. *Strategic Sciences Journal, 22*(30), 285–298.

Vallaeys, F., Cruz, C., & Sasia, P. (2009). *Responsabilidad Social Universitaria. Manual primeros pasos.* Mc Graw Hill.

ADDITIONAL READING

Bueno, E., Salmador, M., & Merino, C. (2008). Génesis, concepto y desarrollo del capital intelectual en la economía del conocimiento: Una reflexión sobre el Modelo Intellectus y sus aplicaciones. *Applied Economics Studies, 26*(2), 43–64.

Burgener, L., & Barth, M. (2018). Sustainability competencies in teacher education: Making teacher education count in everyday school practice. *Journal of Cleaner Production, 74*, 821–826. doi:10.1016/j.jclepro.2017.10.263

Chong, E. (2013). Managerial competencies and career advancement: A comparative study of managers in two countries. *Journal of Business Research, 66*(3), 345–353. doi:10.1016/j.jbusres.2011.08.015

Dagiliute, R., Liobikiene, G., & Minelgaite, A. (2018). Sustainability at universities: Students' perceptions from Green and Non-Green universities. *Journal of Cleaner Production, 181*, 473–482. doi:10.1016/j.jclepro.2018.01.213

Fonseca, T., Faria, P., & Lima, F. (2018). Human capital and innovation: The importance of the optimal organizational task structure. *Research Policy*. doi:10.1016/j.respol.2018.10.010

González, J., & Rodríguez, M. (2010). Modelos de capital intelectual y sus indicadores en la universidad pública. *Notebooks of Administration*, *43*, 113–128.

Hossein, M. (2018). Artificial intelligence and the future of work: Human-AI symbiosis in organizational decision making. *Business Horizons*, *61*(4), 577–586. doi:10.1016/j.bushor.2018.03.007

Kaufmann, L., & Schneider, Y. (2004). Intangibles. A synthesis of a current research. *Journal of Intellectual Capital*, *5*(3), 366–388. doi:10.1108/14691930410550354

Keong, K. (2008). Intellectual capital: Definitions, categorization and reporting models. *Journal of Intellectual Capital*, *9*(4), 609–638. doi:10.1108/14691930810913186

Lara, F., & Salas, A. (2017). Managerial competencies, innovation and engagement in SMEs: The mediating role of organisational learning. *Journal of Business Research*, *79*, 152–160. doi:10.1016/j.jbusres.2017.06.002

Makridakis, S. (2017). The forthcoming Artificial Intelligence (AI) revolution: Its impact on society and firms. *Futures*, *90*, 46–60. doi:10.1016/j.futures.2017.03.006

Malmstrom, M., Wincent, J., & Johansson, J. (2013). Managing competence acquisition and financial performance: An empirical study of how small firms use competence acquisition strategies. *Journal of Engineering and Technology Management*, *30*(4), 327–349. doi:10.1016/j.jengtecman.2013.07.004

Oliveira, A., Sokulsky, C., Silva, A., & Francisco, A. (2018)... *Sustainable Production and Consumption*, *14*, 82–94. doi:10.1016/j.spc.2018.01.005

Prange, C., & Schlegelmilch, B. (2018). Managing innovation dilemmas: The cube solution. *Business Horizons*, *61*(2), 309–322. doi:10.1016/j.bushor.2017.11.014

Ramírez, Y. (2010). Análisis de las principales guías para la presentación de información sobre capital intelectual. *Applied Economics Studies*, *28*(2), 481–491.

Simó, P., & Sallán, J. (2008). Capital intangible y capital intelectual: Revisión, definiciones y líneas de investigación. *Applied Economics Studies*, *26*(2), 65–78.

Trencher, G., Vincent, S., Bahr, K., Kudo, S., Markham, K., & Yamanaka, Y. (2018). Evaluating core competencies development in sustainability and environmental master's programs: An empirical analysis. *Journal of Cleaner Production*, *181*, 829–841. doi:10.1016/j.jclepro.2018.01.164

KEY TERMS AND DEFINITIONS

Human Capital: It is composed of creativity, skill, research potential, knowledge, talent, and experiences of professors, students, researchers, and administrative staff of the educational organization to perform their functions.

Indicator: It is an observable manifestation of a feature or characteristic of one or more variables of interest, susceptible of evaluation, which provides quantitative information about said characteristic.

Intellectual Capital: A set of knowledge, applied experience, organizational technology, customer relationships, and professional skills that give a company a competitive advantage in the market.

Relational Capital: Includes the set of economic, political, and institutional relations developed and maintained between the organization and non-academic partners.

Structural Capital: It is the explicit knowledge related to the internal process of diffusion, communication, and management of scientific and technical knowledge in the organization.

Compilation of References

Acheampong, P., & Kayange, J. J. (2016). University education in Ghana: A privilege or a right? *International Journal of Research Studies in Education*, *6*(3), 17–25. doi:10.5861/ijrse.2016.1563

Adhikari, D. R. (2010). Knowledge management in academic institutions. *International Journal of Educational Management*, *24*(2), 94–104. doi:10.1108/09513541011020918

African National Congress (ANC). (1994). *The Reconstruction and Development programme (RDP): A Policy framework*. Johannesburg: Umanyano Publications.

African National Congress (ANC). (1994). *The Reconstruction and Development Programme: A Policy Framework*. Johannesburg: Umnyano publications.

Alexander, N. (2006). Language, Policy, Symbolic Power and the Democratic Responsibility of the Post-Apartheid University. In R. Pithouse (Ed.), *Asinamali: Understanding Struggles in Post-Apartheid South Africa*. Asmara: Africa World Press Inc.

Allen, W. R. (2005). A forward glance in the mirror: Diversity challenged – access, equity and success in higher education. *Educational Researcher*, *34*(7), 18–23. doi:10.3102/0013189X034007018

Altbach, P. G. (1996). Students and politics. *Comparative Education Review*, *10*(2), 175–187. doi:10.1086/445214

Amtaika, A. (2013). *Local Government in South Africa since 1994: Leadership, Democracy, development and Service Delivery in a Post-Apartheid Era*. Durham, NC: Carolina Academic Press.

ANC. (1994). *The Reconstruction and Development Programme: A Policy Framework*. Johannesburg: Umanyano Publications.

Anderson, B. (2016). Education with Emphasis on South African Education. In Sociology: A South African Perspective (pp. 156-171). Hampshire, UK: Cengage Learning EMEA.

Anderson, B. (2016). Education: With emphasis on South Africa. In Sociology: A South African Perspective (pp. 156-176). CENAGE Learning.

APA. (2018). *Publication Manual of the American Psychological Association* (6th ed.). Washington, DC: Author.

Araujo, A. (2000). *Gestión del conocimiento, Universidad y Empresa.* Paper presented at the University Conference on knowledge management in companies and organizations. Centre for University Knowledge Management. Bilbao.

Area Moreira, M. (2009). *Introduccion a la Tecnología Educativa* (E. Universadad de la Laguna, Ed.). Recuperado el 12 de mayo de 2016, de http://bibliotecadigital.org/bitstream/001/415/5/Introducci%C3%B3n%20a%20la%20tecnolog%C3%ADa%20educativa.pdf

Argyis, C., & Schon, D. A. (1978). *Organizational Learning: A Theory of Action Perspective*. Reading, MA: Addison-Wesley.

Arrieta, N., Gaviria, G., & Consuegra, J. (2017). Papel del capital intelectual en la calidad de las instituciones de educación superior en Colombia. *Education and Educators, 20*(3), 419-433. Retrieved from http://educacionyeducadores.unisabana.edu.co/index.php/eye/article/view/6823/4666

Arrieta, N., Gaviria, G., & Consuegra, J. (2017). Papel del capital intelectual en la calidad de las Instituciones de Educación Superior en Colombia. *Education and Educators*, *20*(3), 419–433. doi:10.5294/edu.2017.20.3.5

Ascanio, A. (1996). *Skandia Navigator model*. Edvinsson.

Association for Educational Communications and Technology. (2008). Definition. In Educational technology: A definition with commentary. New York: Lawrence Erlbaum Associates.

Avedaño, F. (2007). *Cómo gestionar el cambio tecnológico*. Barcelona: Paidós.

Ayres, J. S., & Silvis, A. H. (2011). Principles of Working Together: Developing Relationships that Support Community Development initiatives. Academic Press.

Bahti, T. (1992). The Injured University. In R. Rand (Ed.), *Logomachia: The Conflict of the Faculties*. London: University of Nebraska Press.

Balintulo, M. (2004). The role of the state in the transformation of South African higher education, 1994-2002: Equity and redress revisited. In P. T. Peleza & A. Olukoshi (Eds.), *African Universities in the twenty-first century*. Pretoria: UNISA Press.

Banco Mundial. (2008). Mexico's transitions to a knowledge-bases economy. Challenges and opportunities. Washington, DC: Author.

Barnett, R. (2011). *Being a University*. London: Routledge.

Baškarada, S., & Koronios, A. (2013). Data, Information, Knowledge, Wisdom (DIKW): A Semiotic Theoretical and Empirical Exploration of the Hierarchy and its Quality Dimension. *AJIS. Australasian Journal of Information Systems*, *18*(1), 5–24. doi:10.3127/ajis.v18i1.748

Bautzer, D. (2010). La gestión del capital intelectual y su impacto en la educación superior. *Educational Innovation*, *10*(51), 15–21.

Beciez, D. (2009). *Obtenido de Curso AIU Estrategias de Enseñanza Aprendizaje*. Retrieved from http://cursos.aiu.edu/Estrategias%20de%20Ensenanza%20y%20Apredizaje/PDF/Tema%201.pdf

Bell, S. M., & Carlson, R. (2009). Motivations of Communication Organisations for Service Learning. In The Unheard Voices: Community Organisations and Service Learning (pp. 10-37). Philadelphia: Temple University Press.

Bell, D. (1973). *The coming of post-industrial society*. New York: Basic Books.

Bender, G. (2008). Exploring conceptual models for community engagement at higher education institutions in South Africa. *Perspectives in Education*, *26*(1), 81–95.

Bernstein, H. (1994). *The Rift: The exile experience of South Africans*. London: Jonathan Cape.

Bezhani, I. (2010). Intellectual capital reporting at UK universities. *Journal of Intellectual Capital*, *11*(2), 179–207. doi:10.1108/14691931011039679

Biemans, H., Nieuwenbuis, L., Poell, R., Mulder, M., & Wesselink, R. (2004). Competence based VET in the Netherland. Background and piftalls. *Journal of Vocational Education and Training*, *56*(2), 523–538. doi:10.1080/13636820400200268

Biko, S. (2015). *I write what I like: Selected writings*. University of Chicago Press.

Bloch, G. (2009). *The toxic Mix: What is Wrong with South African Schools and How to Fix It*. Cape Town: NB Publishers.

Bond, P. (2015). Student protesters win as race and class fused in epic battle. *Green Left Weekly, 1075*, 3.

Bontis, N. (1996). There is a price on your head: managing intellectual capital strategically. Business Quaterly, 41-47.

Bontis, N. (1999). Managing organizational knowledge by diagnosing intellectual capital: framing and advancing the state of the field. *International Journal of the Technology Management, 18*(5-8), 433-462.

Bontis, N. (1998). Intellectual capital: An exploratory study that develops measures and models. *Management Decision, 36*(2), 63–76. doi:10.1108/00251749810204142

Bontis, N. (2001). Assessing knowledge assets: A review of the models used to measure intelectual capital. *International Journal of Management Reviews, 3*(1), 41–60. doi:10.1111/1468-2370.00053

Bontis, N. (2002). *National intellectual capital index: Intellectual capital development in the Arab Region*. Ontario: Institute for Intellectual Capital Research.

Bontis, N., & Chua, W. (2000). Intellectual capital and business performance in Malaysian industries. *Journal of Intellectual Capital, 1*(1), 85–100. doi:10.1108/14691930010324188

Bontis, N., Crossan, M., & Hulland, J. (2002). Managing an organizational learning system by aligning stocks and flows. *Journal of Management Studies, 39*(4), 437–469. doi:10.1111/1467-6486.t01-1-00299

Bontis, N., Dragonetti, N., Jacobsen, K., & Roos, G. (1999). The knowledge toolbox: A review of tools available to measure and manage intangible resources. *European Management Journal, 17*(4), 391–402. doi:10.1016/S0263-2373(99)00019-5

Booysen, S. (Ed.). (2016). *FeesMustFall: Student Revolt, Decolonization and Governance in South Africa*. Johannesburg: Wits University Press.

Borrdryk, J. (2002). *Ubuntu: Life Lessons from Africa*. Pretoria: Ubuntu School of Philosophy.

Bosch, T. (2017). Twitter activism and youth in South Africa: The case of #RhodesMustFall. *Information Communication and Society*, *20*(2), 221–231. doi:10.1080/1369118X.2016.1162829

Bozu, Z., & Canto Herrera, P. J. (2009). El profesorado universitario en la sociedad del conocimiento: Competencias profesionales docentes. *Revista de Formación e Innovación Educativa Universitaria*, *2*(2), 87–97.

Bradley, K. (2003). Intellectual capital and the new wealth of nations II. Business Strategy Review, 8(4), 33-44.

Bradley, K. (1997a). Intellectual capital and the new wealth of nations. *Business Strategy Review*, *8*(1), 53–62. doi:10.1111/1467-8616.00007

Bradley, K. (1997b). Intellectual capital and the new wealth of nations II. *Business Strategy Review*, *8*(4), 33–44. doi:10.1111/1467-8616.00046

Braunerhjelm, P. (2010). *Entrepreneurship, Innovation and Economic Growth. Past experiences, current knowledge and policy implications*. Stockholm: Swedish Entrepreneurship Forum and The Royal Institute of Technology.

Breidlid, A. (2009). *Culture, indigenous Knowledge systems and sustainable development: A critical view of education in an African context*. Academic Press.

Breton, P. (2005). La "société de la connaissance": Généalogie d'une double réduction. *Education et Societé*, 45–57.

Brink, C. (2016). Two tales of quality and equality. In *Reflections of South African university leaders*. Cape Town: African Minds.

Brooking, A. (1997b). Intellectual capital. Paidós Empresa.

Brooking, A. (1997a). The management of intellectual capital. *Long Range Planning*, *30*(3), 364–365. doi:10.1016/S0024-6301(97)80911-9

Brown, J. (2015). *South African's Insurgent Citizens On Dissent and the possibility of Politics*. Sunnyside: Jacana Media Ltd.

Brown, J. (2016). *The Road to Soweto: Resistance and the Uprising of 16 June 1996*. Johannesburg: Jacana Media Ltd.

Brown-Martin, G. (2017). *L'education et la quatrième revolution industrielle*. Ontario: Groupe Média TFO.

Buber, M. (1958). *I and thou* (2nd ed.; R. G. Smith, Trans.). New York, NY: Charles Scribner's Sons.

Buccus, I. (2016, October 6). The crisis at universities is escalating. The Mercury, p. 9.

Bueno, E., Salmador, M., & Merino, C. (2008). Genesis, concept and development of intellectual capital in the knowledge economy: A reflection on the Intellectus Model and its applications. *Applied Economics Studies, 26*(2), 43-63. http://hdl.handle.net/10486/669095

Bui, H. T. M., & Baruch, Y. (2012, November). Learning organisations in higher education: An empirical evaluation within an international context. *Management Learning*, *43*(5), 515–544. doi:10.1177/1350507611431212

Burger, P. (2018). *Getting it Right: A New Economy for South Africa*. Sandton: KMM Review Publishing.

Burkart, A., & Medlik, S. (1981). *Tourism: past, present and future* (2nd ed.). Heinemann.

Burkey, S. (1993). *Putting People First: A Guide to Self-Reliant Participatory Rural Development*. London: Zed Books.

Cabero, J. (2007). *Novas Tecnologias na educaión*. Coruña: SecretariaXeral de Análise e Proxeccion de la Xunts de Galicia.

Calderon, E., Flores, F., Gallegos, L., De la Cruz, G., Ramirez, J., & Casteñeda, R. (2016). Laboratorios de ciencias en el bachillerato: Tecnologías digitales y adaptación docente. *Apertura (Guadalajara, Jal.)*, *8*(1), 1–11.

Camisón, C., Palacios, D., & Devece, C. (2000). *A model for the measurement of intellectual capital in the company: the Nova model.* Academic Press.

Cañibano, L., & Sánchez, P. (2008). Intellectual Capital Management and Reporting in Universities and Research Institutions. *Applied Economics Studies*, *26*(2), 7–26.

Cano, M., Sánchez, G., González, M., & Pérez, J. (2014). El rol del capital intelectual en la innovación de las empresas. *European Scientific Journal, 10*(28), 348–366. Retrieved from http://eujournal.org/index.php/esj/ article/viewFile/4405/4202

Carreón y Melgoza. (2012). México: Hacia una sociedad del conocimiento. *Noésis (Pau)*, *21*(41).

Carreon, H., & Melgoza, R. (2012). México hacia una sociedad del conocimiento. Nóesis. *Revista de Ciencias Sociales y Humanidades*, *21*(41), 122–135. doi:10.20983/noesis.2012.1.5

Casas, P.M. (2010). México: sociedad de la información o sociedad del conocimiento. *Virtualis, 1*.

Casillas, M. y. (2016). *La integración de México a la sociedad de la información*. UNAM.

Castell, M. (2001). Universities as dynamic systems of contradictory functions. In Challenges of Globailisation: South African database with Manuel Castells (pp. 206-224). Cape Town: Maskew Miller Longman.

Castell, M. (2003). *Conversations with Manuel Castells*. Oxford, UK: Polity Press.

Castells, M. (1997). *La era de la información. La sociedad red* (Vol. 1). Madrid: Alianza Editorial.

Castel, M. (2000). *End of Millennium* (2nd ed.). Oxford, UK: Blackwell Publishing.

Cebekhlu, A. (2013). *Unhlaba Uyahlaba: The World is Thorny. Wandsbeck*. Reach Publishers.

Cebekhulu, E. (2013). *Umhlaba Uyahlaba: The World is Thorny. Wandsbeck*. Reach Publishers.

Chamber, R. (1993). Participatory rural appraisal (PRA): Analysis of experience. *World Development*, *22*(9), 1253–1268. doi:10.1016/0305-750X(94)90003-5

Chambers, R. (2003). *Whose Reality Counts? Putting the First Last. Warwickshire CV23 9QZ*. ITDG Publishing.

Chávez Márquez, L., & Gutiérrez, M. d. (2015). Redes sociales como facilitadoras del aprendizaje de ciencias exactas en la educación superior. *Apertura (Guadalajara, Jal.)*.

Chetty, N. (2009, June 1). Intellectual freedom the lifeblood of universities. The Mercury.

Chetty, N., & Merrett, C. (2014). *The Struggle for South of a South African University*. The University of KwàZulu-Natal-Academic freedom, corporation and transformation.

Chetty, N., & Merrett, C. (2014). *The Struggle for the South of a South African University: The University of KwaZulu-Natal-Academic freedom, corporatisation and Transformation. Scottsville*. UKZN Press.

Chikane, R. (2018). *Breaking a Rainbow, Building a Nation: The Politics behind #FeesMustFall Movements*. Johannesburg: Picador Africa.

Chiloane, M. (2016). Wits workl 22rd dies after inhaling extinguisher fumes set off during protest. *Eyewitness News*. Retrieved from http://ewn.co.za/2016/09/26/Wits-worker-dies-after-inhaling-extinguisher-fumes

Chinnia, B. (2018). Importance of education. *The Glenwood Weekly Gazette*, *22*, 9.

Chomsky, N. (1983). Language and unconscious knowledge. In *Rules and representations*. FCE.

CID. UNAM. (2018). *Innovación UNAM*. Retrieved from http://www.innova.unam.mx/

CIEBT. IPN. (2018). *Incubadora de empresas*. Retrieved from https://www.ipn.mx/CIEBT/Paginas/Inicio.aspx

Cinque, M. (2016). Lost in translation. Soft skills development in European countries. *Tuning Journal for Higher Education*, *3*(2), 389–427. doi:10.18543/tjhe-3(2)-2016pp389-427

City Press. (2017, January 15). #FeesMustFall: Cool heads are now needed. City Press, p. 2.

Clark, B. R. (1983). *The higher education system*. Berkeley, CA: University of California.

Cloete, N. (2016). *The flawed ideology of "free higher education"*. Retrieved from http://www.universityworldnews. com/article.php?story=20151104111825416

Cloete, N. (2016, September 29). No such thing as 'free higher education. The Mercury, p. 10.

Comisión de las Comunidades Europeas. (1995). *Libro Blanco sobre la educación y la formación. Enseñar y aprender. Hacia la sociedad del conocimiento*. Luxemburgo: CCE.

Commonwealth Expert Group Report. (1991). *Human resource development for a post-apartheid South Africa*. London: Commonwealth Secretariat.

Complexity Labs. (2018). *YouTube*. Retrieved from Knowledge Society Explained: https://www.youtube.com/watch?v=mU3pvZHv-dE

CONACyT. (2016). *Informe general del estado de la Ciencia, la Tecnología y la Innovación*. CONACyT.

CONDUSEF. (2018). *Pierde el miedo*. Retrieved from Condusef: https://www.condusef.gob.mx/Revista/index.php/inversion/otros/303-pierde-el-miedo

Crenshaw, K. (1989). Demarginalising the intersection of race and sex: A black feminist critique of antidiscrimination doctrine, Feminist theory and antiracist politics. *University of Chicago Legal Forum*, *140*, 139–167.

Crossman, P. (2004). 'Perceptions of 'Africanisation' or 'Endogenisation' at African Universities: Issues and Recommendations. In P. T. Zeleza & A. Olukoshi (Eds.), *African Universities in the twenty-first century* (pp. 319–340). Pretoria: UNISA Press.

Daley, J. (2001). The intangible economy and Australia. *Australian Journal of Management*, *26*, 3-19.

Daou, Karuranga, E., & Su, Z. (2014). Towards a better understanding of intelectual capital in Mexicans SMEs. *Journal of Intellectual Capital*, *15*(2), 316–332. doi:10.1108/JIC-08-2013-0092

Davids, N., & Waghid, Y. (2018, April 6). Embrace the ecological university. Mail & Guardian, 27.

Dayile, A. (2018). Aryan Kaganof's Decolonising Wits: A film analysis. In We Are No Longer at Ease: The Struggle for #FeesMustFall (pp. 73-80). Sunnyside: Jakana Media Ltd.

De Gayardon, A., & Bernasconi, A. (2016). *Chilean Universities: Not so tuition-free after all*. Retrieved from http://ejournals.bc.edu/ojs/index.php/ihe/article/view/9372

De Ketele, J. (1996). School Performance Evaluation: What? Why? For what? *Tunisia Journal of Science Education*, *23*, 17-36.

De la Torre, S. C. (2008). *Estrategias didácticas en el aula. Buscando la calidad y la innovación*. Madrid: Universidad Nacional de Educación a Distancia.

Deleuze, G., & Guattari, F. (2004). *A thousand plateaus: Capitalism and schizophrenia*. London: Continuum.

Delors, J. (Ed.). (1996). *La educación encierra un tesoro*. Madrid: Ediciones UNESCO.

Department of Higher Education and Training (DHET). (2013). *Report of the Ministerial Committee for the Review of the Funding of Universities*. Pretoria Department of Higher Education.

Dexter, P. (2017, April 23). Shared economic growth is the only way to go. *City Press*, p. 3.

Díaz Barriga, F. (2000). *Estrategias Docentes: Para un Aprendizaje Significativo*. Mcgraw-Hill Interamericana.

Diaz, E.A. (2011). Información y sociedad del conocimiento en América Latina. *Biblioteca Universitaria, 14*(1).

Dierickx, I., & Cool, K. (1989). Asset stock accumulation and sustainability of competitive advantage. *Management Science, 35*(12), 1504–1511. doi:10.1287/mnsc.35.12.1504

Dinu, M. (2005). *What is knowledge society?* ResearchGate.

Dipholo, K. (2010). *Universities in transition: From Ivory Towers to People-centred Institutions*. Paper presented at the 9th PASCAL international Observatory Conference, Gaborone.

Donnelly, L. (2017, April 21). Limping economy faces uphill. Mail & Guardian, 21.

Drucker, P. (1993). La gerencia en la sociedad futura. Bogotá: Norma.

Drucker, P. (1993). *Post Capitalist Society*. HarperCollins.

Drucker, P. (1969). *The Age of Discontinuity. Guidelines to our changing societies*. New York: Harper & Row.

Drucker, P. (1993). *Post-Capitalist Society*. New York: Harper Business.

Drucker, P. (1997). The Future that Has Already Happened. *Harvard Business Review*, *7*(49), 64–75.

Drucker, P. (2006). *Drucker Para todos los días*. Bogotá: Ed. Norma.

Du Plessis, H., Sehume, J., & Martin, L. (2011). The Concept and Application of Transdisplinarity in Intellectual Discourse and Research. Johannesburg: Mapungubwe Institute for Strategic Reflection (MISTRAN).

Ebong, M. B. (2004). University Industry relations in Nigeria. In African Universities in the Twenty-First Century: Vol. 2. Knowledge and Society (pp. 555-570). Dakar: CODESRIA.

Edvinson, L., & Malone, M. (1999). Intellectual capital: how to identify and calculate the value of the intangible resources of your company. Barcelona: Management 2000.

Edvinson, L., & Malone, M. (1999). *El capital intelectual.* Norma.

Edvinsson, L., & Malone, M. (1999). Intellectual capital, management 2000. Barcelona: Academic Press.

Edvinsson, L. (1997). Developing intellectual capital at Skandia. *Long Range Planning*, *30*(3), 366–373. doi:10.1016/S0024-6301(97)90248-X

Edvinsson, L., & Malone, M. (1998). *El capital intelectual, cómo identificar y calcular el valor inexplorado de los recursos intangibles de su empresa*. Bogotá: Grupo Editorial Norma.

Edvinsson, L., & Stenfelt, C. (1999). Intellectual capital of nations – for future wealth creation. *Journal of Human Resource Costing and Accounting*, *4*(1), 21–33. doi:10.1108/eb029051

Edvinsson, L., & Sullivan, P. (1996). Developing a model for managing intellectual capital. *European Management Journal*, *14*(4), 356–364. doi:10.1016/0263-2373(96)00022-9

Edwards, A. (2010). *Being an Expert Professional Practitioner: The relational turn in expertise*. Dordrecht: Springer. doi:10.1007/978-90-481-3969-9

El Economista. (2019, Feb 4). *Científicos del IPN eliminan 100% del virus del papiloma humano*. Retrieved from https://www.eleconomista.com.mx/arteseideas/Cientificos-del-IPN-eliminan-100-del-virus-del-papiloma-humano-20190204-0058.html

eThekwini Municipality. (2010). *Innovations in Local Sustainability: good Practice from eThekwini*. Durban: eThekwini Municipality Corporate Policy Unit.

Etzkowitz, H. (2003). Research groups as 'quasi-firms': The invention of the entrepreneurial university. *Research Policy*, *32*(1), 109–121. doi:10.1016/S0048-7333(02)00009-4

Euroforum. (1998). *Measurement of Intellectual Capital. Intelect Model*. Euroforum.

European Comission. (2003). *The role of the Universities in the Europe of Knowledge.* Brussels: COM. Retrieved from http://www.ecm.ub.edu/ceuropea/ComUniversidadesES1.pdf

European Commission. (2004). *Key competences for lifelong learning. A European frame of reference.* Implementation of the Education and Training work program 2010. Work group B. Key competences. European Commission. General Directorate of Education and Culture. Retrieved from http://www.educastur.princast.es/info/calidad/indicadores/doc/comision_europea

European Commitee of the Regions. (2018). *The Lisbon Strategy in short.* Retrieved from Europe Monitor 2020 Platform: https://portal.cor.europa.eu/europe2020/Profiles/Pages/TheLisbonStrategyinshort.aspx

European University Association. (2003). *Response to the Communication From the Commission, The Role of the Universities in the Europe of Knowledge.* European University Association.

European University Association. (2003). *Response to the communication from the commission. The Role of the Universities in the Europe of Knowledge.* European University Association.

Everatt, D. (2016). *What must fall: Fees or the South African state?* Retrieved from https://www.enca.com/opinion/whatmust-fall-fees-or-the-south-african-state

Fanon, F. (1952). *Black Skin, White Masks.* London: Pluto Press.

Fanon, F. (1964). *Toward the African Revolution: Political Essays.* New York: Grove Press.

Farias, G. (2010). Espacios de aprendizaje en educación superior: de la profesionalización a la innovación para la transformación social. *Opening*, *2*(2). Retrieved from http://www.udgvirtual.udg.mx/apertura/num13/Articulos/tema2.php

Fengu, M. (2017, January 15). Protest loom over Bursary Funds. City Press, p. 9.

Fernández, E., Montes, J., & Vázquez, C. (1997). The theory of competitive advantage based on resources: synthesis and conceptual structure. *European Journal of Management and Business Administration*, *6*(3), 11-32.

Ferreira, G. (2008). Collective Bargaining and the public sector. *Journal of Public Administration, 43*(2), 191-202.

FitGerald, P., & Seale, O. (2016). Between a Rock and a Hard Place: University Management and the #FEESMUSTFALL Campaign. In Fees-Must-Fall: Student Revolt, Decolonization and Governance in South Africa (pp. 235-255). Johannesburg: Wits University Press.

Fontalvo, T., Quejada, R., & Puello, J. (2011). La gestión del conocimiento y los procesos de mejoramiento. *Dimensión empresarial, 9*(1), 80-87.

Freire, P. (1972). *Pedagogy of the Oppressed.* London: Penguin Books.

Freire, P. (1972). *Pedagogy of the oppressed.* Punguin Books.

Freire, P. (1993). *The Pedagogy of the oppressed.* London: Penguin.

Gibbert, M., Leibold, M., & Voelpe, S. (2001). Rejuvenating corporate intellectual capital by coopting customer competence. *Journal of Intellectual Capital, 2*(2), 109–126. doi:10.1108/14691930110385900

Giddens, A., & Sutton, P. W. (2013). Sociology (7th ed.). Malden, MA: Policy Press.

Gilardi, F., & Radaelli, C. M. (2012). Governance and Learning. In D. Levi-Faur (Ed.), *Oxford Handbook of Governance* (pp. 155–168). Oxford, UK: Oxford University Press.

Godlimpi, Z. (2018). The rise and fall of higher education cost: How 'free' of government's free education policy? In We are No longer at Ease: The Struggle for #FeesMustFall (pp. 182-194). Sunnyside: Jakana Media Ltd.

Godsell & Chikane. (2016). The Roots of the Revolution. In S. Booysen (Ed.), *FeesMustFall: Student Revolt, Decolonization and Governance in South Africa* (pp. 54–73). Johannesburg: Wits University Press.

Gon, S. (2016). Fees can Fall, But First…. Johannesburg: South African Institute of Race Relations (IRR).

González, F., Tamayo, A., & Vargas, E. (2019). Aportaciones para un estado de la cuestión sobre pertinencia en la formación profesional turística. *Iberoamerican Journal of Higher Education, 10*(27), 195–215. doi:10.22201/iisue.20072872e.2019.27

Graham, B. M. (2017). *L'Éducation et la quatriéme révolution industrielle.* Paris: Prépare pour Groupe Média TFO.

Granada, U. d. (2018). *Conecta 13. CANVAS para el Diseño del Entorno de Aprendizaje de una Organización.* Obtenido de Tomado de: http://conecta13.com/canvas/

Grange, L. (2007). Integrated Western and Indigenous Knowledge Systems: The basics for effective science Education in South Africa. *International Review of Education, 53*(5-6), 577–591. doi:10.100711159-007-9056-x

Graue, A. (2009). *Fundamentos de Economía*. Pearson.

Guattari, F. (2005). *The three Ecologies*. London: Continuum.

Gumede, M. (2017, March 26). Curro' tertiary plan just for job. *The Sunday Times*, p. 4.

Guzmán, R., & Adriano, A. (2013). Conocimiento, economía, desarrollo y sociedad: trazos desde la complejidad. *In-keys of Thought, 7*(14), 123-143. Retrieved from http://www.scielo.org.mx/scielo.php?script=sci_arttext&pid=S1870-879X2013000200006&lng=es&tlng=es

Habib, A. (2019). *Rebels and Rage: Reflecting on #FeesMustFall*. Johannesburg: Jonathan Balls Publisher.

Habib, A. (2019, March 18). Free higher education a vehicle for class mobility. *The Star*, p. 8.

Haghshenas, H., & Barzegar, G. (2014). *Intellectual Capital and Knowledge Assets for Value Creation M.A.* Islamic Azad University, South-Tehran Branch. Faculty Member at University of Mazandaran. Retrieved from http://zolcat.com/press/journal/sn/vol3/no1/sn.3.1.5.pdf

Hallowes, D., & Munnik, V. (2006). *Poisoned Spaces: Manufacturing wealth, producing poverty*. Pietermaritzburg: Groundwork.

Halvorsen, T., Ibsen, H., Evans, H. C., & Penderis, S. (2017). Introduction. In Knowledge for justice: Critical perspectives from Southern African-Nordic research partnerships. Somerset West: African Minds.

Halvorsen, T. (2017). The Sustainable Development Goals, knowledge production and the global struggle over values. In T. Halvorsen, H. Ibsen, H. Evans, & S. Penderis (Eds.), *Knowledge for justice: Critical perspectives rom southern African-Nordic research partnerships*. African Minds.

Handleman, H. (1996). *The Challenge ofThird World Development*. Simon & Schuster.

Harvey, M. G., & Lusch, R. F. (1999). Balancing the intellectual capital books: Intangible liabilities. *European Management Journal, 17*(1), 85–92. doi:10.1016/S0263-2373(98)00065-6

Heinz, K. (2004). Intellectual capital reporting for universities: Conceptual background and application for Austrian universities. *Research Evaluation, 3*(2), 129–140. doi:10.3152/147154404781776464

Henao, E., López, M., & Garcés, R. (2014). Medición de capacidades en investigación e innovación en instituciones de educación superior: Una mirada desde el enfoque de las capacidades dinámicas. *Framework, 10*(1), 252–271.

Hicks, J., & Buccus, I. (2016). Public participation in South Africa: Strengthening state accountability in a dominant party system. In State, governance and development in Africa (pp. 100-122). Claremont: UCT Press.

Higgins, J. (2013). *Academic Freedom in a Democratic South Africa: Essays and Interviews on higher Education and the Humanities*. Johannesburg: Wits University Press.

Higgs, P. (2002). Indigenous knowledge as a System of African knowledge: An Educational Perspective. *Indilinga: African Journal of Indigenous knowledge, 1*(1), 27-36.

Higgs, P. (2008). Towards an Indigenous African Educational Discourse: A Philosophical Reflection. *International Review of Education, 44*(3,4), 455-458.

Higgs, P. (2003). African philosophy and transformation of educational discourse in South Africa. *Journal of Education, 30*, 5–22.

Higgs, P., & Smith, J. (2015). *Philosophy of Education Today: An Introduction*. Cape Town: Juta and Company Ltd.

Honwana, A. (2013). *The Time of Youth: Work, Social Change and Politics in Africa*. Boulder, CO: Kumarian Press.

Hoppers, C. O. (2001). Indigenous knowledge and academic institutions in South Africa. *Perspectives in Education, 19*(1), 73–85.

Hudson, M. (1999). *Managing without profit: Art of Managing Third-Sector Organisations*. London: Penguin Books.

Hull, G. (2015). *Free university education is not the route to social justice*. Retrieved from http://theconversation.com/free-university-education-is-not-the-route-to-social-justice-49755

Huws, U. (1995). *Social Europe follow-up to the white paper*. EC Publication.

Inmersys. (2018, Oct 13). *Inicio*. Retrieved from https://www.inmersys.com/

Instituto Politecnico Nacional. (2019, Feb 15). *Pone en marcha IPN primer laboratorio nacional del agua*. Retrieved from https://www.ipn.mx/CCS/comunicados/ver-comunicado.html?y=2019&n=18

INTELF. (2018). *MOOC Aprendizaje Basado en Proyectos*. Obtenido de http://docentesinnovadores.perueduca.pe/?get_group_doc=104/1498096235-aprendizaje-basado-en-proyectos.pdf

IPN. (2010). *Manual: Operatividad del proyecto aula*. IPN.

Ishengoma, J. M. (2013). Funding Higher Education in Tanzania: Modalities, Challenges, Prospects and a Proposal for New Funding Modalities. In D. Teferra (Ed.), *Funding Higher Education in Sub-Saharan Africa* (pp. 214–246). New York: Palgrave Macmillan. doi:10.1057/9781137345783_9

Jansen, J. (2003). Changes and continuities in South Africa's higher education system, 1994–2004. In L. Chisholm (Ed.), *Changing Class: Education and Social Change in Post-Apartheid*. Cape Town: HSRC Press.

Jeffery, A. (2010). *Chasing the rainbow: South Africa's Move from Mandela to Zuma*. Johannesburg: South African Institute of Race Relations.

Jeffery, A. (2010). *Chasing the Rainbow: South Africa's Move from Mandela to Zuma*. Johannesburg: South African Institute of Race Relations.

Johnson, K., & Jacobs, S. (2012). Encyclopedia of South Africa. Scottsville: University of KwaZuku-Natal.

Johnson, P. (2013). The passive revolution and the post-apartheid university-Black Skin, White Masks. In Beyond the Apartheid University: Critical voices on Transformation in the university sector (pp. 55-68). University of Fort Hare Press.

Johnson, S. (2010). *TED: ¿De dónde vienen las buenas ideas?* [Vídeo] Retrieved from http://www. ted.com/talks/steven_johnson_where_good_ideas_come_from

Johnson, K., & Jacobs, S. (Eds.). (2012). *Encyclopedia of South Africa. Scottsville.* University of KwaZulu-Natal Press.

Johnson, K., & Jacobs, S. (Eds.). (2012). *Encyclopedia of South Africa. Scottville.* University of KwaZulu-Natal Press.

Johnston, P. Y Nolan, J. (2000). eWork 2000. *Status report on new ways to work in the information society*. Comisión Europea, Dirección General de la Sociedad de la Información.

JuluMed. (2018, Oct 13). *Inicio*. Retrieved from http://julumed.com/nuestrocasco

Kaplan, R. S. Y., & Norton, D. P. (1992). The balanced scorecard - measures that drive performance. *Harvard Business Review*, 71–79. PMID:10119714

Kaplan, R. S. Y., & Norton, D. P. (1993). Putting the balance scorecard to work. *Harvard Business Review*, 135–147.

Kgosiemang, M. L. (2018). University transformation re-imagined: Discourses resulting after the Fallist movement. In We are No longer at Ease: The Struggle for #FeesMustFall (pp. 167-174). Sunnyside: Jakana Media Ltd.

Khor, M., & Lin, L. L. (2001). *Good Practices & Innovative Experiences in the South: Social Policies, Indigenous Knowledge and Appropriate Technology*. London: Zed Books.

Kimble, C., & Li, F. (2010). Effective virtual Working through Community of Practice. In S. Dasgupta (Ed.), *Encyclopedia of Virtual Communities and Technologies*. IGI Publishing.

Kinti, I., & Hayward, G. (2015). Developing skills for Collaborative, Relational Research in Higher education: A Cultural Historical Analysis. In Pedagogy in Higher Education: A Cultural Historical Approach (pp. 181-197). Cambridge, UK: Cambridge University Press.

Kolb, D. (1994). *Experiential learning: Experiences as the sources of learning and development*. Englewood Cliffs, NJ: Prentice Hall.

Kondlo, K. (2017). The context of South African government and politics. In C. Landsberg & S. Graham (Eds.), *Government and Politics in South Africa: Coming of Age* (5th ed.). Hatfield: Van Schaick Publishers.

Kpmg Peat Marwick. (1999). The incorporation of intellectual capital as a key element of a company's market value. In *Seminar on knowledge management ´99*. Recoletos.

Kretzmann, J. P., & McKnight, J. L. (1993). *Building Communities from the Inside Out: A Path toward finding and Mobilising a community's asset*. Chicago: ACTA Publications.

Kuznetsov, Y., & Dahlman, C. (2008). *Mexico's transition to a knowledge-based economy. Challenges and opportunities*. Washington, DC: The International Bank for Reconstruction and Development / The World Bank.

Langa, P., Wangenge-Ouma, G., Jungblut, J., & Cloete, N. (2016). *South Africa and the illusion of free higher education*. Retrieved from http://www.universityworldnews.com/article.php?story=20160223145336908

Latour, B. (1988). *The pasteurization of France* (A. Sheridan & J. Law, Trans.). Cambridge, MA: Harvard University Press.

Laurenti, T. (2008). Modelling Exogenous Variables in Human Capital Formation throught a Heteroscedastic Stochastic Frontier. *International Atlantic Economic Society*, *14*, 76–89.

Lave, J., & Wenger, E. (1991). *Situated Learning: Legitimate Peripheral Participation*. Cambridge, UK: Cambridge University Press. doi:10.1017/CBO9780511815355

Leal, F. W., Úbelis, A., & Berzina, D. (2015). *Sustainable development, knowledge society and smart future manufacturing technologies*. Springer.

Lebakeng, T. J. (2016). Reversing Epistemicide and the quest for relevant Social Sciences and Humanities. In Decolonizing the University, Knowledge systems and Disciplines in Africa (pp. 47-63). Carolina Academic Press, LLC.

Ledwith, M., & Springett, J. (2010). *Participatory practice: Community-based action for transformative change. Bristol BS8 1QU*. The Policy Press.

Ledwith, M., & Springett, J. (2010). *Participatory practice: Community-based action for transformative change*. The Policy Press.

Leitner, K., Bornemann, M., & Schneider, U. (2002). *Development and Implementation of an Intellectual Capital Report for a Research Technology Organisation*. Paper presented at the World Congress on Intellectual Capital Readings. 10.1016/B978-0-7506-7475-1.50018-X

Lev, B. (2001). *Intangibles. Management, measurement and reporting*. Washington, DC: Brookings Institution.

Lev, B., & Zambon, S. (2003). Intangibles and intellectual capital: An introduction to a special issue. *European Accounting Review*, *12*(4), 597–603. doi:10.1080/0963818032000162849

Lindsey, G., Ottensmann, J., Palmer, J., Wilson, J., & Tutterrow, J. (2005). Encouraging Smart Growth in a Skeptical state: University-Stakeholder Collaboration in Central Indiana. In W. Wiewel & G. J. Knaap (Eds.), *Partnerships for Smart Growth: University-Community Collaboration for Better Public Places* (pp. 95–114). London: Routledge.

London, T. (2017, January 15). Education inherently evolves. Saturday Star, p. 9.

López, C., & Leal, D. (2002). Cómo aprender en la sociedad del conocimiento. Barcelona. *Gestion.*

Lovece, S. (2009). *E-Learning e società della conoscenza*. Bologna: Università di Bologna.

Luyat, Y. G. (2003). The Development of Higher Education in Africa: A Historical Survey. In D. Teferra & P. G. Altbach (Eds.), *African Higher Education: An International Reference Handbook* (pp. 15–43). Bloomington, IN: Indiana University Press.

Maake, N. (2011). *Barbarism in Higher Education: Once Upon a time in a University*. Johannesburg: Ekaam Books CC.

Maake, N. (2011). *Barbarism in Higher Education: Once Upon a Time in a University*. Johannesburg: Ekaam Books CC.

Madrigal, T.B. (2009). Capital humano e intelectual: su evaluación. *Revista Observatorio Laboral, 2*(3).

Maisel, L. (1992). Performance measurement. The balanced scorecard approach. *Journal of Cost Management*, *6*(2), 47–52.

Majó, J. (2005). Skills or professional skills that new degrees must provide to the Tourism System in Harmonization of Tourism studies in the European Higher Education Area. In *XL National and International Congress of Tourism Schools*. European University Miguel de Cervantes.

Majozi, P. (2016). *Quality education isn't free. Expect a fallout, either way*. Retrieved from http://www.biznews.com/thought-leaders/2016/09/28/phumlani-majozi-quality-education-isnt-free-expect-a-fallout-eitherway

Makgoba, M. W., & Chetty, C. (2010). The History and context of Higher Education in South Africa post-1994. In The Creation of the University of KwaZulu-Natal: Reflections on a Merger and Transformation Experience (pp. 1-23). Excel Books.

Malhotra, Y. (2000). Knowledge assets in the global economy: Assessment of national intellectual capital. *Journal of Global Information Management*, *8*(3), 5–15. doi:10.4018/jgim.2000070101

Mamdani, M. (1989). *Social movements and constitutionalism in the African context*. Centre for Basic Research Working Paper 2, Centre for Basic Research.

Maneta, R. (2018). 2015, the year of the student: A personal account. In We Are No Longer at Ease: The Struggle for #FeesMustFall (pp. 125-127). Sunnyside: Jakana Media Ltd.

Manik, S. (2017). What Is Being done? 'Ubuntu' in Student Support Programs in Public Higher Education Institutions in South Africa. In M. Shaw & G. Whiteford (Eds.), *Bridges, Pathways and Transitions: International Innovations in Widening Participation*. Chippenham: Elsevier Ltd. doi:10.1016/B978-0-08-101921-4.00012-9

Manson, C., & Ross, B. (2013). *Entrepreneurial Ecosystems and Growth Oriented Entrepreneurship*. The Hague: OECD LEED Programme and the Dutch Ministry of Economic Affairs.

Marginson, S. (2013). La Educación Superior como autoformación: El caso de estudiantes transfronterizos. *High School Journal*, *43*(169), 7–24. Retrieved from http://www.scielo.org.mx/pdf/resu/v43n169/v43n169a2.pdf

Marginson, S., & Marjijk, W. (2007). *Globalization and Higher Education*. Paris: Organisation for Economic Co-operation and Development.

Margison, S. (2006). Putting "public" back into the public universities. *Thesis Eleven, 84*.

Margison, S., & Considine, M. (2011). *The Enterprise University: Power, Governance and Reinvention in Australia*. Cambridge, UK: Cambridge University Press.

Marquart, M. J. (2011). *Building the Learning Organisation: Achieving Strategic Advantage through a Commitment to Learning* (3rd ed.). Boston, MA: Nicholas Brealey Publishing.

Martínez, P., & Echeverría, B. (2009). Formación basada en competencias. *Educational Research Journal*, *27*(1), 125–147. doi:10.6018/rie.27.1.94331

Marwala, T. (2018, June 24). Will AI affect our standard of living. The Sunday Independent, p. 15.

Marwala, T. (2018, March 25). The fourth industrial revolution. *The Sunday Independent*, p. 17.

Maseremule, M. H. (2016b, November 3). Free higher education fails to test. The Mercury, p. 9.

Maseremule, M. H. (2016a, November 4). Narrative of free higher education has been twisted. *The New Age*, p. 19.

Maslow, A. H. (1943). A Theory of Human Motivation. *Psychological Review*, *50*(4), 370–396. doi:10.1037/h0054346

Mas-Torelló, O. y. (2019). El Profesor universitario en el espacio europeo de educación superior: La autopercepción de sus competencias docentes actuales y orientaciones para su formación pedagógica. *Revista Mexicana de Investigación Educativa*, 437–470.

Matolino, B. (2017). Return the Source? Challenges and Prospects. In P. Ngulube (Ed.), *Handbook of Research on Social, Cultural and Educational Considerations of Indigenous Knowledge in Developing Countries* (pp. 36–58). Hershey, PA: IGI Global. doi:10.4018/978-1-5225-0838-0.ch001

Maurrasse, D. J. (2001). *Beyond the campus: How Colleges and Universities form Partnerships with their Communities*. New York: Routledge.

Max-Neef, M. A. (1991). *Human Scale Development: conception, application and further flections*. New York: Apex.

Maxwele, C. (2017, March 26). Campaign for a free education. *The Sunday Independent*, p. 17.

Mazibuko, F., Chetty, D., & Mneney, E. (2010). Establishing a New Institutional Identity. In The Creation of the University of KwaZulu-Natal: Reflections on a Merger and Transformation Experience (pp. 73-93). New Delhi: Excel Books.

Mbeki, T. (2004). Meeting the Challenge for the Second Economy. *New Agenda: South African Journal of Social and Economic Policy, 14*.

Mbigi, L., & Maree, J. (2005). *Ubuntu: The Spirit of African Transformation Management*. Randburg: Knowres Publishing.

McClelland, D. C. (1973). Testing for Competencies rather than intelligence. *The American Psychologist*, *28*(1), 1–14. doi:10.1037/h0034092 PMID:4684069

Medi-Print. (2018, Oct 13). *Inicio*. Retrieved from https://mediprint3d.com.mx/

Mercado, P., Gil, P., & Cernas, D. (2016). Validez inicial de una escala de medición del capital intelectual en universidades. *Universitas Psychologica*, *15*(2), 109–120. doi:10.11144/Javeriana.upsy15-2.viem

Meyer, K. (2002). *Quality in diistance education. Focus on On-line learning.* Hoboken, NJ: Academic Press.

Midgley, J. (1986). Community participation: History, concepts and controversies. In J. Migley (Ed.), *Community participation, social development and the state*. London: Methuen.

Minkler, M., & Wallenstein, N. (2003). Introduction to community based participatory research. In M. Minkler, N. Wallenstein, & B. Hall (Eds.), *Community-based Participatory Research for Health* (pp. 3–26). San Francisco, CA: Jossey-Bass Wiley.

Minogue, K. (2005). The concept of a university. Transaction.

Mji, G., Kalenga, R., Ned, L., Alpersteisn, M., & Banda, D. (2017). Indigenous Knowledge Exclusion in Education Systems of Africans: Impact of Beingness and Becoming an African. In P. Ngulube (Ed.), *Handbook of Research on Social, Cultural and Educational Considerations of Indigenous Knowledge in Developing Countries* (pp. 36–58). Hershey, PA: IGI Global. doi:10.4018/978-1-5225-0838-0.ch003

Mlatsheni, C. (2012). The Challenges Unemployment imposes on Youth. In H. Perold, C. Cloete, & J. Papier (Eds.), *Shaping the future of South Africa's Youth: Rethinking post-school education and skills training* (pp. 31–41). Somerset West: African Minds.

Modupe, T. (2018). What does a revolutionary look like? In We Are No Longer at Ease: The Struggle for #FeesMustFall (pp. 121-124). Sunnyside: Jakana Media Ltd.

Moerane, B. (2015). *SA far from free tertiary education: Economist*. Retrieved from http://www.sabc.co.za/news/a/76b40b004b239e5bbb38fb445cadceaa/SA-far-from-free-tertiary-education:-Economist20153112

Molina, P., Arango, M. & Botero, S. (2010). Análisis del valor agregado del conocimiento. Caso aplicado en una Institución de Educación Superior. *Journal Faculty of Economic Sciences: Research and Reflection*, *18*(2), 95 – 105.

Moloi, K. C. (2009). *The School as a Learning Organisation: Reconceptualising school practice in South Africa* (2nd ed.). Pretoria: Van Schaik Publishers.

Mooney, L. A., & Edwards, B. (2001). Experiential learning in sociology: Service learning and other community-based learning initiatives. *Teaching Sociology*, *29*(2), 181–194. doi:10.2307/1318716

Morrow, S. (2008). Race, Redress and Historically Black Universities. In A. Habib & K. Bentley (Eds.), *Racial Redress & Citizenship in South Africa* (pp. 263–288). Cape Town: HSRC Press.

Mosoetsa, S. (2018, November 9). Transformation taking place in the higher education system. Mail & Guardian, 36.

Mpofu-Walsh, S. (2017). *Democracy & Delusion: 10 Myths in South Africa Politics*. Cape Town: Tafelberg.

Mpofu-Walsh, S. (2017). *Democracy & Delusion: 10 Myths in South African Politics*. Cape Town: NB Publishers.

Msila, V. (2007). From Apartheid Education to the Revised National Curriculum Statement: Pedagogy for Identity Formation and Nation Building in South Africa. *Nordic Journal of African Studies*, *16*(2), 146–160.

Msila, V. (2017). Of African Philosophy and African Renaissance: Redeeming Education. In V. Msila (Ed.), *Decolonising knowledge for African's Renewal: Examining African Perspectives and Philosophies* (pp. 21–33). Randburg: KR Publishing.

Mubangizi, J., & Kaya, H. (2015). African Indigenous knowledge systems and Human rights: Implications for Higher Education, Based on the South African experience. *International Journal of African Renaissance Studies*, *10*(2), 125–142. doi:10.1080/18186874.2015.1107985

Mupepi, M. G. (2017). Developing Democratic Paradigms to Effectively Manage Business, government and Civil Society. In Handbook of Research on Sub-National Governance and Development (pp. 432-462). Hershey, PA: IGI Global. doi:10.4018/978-1-5225-1645-3.ch020

Musau, Z. (2017, March 28). Universities fund entrepreneurial graduates. The Mercury, p. 16.

Mzileni, P. (2018, September 21). Sasco must introspect to succeed. Mail & Guardian, 34.

Nakata, M. (2002). Indigenous Knowledge and the Cultural Interface: Underlying issues at the intersection of knowledge and information systems. *OFLA Journal, 28*(5/6), 281–291.

Nakpodia, E. D. (2009). Implications and Challenges of Nigerian Universities as Learning Organisations. *Academic Leadership Journal, 7*(3), 1–8.

National Development Plan (NDP). (2011). *National Development Plan; Vision for 2030*. Pretoria: National Planning Commission.

Nava, R., Mercado, P., & Demuner, M. (2012). Indicadores de capital intelectual para instituciones públicas de educación superior. In El capital intelectual en las organizaciones: una agenda de investigación. Universidad Autónoma del Estado de México.

Nava, R., & Mercado, P. (2010). Evaluación de la calidad métrica para indicadores de capital intelectual generados a partir de bases estadísticas. *The Journal of Higher Education, 39*(155).

Ndlovu-Gathseni, S. J. (2013). *Empire, Global Coloniality and African Subjectivity*. New York, Oxford, UK: Berghahn Books.

Ndlovu-Gathseni, S. J. (2017). Foreword: The Case for a Decolonised/Africanised Africa. In V. Msila (Ed.), *Decolonising Knowledge for Africa's Renewal: Examining African Perspectives and Philosophies* (pp. x–xv). Randburg: KR Publishing.

Ndlovu-Gatsheni, S. (2013). Decolonising the university in Africa. *Think, 51*, 46–51.

Ndlovu-Gatsheni, S. J. (2016). The Imperative of decolonised the Modern Westernised University. In S. J. Ndlovu-Gatsheni & S. Zondi (Eds.), *Decolonizing the University, Knowledge Systems and Disciplines in Africa*. Durham, NC: Carolina Academic Press.

Ndlovu-Gatsheni, S. J. (2017). The Imperative of Decolonizing the Modern Westernised University. In S. J. Ndlovu-Gatsheni & S. Zondi (Eds.), *Decolonising the university, Knowledge systems and disciplines in Africa* (pp. 27–45). Durham, NC: Carolina Academic Press.

Nengwekhulu, R. H. (2009). Public service delivery challenges facing South African public service. *Journal of Public Administration., 44*(20), 341–363.

Nevado, D., & López, V. (2002b). A model and accounting report for the measurement of capital intellectual development and applications. Journal of Accounting and Taxation, 229, 161-206.

Nevado, D., & López, V. (2002a). *Intellectual capital: evaluation and measurement*. Madrid: Prentice Hall.

Ngcaweni, W & Ngcaweni, B. (2018). *We are No longer at Ease: The Struggle for #FeesMustFall*. Sunnyside: Jakana Media Ltd.

Ngcobo, Z., Manyathela, C., & Bateman, B. (2016). *FeesMustFall protests turn violent, bus set alight in Jhb CBD*. Retrieved from http://ewn.co.za/2016/10/10/Bus-set-alight-during-Wits-protests

Ngubane, S. (2017, June 2). Revolution or repression? Continent must choose. *Daily News*, p. 13.

Nichol, V. (2010). *Exploring Community Benefits in Community-Based Learning: A Study of International Community-Based Learning Initiatives in Wentworth, Durban* (Master's thesis). University of KwaZulu-Natal.

Nicolescu, B. (2005). *Towards Transdisciplinary Education and Learning*. Paper prepared for conference on Science and Religion: Global Perspectives. Philadelphia: Metanexus Institute.

Nicolson, G. (2015). Luister: The viral film exposing South Africa's ongoing racism problem. *TheGuardian*. Retrieved from https://www.theguardian.com/world 2015/Sep/07/luister-south-Africa-film-racism-Stellenbosch

Niven, P. (2003). The scorecard step by step. Management 2000, Barcelona, Spain.

Nkondo, M. (2017, April 23). Academic capitalism and state capture in higher education. The Sunday Independent, p. 19.

Nkuna, N. W., & Sebola, M. P. (2015). Developmental Local government and the State of Public Administration: Theoretical Discourse in South Africa. In M. P. Sebola (Ed.), *Local Government Administration Post-Apartheid South Africa: Some Critical Perspectives. Polokwane*. Batalea Publishers.

Nombembe, P. (2017, January 15). Blade's plan falls flat with #FeesMustFall. *Sunday Times*, p. 8.

Nonaka, I., & Takeuchi, H. (1995). *The Knowledge-Creating Company*. Oxford, UK: Oxford University Press.

Nonaka, I., & Takeuchi, H. (1995). *The knowledge-creating company: How Japanese Companies Create the Dynamics of Innovation*. New York: Oxford University Press.

North Western University. (2018). *Indigenous Knowledge Systems Centre Brochure: Reclaiming our Origin, Charting our Destiny*. Accessed from http://natural-sciences.nwu.ac.za/indigenous-knowledge-systems-centre/about-us

Noxon, J. (2011). *Higher Education and the Public good: Imagining the University*. London: Continuum.

Nshemererwe, C. (2016, November 4). Transforming from oppressed to truly liberated. *African Independent*, p. 9.

Ntsaluba, S. (2017, April 23). Rating downgrade has to be taken very, very seriously. *Sunday Times*, p. 15.

Nuñez, S. A. (2017). The developmente of critical thinking abilities in university students by means of problem-base learning. *Revista iberoamericana de educación media superior*, 84-103.

Nussbaum, M. C. (1998). *Cultivating humanity: A classical defence of reform in liberal education*. Cambridge, MA: Harvard University Press.

Nyamnjoh, F. (2016). *RhodesMustFall: Nibbling at Resilient Colonialism in South Africa*. Bamenda, Cameroon: Langaa Research and Publishing Common Initiative Group.

Nymnjoh, F. B. (2012). 'Potted plants in greenhouses': A critical reflection on the resilience of colonial education in Africa. *Journal of Asian and African Studies*.

OCDE. (2004). *Innovation in the Knowledge Economy: Implications for Education and Learning*. Paris: OCDE.

OCDE. (2007). *Insights Human Capital: How what you know shapes your life*. Paris: OCDE.

OCDE. (2015). *Start-up America Latina. Construyendo un futuro innovador*. París: OCDE.

Odoro-Hoppers, C. A. (2001). *Decolonising the curriculum, indigenous knowledge systems and globalisation*. Unpublished paper delivered at the Gauteng Institute for curriculum development.

OECD. (2009). *Education at a Glance 2009*. Paris: OECD. Retrieved from http://www.oecd.org/education/skills-beyond-school/43636332.pdf

OECD. (2013). *Panorama of education 2013 Indicators of the OECD*. Santillana.

OECD. (2015a). *Students, Computer y Learning: Making the conection PISA*. Obtenido de http://goo.gl3X8cam

OECD. (2015b). *Teaching with Tecnology. Teaching in Focus Report*. Obtenido de http://goo.gl/NgxYKy

OECD. (2018). *OECD Tourism Trends and Policies 2018*. OECD Publishing; doi:10.1787/tour-2018-

Olalde, M. (2017, January 14). Education funding riddle. *Saturday Star*, p. 9.

Olve, N., Roy, J., & Wetter, M. (2000). Implementing and managing the scorecard (Performance drivers). Management 2000, Barcelona, Spain.

OMT Themis Foundation. (n.d.). *UNWTO Certification System*. TedQual. Madrid: OMT. Retrieved from http://themis.unwto.org/en/content/sistema-de-certificacion-unwtotedqual

OMT. (1994). *Introduction to Tourism*. Retrieved from https://pub.unwto.org/WebRoot/Store/Shops/.../1128/9284402697.pdf

OMT. (2014). *Understanding tourism Basic Glossary*. Retrieved from http://media.unwto.org/en/content/entender-el-turismo-glosario-basico

OMT. (2017). *OMT panorama of international tourism. Edition 2017*. Madrid: World Tourism Organization. Retrieved from https://www.e-unwto.org/doi/pdf/10.18111/9789284419043

Ontoria, A., Gomez, J., & Molina, A. (2000). *Potenciar la Capacidad de Aprender y Pensar.* Madrid: Narcea, S.A. de Ediciones.

Ordóñez, P. (1999). *Strategic importance of the measurement of intellectual capital in organizations*. Magazine Injet.com.

Ordóñez, P. (2001). *Intellectual capital, human resource management system and knowledge management: influence on organizational outcomes* (Doctoral thesis). Oviedo University.

Ordóñez, P. (2002). Evidence of intellectual capital measurement from Asia, Europe and the Middle East. *Journal of Intellectual Capital*, *3*(3), 287–302. doi:10.1108/14691930210435624

Ordóñez, P. (2003). Intellectual capital reporting in Spain: A comparative review. *Journal of Intellectual Capital*, *4*(1), 61–81. doi:10.1108/14691930310455397

Organization for Economic Cooperation and Development (OECD). (1998). Human Capital Investment. An International Comparison. Paris: OECD.

Organization for Economic Cooperation and Development (OECD). (2011). *Skills for innovation and Research*. Retrieved from https://biobs.jrc.ec.europa.eu/sites/ default/ files/generated/files/policy/OECD%202011%20Skills%20for%20Innovation%20 and%20Research.pdf

Organization for Economic Cooperation and Development (OECD). (2012). Better Skills, Better Jobs, Better Lives: A Strategic Approach to Skills Policies. Paris: OECD. doi:10.1787/9789264177338-en

Paredes, R. (2016). Una estrategia de enseñanza de educación ambiental, en estudiantes de un liceo municipal de Cañete. *Revista electrónica educare*, 1-26.

Pasher, E. (1999). The Intellectual Capital of the State of Israel: A look to the Future – The Hidden Values of the Desert. Ed. Pasher&Co, Herzlia Pituach.

Pather, D. (2017, April 23). Why SA is a stressed society. *Sunday Tribune*, p. 18.

Pérez, G. (2000). Intellectual capital and knowledge innovation. *X National Congress of ACEDE: Economic integration, competitiveness and institutional environment of the company*.

Perrenoud, P. (2007). *Ten new competences to teach* (4th ed.). Barcelona: Graó.

Petrash, G. (2001). The intellectual assets management. In Monetize intellectual capital. Techniques to optimize the value of the Organization. Barcelona: Paidós Company.

Petrash, G. (1996). Dow's Journey to a knowledge value management culture. *European Management Journal*, *14*(4), 365–373. doi:10.1016/0263-2373(96)00023-0

Petty, R., & Guthrie, J. (2000). Intellectual capital literature review. Measurement, reporting and management. *Journal of Intellectual Capital*, *1*(2), 155–176. doi:10.1108/14691930010348731

Phungo, R. (2015). *University fees: Free higher education is possible in South Africa*. Retrieved from https://www.dailymaverick.co.za/article/2015-10-21-university-fees-free-higher-education-ispossible-in-south-africa/#.WRG5qOWGPcs

Picard, L. A. (2005). *The State of the State: Institutional Transformation Capacity and Political Change in South Africa*. Johannesburg: Wits University Press.

Pillay, P. (2016). Financing of Universities: Promoting Equity or Reinforcing Inequality. In S. Booysen (Ed.), *Fees Must Fall: Student Revolt, Decolonization and Governance in South Africa* (pp. 256–268). Johannesburg: Wits University Press. doi:10.18772/22016109858.17

Pimienta, P. J. (2012). *Estrategias de Enseñanza Aprendizaje docencia universitaria basada en competencias*. Pearson Educación.

Punie, Y. (2007). Learning Spaces: An ICT-enabled model of future learning in the Knowledge-based Society. *European Journal of Education, 42*(2), 187. doi:10.1111/j.1465-3435.2007.00302.x

RAE. (2018). *Spanish dictionary. Edition of the Tercentenary*. Madrid: Royal Spanish Academy. Retrieved from http://dle.rae.es/?id=A0fanvT|A0gTnnL

Ramírez, O. y. (2015). El aprendizaje basado en problemas y su utilidad en el desarrollo de las ciencias de la salud. *Revista de la Facultad de Medicina (Caracas), 63*(2), 325–330. doi:10.15446/revfacmed.v63n2.49171

Ramírez, Y., & Santos, J. (2013). Propuesta de un Informe de Capital Intelectual para las instituciones de educación superior españolas. *Applied Economics Studies, 31*(2), 525–554.

Ramose, M. B. (2005). *African Philosophy through Ubuntu*. Harare: Mond Books Publishers.

Ramphele, M. (2008). *Laying Ghosts to rest in South Africa: Dilemmas of the Transformation in South Africa*. Cape Town: Tafelberg.

Ramphele, M. (2008). *Laying Ghosts to Rest: Dilemmas of the Transformation in South Africa*. Cape Town: Tafelburg.

Ramphele, M. (2012). *Conservations with my Sons and Daughters. Parktown*. Penguin Books.

Ray, M. (2016). *Free Fall: Why South Africa Universities are in Race Against Time*. Johannesburg: Bookstorm.

Ray, M. (2016). *Free Fall; why South African Universities are in a Race Against Time*. Johannesburg: Bookstorm Ltd.

Real Academia Española. (2017). *Diccionario de la lengua española*. Madrid: RAE.

Red De Recursos Humanos. (2002). *Some clarification of concepts of fashion*. Author.

Republic of South Africa. (1997). *White Paper on Higher Education and Training*. Pretoria: Department of Education.

Ritkin, S., & Camphell, C. (2001). *Partners in Planning: Information, participation and empowerment*. London: TALC & Macmillan Education.

Rivas, G., & Sebastian, R. (2014). *Nuevas instituciones para la innovación: Prácticas y experiencias en América Latina. Santiago de Chile: CEPAL; Alis*. Cooperación Alemana.

Rivero, D. (2009). *Conceptual model for the measurement of intellectual capital and a procedure for its implementation. Hospitality Case* (PhD thesis). Matanzas, Cuba: University of Matanzas.

Robinsion, J. W., & Green, G. P. (2011). Developing communities. In Introduction to Community Development: theory, Practice and Service Learning. Los Angeles, CA: Sage.

Robinson, G., & Kleiner, B. (1996). How to measure an organization's intellectual capital. *Managerial Auditing Journal*, *11*(8), 36–39. doi:10.1108/02686909610131675

Rodney, W. (2009). *How European underdeveloped Africa*. Panaf Publishing.

Rodov, I., & Leliaert, P. (2002). FiMIAM: Financial method of intangible assets measurement. *Journal of Intellectual Capital*, *3*(3), 323–336. doi:10.1108/14691930210435642

Rodríguez, D., & Gairín, J. (2015). Innovación, aprendizaje organizativo y gestión del conocimiento en las instituciones educativas. *Education*, *24*(46), 73–90.

Roegiers, X. (2000). *The future of competitions*. Brussels: De Boeck.

Rogoff, B. (1995). Observing sociocultural activity on three planes: Participatory appropriation guided participation, and apprenticeship. In J. V. Wertsch, A. Alvarez, & P. De Rio (Eds.), *Sociocultural Studies of Mind* (pp. 139–164). New York: Cambridge University Press. doi:10.1017/CBO9781139174299.008

Romero, G. (2018). Calidad educativa: Engranaje entre la gestión del conocimiento, la gestión educativa, la innovación y los ambientes de aprendizaje. *Journal of Studies and Experiences in Education*, *17*(35), 91–103. Retrieved from http://www.rexe.cl/ojournal/index.php/rexe/article/view/597/472

Romo, A., Villalobos, M., & Guadalupe, L. (2012). Gestión del Conocimiento: Estrategia para la Formación de Investigadores. *Sinéctica*, 38.

Ronca, C. (2010). *Società della Conoscenza, sviluppo locale e competitività delle imprese. Modelli e metriche di valorizzazione degli intangibili di impresa*. Roma: Fondazione Adriano Olivetti.

Roos, J., Roos, G., Dragonetti, N., & Edvinsson, L. (2001). Intellectual capital. The intangible value of the company. Paidós Company.

Roos, G., Bainbridge, A., & Jacobsen, K. (2001). Intellectual capital as a strategic tool. *Strategy and Leadership*, *29*(4), 21–26. doi:10.1108/10878570110400116

Roos, G., & Roos, J. (1997). Measuring your company's intellectual performance. *Long Range Planning*, *30*(3), 413–426. doi:10.1016/S0024-6301(97)90260-0

Rothblatt, S. (2006). *The Modern University and its Discontents: the fate of Newman's legacies in Britain and America*. Cambridge, UK: Cambridge University Press.

Rowntree, K., & Fox, R. (2017). Contributing to the agenda for sustainable development through North-South educational partnerships: An analysis of two Linnaeus-Palme staff-student exchanges between Sweden and South Africa. In Knowledge for justice: Critical perspectives from southern African-Nordic research partnerships (pp. 131-146). Cape Town: African Minds.

Ruiz Ortega, F. (2007). Modelos didácticos para la enseñanza de las ciencias naturales. *Revista Latinoamericana de Estudios Educativos, 3*(2), 41-60.

SABC News. (2016). *Free education for all not feasible: Manana*. Retrieved from http://www.sabc.co.za/news/a/cd65af004c50f448a2cdbe8be7d9f0df/Free-education-for-all-not-feasible:-Manana20160407

Salinas, J. (2004). Cambios metodologicos con las TIC. *Estrategias didacticas y entornos virtuales de enseñanza-aprendizaje, 56*, 3-4.

Samsung NewsRoom Mexico. (2018). *Samsung y el IPN presentan la edición 2018 del concurso Soluciones para el Futuro*. Retrieved from https://news.samsung.com/mx/samsung-y-el-ipn-presentan-la-edicion-2018-del-concurso-soluciones-para-el-futuro

Sánchez, P., Elena, S., & Castrillo, R. (2006). The Intellectual Capital Report of Universities. Guidelines for disclosing IC information. Observatory of the European University: PRIME-OEU Methodological Guide, 223-251.

Sánchez, P., Chaminade, C., & Olea, M. (2000). Management of intangibles. An attempt to build a theory. *Journal of Intellectual Capital, 1*(4), 312–327. doi:10.1108/14691930010359225

Sánchez, P., Elena, S., & Castrillo, R. (2009). Intellectual capital dynamics in universities: A reporting model. *Journal of Intellectual Capital, 10*(2), 307–324. doi:10.1108/14691930910952687

Sarur, M. (2013). The importance of intellectual capital in organizations. *Administrative Sciences, 1*, 39–45.

Saurombe, A. (2017). Towards a Regional Policy and legal Instrument for the Protection of Indigenous knowledge Systems in Southern Africa. In P. Ngulube (Ed.), *Handbook of Research on Social, Cultural and Educational Considerations of Indigenous Knowledge in Developing Countries* (pp. 16-35). Hershey, PA: IGI Global.

Schenck, R., Nel, H., & Louw, H. (2010). *Introduction to participatory community practice*. Pretoria: Unisa Press.

Schoeman, M., & Graham, S. (2017). The political economy of south Africa in a global Context. In C. Landsberg & S. Graham (Eds.), *Government and Politics in South Africa: Coming of Age* (5th ed.). Hatfield: Van Schaick Publishers.

Schumpeter, J. A. (1964). *Business Cycles*. New York: McGraw Hill.

Scott, J. (2007). *Fifty Key Sociologists: The Contemporary Theorists*. London: Routledge.

Segalo, P. (2017). Decolonising Social Psychology in Africa. In Decolonising the university, Knowledge systems and disciplines in Africa (pp. 165-178). Durham, NC: Carolina Academic Press.

SEGOB. (2018). *El Conacyt*. Retrieved from Conacyt: https://www.conacyt.gob.mx/index.php/el-conacyt

Sehume, J. (2018). Solving poverty, unemployment and inequality. *The Sunday Independent, 24*(June), 15.

Selapisa, L. (2017). Free education must have 5 components. *The NewAge, 23*(March), 2.

Selapisa, L., Tshikalange, S., & Mahlo, A. (2017). Students turn NSFAS book cards into 'spaza vouchers. *The New Age*, *22*(May), 1.

Sen, A. (1999). *Development as freedom*. New York: Albert Knopf.

Senge, P. M. (1990). *Fifth Discipline: The Art & Practice of Learning Organisation*. Croydon: CPI Group.

Senge, P. M. (2006). *The Fifth Discipline: The Art & Practice of the Learning Organisation*. London: Random House Business Books.

SEP. (2010). *Programa de Formación de Recursos Humanos Basado en Competencias*. Cd.de México: SEP.

SEP. (2011). *Generic competences that express the profile of the graduate of upper secondary education*. Retrieved from https://www.uv.mx/dgdaie/files/2013/09/COMPETENCIAS-GENERICAS-QUE-EXPRESAN-EL-PERFIL-DEL-EGRESADO.pdf

Seroto, J. (2018). Dynamics of Decoloniality in South Africa: A Critique of the History of Swiss Mission Education for Indigenous People. *Studia Historiae Ecclesiastacae*, *44*(3), 1–14.

Shava, S., & Nkopodi, N. (2017). Indigenous the University Curriculum in Sothern Africa. In P. Ngulube (Ed.), *Handbook of Research on Social, Cultural and Educational Considerations of Indigenous Knowledge in Developing Countries* (pp. 80–91). Hershey, PA: IDGI Global. doi:10.4018/978-1-5225-0838-0.ch005

Silva, J., Barahona, P., & Galleguillos, C. (2014). Valoración prospectiva del capital intelectual de la Universidad de Atacama, mediante la técnica Delphi. *Ingeniare. Chilean Journal of Engineering*, *22*(4), 567–574. Retrieved from https://scielo.conicyt.cl/pdf/ingeniare/v22n4/art12.pdf

Simanowitx, A., & Knotts, K. (2015). *The Business of Doing Good: Insights from one social enterprise's journey to delivery on good intentions*. Practical Action Publishing Ltd. doi:10.3362/9781780448640

Skandia. (1996). *Supplement to the Annual Report, Customer Value*. Stockholm: Author.

Skilton, M., & Hovsepian, F. (2018). *The Forth Industrial Revolution. Responding to the impact of Artificial Intelligence on Business*. Palgrave Macmillan.

Skovdal, M., & Cornish, F. (2015). *Qualitative Research for Development: A Guide for Practitioners*. Practical Action Publishing. doi:10.3362/9781780448534

Smolentseva, A. (2015). *Will there be free higher education in Russia?* Retrieved from https://ejournals.bc.edu/ojs/index.php/ihe/article/viewFile/7485/6680

Soedien, C. (2016). Leading in the South African Higher Education. In Leadership: Perspectives from the Front Line (pp. 205-219). Ransburg: KR Publishing.

Spreen, C. A., & Vally, S. (2006). Education rights, education policies and equality in South Africa. *International Journal of Educational Development*, *26*(4), 352–362. doi:10.1016/j.ijedudev.2005.09.004

Stam, E., & Spigen, B. (2016). *Entrepreneurial Ecosystems*. Utrecht: Utrecht School of Economics.

Staniland, M. (1985). *What is political economy: A study of social theory & underdevelopment*. New Haven, CT: Yale University Press.

Stewart, T. (1991). Brainpower: how intellectual capital becoming America's most valuable asset. Fortune, 2, 44-60.

Stewart, P. (2007). Re-envisioning the academic profession in the shadow of corporate managerialism. *The Journal of Higher Education*, *5*(1), 141.

Stewart, T. (1998). *The new wealth of organizations: intellectual capital*. Barcelona: Granica.

Stoecker, R. (2016). *Liberating Service Learning and the Rest of Higher Education Civic Engagement*. Philadelphia: Temple University Press.

Stoeker, R. (2009), Unheard Voices: Community Organisations and Service Learning. In The Unheard Voices: Community Organisations and Service Learning (pp. 10-37). Philadelphia: Temple University Press.

Stone, D. (2012). Agents of Knowledge. In D. Levi-Faur (Ed.), Oxford Handbook of Governance (pp. 339-351). Oxford, UK: Oxford University Press. doi:10.1093/oxfordhb/9780199560530.013.0024

Stone, D. (2012). Agents of Knowledge. In D. Levi-Faur (Ed.), *The Oxford Handbook of Governance* (pp. 338–352). Oxford, UK: Oxford University Press.

Sullivan, P. (1999). Profiting from intellectual capital. *Journal of Knowledge Management, 3*(2), 132–142. doi:10.1108/13673279910275585

Sullivan, P. (2001). *Value-Driven Intellectual Capital – How To Convert Intangible Corporate Assets into Market Value*. New York: Wiley.

Sullivan, P. (2001a). Introduction to the management of intellectual capital. In P. H. Sullivan (Ed.), *Monetize intellectual capital. Techniques to optimize the value of the Organization. Paidós Company.*

Sullivan, P. (2001b). Definitions and basic concepts. In P. H. Sullivan (Ed.), *Monetize intellectual capital. Techniques to optimize the value of the Organization. Paidós company.*

Sunkel, G. (2006). Las tecnologias de la información y comunicación (TIC) en la educación en America Látina. Una exploracion de indicadores (Serie de Politicas Sociales ed.). Santiago de Chile: CEPAL UNESCO.

Sveiby, K. (1998). *Measuring intangibles and intellectual capital - An emerging first standard*. Documento obtenido en Internet: http://www.sveiby.com/articles/EmergingStandard.html

Sveiby, K. (2000). The new wealth of the companies. Management 2000, Barcelona, Spain.

Sveiby, K. (2001b). *The intangible Assets Monitor*. Academic Press.

Sveiby, K. (1989). *The invisible balance sheet*. Stockholm: Affersvaerlden/Ledarskap.

Teferra, D. (2013). Introduction. In D. Teferra (Ed.), Funding Higher Education in Sub-Saharan African (pp. 1-12). London: Palgrave Macmillan.

Teferra, D. (2016). *Why free education is a folly in an unequal society*. Retrieved from http://theconversation.com/whyfree-education-is-a-folly-in-an-unequal-society-54515

Teferra, D., & Altbach, P. G. (2003). Trends and perspectives in African Higher education. In African higher Education: An International Reference Handbook (pp. 3-14). Bloomington, IN: Indiana University Press.

Teferra, D., & Altbach, P. G. (2003). Trends and Perspectives in African Higher Education. In D. Teferra & P. Altbach (Eds.), *African Higher Education: An International Reference Handbook* (p. 314). Bloomington, IN: Indiana University Press.

Tererra, D., & Altbach, P. G. (2003). Trends and Perspectives in African Higher Education. In African Higher Education: An International Reference Handbook (pp. 3-14). Bloomington, IN: Indiana University Press.

Terreblanche, S. (2012). *Lost in Transformation: South Africa's Search for a New Future since 1986*. Johannesburg: KMM Review Publishing Company.

Thiongo, N. (2005). *Decolonising the Mind: The Politics of Language in African Literature*. Nairobi: East African Educational Publishers.

Torres Gastelun, C., & Moreno Coatzozón, G. (2013). Inclusión de las TIC en los escenarios de aprendizaje universitario. *Apertura, 5,* 48-65.

Trillo, M., & Fernández, M. (2013). Caracterización de la innovación en Spin-Off de base tecnológica. *Industrial Economy*, *388*, 67–78.

Tseng, C., & James Goo, Y. (2005). Intellectual capital and corporate value in an emerging economy: Empirical study of Taiwanese manufacturers. *R & D Management*, *35*(2), 187–201. doi:10.1111/j.1467-9310.2005.00382.x

Tshishonga, N. (2017). Operation Sukuma Sakhe: A New Social Contract for Decentralised Service Delivery and Responsive Governance in KwaZulu-Natal. In Handbook of Research on Sub-National Governance and Development (pp. 304-323). Hershey, PA: IGI Global. doi:10.4018/978-1-5225-1645-3.ch014

Tshiwula, L., & Magopeni, N. (2014). A return to basics: selected views on factors preventing access to higher education in South Africa. In M. Speckman & M. Mandew (Eds.), *Perspectives on Student Affairs in South Africa*. Somerset West: African Minds.

UNESCO. (2005). *Toward knowledge societies. UNESCO world report*. UNESCO.

UNESCO. (2009). *World Conference on Higher Education 2009 Final Report*. París: UNESCO.

UNICEF. (2008). *Education and evaluation by competences: a challenge for the Latin American Laboratory for the Evaluation of the Quality of Education (LLECE)*. Retrieved from http://www.unesco.org/new/es/santiago/press-room/newsletters/newsletter-laboratory-for-assessment-of-the-quality-of-education-llece/n12/education-and- assessment-by-competences /

Unión Fenosa. (1999). *Annual report 1999*. Madrid: Unión FENOSA.

United Nations Development Programme (UNDP). (1990). *The Nature of States Parties Obligations*. Oxford University Press.

United Nations Development Programme (UNDP). (2000). *South Africa: Transformation for Human Development*. Pretoria: UNDP.

United Nations Educational, Scientific and Cultural Organization (UNESCO). (1998). *La educación superior en el Siglo XXI: visión y acción*. Retrieved from http://www.unesco.org/education/educprog/wche/declaration_spa.htm

United Nations Educational, Scientific and Cultural Organization (UNESCO). (2005). Educación para todos: el imperativo de la calidad. Informe de Seguimiento de Educación para Todos en el Mundo. Paris, France: UNESCO.

United Nations Educational, Scientific and Cultural Organization (UNESCO). (2013). *Gestión Educativa Estratégica*. Buenos Aires: Instituto Superior de Planeamiento de la Educación - Ministerio de Educación de la Nación. Retrieved from http://www.buenosaires.iipe.unesco.org/sites/default/iles/modulo02_0.pdf

Uys, L., De Kadt, E., Bawa, A., & Mazibuko, F. (2010). 'Core business (Teaching/Research /Community Engagement). In M. Makgoba & J. C. Mubangizi (Eds.), *The Creation of the University of KwaZulu-Natal: Reflections on a Merger and Transformation Experience* (pp. 177–198). New Delhi: Excel Books.

Valencia, M., Estrada, J., Bedoya, I., Tuttle, S., & Gaviria, F. (2013). Indicadores del capital intelectual en el área de ingenierías de una universidad. *Strategic Sciences Journal*, *22*(30), 285–298.

Välimaa, J., & Hoffman, D. (2008). Knowledge society discourse and higher education. *Higher Education*, *56*(3), 265–285. doi:10.100710734-008-9123-7

Vallaeys, F., Cruz, C., & Sasia, P. (2009). *Responsabilidad Social Universitaria. Manual primeros pasos*. Mc Graw Hill.

Van Rensburg, G. (2007). *The Leadership Challenge in Africa*. Pretoria: Van Schaik Publishers.

Van Rhyn, L., McMillan, G., & Ndlebe, J. (2016). School Leadership. In Leadership: Perspectives from the Front Line (pp. 189-204). Ransburg: KR Publishing.

Van Schalkwyk, F. (2013). Beyond Engagement: Exploring tensions between the academic core and engagement activities at Nelsomn Mandela Metropolitan University. Academic Press.

Vandenberghe, V. (2005). *Free higher education. Regressive transfer or implicit loan?* Discussion Paper 31. UC Louvain, Department des Sciences Economiques.

Velthuizen, A. (2017). Engaging with the African ground: Towards a new research paradigm for conflict studies in Africa. In V. Msila (Ed.), *Decolonising knowledge for Africa's renewal: Examining African Perspectives and Philosophies* (pp. 73–86). Randburg: KR Publishing.

Venetoulis, J. (2001). Assessing the ecological impact of a university: The ecological footprint for the University of Redlands. *International Journal of Sustainability in Higher Education*, *2*(2), 180–196. doi:10.1108/14676370110388381

Vera, F. (2016). Infusión de habilidades blandas en el currículo de la educación superior: Clave para el desarrollo de capital humano avanzado. *Akademéia Journal*, *7*(1), 53–73.

Viedma, J. (2001). ICBS – Intellectual Capital Benchmarking System. *Journal of Intellectual Capital*, *2*(2), 148–165. doi:10.1108/14691930110385937

Walker, G., & MacDonald, J. R. (2001). Designing and implementing an HR scorecard. *Human Resource Management*, *40*(4), 365–377. doi:10.1002/hrm.1025

Wangenge-Ouma, G. (2012). Tuition fees and the challenge of making higher education a popular commodity in South Africa. *Higher Education*, *64*(6), 831–844. doi:10.100710734-012-9531-6

Warden, C. (2004). *Valuation and Evaluation of Intangibles in Universities & Research Centres.* Academic Press.

Wells, G., & Edwards, A. (2015). Introduction: The Changing Face of Higher Education. In Pedagogy in Higher Education: A Cultural Historical Approach (pp. 1-17). Cambridge, UK: Cambridge University Press.

Wenger, E. (1998). *Communities of practice: Learning, meaning and identity.* Cambridge, UK: Cambridge University Press. doi:10.1017/CBO9780511803932

Wenger, E., & Synder, W. (2000). Communities of practice: The organisational Frontier. *Harvard Business Review*, 139–145.

Wiig, K. (1997). Integrating intellectual capital and knowledge management. *Long Range Planning*, *30*(3), 399–405. doi:10.1016/S0024-6301(97)90256-9

World Bank Group. (2018). *An Incomplete Transition: Overcoming the Legacy of Exclusion in South Africa*. Cape Town: UCT Press.

World Bank. (1998). *Indigenous knowledge for development: A Framework for Action*. Retrieved from www.Worldbank.org/afh/ik/ik.pdg

World Economic Forum. (2014). *Entrepreneurial Ecosystems Around the Globe and Early-Stage Company Growth Dynamics*. Geneva: World Economic Forum.

World Economic Forum. (2016). *The Future of Jobs, Employment, Skills, and Workforce Strategy for the Forth Industrial Revolution*. Global Challenge Insight Report. Author.

World Economic Forum. (2016). *The future of Jobs. Employment, skills and workforce strategy for the fourth industrial revolution*. WEF.

Yakubu, H. (2017). Higher Education for Innovation and Development. In Innovating University Education: Issues in Contemporary African Higher Education. Kampala: Fountain Publishers.

Yakubu, H. (2017). Higher Education and Development. In J. Ssempebwa, P. Neema-Abooki, & J. C. S. Musaaki (Eds.), *Innovating Higher Education: Issues in Contemporary African Higher Education* (pp. 1–17). Kampala: Fountain Publishers.

Yigezu, M. (2013). Funding Higher Education in Ethiopia: Modalities, Challenges, Opportunities and Prospects. In D. Teferra (Ed.), *Funding Higher Education in Sub- Saharan Africa* (pp. 38–71). Basingstoke, UK: Palgrave Macmillan. doi:10.1057/9781137345783_3

Related References

To continue our tradition of advancing academic research, we have compiled a list of recommended IGI Global readings. These references will provide additional information and guidance to further enrich your knowledge and assist you with your own research and future publications.

Aburezeq, I. M., & Dweikat, F. F. (2017). Cloud Applications in Language Teaching: Examining Pre-Service Teachers' Expertise, Perceptions and Integration. *International Journal of Distance Education Technologies, 15*(4), 39–60. doi:10.4018/IJDET.2017100103

Adera, B. (2017). Supporting Language and Literacy Development for English Language Learners. In J. Keengwe (Ed.), *Handbook of Research on Promoting Cross-Cultural Competence and Social Justice in Teacher Education* (pp. 339–354). Hershey, PA: IGI Global. doi:10.4018/978-1-5225-0897-7.ch018

Ahamer, G. (2011). How Technologies Can Localize Learners in Multicultural Space: A Newly Developed "Global Studies" Curriculum. *International Journal of Technology and Educational Marketing, 1*(2), 1–24. doi:10.4018/ijtem.2011070101

Ahamer, G. (2015). Conclusions from Social Dynamics in Collaborative Environmental Didactics. *International Journal of Technology and Educational Marketing, 5*(2), 68–92. doi:10.4018/IJTEM.2015070105

Ahamer, G. (2015). Designing and Analyzing Social Dynamics for Collaborative: Environmental Didactics. *International Journal of Technology and Educational Marketing, 5*(2), 46–67. doi:10.4018/IJTEM.2015070104

Ahamer, G. (2017). Quality Assurance for a Developmental "Global Studies" (GS) Curriculum. In I. Management Association (Ed.), Educational Leadership and Administration: Concepts, Methodologies, Tools, and Applications (pp. 438-477). Hershey, PA: IGI Global. doi:10.4018/978-1-5225-1624-8.ch023

Ahamer, G. (2017). Quality Assurance for a Developmental "Global Studies" (GS) Curriculum. In I. Management Association (Ed.), Educational Leadership and Administration: Concepts, Methodologies, Tools, and Applications (pp. 438-477). Hershey, PA: IGI Global. doi:10.4018/978-1-5225-1624-8.ch023

Alegre de la Rosa, O. M., & Angulo, L. M. (2017). Social Inclusion and Intercultural Values in a School of Education. In S. Mukerji & P. Tripathi (Eds.), *Handbook of Research on Administration, Policy, and Leadership in Higher Education* (pp. 518–531). Hershey, PA: IGI Global. doi:10.4018/978-1-5225-0672-0.ch020

Ambikairajah, E., Sethu, V., Eaton, R., & Sheng, M. (2014). Evolving Use of Educational Technologies: Enhancing Lectures. In F. Alam (Ed.), *Using Technology Tools to Innovate Assessment, Reporting, and Teaching Practices in Engineering Education* (pp. 241–258). Hershey, PA: IGI Global. doi:10.4018/978-1-4666-5011-4.ch018

Anderson, K. M. (2017). Preparing Teachers in the Age of Equity and Inclusion. In I. Management Association (Ed.), Medical Education and Ethics: Concepts, Methodologies, Tools, and Applications (pp. 1532-1554). Hershey, PA: IGI Global. doi:10.4018/978-1-5225-0978-3.ch069

Awdziej, M. (2017). Case Study as a Teaching Method in Marketing. In D. Latusek (Ed.), *Case Studies as a Teaching Tool in Management Education* (pp. 244–263). Hershey, PA: IGI Global. doi:10.4018/978-1-5225-0770-3.ch013

Bain, B. (2014). Exploring Assessment of Critical Thinking Learning Outcomes in Online Higher Education. In V. Wang (Ed.), *Handbook of Research on Education and Technology in a Changing Society* (pp. 1191–1202). Hershey, PA: IGI Global. doi:10.4018/978-1-4666-6046-5.ch089

Banas, J. R., & York, C. S. (2017). Pre-Service Teachers' Motivation to Use Technology and the Impact of Authentic Learning Exercises. In L. Tomei (Ed.), *Exploring the New Era of Technology-Infused Education* (pp. 121–140). Hershey, PA: IGI Global. doi:10.4018/978-1-5225-1709-2.ch008

Bariso, E. U. (2015). Educational Policy Analysis Debates and New Learning Technologies in England. In M. Khosrow-Pour (Ed.), *Encyclopedia of Information Science and Technology* (3rd ed.; pp. 2371–2378). Hershey, PA: IGI Global. doi:10.4018/978-1-4666-5888-2.ch230

Beycioglu, K., & Wildy, H. (2015). Principal Preparation: The Case of Novice Principals in Turkey. In K. Beycioglu & P. Pashiardis (Eds.), *Multidimensional Perspectives on Principal Leadership Effectiveness* (pp. 1–17). Hershey, PA: IGI Global. doi:10.4018/978-1-4666-6591-0.ch001

Beycioglu, K., & Wildy, H. (2017). Principal Preparation: The Case of Novice Principals in Turkey. In I. Management Association (Ed.), Educational Leadership and Administration: Concepts, Methodologies, Tools, and Applications (pp. 1152-1169). Hershey, PA: IGI Global. doi:10.4018/978-1-5225-1624-8.ch054

Bharwani, S., & Musunuri, D. (2018). Reflection as a Process From Theory to Practice. In M. Khosrow-Pour, D.B.A. (Ed.), Encyclopedia of Information Science and Technology, Fourth Edition (pp. 1529-1539). Hershey, PA: IGI Global. doi:10.4018/978-1-5225-2255-3.ch132

Bisschoff, T., & Rhodes, C. (2011). Transformation through Marketing: A Case of a Secondary School in South Africa. In P. Tripathi & S. Mukerji (Eds.), *Cases on Innovations in Educational Marketing: Transnational and Technological Strategies* (pp. 263–272). Hershey, PA: IGI Global. doi:10.4018/978-1-60960-599-5.ch016

Bodomo, A. B. (2010). Educational Technologies (WebCT): Creating Constructivist and Interactive Learning Communities. In A. Bodomo (Ed.), *Computer-Mediated Communication for Linguistics and Literacy: Technology and Natural Language Education* (pp. 252–290). Hershey, PA: IGI Global. doi:10.4018/978-1-60566-868-0.ch010

Bohjanen, S. L., Cameron-Standerford, A., & Meidl, T. D. (2018). Capacity Building Pedagogy for Diverse Learners. In J. Keengwe (Ed.), *Handbook of Research on Pedagogical Models for Next-Generation Teaching and Learning* (pp. 195–212). Hershey, PA: IGI Global. doi:10.4018/978-1-5225-3873-8.ch011

Brewer, J. C. (2018). Measuring Text Readability Using Reading Level. In M. Khosrow-Pour, D.B.A. (Ed.), Encyclopedia of Information Science and Technology, Fourth Edition (pp. 1499-1507). Hershey, PA: IGI Global. doi:10.4018/978-1-5225-2255-3.ch129

Brown, S. L. (2017). A Case Study of Strategic Leadership and Research in Practice: Principal Preparation Programs that Work – An Educational Administration Perspective of Best Practices for Master's Degree Programs for Principal Preparation. In V. Wang (Ed.), *Encyclopedia of Strategic Leadership and Management* (pp. 1226–1244). Hershey, PA: IGI Global. doi:10.4018/978-1-5225-1049-9.ch086

Brzozowski, M., & Ferster, I. (2017). Educational Management Leadership: High School Principal's Management Style and Parental Involvement in School Management in Israel. In V. Potocan, M. Üngan, & Z. Nedelko (Eds.), *Handbook of Research on Managerial Solutions in Non-Profit Organizations* (pp. 55–74). Hershey, PA: IGI Global. doi:10.4018/978-1-5225-0731-4.ch003

Cannaday, J. (2017). The Masking Effect: Hidden Gifts and Disabilities of 2e Students. In P. Dickenson, P. Keough, & J. Courduff (Eds.), *Preparing Pre-Service Teachers for the Inclusive Classroom* (pp. 220–231). Hershey, PA: IGI Global. doi:10.4018/978-1-5225-1753-5.ch011

Capobianco, B. M., & Lehman, J. D. (2010). Fostering Educational Technology Integration in Science Teacher Education: Issues of Teacher Identity Development. In J. Yamamoto, J. Kush, R. Lombard, & C. Hertzog (Eds.), *Technology Implementation and Teacher Education: Reflective Models* (pp. 245–257). Hershey, PA: IGI Global. doi:10.4018/978-1-61520-897-5.ch014

Chao, G. H., Hsu, M. K., & Scovotti, C. (2013). Predicting Donations from a Cohort Group of Donors to Charities: A Direct Marketing Case Study. In J. Wang (Ed.), *Optimizing, Innovating, and Capitalizing on Information Systems for Operations* (pp. 196–214). Hershey, PA: IGI Global. doi:10.4018/978-1-4666-2925-7.ch010

Chauhan, A. (2015). Beyond the Phenomenon: Assessment in Massive Open Online Courses (MOOCs). In E. McKay & J. Lenarcic (Eds.), *Macro-Level Learning through Massive Open Online Courses (MOOCs): Strategies and Predictions for the Future* (pp. 119–140). Hershey, PA: IGI Global. doi:10.4018/978-1-4666-8324-2.ch007

Coffman, T. L., & Klinger, M. B. (2013). Managing Quality in Online Education. In G. Kurubacak & T. Yuzer (Eds.), *Project Management Approaches for Online Learning Design* (pp. 220–233). Hershey, PA: IGI Global. doi:10.4018/978-1-4666-2830-4.ch011

Contreras, E. C., & Contreras, I. I. (2018). Development of Communication Skills through Auditory Training Software in Special Education. In M. Khosrow-Pour, D.B.A. (Ed.), Encyclopedia of Information Science and Technology, Fourth Edition (pp. 2431-2441). Hershey, PA: IGI Global. doi:10.4018/978-1-5225-2255-3.ch212

Cook, R. G. (2011). Educational Marketing: Coming Down from the Cloud Using Landing Gear. In U. Demiray & S. Sever (Eds.), *Marketing Online Education Programs: Frameworks for Promotion and Communication* (pp. 26–31). Hershey, PA: IGI Global. doi:10.4018/978-1-60960-074-7.ch003

Cook, R. G., & Ley, K. (2015). Past, Future and Presents: Meeting New Online Challenges with Primal Marketing Solutions. *International Journal of Technology and Educational Marketing*, *5*(2), 19–33. doi:10.4018/IJTEM.2015070102

Cooley, D., & Whitten, E. (2017). Special Education Leadership and the Implementation of Response to Intervention. In F. Topor (Ed.), *Handbook of Research on Individualism and Identity in the Globalized Digital Age* (pp. 265–286). Hershey, PA: IGI Global. doi:10.4018/978-1-5225-0522-8.ch012

Cosner, S., Tozer, S., & Zavitkovsky, P. (2017). Enacting a Cycle of Inquiry Capstone Research Project in Doctoral-Level Leadership Preparation. In I. Management Association (Ed.), Educational Leadership and Administration: Concepts, Methodologies, Tools, and Applications (pp. 1460-1481). Hershey, PA: IGI Global. doi:10.4018/978-1-5225-1624-8.ch067

Crawford, C. M. (2018). Instructional Real World Community Engagement. In M. Khosrow-Pour, D.B.A. (Ed.), Encyclopedia of Information Science and Technology, Fourth Edition (pp. 1474-1486). Hershey, PA: IGI Global. doi:10.4018/978-1-5225-2255-3.ch127

Crosby-Cooper, T., & Pacis, D. (2017). Implementing Effective Student Support Teams. In P. Dickenson, P. Keough, & J. Courduff (Eds.), *Preparing Pre-Service Teachers for the Inclusive Classroom* (pp. 248–262). Hershey, PA: IGI Global. doi:10.4018/978-1-5225-1753-5.ch013

Curran, C. M., & Hawbaker, B. W. (2017). Cultivating Communities of Inclusive Practice: Professional Development for Educators – Research and Practice. In C. Curran & A. Petersen (Eds.), *Handbook of Research on Classroom Diversity and Inclusive Education Practice* (pp. 120–153). Hershey, PA: IGI Global. doi:10.4018/978-1-5225-2520-2.ch006

Dass, S., & Dabbagh, N. (2018). Faculty Adoption of 3D Avatar-Based Virtual World Learning Environments: An Exploratory Case Study. In I. Management Association (Ed.), Technology Adoption and Social Issues: Concepts, Methodologies, Tools, and Applications (pp. 1000-1033). Hershey, PA: IGI Global. doi:10.4018/978-1-5225-5201-7.ch045

Davison, A. M., & Scholl, K. G. (2017). Inclusive Recreation as Part of the IEP Process. In C. Curran & A. Petersen (Eds.), *Handbook of Research on Classroom Diversity and Inclusive Education Practice* (pp. 311–330). Hershey, PA: IGI Global. doi:10.4018/978-1-5225-2520-2.ch013

DeCoito, I. (2018). Addressing Digital Competencies, Curriculum Development, and Instructional Design in Science Teacher Education. In M. Khosrow-Pour, D.B.A. (Ed.), Encyclopedia of Information Science and Technology, Fourth Edition (pp. 1420-1431). Hershey, PA: IGI Global. doi:10.4018/978-1-5225-2255-3.ch122

DeCoito, I., & Richardson, T. (2017). Beyond Angry Birds™: Using Web-Based Tools to Engage Learners and Promote Inquiry in STEM Learning. In I. Levin & D. Tsybulsky (Eds.), *Digital Tools and Solutions for Inquiry-Based STEM Learning* (pp. 166–196). Hershey, PA: IGI Global. doi:10.4018/978-1-5225-2525-7.ch007

Delmas, P. M. (2017). Research-Based Leadership for Next-Generation Leaders. In R. Styron Jr & J. Styron (Eds.), *Comprehensive Problem-Solving and Skill Development for Next-Generation Leaders* (pp. 1–39). Hershey, PA: IGI Global. doi:10.4018/978-1-5225-1968-3.ch001

Demiray, U., & Ekren, G. (2018). Administrative-Related Evaluation for Distance Education Institutions in Turkey. In K. Buyuk, S. Kocdar, & A. Bozkurt (Eds.), *Administrative Leadership in Open and Distance Learning Programs* (pp. 263–288). Hershey, PA: IGI Global. doi:10.4018/978-1-5225-2645-2.ch011

Dickenson, P. (2017). What do we Know and Where Can We Grow?: Teachers Preparation for the Inclusive Classroom. In P. Dickenson, P. Keough, & J. Courduff (Eds.), *Preparing Pre-Service Teachers for the Inclusive Classroom* (pp. 1–22). Hershey, PA: IGI Global. doi:10.4018/978-1-5225-1753-5.ch001

Dickerson, J., & Coleman, H. V. (2012). Technology, E-Leadership and Educational Administration in Schools: Integrating Standards with Context and Guiding Questions. In V. Wang (Ed.), *Encyclopedia of E-Leadership, Counseling and Training* (pp. 408–422). Hershey, PA: IGI Global. doi:10.4018/978-1-61350-068-2.ch030

Dickerson, J., Coleman, H. V., & Geer, G. (2012). Thinking like a School Technology Leader. In V. Wang (Ed.), *Technology and Its Impact on Educational Leadership: Innovation and Change* (pp. 53–63). Hershey, PA: IGI Global. doi:10.4018/978-1-4666-0062-1.ch005

Donne, V., & Hansen, M. (2017). Teachers' Use of Assistive Technologies in Education. In L. Tomei (Ed.), *Exploring the New Era of Technology-Infused Education* (pp. 86–101). Hershey, PA: IGI Global. doi:10.4018/978-1-5225-1709-2.ch006

Donne, V., & Hansen, M. A. (2018). Business and Technology Educators: Practices for Inclusion. In I. Management Association (Ed.), Business Education and Ethics: Concepts, Methodologies, Tools, and Applications (pp. 471-484). Hershey, PA: IGI Global. doi:10.4018/978-1-5225-3153-1.ch026

Dreon, O., Shettel, J., & Bower, K. M. (2017). Preparing Next Generation Elementary Teachers for the Tools of Tomorrow. In M. Grassetti & S. Brookby (Eds.), *Advancing Next-Generation Teacher Education through Digital Tools and Applications* (pp. 143–159). Hershey, PA: IGI Global. doi:10.4018/978-1-5225-0965-3.ch008

Drinka, D., Voge, K., & Yen, M. Y. (2005). From Principles to Practice: Analyzing a Student Learning Outcomes Assessment System. *Journal of Cases on Information Technology*, *7*(3), 37–56. doi:10.4018/jcit.2005070103

Durak, H. Y., & Güyer, T. (2018). Design and Development of an Instructional Program for Teaching Programming Processes to Gifted Students Using Scratch. In J. Cannaday (Ed.), *Curriculum Development for Gifted Education Programs* (pp. 61–99). Hershey, PA: IGI Global. doi:10.4018/978-1-5225-3041-1.ch004

Egorkina, E., Ivanov, M., & Valyavskiy, A. Y. (2018). Students' Research Competence Formation of the Quality of Open and Distance Learning. In V. Mkrttchian & L. Belyanina (Eds.), *Handbook of Research on Students' Research Competence in Modern Educational Contexts* (pp. 364–384). Hershey, PA: IGI Global. doi:10.4018/978-1-5225-3485-3.ch019

Ekren, G., Karataş, S., & Demiray, U. (2017). Understanding of Leadership in Distance Education Management. In I. Management Association (Ed.), Educational Leadership and Administration: Concepts, Methodologies, Tools, and Applications (pp. 34-50). Hershey, PA: IGI Global. doi:10.4018/978-1-5225-1624-8.ch003

Elmore, W. M., Young, J. K., Harris, S., & Mason, D. (2017). The Relationship between Individual Student Attributes and Online Course Completion. In K. Shelton & K. Pedersen (Eds.), *Handbook of Research on Building, Growing, and Sustaining Quality E-Learning Programs* (pp. 151–173). Hershey, PA: IGI Global. doi:10.4018/978-1-5225-0877-9.ch008

Ercegovac, I. R., Alfirević, N., & Koludrović, M. (2017). School Principals' Communication and Co-Operation Assessment: The Croatian Experience. In I. Management Association (Ed.), Educational Leadership and Administration: Concepts, Methodologies, Tools, and Applications (pp. 1568-1589). Hershey, PA: IGI Global. doi:10.4018/978-1-5225-1624-8.ch072

Everhart, D., & Seymour, D. M. (2017). Challenges and Opportunities in the Currency of Higher Education. In K. Rasmussen, P. Northrup, & R. Colson (Eds.), *Handbook of Research on Competency-Based Education in University Settings* (pp. 41–65). Hershey, PA: IGI Global. doi:10.4018/978-1-5225-0932-5.ch003

Farmer, L. S. (2017). Managing Portable Technologies for Special Education. In V. Wang (Ed.), *Encyclopedia of Strategic Leadership and Management* (pp. 977–987). Hershey, PA: IGI Global. doi:10.4018/978-1-5225-1049-9.ch068

Farmer, L. S. (2018). Optimizing OERs for Optimal ICT Literacy in Higher Education. In J. Keengwe (Ed.), *Handbook of Research on Mobile Technology, Constructivism, and Meaningful Learning* (pp. 366–390). Hershey, PA: IGI Global. doi:10.4018/978-1-5225-3949-0.ch020

Fındık, L. Y. (2017). Self-Assessment of Principals Based on Leadership in Complexity. In I. Management Association (Ed.), Educational Leadership and Administration: Concepts, Methodologies, Tools, and Applications (pp. 978-991). Hershey, PA: IGI Global. doi:10.4018/978-1-5225-1624-8.ch047

Flor, A. G., & Gonzalez-Flor, B. (2018). Dysfunctional Digital Demeanors: Tales From (and Policy Implications of) eLearning's Dark Side. In I. Management Association (Ed.), The Dark Web: Breakthroughs in Research and Practice (pp. 37-50). Hershey, PA: IGI Global. doi:10.4018/978-1-5225-3163-0.ch003

Floyd, K. K., & Shambaugh, N. (2017). Instructional Design for Simulations in Special Education Virtual Learning Spaces. In T. Kidd & L. Morris Jr., (Eds.), *Handbook of Research on Instructional Systems and Educational Technology* (pp. 202–215). Hershey, PA: IGI Global. doi:10.4018/978-1-5225-2399-4.ch018

Giovannini, J. M. (2017). Technology Integration in Preservice Teacher Education Programs: Research-based Recommendations. In M. Grassetti & S. Brookby (Eds.), *Advancing Next-Generation Teacher Education through Digital Tools and Applications* (pp. 82–102). Hershey, PA: IGI Global. doi:10.4018/978-1-5225-0965-3.ch005

Good, S., & Clarke, V. B. (2017). An Integral Analysis of One Urban School System's Efforts to Support Student-Centered Teaching. In J. Keengwe & G. Onchwari (Eds.), *Handbook of Research on Learner-Centered Pedagogy in Teacher Education and Professional Development* (pp. 45–68). Hershey, PA: IGI Global. doi:10.4018/978-1-5225-0892-2.ch003

Grobler, B. (2015). The Relationship between Emotional Competence and Instructional Leadership and Their Association with Learner Achievement. In K. Beycioglu & P. Pashiardis (Eds.), *Multidimensional Perspectives on Principal Leadership Effectiveness* (pp. 373–407). Hershey, PA: IGI Global. doi:10.4018/978-1-4666-6591-0.ch017

Hamidi, F., Owuor, P. M., Hynie, M., Baljko, M., & McGrath, S. (2017). Potentials of Digital Assistive Technology and Special Education in Kenya. In C. Ayo & V. Mbarika (Eds.), *Sustainable ICT Adoption and Integration for Socio-Economic Development* (pp. 125–151). Hershey, PA: IGI Global. doi:10.4018/978-1-5225-2565-3.ch006

Heavin, C., & Neville, K. (2015). Addressing the Learning Needs of Future IS Security Professionals through Social Media Technology. In M. Khosrow-Pour (Ed.), *Encyclopedia of Information Science and Technology* (3rd ed.; pp. 4766–4775). Hershey, PA: IGI Global. doi:10.4018/978-1-4666-5888-2.ch468

Henderson, L. K. (2017). Meltdown at Fukushima: Global Catastrophic Events, Visual Literacy, and Art Education. In R. Shin (Ed.), *Convergence of Contemporary Art, Visual Culture, and Global Civic Engagement* (pp. 80–99). Hershey, PA: IGI Global. doi:10.4018/978-1-5225-1665-1.ch005

Hismanoglu, M. (2012). Important Issues in Online Education: E-Pedagogy and Marketing. In I. Management Association (Ed.), E-Marketing: Concepts, Methodologies, Tools, and Applications (pp. 676-701). Hershey, PA: IGI Global. doi:10.4018/978-1-4666-1598-4.ch041

Howard, B. C. (2008). Common Features and Design Principles Found in Exemplary Educational Technologies. *International Journal of Information and Communication Technology Education*, *4*(4), 31–52. doi:10.4018/jicte.2008100104

Howard, B. C., & Tomei, L. A. (2008). The Classroom of the Future and Emerging Educational Technologies: Introduction to the Special Issue. *International Journal of Information and Communication Technology Education*, *4*(4), 1–8. doi:10.4018/jicte.2008100101

Hudgins, T., & Holland, J. L. (2018). Digital Badges: Tracking Knowledge Acquisition Within an Innovation Framework. In I. Management Association (Ed.), Wearable Technologies: Concepts, Methodologies, Tools, and Applications (pp. 1118-1132). Hershey, PA: IGI Global. doi:10.4018/978-1-5225-5484-4.ch051

Ion, G., Tomàs, M., Castro, D., & Salat, E. (2015). Analysis of the Tasks of School Principals in Secondary Education in Catalonia: Case Study. In K. Beycioglu & P. Pashiardis (Eds.), *Multidimensional Perspectives on Principal Leadership Effectiveness* (pp. 39–58). Hershey, PA: IGI Global. doi:10.4018/978-1-4666-6591-0.ch003

Janus, M., & Siddiqua, A. (2018). Challenges for Children With Special Health Needs at the Time of Transition to School. In I. Management Association (Ed.), Autism Spectrum Disorders: Breakthroughs in Research and Practice (pp. 339-371). Hershey, PA: IGI Global. doi:10.4018/978-1-5225-3827-1.ch018

Jesus, R. A. (2018). Screencasts and Learning Styles. In M. Khosrow-Pour, D.B.A. (Ed.), Encyclopedia of Information Science and Technology, Fourth Edition (pp. 1548-1558). Hershey, PA: IGI Global. doi:10.4018/978-1-5225-2255-3.ch134

Kaplan-Rakowski, R., & Rakowski, D. (2011). Educational Technologies for the Neomillennial Generation. In E. Dunkels, G. Franberg, & C. Hallgren (Eds.), *Interactive Media Use and Youth: Learning, Knowledge Exchange and Behavior* (pp. 12–31). Hershey, PA: IGI Global. doi:10.4018/978-1-60960-206-2.ch002

Karpinski, A. C., D'Agostino, J. V., Williams, A. K., Highland, S. A., & Mellott, J. A. (2018). The Relationship Between Online Formative Assessment and State Test Scores Using Multilevel Modeling. In M. Khosrow-Pour, D.B.A. (Ed.), Encyclopedia of Information Science and Technology, Fourth Edition (pp. 5183-5192). Hershey, PA: IGI Global. doi:10.4018/978-1-5225-2255-3.ch450

Kats, Y. (2017). Educational Leadership and Integrated Support for Students with Autism Spectrum Disorders. In I. Management Association (Ed.), Educational Leadership and Administration: Concepts, Methodologies, Tools, and Applications (pp. 101-114). Hershey, PA: IGI Global. doi:10.4018/978-1-5225-1624-8.ch007

Kaya, G., & Altun, A. (2018). Educational Ontology Development. In M. Khosrow-Pour, D.B.A. (Ed.), Encyclopedia of Information Science and Technology, Fourth Edition (pp. 1441-1450). Hershey, PA: IGI Global. doi:10.4018/978-1-5225-2255-3.ch124

Keough, P. D., & Pacis, D. (2017). Best Practices Implementing Special Education Curriculum and Common Core State Standards using UDL. In P. Dickenson, P. Keough, & J. Courduff (Eds.), *Preparing Pre-Service Teachers for the Inclusive Classroom* (pp. 107–123). Hershey, PA: IGI Global. doi:10.4018/978-1-5225-1753-5.ch006

Kilburn, M., Henckell, M., & Starrett, D. (2018). Factors Contributing to the Effectiveness of Online Students and Instructors. In M. Khosrow-Pour, D.B.A. (Ed.), Encyclopedia of Information Science and Technology, Fourth Edition (pp. 1451-1462). Hershey, PA: IGI Global. doi:10.4018/978-1-5225-2255-3.ch125

Konecny, L. T. (2017). Hybrid, Online, and Flipped Classrooms in Health Science: Enhanced Learning Environments. In I. Management Association (Ed.), Flipped Instruction: Breakthroughs in Research and Practice (pp. 355-370). Hershey, PA: IGI Global. doi:10.4018/978-1-5225-1803-7.ch020

Kowch, E. G. (2013). Towards Leading Diverse, Smarter and More Adaptable Organizations that Learn. In J. Lewis, A. Green, & D. Surry (Eds.), *Technology as a Tool for Diversity Leadership: Implementation and Future Implications* (pp. 11–34). Hershey, PA: IGI Global. doi:10.4018/978-1-4666-2668-3.ch002

Krezmien, M., Powell, W., Bosch, C., Hall, T., & Nieswandt, M. (2017). The Use of Tablet Technology to Support Inquiry Science for Students Incarcerated in Juvenile Justice Settings. In I. Levin & D. Tsybulsky (Eds.), *Optimizing STEM Education With Advanced ICTs and Simulations* (pp. 267–295). Hershey, PA: IGI Global. doi:10.4018/978-1-5225-2528-8.ch011

Leach, L. F., Winn, P., Erwin, S., & Benedict, L. P. (2015). What 21st Century Students Want: Factors that Influence Student Selection of Educational Leadership Graduate Programs. *International Journal of Technology and Educational Marketing*, *5*(1), 15–28. doi:10.4018/ijtem.2015010102

Leng, H. K. (2014). An Update on the Use of Facebook as a Marketing Tool by Private Educational Institutions in Singapore. In I. Lee (Ed.), *Trends in E-Business, E-Services, and E-Commerce: Impact of Technology on Goods, Services, and Business Transactions* (pp. 191–205). Hershey, PA: IGI Global. doi:10.4018/978-1-4666-4510-3.ch011

Leone, S. (2018). An Open Learning Format for Lifelong Learners' Empowerment. In M. Khosrow-Pour, D.B.A. (Ed.), Encyclopedia of Information Science and Technology, Fourth Edition (pp. 1517-1528). Hershey, PA: IGI Global. doi:10.4018/978-1-5225-2255-3.ch131

Ley, K., & Gannon-Cook, R. (2010). Marketing a Blended University Program: An Action Research Case Study. In S. Mukerji & P. Tripathi (Eds.), *Cases on Technology Enhanced Learning through Collaborative Opportunities* (pp. 73–90). Hershey, PA: IGI Global. doi:10.4018/978-1-61520-751-0.ch005

Loose, W., & Marcos, T. (2016). Instructional Design for Millennials: Instructor Efficiency in Streamlining Content, Assignments, and Assessments. In P. Dickenson & J. Jaurez (Eds.), *Increasing Productivity and Efficiency in Online Teaching* (pp. 1–25). Hershey, PA: IGI Global. doi:10.4018/978-1-5225-0347-7.ch001

Lovell, K. L. (2017). Development and Evaluation of Neuroscience Computer-Based Modules for Medical Students: Instructional Design Principles and Effectiveness. In J. Stefaniak (Ed.), *Advancing Medical Education Through Strategic Instructional Design* (pp. 262–276). Hershey, PA: IGI Global. doi:10.4018/978-1-5225-2098-6.ch013

Manuel, N. N. (2016). Angolan Higher Education, Policy, and Leadership: Towards Transformative Leadership for Social Justice. In N. Ololube (Ed.), *Handbook of Research on Organizational Justice and Culture in Higher Education Institutions* (pp. 164–188). Hershey, PA: IGI Global. doi:10.4018/978-1-4666-9850-5.ch007

Marouchou, D. V. (2015). The Impact of Academic Beliefs on Student Learning. In M. Khosrow-Pour (Ed.), *Encyclopedia of Information Science and Technology* (3rd ed.; pp. 4796–4804). Hershey, PA: IGI Global. doi:10.4018/978-1-4666-5888-2.ch471

McCormack, V. F., Stauffer, M., Fishley, K., Hohenbrink, J., Mascazine, J. R., & Zigler, T. (2018). Designing a Dual Licensure Path for Middle Childhood and Special Education Teacher Candidates. In D. Polly, M. Putman, T. Petty, & A. Good (Eds.), *Innovative Practices in Teacher Preparation and Graduate-Level Teacher Education Programs* (pp. 21–36). Hershey, PA: IGI Global. doi:10.4018/978-1-5225-3068-8.ch002

McDaniel, R. (2017). Strategic Leadership in Instructional Design: Applying the Principles of Instructional Design through the Lens of Strategic Leadership to Distance Education. In V. Wang (Ed.), *Encyclopedia of Strategic Leadership and Management* (pp. 1570–1584). Hershey, PA: IGI Global. doi:10.4018/978-1-5225-1049-9.ch109

Memon, R. N., Ahmad, R., & Salim, S. S. (2018). Critical Issues in Requirements Engineering Education. In I. Management Association (Ed.), Computer Systems and Software Engineering: Concepts, Methodologies, Tools, and Applications (pp. 1953-1976). Hershey, PA: IGI Global. doi:10.4018/978-1-5225-3923-0.ch081

Mendenhall, R. (2017). Western Governors University: CBE Innovator and National Model. In K. Rasmussen, P. Northrup, & R. Colson (Eds.), *Handbook of Research on Competency-Based Education in University Settings* (pp. 379–400). Hershey, PA: IGI Global. doi:10.4018/978-1-5225-0932-5.ch019

Mense, E. G., Griggs, D. M., & Shanks, J. N. (2018). School Leaders in a Time of Accountability and Data Use: Preparing Our Future School Leaders in Leadership Preparation Programs. In E. Mense & M. Crain-Dorough (Eds.), *Data Leadership for K-12 Schools in a Time of Accountability* (pp. 235–259). Hershey, PA: IGI Global. doi:10.4018/978-1-5225-3188-3.ch012

Mense, E. G., Griggs, D. M., & Shanks, J. N. (2018). School Leaders in a Time of Accountability and Data Use: Preparing Our Future School Leaders in Leadership Preparation Programs. In E. Mense & M. Crain-Dorough (Eds.), *Data Leadership for K-12 Schools in a Time of Accountability* (pp. 235–259). Hershey, PA: IGI Global. doi:10.4018/978-1-5225-3188-3.ch012

Mestry, R., & Naicker, S. R. (2017). Exploring Distributive Leadership in South African Public Primary Schools in the Soweto Region. In I. Management Association (Ed.), Educational Leadership and Administration: Concepts, Methodologies, Tools, and Applications (pp. 1041-1064). Hershey, PA: IGI Global. doi:10.4018/978-1-5225-1624-8.ch050

Monaghan, C. H., & Boboc, M. (2017). (Re) Defining Leadership in Higher Education in the U.S. In V. Wang (Ed.), *Encyclopedia of Strategic Leadership and Management* (pp. 567–579). Hershey, PA: IGI Global. doi:10.4018/978-1-5225-1049-9.ch040

Muthee, J. M., & Murungi, C. G. (2018). Relationship Among Intelligence, Achievement Motivation, Type of School, and Academic Performance of Kenyan Urban Primary School Pupils. In M. Khosrow-Pour, D.B.A. (Ed.), Encyclopedia of Information Science and Technology, Fourth Edition (pp. 1540-1547). Hershey, PA: IGI Global. doi:10.4018/978-1-5225-2255-3.ch133

Naranjo, J. (2018). Meeting the Need for Inclusive Educators Online: Teacher Education in Inclusive Special Education and Dual-Certification. In D. Polly, M. Putman, T. Petty, & A. Good (Eds.), *Innovative Practices in Teacher Preparation and Graduate-Level Teacher Education Programs* (pp. 106–122). Hershey, PA: IGI Global. doi:10.4018/978-1-5225-3068-8.ch007

Nkabinde, Z. P. (2017). Multiculturalism in Special Education: Perspectives of Minority Children in Urban Schools. In J. Keengwe (Ed.), *Handbook of Research on Promoting Cross-Cultural Competence and Social Justice in Teacher Education* (pp. 382–397). Hershey, PA: IGI Global. doi:10.4018/978-1-5225-0897-7.ch020

Nkabinde, Z. P. (2018). Online Instruction: Is the Quality the Same as Face-to-Face Instruction? In J. Keengwe (Ed.), *Handbook of Research on Digital Content, Mobile Learning, and Technology Integration Models in Teacher Education* (pp. 300–314). Hershey, PA: IGI Global. doi:10.4018/978-1-5225-2953-8.ch016

O'Connor, J. R. Jr, & Jackson, K. N. (2017). The Use of iPad® Devices and "Apps" for ASD Students in Special Education and Speech Therapy. In Y. Kats (Ed.), *Supporting the Education of Children with Autism Spectrum Disorders* (pp. 267–283). Hershey, PA: IGI Global. doi:10.4018/978-1-5225-0816-8.ch014

Okolie, U. C., & Yasin, A. M. (2017). TVET in Developing Nations and Human Development. In U. Okolie & A. Yasin (Eds.), *Technical Education and Vocational Training in Developing Nations* (pp. 1–25). Hershey, PA: IGI Global. doi:10.4018/978-1-5225-1811-2.ch001

Paciga, K. A., & Hoffman, J. L. (2015). Realizing the Potential of e-Books in Early Education. In M. Khosrow-Pour (Ed.), *Encyclopedia of Information Science and Technology* (3rd ed.; pp. 4787–4795). Hershey, PA: IGI Global. doi:10.4018/978-1-4666-5888-2.ch470

Paulson, E. N. (2017). Adapting and Advocating for an Online EdD Program in Changing Times and "Sacred" Cultures. In I. Management Association (Ed.), Educational Leadership and Administration: Concepts, Methodologies, Tools, and Applications (pp. 1849-1876). Hershey, PA: IGI Global. doi:10.4018/978-1-5225-1624-8.ch085

Petersen, A. J., Elser, C. F., Al Nassir, M. N., Stakey, J., & Everson, K. (2017). The Year of Teaching Inclusively: Building an Elementary Classroom for All Students. In C. Curran & A. Petersen (Eds.), *Handbook of Research on Classroom Diversity and Inclusive Education Practice* (pp. 332–348). Hershey, PA: IGI Global. doi:10.4018/978-1-5225-2520-2.ch014

Pfannenstiel, K. H., & Sanders, J. (2017). Characteristics and Instructional Strategies for Students With Mathematical Difficulties: In the Inclusive Classroom. In C. Curran & A. Petersen (Eds.), *Handbook of Research on Classroom Diversity and Inclusive Education Practice* (pp. 250–281). Hershey, PA: IGI Global. doi:10.4018/978-1-5225-2520-2.ch011

Preast, J. L., Bowman, N., & Rose, C. A. (2017). Creating Inclusive Classroom Communities Through Social and Emotional Learning to Reduce Social Marginalization Among Students. In C. Curran & A. Petersen (Eds.), *Handbook of Research on Classroom Diversity and Inclusive Education Practice* (pp. 183–200). Hershey, PA: IGI Global. doi:10.4018/978-1-5225-2520-2.ch008

Randolph, K. M., & Brady, M. P. (2018). Evolution of Covert Coaching as an Evidence-Based Practice in Professional Development and Preparation of Teachers. In V. Bryan, A. Musgrove, & J. Powers (Eds.), *Handbook of Research on Human Development in the Digital Age* (pp. 281–299). Hershey, PA: IGI Global. doi:10.4018/978-1-5225-2838-8.ch013

Rawlins, P., & Kehrwald, B. (2010). Education Technology in Teacher Education: Overcoming Challenges, Realizing Opportunities. In R. Luppicini & A. Haghi (Eds.), *Cases on Digital Technologies in Higher Education: Issues and Challenges* (pp. 50–63). Hershey, PA: IGI Global. doi:10.4018/978-1-61520-869-2.ch004

Rell, A. B., Puig, R. A., Roll, F., Valles, V., Espinoza, M., & Duque, A. L. (2017). Addressing Cultural Diversity and Global Competence: The Dual Language Framework. In L. Leavitt, S. Wisdom, & K. Leavitt (Eds.), *Cultural Awareness and Competency Development in Higher Education* (pp. 111–131). Hershey, PA: IGI Global. doi:10.4018/978-1-5225-2145-7.ch007

Riel, J., Lawless, K. A., & Brown, S. W. (2017). Defining and Designing Responsive Online Professional Development (ROPD): A Framework to Support Curriculum Implementation. In T. Kidd & L. Morris Jr., (Eds.), *Handbook of Research on Instructional Systems and Educational Technology* (pp. 104–115). Hershey, PA: IGI Global. doi:10.4018/978-1-5225-2399-4.ch010

Roberts, C. (2017). Advancing Women Leaders in Academe: Creating a Culture of Inclusion. In S. Mukerji & P. Tripathi (Eds.), *Handbook of Research on Administration, Policy, and Leadership in Higher Education* (pp. 256–273). Hershey, PA: IGI Global. doi:10.4018/978-1-5225-0672-0.ch012

Rodgers, W. J., Kennedy, M. J., Alves, K. D., & Romig, J. E. (2017). A Multimedia Tool for Teacher Education and Professional Development. In C. Martin & D. Polly (Eds.), *Handbook of Research on Teacher Education and Professional Development* (pp. 285–296). Hershey, PA: IGI Global. doi:10.4018/978-1-5225-1067-3.ch015

Romanowski, M. H. (2017). Qatar's Educational Reform: Critical Issues Facing Principals. In I. Management Association (Ed.), Educational Leadership and Administration: Concepts, Methodologies, Tools, and Applications (pp. 1758-1773). Hershey, PA: IGI Global. doi:10.4018/978-1-5225-1624-8.ch080

Ruffin, T. R., Hawkins, D. P., & Lee, D. I. (2018). Increasing Student Engagement and Participation Through Course Methodology. In M. Khosrow-Pour, D.B.A. (Ed.), Encyclopedia of Information Science and Technology, Fourth Edition (pp. 1463-1473). Hershey, PA: IGI Global. doi:10.4018/978-1-5225-2255-3.ch126

Rutaisire, J. (2011). Innovations in Technology for Educational Marketing: Stakeholder Perceptions and Implications for Examinations System in Rwanda. In P. Tripathi & S. Mukerji (Eds.), *Cases on Innovations in Educational Marketing: Transnational and Technological Strategies* (pp. 214–233). Hershey, PA: IGI Global. doi:10.4018/978-1-60960-599-5.ch013

Sabina, L. L., Curry, K. A., Harris, E. L., Krumm, B. L., & Vencill, V. (2017). Assessing the Performance of a Cohort-Based Model Using Domestic and International Practices. In I. Management Association (Ed.), Educational Leadership and Administration: Concepts, Methodologies, Tools, and Applications(pp. 913-929). Hershey, PA: IGI Global. doi:10.4018/978-1-5225-1624-8.ch044

Santamaría, A. P., Webber, M., & Santamaría, L. J. (2017). Effective School Leadership for Māori Achievement: Building Capacity through Indigenous, National, and International Cross-Cultural Collaboration. In I. Management Association (Ed.), Educational Leadership and Administration: Concepts, Methodologies, Tools, and Applications (pp. 1547-1567). Hershey, PA: IGI Global. doi:10.4018/978-1-5225-1624-8.ch071

Santamaría, L. J. (2017). Culturally Responsive Educational Leadership in Cross-Cultural International Contexts. In I. Management Association (Ed.), Educational Leadership and Administration: Concepts, Methodologies, Tools, and Applications (pp. 1380-1400). Hershey, PA: IGI Global. doi:10.4018/978-1-5225-1624-8.ch064

Sarafidou, J., & Xafakos, E. (2015). Transformational Leadership and Principals' Innovativeness: Are They the "Keys" for the Research and Innovation Oriented School? In K. Beycioglu & P. Pashiardis (Eds.), *Multidimensional Perspectives on Principal Leadership Effectiveness* (pp. 324–348). Hershey, PA: IGI Global. doi:10.4018/978-1-4666-6591-0.ch015

Segredo, M. R., Cistone, P. J., & Reio, T. G. (2017). Relationships Between Emotional Intelligence, Leadership Style, and School Culture. *International Journal of Adult Vocational Education and Technology*, *8*(3), 25–43. doi:10.4018/IJAVET.2017070103

Shaik, N., & Ritter, S. (2012). Social Media Based Relationship Marketing. In I. Management Association (Ed.), E-Marketing: Concepts, Methodologies, Tools, and Applications (pp. 88-110). Hershey, PA: IGI Global. doi:10.4018/978-1-4666-1598-4.ch006

Shalev, N. (2017). Empathy and Leadership From the Organizational Perspective. In Z. Nedelko & M. Brzozowski (Eds.), *Exploring the Influence of Personal Values and Cultures in the Workplace* (pp. 348–363). Hershey, PA: IGI Global. doi:10.4018/978-1-5225-2480-9.ch018

Siamak, M., Fathi, S., & Isfandyari-Moghaddam, A. (2018). Assessment and Measurement of Education Programs of Information Literacy. In R. Bhardwaj (Ed.), *Digitizing the Modern Library and the Transition From Print to Electronic* (pp. 164–192). Hershey, PA: IGI Global. doi:10.4018/978-1-5225-2119-8.ch007

Siozos, P. D., & Palaigeorgiou, G. E. (2008). Educational Technologies and the Emergence of E-Learning 2.0. In D. Politis (Ed.), *E-Learning Methodologies and Computer Applications in Archaeology* (pp. 1–17). Hershey, PA: IGI Global. doi:10.4018/978-1-59904-759-1.ch001

Siu, K. W., & García, G. J. (2017). Disruptive Technologies and Education: Is There Any Disruption After All? In I. Management Association (Ed.), Educational Leadership and Administration: Concepts, Methodologies, Tools, and Applications (pp. 757-778). Hershey, PA: IGI Global. doi:10.4018/978-1-5225-1624-8.ch037

Skibba, K., Moore, D., & Herman, J. H. (2013). Pedagogical and Technological Considerations Designing Collaborative Learning Using Educational Technologies. In J. Keengwe (Ed.), *Research Perspectives and Best Practices in Educational Technology Integration* (pp. 1–27). Hershey, PA: IGI Global. doi:10.4018/978-1-4666-2988-2.ch001

Slagter van Tryon, P. J. (2017). The Nurse Educator's Role in Designing Instruction and Instructional Strategies for Academic and Clinical Settings. In J. Stefaniak (Ed.), *Advancing Medical Education Through Strategic Instructional Design* (pp. 133–149). Hershey, PA: IGI Global. doi:10.4018/978-1-5225-2098-6.ch006

Slattery, C. A. (2018). Literacy Intervention and the Differentiated Plan of Instruction. In *Developing Effective Literacy Intervention Strategies: Emerging Research and Opportunities* (pp. 41–62). Hershey, PA: IGI Global. doi:10.4018/978-1-5225-5007-5.ch003

Smith, A. R. (2017). Ensuring Quality: The Faculty Role in Online Higher Education. In K. Shelton & K. Pedersen (Eds.), *Handbook of Research on Building, Growing, and Sustaining Quality E-Learning Programs* (pp. 210–231). Hershey, PA: IGI Global. doi:10.4018/978-1-5225-0877-9.ch011

Souders, T. M. (2017). Understanding Your Learner: Conducting a Learner Analysis. In J. Stefaniak (Ed.), *Advancing Medical Education Through Strategic Instructional Design* (pp. 1–29). Hershey, PA: IGI Global. doi:10.4018/978-1-5225-2098-6.ch001

Spring, K. J., Graham, C. R., & Ikahihifo, T. B. (2018). Learner Engagement in Blended Learning. In M. Khosrow-Pour, D.B.A. (Ed.), Encyclopedia of Information Science and Technology, Fourth Edition (pp. 1487-1498). Hershey, PA: IGI Global. doi:10.4018/978-1-5225-2255-3.ch128

Stocklin, S. (2015). Building Capacity by Managing a Mission. In J. Feng, S. Stocklin, & W. Wang (Eds.), *Educational Strategies for the Next Generation Leaders in Hotel Management* (pp. 115–139). Hershey, PA: IGI Global. doi:10.4018/978-1-4666-8565-9.ch005

Storey, V. A., Anthony, A. K., & Wahid, P. (2017). Gender-Based Leadership Barriers: Advancement of Female Faculty to Leadership Positions in Higher Education. In V. Wang (Ed.), *Encyclopedia of Strategic Leadership and Management* (pp. 244–258). Hershey, PA: IGI Global. doi:10.4018/978-1-5225-1049-9.ch018

Stottlemyer, D. (2018). Develop a Teaching Model Plan for a Differentiated Learning Approach. In *Differentiated Instructional Design for Multicultural Environments: Emerging Research and Opportunities* (pp. 106–130). Hershey, PA: IGI Global. doi:10.4018/978-1-5225-5106-5.ch005

Stottlemyer, D. (2018). Developing a Multicultural Environment. In *Differentiated Instructional Design for Multicultural Environments: Emerging Research and Opportunities* (pp. 1–27). Hershey, PA: IGI Global. doi:10.4018/978-1-5225-5106-5.ch001

Swami, B. N., Gobona, T., & Tsimako, J. J. (2017). Academic Leadership: A Case Study of the University of Botswana. In N. Baporikar (Ed.), *Innovation and Shifting Perspectives in Management Education* (pp. 1–32). Hershey, PA: IGI Global. doi:10.4018/978-1-5225-1019-2.ch001

Swanson, K. W., & Collins, G. (2018). Designing Engaging Instruction for the Adult Learners. In M. Khosrow-Pour, D.B.A. (Ed.), Encyclopedia of Information Science and Technology, Fourth Edition (pp. 1432-1440). Hershey, PA: IGI Global. doi:10.4018/978-1-5225-2255-3.ch123

Swartz, B. A., Lynch, J. M., & Lynch, S. D. (2018). Embedding Elementary Teacher Education Coursework in Local Classrooms: Examples in Mathematics and Special Education. In D. Polly, M. Putman, T. Petty, & A. Good (Eds.), *Innovative Practices in Teacher Preparation and Graduate-Level Teacher Education Programs* (pp. 262–292). Hershey, PA: IGI Global. doi:10.4018/978-1-5225-3068-8.ch015

Taliadorou, N., & Pashiardis, P. (2015). Emotional Intelligence and Political Skill Really Matter in Educational Leadership. In K. Beycioglu & P. Pashiardis (Eds.), *Multidimensional Perspectives on Principal Leadership Effectiveness* (pp. 228–256). Hershey, PA: IGI Global. doi:10.4018/978-1-4666-6591-0.ch011

Taliadorou, N., & Pashiardis, P. (2017). Emotional Intelligence and Political Skill Really Matter in Educational Leadership. In I. Management Association (Ed.), Educational Leadership and Administration: Concepts, Methodologies, Tools, and Applications (pp. 1274-1303). Hershey, PA: IGI Global. doi:10.4018/978-1-5225-1624-8.ch060

Tam, F. W., & Kwan, P. Y. (2011). School Images, School Identity, and How Parents Select Schools for Their Children: The Case of Hong Kong. In P. Tripathi & S. Mukerji (Eds.), *Cases on Innovations in Educational Marketing: Transnational and Technological Strategies* (pp. 87–103). Hershey, PA: IGI Global. doi:10.4018/978-1-60960-599-5.ch005

Tandoh, K. A., & Ebe-Arthur, J. E. (2018). Effective Educational Leadership in the Digital Age: An Examination of Professional Qualities and Best Practices. In J. Keengwe (Ed.), *Handbook of Research on Digital Content, Mobile Learning, and Technology Integration Models in Teacher Education* (pp. 244–265). Hershey, PA: IGI Global. doi:10.4018/978-1-5225-2953-8.ch013

Tinoca, L., Pereira, A., & Oliveira, I. (2014). A Conceptual Framework for E-Assessment in Higher Education: Authenticity, Consistency, Transparency, and Practicability. In S. Mukerji & P. Tripathi (Eds.), *Handbook of Research on Transnational Higher Education* (pp. 652–673). Hershey, PA: IGI Global. doi:10.4018/978-1-4666-4458-8.ch033

Tobin, M. T. (2018). Multimodal Literacy. In M. Khosrow-Pour, D.B.A. (Ed.), Encyclopedia of Information Science and Technology, Fourth Edition (pp. 1508-1516). Hershey, PA: IGI Global. doi:10.4018/978-1-5225-2255-3.ch130

Torres, M. L., & Ramos, V. J. (2018). Music Therapy: A Pedagogical Alternative for ASD and ID Students in Regular Classrooms. In P. Epler (Ed.), *Instructional Strategies in General Education and Putting the Individuals With Disabilities Act (IDEA) Into Practice* (pp. 222–244). Hershey, PA: IGI Global. doi:10.4018/978-1-5225-3111-1.ch008

Toulassi, B. (2017). Educational Administration and Leadership in Francophone Africa: 5 Dynamics to Change Education. In S. Mukerji & P. Tripathi (Eds.), *Handbook of Research on Administration, Policy, and Leadership in Higher Education* (pp. 20–45). Hershey, PA: IGI Global. doi:10.4018/978-1-5225-0672-0.ch002

Umair, S., & Sharif, M. M. (2018). Predicting Students Grades Using Artificial Neural Networks and Support Vector Machine. In M. Khosrow-Pour, D.B.A. (Ed.), Encyclopedia of Information Science and Technology, Fourth Edition (pp. 5169-5182). Hershey, PA: IGI Global. doi:10.4018/978-1-5225-2255-3.ch449

Usman, L. M. (2011). Adult Education and Sustainable Learning Outcome of Rural Widows of Central Northern Nigeria. *International Journal of Adult Vocational Education and Technology, 2*(2), 25–41. doi:10.4018/javet.2011040103

Vettraino, L., Castello, V., Guspini, M., & Guglielman, E. (2018). Self-Awareness and Motivation Contrasting ESL and NEET Using the SAVE System. In M. Khosrow-Pour, D.B.A. (Ed.), Encyclopedia of Information Science and Technology, Fourth Edition (pp. 1559-1568). Hershey, PA: IGI Global. doi:10.4018/978-1-5225-2255-3.ch135

Wang, V. C. (2013). Marketing Educational Programs through Technology and the Right Philosophies. In P. Tripathi & S. Mukerji (Eds.), *Marketing Strategies for Higher Education Institutions: Technological Considerations and Practices* (pp. 15–24). Hershey, PA: IGI Global. doi:10.4018/978-1-4666-4014-6.ch002

Wiemelt, J. (2017). Critical Bilingual Leadership for Emergent Bilingual Students. In I. Management Association (Ed.), Educational Leadership and Administration: Concepts, Methodologies, Tools, and Applications (pp. 1606-1631). Hershey, PA: IGI Global. doi:10.4018/978-1-5225-1624-8.ch074

Williams, D. D. (2006). Measurement and Assessment Supporting Evaluation in Online Settings. In D. Williams, M. Hricko, & S. Howell (Eds.), *Online Assessment, Measurement and Evaluation: Emerging Practices* (pp. 1–9). Hershey, PA: IGI Global. doi:10.4018/978-1-59140-747-8.ch001

Wolf, F., Seyfarth, F. C., & Pflaum, E. (2018). Scalable Capacity-Building for Geographically Dispersed Learners: Designing the MOOC "Sustainable Energy in Small Island Developing States (SIDS)". In U. Pandey & V. Indrakanti (Eds.), *Open and Distance Learning Initiatives for Sustainable Development* (pp. 58–83). Hershey, PA: IGI Global. doi:10.4018/978-1-5225-2621-6.ch003

Woodley, X. M., Mucundanyi, G., & Lockard, M. (2017). Designing Counter-Narratives: Constructing Culturally Responsive Curriculum Online. *International Journal of Online Pedagogy and Course Design*, *7*(1), 43–56. doi:10.4018/IJOPCD.2017010104

Woods, P. A., & Woods, G. J. (2011). Lighting the Fires of Entrepreneurialism?: Constructions of Meaning in an English Inner City Academy. *International Journal of Technology and Educational Marketing*, *1*(1), 1–24. doi:10.4018/ijtem.2011010101

Yell, M. L., & Christle, C. A. (2017). The Foundation of Inclusion in Federal Legislation and Litigation. In C. Curran & A. Petersen (Eds.), *Handbook of Research on Classroom Diversity and Inclusive Education Practice* (pp. 27–52). Hershey, PA: IGI Global. doi:10.4018/978-1-5225-2520-2.ch002

Zhao, J. (2011). China Special Education: The Perspective of Information Technologies. In P. Ordóñez de Pablos, J. Zhao, & R. Tennyson (Eds.), *Technology Enhanced Learning for People with Disabilities: Approaches and Applications* (pp. 34–43). Hershey, PA: IGI Global. doi:10.4018/978-1-61520-923-1.ch003

Zinger, D. (2016). Developing Instructional Leadership and Communication Skills through Online Professional Development: Focusing on Rural and Urban Principals. In A. Normore, L. Long, & M. Javidi (Eds.), *Handbook of Research on Effective Communication, Leadership, and Conflict Resolution* (pp. 354–370). Hershey, PA: IGI Global. doi:10.4018/978-1-4666-9970-0.ch019

Zutshi, A., Pogrebnaya, M., & Fermelis, J. (2014). Wellness Programs in Higher Education: An Australian Case. In N. Baporikar (Ed.), *Handbook of Research on Higher Education in the MENA Region: Policy and Practice* (pp. 391–419). Hershey, PA: IGI Global. doi:10.4018/978-1-4666-6198-1.ch017

About the Contributors

Edgar Oliver Cardoso Espinosa, PhD, is Professor - Researcher since 2009 on la Sección de Estudios de Posgrado e Investigación of the Escuela Superior de Comercio y Administración (ESCA) of the Instituto Politécnico Nacional (IPN), Mexico City. In his position conducts research projects focused on the management and development of education in educational programs at senior level. PhD Cardoso belongs to the National System of Researchers of CONACyT with the distinction I He teaches courses Methodological Seminar I, II, III and Statistics for Educational Research to Master's and Research Seminars I, II and III as well as Research Visits I, II, III and IV to PhD level. Dr. Cardoso earned his doctorate at the IPN. He has a master of science in management and development of education in the ESCA-IPN. His research includes evaluation of educational programs and executive education. He belongs to the National System of Researchers with the level I distinction in the CONACyT of Mexico. He has directed several research projects in the area of educational management. He has conducted thesis addresses at the master's and doctoral level in the educational area.

* * *

Ingrid Cuevas Zuñiga, PhD Administrative Sciences, is specialist in innovation and sustainability; her research focuses on the incorporation of the premise of sustainable development into the business strategy in organizations, specifically through innovation. She is head of the Research Department and teacher of the ESCA Santo Tomás Unit of the Instituto Politécnico Nacional in Mexico City. And it was awarded the Presencia Lázaro Cárdenas, the highest distinction granted by the Institute to the most outstanding members of its community.

Susana Asela Garduño Román is a specialist in innovation and technological change and focuses his research on the need to innovate have enterprises as a pillar of the economic growth and development of any country.

Rosa María Rivas García, PhD, is Professor - Researcher on the Escuela Superior de Turismo (EST) of the Instituto Politécnico Nacional (IPN), Mexico City. She has a PhD in Administrative Sciences from the Higher School of Commerce and Administration

Miguel Mendoza Pérez is a student of master in business administration for sustainability at the Instituto Politécnico Nacional and Professor of foreign languages at the same institution.

Sandra Viridiana Cortés Ruíz, Computer Systems Engineer from the University of the Valley of Mexico, currently is a student of specific purpose courses of the Master in Administration in Management and Development of the Education at the Instituto Politécnico Nacional.

Maria del Rocio Soto Flores is a specialist in the economics of technological change and competitiveness and industrial innovation and focuses his research on the need to innovate have enterprises as a pillar of the economic growth and development of any country. He is Professor of the Instituto Politécnico Nacional in the city of Mexico. And is member founder of the network of research on teaching and innovation technology. He was also member of the network of centers in support of innovation, funded by the CyTED of Spain. He served as Director for Mexico of the Latino-Iberoamericana Association of technology management.

Ndwakhulu Tshishonga holds a BA, BA (Hons) in Development Studies (UNISA); an MA in Applied Anthropology (Goldsmith College, University of London), MM in Public Development and Management (WITS) and MPA-Public Administration (UWC), Advanced Diploma (UWC-Adult Education) and Social Reconstruction and Development Certificate (SADEP-UWC). His interests are in citizenship and local government and local governance, Intergovernmental Relations, Social Movements and Protests, etc. His teaching interests range from Alternative Models of Development, Project Management and Development Planning to Micro Level Strategies in Economic Community Development, Co-operatives. His current research is on Intergenerational poverty, Inclusive and Exclusive Citizenship and Local Governance, Youth and Gender development as well as poverty issues and food security, politics of service delivery & social movements, Indigenous knowledge systems. His research output entails scholarly conference presentations and publication in journals such as Journal of Public Administration, Agenda, African Journal of Public Affairs, and Journal of African & Asian Local Government Studies. He has published more than 20 book chapters and journal papers nationally and internationally.

Jésica Alhelí Cortés Ruíz, PhD, is Professor - Researcher since 2018 on the Sección de Estudios de Posgrado e Investigación of the Escuela Superior de Comercio y Administración (ESCA) of the Instituto Politécnico Nacional (IPN), Mexico City. PhD in Administrative Sciences from the Higher School of Commerce and Administration, Master of Science in Systems Engineering from the Higher School of Mechanical and Electrical Engineering. She is a specialist in transdisciplinary systemic and has been the author of chapters of dissemination books, as well as various articles in research journals. Her systemic training and dedication to the knowledge society has allowed her to teach In the International Business Degree, the Master in Administration in Management and Development of Education, The Master in Business Administration for Sustainability and the Master of Science in Business Administration.

Index

I

K

L

M

N

P

Q

R

S

www.ingramcontent.com/pod-product-compliance
Lightning Source LLC
LaVergne TN
LVHW081339300926
849161LV00008B/2019